Small Group
COMMUNICATION SYNERGY

Peter A. DeCaro

California State University-Stanislaus

Kendall Hunt
publishing company

Book Team

Chairman and Chief Executive Officer   Mark C. Falb
President and Chief Operating Officer   Chad M. Chandlee
Vice President, Higher Education   David L. Tart
Director of Publishing Partnerships   Paul B. Carty
Editorial Manager   Georgia Botsford
Senior Editor   Angela Willenbring
Vice President, Operations   Timothy J. Beitzel
Assistant Vice President, Production Services   Christine E. O'Brien
Senior Production Editor   Charmayne McMurray
Permissions Editor   Caroline Kieler
Cover Designer   Heather Richman
Web Project Editor   Sheena Reed

Cover image © Shutterstock, Inc.

Kendall Hunt
publishing company
www.kendallhunt.com
Send all inquiries to:
4050 Westmark Drive
Dubuque, IA 52004-1840

Dedication

This text is dedicated to Dr. Daniel J. Montgomery—mentor, friend, and colleague. May your students continue in your footsteps.

Brief Contents

Contents

Preface

Many small group communication texts focus on the *process* of communication as the end product, or the ultimate goal for small group work. This text is a departure from that view. I hold the philosophy that the ultimate goal of small group or team work is *performance;* I view communication as the tool we use to increase individual and group performance. After all, isn't that the purpose of group work, to provide the best possible outcome, one that is performance-driven? Therefore, this text emphasizes two perspectives within the group context—*performance and communication.* We understand that groups serve a multitude of purposes in society; probably two of the most typical purposes are decision making and problem solving. At one time, face-to-face communication was the only way to achieve these two purposes; however, technology has given group and team work alternatives.

Another aspect of this text that is a departure from many other texts is the fact that we refer to many of the original theorists and their works in explaining why and how individual members interact in a group setting instead of referring to multiple interpretations by others. For example, in order to understand the field of group dynamics, we explore the work of Kurt Lewin and the impact he had on social psychology. Lewin is best known for his work in the field of organization behavior and the study of group dynamics, especially the study of leadership patterns and their influence on groups and group members. Similarly, we investigate Robert Bales' Interaction Process Analysis, a theory which aims to explain the pattern of responses in which groups work toward a goal of a group decision-making problem. We discover George C. Homans' behavioral theories in small groups, in which he viewed groups as social systems of interacting individuals and was interested in understanding how groups got their power to control individual behavior. And we look at Stanley Milgram's Agency Theory in which Milgram analyzed power by creating and studying small groups in his laboratory at Yale University. These are just some examples of the theorists cited.

This text is intended for students studying small group communication. Although we focus on particular theorists, this text is not theory driven; rather, we incorporate theory where necessary to help you, the student, understand *why* and *how* people behave the way they do in a group setting, as simply and clearly as we can. This text also incorporates leadership with performance management. A good leader is one who can direct the group to perform at its best with the least amount of direction.

Chapter 1: Role of Communication in Groups and Teams

Understanding the communication process in groups and interpersonal communication is central to successful group work. This chapter discusses the elements of verbal and nonverbal communication, the importance of ethics, the cultural influence, and gender differences.

Chapter 2: Developing Effective Groups and Teams

The role of performance in groups is explained, as well as what constitutes a group or team. This chapter explores how to team build and how theory explains group work. It distinguishes the various elements of a system and describes the Myers-Briggs Type Indicator.

Chapter 3: Power Roles: Members, Leaders, and Ethics

This chapter explains the types of power in groups and how members can influence group behavior. It explains the structural process of individual power and introduces coercive forms of power. The two basic types of leadership in groups are distinguished. The importance of power and ethics is explored.

Chapter 4: Member Roles and Responsibilities

Becoming familiar with the many types and functions of roles in group work and how roles affect individual and group performance is the focus of this chapter. It also discusses how roles influence the individual behavior and taking responsibility for one's behavior.

Chapter 5: Leadership and Leadership Styles

The various leadership styles and the three competencies of leadership are described in this chapter. It also explains the meaning of leadership and its characteristics.

Chapter 6: Leadership, Persuasion, and Motivation

This chapter provides information on the cognitive structures that influence persuasion and how persuasive theories explain behavior change. It explores compliance-gaining strategies and how motivational theories actuate behavior.

Chapter 7: Leadership and Performance Management

Understanding the principles of performance management, how the ABC Model of behavior change works, and reinforcement strategies is the focus of this chapter.

Chapter 8: Leadership and Team Building

The purpose and roles of leadership, as well as the decision-making and problem-solving processes are explained. Working with a leader in teams and groups and modeling behavior and leadership is explored.

Chapter 9: Interpersonal Communication for Leaders

The role that relationships play within group settings and the model of dialectical tensions in group interaction is explored. The factors affecting individual responses and motivations to share information are identified. The symbolic constitution of meaning and its role in organizations is explained, as well as the critical listening process. The factors that shape communication climates are described. Social and cultural factors on group interaction are explained.

Chapter 10: Goal Setting

Locke's goal-setting theory is described, along with how to set and attain goals and objectives. Understanding the group charge and achieving your checkpoints is also explained. This chapter familiarizes you with the goal-writing process and how to set good goals.

Chapter 11: Critical Thinking, Problem Solving, and Decision Making

This chapter describes the critical thinking process and its role in group decision making. The symptoms of groupthink and structural barriers to decision making are identified. The five-step problem solving process is described along with how group processes can prevent barriers to decision making.

Chapter 12: Conflict Management

This chapter discusses how conflict arises in groups, the patterns of conflict, and how to identify the signs and stages of conflict. It defines the conflict continuum and the various coping styles, as well as the diversity of viewpoints and experiences. Assuming the role of mediator as a leader is discussed, as well as power in groups.

Chapter 13: Virtual Groups

The function of mediated groups in an electronic age is explored in this chapter, as well as information literacy and virtual dimensions. It explains how to build a virtual group and conduct a virtual meeting, along with virtual rules.

Student-Oriented Pedagogy

Because assessing student learning is imperative, this text includes features that facilitate student learning and help instructors measure learning outcomes.

- Chapter Objectives help students focus on the overall concepts, theories, and skills discussed.
- Key Terms list important concepts.
- Chapter Outlines serve as a map to guide students through the content of the chapter and focus on key points.
- Running Glossary provides a quick definition of key terms within the text.
- Figures and Tables visually illustrate chapter concepts.
- Cartoons offer a humorous break in the content.
- Summary effectively reviews elements presented throughout the chapter.
- Discussion Questions encourage students to further explore the concepts they learned.
- Notes document the extensive research cited in the text.

Instructional Online Enhancements

Both students and instructors have access to online content that is integrated with the chapters of the text to enrich student learning. The Web access code is included on the inside front cover of the textbook.

Look for the Web icon in the text margins to direct you to various interactive tools.

- **Flash cards** offer an interactive version of the key terms and their definitions.
- **Activities** provide extensive content review and application of concepts.
- **PowerPoint slides** illustrate important chapter concepts.
- **Comprehensive Test Bank** offers different question formats to better assess student knowledge.

Acknowledgments

Seldom can an academician claim to be the sole author of his or her text. Like many before me, I did not write this alone. I would like to acknowledge the help from Keith Nainby, Ph.D., a brilliant colleague who authored Chapters 9 and 11, and who has been instrumental in assisting me with this endeavor. He complements my perspective to small-group work. I also want to recognize Alina R. Martin, a student majoring in communication at CSUS, who made a significant contribution to Chapter 9. And I would like to give a special thank you to Dr. Fred P. Hilpert, my esteemed colleague, who provided support, guidance, and original materials for this text. Thank you so much, Fred; you have been an inspiration!

I must also note that while attending graduate school at The Florida State University, Tallahassee, Florida, I had the pleasure of meeting Aubrey C. Daniels, Ph.D., who is the world's foremost authority on performance management. My mentor at FSU, Dr. Daniel J. Montgomery, a colleague and friend of Dr. Daniels, afforded me an opportunity to meet him. Listening to Dr. Daniels speak about PM was an aspiring, rewarding, and memorable experience, to say the least.

This text would not have been published if not for the patience of Paul Carty and Angela Willenbring, my editors at Kendall Hunt Publishing Company, and the many unnamed Kendall Hunt personnel who helped put this text together.

Finally, I hope that you, the reader, discover this text to be as rewarding and informative to read as it was for me to write.

I gratefully acknowledge the constructive comments of the colleagues who provided content reviews. They include:

Patricia Amason	University of Arkansas	Claire Ferraris	Western Oregon University
Carolyn Anderson	University of Akron	Diane Ferrero-Paluzzi	Iona College
Isolde Anderson	Hope College	Richard Fiordo	University of North Dakota
Ronnie Arnett	University of Alaska-Anchorage	John Fisher	Northwest Missouri State University
Susan Baker	Oakland University	David Foster	The University of Findlay
Kaylene Barbe	Oklahoma Baptist University	Philip Frazier	Bethel University
William Barber, III	Ohio University Zanesville	Skye Gentile	Cabrillo College
Polly Begley	Fresno City College	Eletra Gilchrist	Middle Tennessee State University
Sally Bishai	Florida State University	Lauren Gragg	University of Toledo and Oakland University
Deena Bisig	Clark College		
Lisa Boragine	Cape Cod Community College	Donyale Griffin	Wayne State University
Jay Bourne	University of the Cumberlands	Adam Gutschmidt	North Carolina State University
Anne Brackin	Palm Beach Atlantic University	Kim Gyuran	Modesto Junior College
Camilla Brammer	Marshall University	Kim Haimes-Korn	Southern Polytechnic State University
Dana Burnside	Lehigh Carbon Community College		
Amy Capwell Burns	University of Toledo	Cheri Hampton-Farmer	The University of Findlay
Maria Christian	Oklahoma State University-Okmulgee	Sandy Hanson	University of North Carolina-Charlotte
JackCiak	Seton Hill University	Ryan Harrington	SUNY-Oneonta
Janis Crawford	Butler University	Robert Harrison	Gallaudet University
Randy Cullen	Oakland University	Nola Heidlebaugh	SUNY-Oswego
Dan DuBray	Cosumnes River College	Katherine Hendrix	University of Memphis
Tresha Dutton	Whatcom Community College	Stephen Hinerman	San Jose State University
Thomas Endres	University of Northern Colorado	Rick Hogrefe	Crafton Hills College

Cary Horvath — Youngstown State University

Ron Howell — Illinois Central College

Megan Hudson — Boise State University

Mike Ingram — Whitworth University

Rick Isaacson — San Francisco State University

Nancy Jennings — Cuyamaca College

Valerie Jensen — Central Arizona College

Linda Joesting — Long Beach City College

Clifford Johnson — Cedarville University

A. Todd Jones — Bakersfield College

Bernadette Kapocias — Southwestern Oregon Community College

Tressa Kelly — University of West Florida

Virginia Kidd — California State University-Sacramento

Amy Lenoce — Naugatuck Valley Community College

Jason Lesko — Ball State University

Marifran Mattson — Purdue University

Julie Mayberry — Meredith College

John McArthur — Clemson University

Beverly McCall — Grossmont College/Vincennes University

Suzanne McCorkle — Boise State University

Anthony McGill — The University of Michigan-Flint

Heidi Muller — University of Northern Colorado

Gregory Olson — University of Wisconsin-Oshkosh

Ray Ozley — University of Montevallo

Jean Perry — Glendale Community College

Patricia Rockwell — University of Louisiana at Lafayette

Margaret Sargent — Southern Connecticut State University

Charlotte Schell — Portland State University

Carsten Schmidtke — Oklahoma State University-Okmulgee

Juliann Scholl — Texas Tech University

Will Scott — Green River Community College

Gerri Smith — California State University-Sacramento

Tim Steckline — Black Hills State University

Tim Steffensmeier — Kansas State University

Roxane Sutherland — Clark College

Beatriz Torres — Keene State College

Paula Marie Usrey — Umpqua Community College

Charles Veenstra — Dordt College

Michael Wallinger — Frostburg State University

M. James Warnemuende — California State University-Chico

Joel A. Weiss — Penn State University-Altoona College

C. E. Wilson — University of South Carolina-Aiken

Kimberlee Wirig — Grossmont College/San Diego City College

Catherine Woells — Bellevue University

Melinda Womack — Santiago Canyon College

Debra L. Worthington — Auburn University

Catherine Wright — George Mason University

Steven Ybarra — Sacramento City College

Paul Yelsma — Western Michigan University

Stephen Yungbluth — Northern Kentucky University

Raymond Zeuschner — California Polytechnic State University

Julie Zink — University of Southern Maine

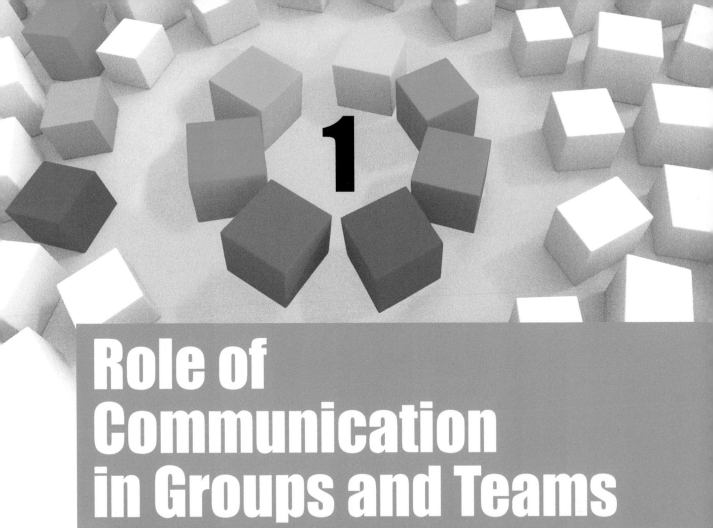

1

Role of Communication in Groups and Teams

CHAPTER OBJECTIVES

- Understand the communication process in groups
- Be familiar with the elements of verbal communication
- Know what constitutes nonverbal communication
- Understand interpersonal communication competence
- Comprehend the importance of ethics
- Understand how culture influences communication
- Know the differences of gender communication

KEY TERMS

Communication
Transactional process
Concepts
Conception
Denotative meaning
Connotative meaning
Kinesics
Culture
Cultural norms
Values
Terminal values

Instrumental values
Concrete language
Abstract words
Self-monitoring
Cultural assumptions
Ethics

CHAPTER OUTLINE

CHARACTERISTICS OF HUMAN COMMUNICATION

One of the most overlooked, if not the most overlooked, aspects of small group communication is the role that human communication plays in groups and teams. We tend to forget that groups don't communicate with one another; the people in those groups do. Communication occurs on an interpersonal level and has many complex dynamics, both internal (what we call the cognitive process) and external, occurring simultaneously. But before we can explore the communication process, we should first define communication. What communication means to you may be quite different than what it means to the other individuals in your group. Many years ago, I was a member of a committee on race relations in Tallahassee, Florida. I distinctly remember the first meeting we had when eleven of us, all from different walks of life and ethnicities, sat down to discuss how we could improve race relations in Tallahassee. During the initial two hour meeting, we spent the first one and a half hours arguing about race relations in general. We were angry with one another and going nowhere fast. Finally, I asked each member of the group what he or she understood race relations to be. We wasted most of the first meeting because none of us perceived race relations the same. We assumed everyone was on the same page. Boy, were we wrong! Once we established a working definition, we were able to effectively communicate our ideas to one another, and the group, from that point on, worked well together because we learned a very valuable lesson—make sure that all members share the same working definition of a word, concept, or phrase. This will eliminate a lot of confusion, misunderstanding, and ill will.

Communication as a Transactional Process

So, what is human communication? There are many definitions of the term, but the one I prefer defines **communication** as the process by which people create and transmit messages that are received, interpreted, and responded to by other people. We refine this definition somewhat for small group communication as the process by which individuals create and transmit messages that are simultaneously received and interpreted by group members, who then create and transmit messages in response to the sender. We refer to this communication as a **transactional process**. Much of small group work demands that members respond, cooperate, and work together to achieve common meaning and understanding. It engages group members to become interactive. The transactional process emphasizes the reciprocal, multidirectional interaction in the communication environment and the responsiveness of communicative members. This interactivity has the potential to positively affect member behavior and attitudes. This, in turn, can affect the quality and nature of group interaction and the successful completion of the group's charge.

This analysis of communication as a transactional process provides us with three conclusions.[1] First, the emphasis on reciprocal and multidirectional interaction tells us that the process is **complex** and **dynamic**. Transactions are contextual and therefore irreversible, unique, and unrepeatable. Group members interpret other members' communication and behavior based on each of their experiences and circumstances with one another. Once an episode occurs, the particular set of events cannot be repeated in the identical form. Second, as a process, communication has no necessary beginning or end, so labeling one member as a sender and another as a receiver is an arbitrary distinction. We can assign the role of sender in a particular situation, but almost all group communication occurs in the context of ongoing activities, relationships, and goals. Third, everyone can be simultaneously affected and can affect other members of the transaction. In other words, we are sending and receiving messages at the same time. The fundamental assumption of the transactional model is that group communication is facilitated by the reciprocal, multidirectional interaction of its members in a communicative environment. This paves the way for group cohesion, interdependency, cooperation, and synergy.

Communication as Shared Meaning

It has been said that the boundary that separates humans from animals is language. The ability to express ourselves—our ideas, feelings, needs, wants, and desires—is unique to humans. It has been argued that language brought about the dawn of humanity. Throughout human history, our ability to create symbols has given mankind opportunities to advance civilization. It wasn't simply the advent of symbols that brought about these advancements, but the creation of language, both oral and written. (While language is the clearest example of symbolic communication, many nonverbal cues are also used symbolically. We call this nonverbal communication.) When we look at communication as shared meaning, we must first understand the *meaning* of meaning. In everyday

 **Communication**
The process by which people create and transmit messages that are received, interpreted, and responded to by other people.

Transactional process
The process by which individuals create and transmit messages that are simultaneously received and interpreted by group members, who then create and transmit messages in response to the sender.

discussions, we use the term *meaning* without giving it much thought. For example, have you ever said any of the following?

"I meant to write you."
"What's that supposed to mean?"
"A red light means stop."
"I didn't mean to hurt his feelings."
"Baseball means everything to me."
"...if you take my meaning."
"What's the meaning of this?"
"...if you know what I mean."
"...I mean...you know what I mean."

You can see that we don't use the word meaning with the same meaning every time. How can we account for the many differences in its use? Between a thought and a symbol there exists what we call **causal relations**. When we speak, the symbolism we use is caused partly by the reference we are making and partly by social and psychological factors; that is, the reason we are making the reference, the proposed effect of our symbols on other people, and our own attitude. This means that words and images have many meanings, not just one.[2] When we think about communication, in reality, we are thinking about the process of making word symbols—the use of language. **Symbolic reality** is the interpretation of physical reality.[3] Language is the way we share meanings and interpretations. Because of this, we live in what we call a **symbolic universe**. We do not deal with an actual object; we deal with our perception of it. When we say that one thing represents something else, we are referring to symbols. Humans think conceptually through the use of symbols; they are necessary for thought. Without symbols, we cannot take an idea or a concept from our environment and put it in our brain, or from one part of our brain to another part, nor from one person to another.[4] As symbols, words are instruments for describing past events, making predictions, talking about happenings in other places, and giving a group its own identity.

An important characteristic of symbols is that they are arbitrary. Symbols and their meanings are culture-specific; that is, a symbol is created by members of a culture and those members assign meaning to that symbol. Suzanne Langer (1942) states that, "Symbols are not proxy of their objects but are vehicles for the conception of objects." (p. 61).[5] The use of symbols allows an individual to think about an object, person, place, idea, or event without being within its proximity. Langer claims that this makes symbols "an instrument of thought" (p. 63). We can conceptualize our thoughts into concepts, label them, and then explain them. Each new concept adds to our reality, and we use communication to share that reality. This is one way in which we are able to share meaning.

Because symbols are arbitrarily assigned to the things they represent, their meanings must be agreed upon, or conventionalized, in order for us to use them to communicate with others. This conventionalization allows us to communicate with a common understanding of what that symbol represents. As we observe phenomena, we create new symbols in order to explain them; therefore, symbol-making is a continuous human process. In group work, we can attribute

a good part of a member's behavior by understanding that member's symbolic need. Our view of the world may change as our symbol system is modified through interaction with others.

Symbols work in two basic ways: (1) they communicate a concept, a general idea, pattern, or form. **Concepts** are shared meanings among communicators; (2) each communicator has his or her own private understanding, image, or meaning idiosyncratically assigned that he or she uses to fill in the blank details. This private or personal understanding is called a **conception**. Therefore, meaning is a combination of a communicator's shared understanding of the concept and his or her own private conception.

How do symbols, then, affect thought? We create symbols as a means to effectively communicate. Symbols function in a number of ways: (1) They allow us to convey our thoughts about things that are not in our immediate presence. When we use symbols to communicate about things that are not in our presence, "we can communicate across barriers of time and space."[6] In other words, we can talk about things we did in the past and what we plan on doing in the future. Time and space do not constrain our thoughts. (2) They are vehicles for expanding knowledge and understanding; we learn, in part, through symbols. Words, for example, are symbols; and words such as freedom, love, and compassion do not have a referent. We cannot point to an object and call it love or compassion, but we use these words to express our feelings and thoughts. (3) We use symbols to think abstractly. Single abstract terms, such as building, allow us to categorize a number of differing structures. They also allow us to make it easier to reason from specific events to general conclusions, and abstractions also allow us to make comparisons within categories and between categories.[7] For example, we can determine the differences between a glass building from one that is concrete or steel. (4) We create a shared social reality through them. Through shared and similar meanings for symbols, we can communicate our thoughts, feelings, and ideas to others. This is how we create groups, societies, and cultures.

Communication theorist David Berlo (1960)[8] made a number of thought-provoking statements about the nature of meaning:

1. **Meanings are in people.** Though many different pairs of people may say the same thing (linguistically) on different occasions in conversation, each occasion, as an event, is observably different in many aspects from the

Concepts
Shared meanings among communicators.

Conception
The private or personal understanding of a symbol.

others; such differences depend upon people's accents, their past experiences, their present states of mind, the environment, the future consequences
of interpreting the message, knowledge of each other, and many other factors. What Berlo refers to when he says that meanings are in people is that
the meaning we assign to a word is determined by many factors, some of
which include who we are (all of those experiences, family, friends, education, etc., that have given us our world view), who we communicate with,
where we communicate (the context), the language we use to communicate,
our mood and that of the people we are communicating with at the time,
and how well we know the other people.

2. **Words do not mean at all; only people mean.** People do not mean the
same by all words. Simply transmitting messages doesn't ensure that we
transmit meaning. We have to make allowances for the different meanings
people have if we want to be reasonably successful in communicating with
others. This relates to meanings are in people. Just because we say something doesn't guarantee that the meaning we wanted to attach to the message is the same meaning received by the person we intended the message
for. We need to remember that meaning resides in each person, and each
person interprets meanings differently.

3. **Communication does not consist of the transmission of meanings but of
the transmissions of messages.** The elements and structure of language
do not themselves have meaning. They are only symbols, sets of symbols,
or cues that cause us to assign our own meanings, think about those meanings, reassign meaning, etc. Even if the elements of messages are received
with 100 percent fidelity, there is certainly no guarantee that their intended
meanings will be received. By and large, we agree on what the signs of a
code mean. If there weren't broad agreement, then codes would be quite
useless. But our individual understanding of messages will be affected by
a variety of factors. We can't refer to the dictionary to find out the right
meaning of a word, because there isn't a right meaning. Meanings were not
assigned when our language codes were invented; they are a product of our
social process and therefore change and evolve as society changes, and they
can be quite different from one section of society to another.

When we communicate, we are sending messages. These messages consist
of symbols—words—and these words lack any type of meaning until the
receiver assigns meaning to them, even if the receiver heard every word the
person said. We know that words have conventional meanings, that there is
a general understanding of what a given word means; if not, then language
is useless. However, successful communication doesn't occur until the receiver assigns meaning to the message, the same meaning that the sender
intended when coding the message.

4. **Meanings are not in the message; they are in the message users.** We interpret the world around us through our own lenses, our perspectives about
things. This can make communication with another person quite difficult.
Words do not mean the same thing to all people. In fact, it is not words that
hold meaning; it is the person. Messages in and of themselves do not have
meaning. They hold a conventional definition, but their meanings lie within

the person who interprets the message. We interpret through our frames of mind, our lenses of who we are, our accumulated knowledge and experiences. As stated earlier, no two people share the exact same world view and experiences. For example, if I softly whispered to you, "Come here," past experiences with that particular tone of voice signals that I probably am not angry with you. But, if I yelled very loudly, and in a sharp and angry voice, "Come here!" those same past experiences would probably signal that there is something wrong; there is urgency about the way I said it. And if I wrote, "Come here" on a piece of paper, you would probably be wondering if something was wrong.

5. **People can have similar meanings only to the extent that they have had or can anticipate having similar experiences.** Through each new experience, each new word, we learn as we go through life, we attach meanings to them. Since no two individuals perceive a shared experience or learn a new word the same way, there will always be some differences in the meanings people have for the same word.

6. **Meanings are never fixed; as experiences change, meanings change.** A language system such as ours is always in a state of change. Each generation creates its own words and changes meanings in existing words. Because of technological changes, and social, educational, and economic changes, each generation experiences society differently from the previous generation. When I was in high school, and someone called you "fat," that meant you were overweight. Today, if someone calls you fat, you have to ask if that is spelled "fat" or "phat." They have two completely different meanings. I think I'd rather be called "phat."

7. **No two people can have exactly the same meaning for anything.** We create many of our own communication problems because we assume that the meaning we attach to our message is received by the other person in the same way. We think that everybody understands the meanings the same way we do. You tell them what you meant, but they, without a doubt, understood what they meant. If we believe that meanings do not lie in messages, but come about only during an encounter, then we must assume that the act of communication is unpredictable and filled with uncertainty. If this is so, then we must always be careful of what we say, when we say it, and to whom we say it. This is called self-monitoring. Let's see how we use symbols to create shared meaning in verbal and nonverbal communication.

VERBAL COMMUNICATION

Words are amazing things. We accomplish so much because of language, and we seldom give it a second thought. Think about all of the things you normally do with language. For example, you explain to your boss why you were late for work; you describe to your teacher how your dog ate your homework; you ask your mother to tell your father that you put a dent in his brand new car; or you attempt to explain to the police officer why you didn't see the red light you just ran. In each example, you are trying to convey some kind of meaning—you are goal-directed; you have an agenda; you are responsible for your actions;

and you're looking for some form of cooperation from others. What you have yet to achieve is a solution to these problems. In each example, you are sharing meaning that you hope will be interpreted the way you intended. Groups are the same; they are goal-directed; they have an agenda; members are responsible for their actions; they require cooperation; and they find solutions. Like you, groups cannot function without language, and they cannot function without having shared meaning. There is an old Chinese proverb that says, "If you don't know where you're going, any road will take you there." Generally speaking, groups need to know where they are going, how they will get there, the role each member will play, and what each member needs to do along the way; and they will need to know when they have completed their task.

To further help understand how meaning is conveyed, we need to consider two kinds of word meanings: **denotative** and **connotative**.

Denotative meaning, also known as referential meaning, refers to the literal meaning of a word, the dictionary definition. It is the most specific or direct meaning of a word. For example, if you look up the word snake in the *Webster's Unabridged Dictionary,* you will discover that one of its denotative meanings is "any of numerous limbless, scaly, elongate reptiles comprising venomous and non-venomous species inhabiting tropical and temperate areas."

Connotative meaning, in contrast to denotative, is its figurative or associated meaning. It refers to the associations that are connected to a certain word or the emotional suggestions related to that word. The connotations for the word snake in the *Webster's Unabridged Dictionary* include, "a treacherous person; an insidious enemy." You can see that the connotative meaning of snake lacks any reference to its denotative meaning. However, they are inseparable; the connotative meanings of a word exist together with the denotative meanings.

According to Berlo (1960), there are five verbal communication skills.

Two are encoding skills:

  1. speaking
  2. writing

Two are decoding skills:

  3. listening
  4. reading

The fifth is critical to both encoding and decoding:
  5. reasoning

You should master all five if you want to become an effective communicator.

Now that I've explained what verbal communication is, let me say that, in my opinion, verbal communication is probably the single most important influence on how a group operates and what it achieves. Talking and listening are the substance of problem-solving.[9] Individuals come together to form a group so they can talk, listen, and respond to one another. Verbal communication is immediate and responsive. As we will see when we talk about dialectics and dialogue, verbal communication is much more effective in discussing ideas, identifying feelings, and expressing beliefs and values, than writing them on a

Denotative meaning

The literal meaning of a word.

Connotative meaning

In contrast to denotative, is a word's figurative or associated meaning.

piece of paper for members to read. Face-to-face communication in a group setting allows people to negotiate and bargain in the interest of all members.

However, in just about every group, you have one or two individuals who like to dominate the discussions. They're the ones who know everything, talk the most, waste time, and tell irrelevant stories. These people prevent the group from being effective and productive. They talk too much and rarely listen. My grandfather used to tell me, "You learn more by listening than talking. So be quiet and learn." He was right; we do learn more by listening and very little, if anything, by talking. We need a balance between the quantity and quality of participation and listening (which we will discuss in Chapter 8) must be recognized as an integral element of effective communication.

Verbal communication allows members to express important and useful ideas. There also is a tendency for members to listen thoughtfully, offer suitable criticism, and engage in important arguments. Verbal communication gives everyone an opportunity to participate equally in the process. When individuals participate in the process, they are more likely to become committed to the group and its outcomes. A problem-solving group needs all of these and more if it is going to be successful. When people feel that they have had a fair opportunity to be heard, they become vested in the process; and they invest more time, energy, and thought in their tasks. A balance in the communicative process is critical for making each member feel that he or she is a valuable part of the group. There is no question that there is a connection between active, balanced participation and successful group work.[10]

Participation in the group system is made up of various communication roles performed by its members. Effective problem-solving discussion requires three basic communication roles that address the group's task, procedure, and climate.[11]

Task roles, or task ordering, focus on communication about the information that forms the basis of problem-solving: asking for ideas and information, giving ideas and information, elaborating and evaluating information that has been introduced into deliberations. Each of these task roles is designed to help a group find valid, reliable information that is necessary for sound decision making. Task roles tell us *what* we should say.

Procedural roles, or process orientation, organize the group's collective efforts: this includes establishing and maintaining an agenda coordinating the many ideas offered by group members, summarizing progress, and recording ideas and agreements. Procedural roles rely on comments that help members stay on a common train of thought. Procedural roles tell us *how* something should be said.

Climate roles principally create and maintain a viable, cooperative atmosphere in group interaction so the group can pursue productive discussion. Climate roles include recognizing others' ideas and proposals, managing conflict, using humor and other rhetorical devices to release group tension, and pointing out collective group goals and values.

Every member bears the responsibility for contributing to balanced participation. Effective group discussion makes it possible for reluctant members to participate and discourages those who talk too much from dominating discussion. These roles are not fixed; that is, each member can choose any one of these roles at any time in group discussion.

NONVERBAL COMMUNICATION

All human behavior has the potential to create meaning. Does that make all behavior communication? Nonverbal communication is a behavior. Does that make all nonverbal behavior communication? There has been an ongoing argument among communication theorists as to what defines nonverbal communication. Some theorists claim that any nonverbal behavior intentionally sent or not, is a form of communication. Others disagree, limiting it to strictly an intentional behavior. These theorists argue that in order for nonverbal behavior to be considered a form of communication, it must fulfill three criteria: (1) the message must be perceived consciously by either the sender or receiver; (2) the sender intended it to be a message; and (3) it has to be interpreted by the receiver as a message.[12] There is a middle ground, though. Some nonverbal communication is unintentional, while most is intentional. We know that an unintended message can have powerful effects on the receiver, even though the sender did not consciously intend to send a message. (Intentionality in nonverbal communication may be difficult to determine in many instances.) We can define nonverbal communication as any instance in which a stimulus other than words creates meaning in either a sender's or a receiver's mind.[13] What constitutes a stimulus? A stimulus can be a single behavior or a group of particular behaviors. The most common forms of nonverbal communication are:

1. **Facial displays.** We are all familiar with facial displays. We use them to express our emotions and our thoughts. There are many forms of facial displays. Crying is a facial display that can be an expression of sadness or happiness. How is that, you ask? We can use Yecenia as an example. Yecenia has been impatiently waiting to hear if she is going to be accepted into college. One day, she receives a letter from one of the schools she applied to and opens it. It says, "Dear Yecenia, we are sorry to inform you..." She breaks down and sobs after reading the letter. She obviously is sad. We know she is sad because she is crying. The next day, Yecenia receives a letter from another college; she opens it and cries. But this time, she is jumping up and down at the same time. Is Yecenia happy or sad? The letter reads, "Dear Yecenia, congratulations on your acceptance to...". She is happy, of course, but could you determine that by observing her crying? Yecenia didn't know she was being watched by us during either occasion. She didn't intend to send us any nonverbal messages, but they were sent nevertheless. Are these instances

© Orange Line Media, 2011. Under license from Shutterstock, Inc.

of nonverbal communication? Yes, they are. Although she didn't intend to send the messages, we interpreted them as such because we were stimulated by her behavior.

2. **Eye behavior.** Have you ever been told, or have you ever told someone else, "Don't roll your eyes at me?" And you respond or were responded to, "I'm not rolling my eyes at you!" Of course you have, thousands of times. And of course, you rolled your eyes. Eyes have a way of telling on us, whether we like it or not. They have a tendency to reflect our thoughts and responses. In our culture, we believe that you must be able to look the other person in the eyes when spoken to; otherwise, you can't be trusted. Haven't you been told, "Look me in the eyes when I speak to you?" Sure you have. The person thinks that by looking him or her in the eyes, you receive and understand the message. We associate eye behavior with specific character traits. People who make frequent eye contact are consider trustworthy, friendly, and sincere, compared to those who avoid eye contact. We have a tendency to be suspicious of people who can't look us in the eyes when speaking.

3. **Eyebrows.** They are a part of facial displays, and one can argue, part of eye contact. But let's talk about eyebrows for a moment. We raise and lower our eyebrows both intentionally and unintentionally. We intentionally raise them to show approval or an emotion, and we unintentionally raise them when we are surprised. We intentionally lower our eyebrows to show disapproval or dissatisfaction, and we unintentionally lower them when we aren't sure about something.

4. **Paralanguage.** This is how we say something. It is the connotative meaning that the sender assigns to the actual words used when delivering a message. Paralanguage includes vocal qualities such as loudness, pitch, inflection, tempo, rhythm, intensity, articulation, resonance, dialects, accents, pauses, and silences. At times, we may augment these by crying, laughing, moaning, yelling, or whining. Group members often use paralanguage to let other members know that they agree or disagree, approve, or are uncertain about member contributions. The voice is often used to imply personality traits.

5. **Body language.** This consists of body movements such as gestures, posture, and head, trunk, and limb movements. The study of body movements is known as **kinesics**. Body movements are internal indicators; they often reflect our emotional states and what we are thinking. We automatically turn away from people we don't want to speak or associate with. When we are uncomfortable with something someone has said or in the presence of someone we don't want to be with, we fidget; that is, we seem to nervously move our body. Slouching in our seats while someone is speaking and looking around the room aimlessly are cues that we are bored.

Kinesics
The study of body movements.

Body language can indicate whether group members are attentive. For example, if one or more members are looking around the room, doodling on paper,

By permission of Leigh Rubin and Creators Syndicate, Inc.

That day, Koko learned a new hand gesture not usually found in the standard curriculum.

frequently yawning, or checking their fingernails, these are cues that they are bored and disengaged from the group process.

We can summarize aspects of nonverbal communication as **interaction cues**. In group discussions, they provide many cues for interactions. Facial gestures, tone of voice, posture, and eye behavior indicate feelings and levels of interest. At times, nonverbal cues are complete messages in themselves. Without having to say a word, a simple nod of the head may indicate agreement or disagreement. In other circumstances, nonverbal cues supplement verbal messages—for example, telling someone you disagree with him or her while simultaneously waving a pointed finger from side to side.

We use nonverbal cues to regulate or control interaction in groups. The flow of discussion is usually regulated by the leader pointing a finger at the next speaker. When a speaker allows for someone else to interrupt, there is usually a longer than normal pause, which signals that it is OK to speak.

We know that verbal communication directs the task, process, and climate aspects of the group discussion. How does nonverbal communication play a role in this as an interactive group process?

VERBAL AND NONVERBAL COMMUNICATION INTERCONNECTEDNESS

The words that we use, the way in which we put them together, and the way we express them affect what we think and how we think. Communication competence is more than just having a good vocabulary or speaking well. It is the ability to command both verbal and nonverbal communication to produce effective messages. When we see others doing this, we call them communicators, and sometimes we call them leaders. The first step to becoming a good communicator is to know how to effectively *connect* verbal and nonverbal messages.

Communication as a Regulatory Function

We use language to regulate our thoughts and behaviors. In small-group communication, we can identify at least seven functions of language in this process.[14]

1. **Language allows us to express and control emotion.** During periods of stressful discussion, we talk simply in an attempt to reduce inner tension. At other times, we may want to withhold emotional venting, preventing us from shouting or yelling at other members. In effect, we talk ourselves out of blowing our tops. Regulating our emotions enables us to create and

maintain good working relationships with our colleagues. It helps us to remain focused on our charge. And it is a sign of maturity.

2. **Language can reveal or camouflage our thoughts and motives.** Nobody knows what we are thinking until we choose to tell them or act it out through our behavior. Only if we communicate our thoughts can members know what we are thinking and why. On the other hand, we can combine nonverbal with verbal communication to camouflage our thoughts. We may want to yell at the group, but a simple wave of the hand and a "nothing's wrong" masks our true intentions.

3. **Language permits us to make and avoid contact.** Language is our connection to others, and it can also be a wall. We use language to reach out to our colleagues, to connect with them, to form bonds. We also use language to separate ourselves from others, to create walls when we don't want to communicate.

4. **Language enables us to assert individual and social identity.** Each of us is unique, and language enables us to present ourselves and an image of how we want to be perceived by others. When members come together to form a group, one of the first things we do is talk about ourselves—who we are, our backgrounds, likes and dislikes, etc. And when the group reaches a synergy, it creates an identity all of its own, in which members proudly relate to others.

5. **Language may be used to give or seek information.** Language is the primary medium for information exchange. It allows us to gather, organize, evaluate, and share information. Through language, we can discover, describe, interpret, classify, recognize, identify, explain, state, analyze, and synthesize the information around us. Language also affords us the ability to comprehend and understand meanings and ideas.

6. **Language allows us to control and be controlled.** It is power. We use language to influence, regulate, persuade, or dominate group members. From making a good impression at the first meeting to asserting ourselves as leaders, we use language to control group roles and group work. Language also controls us because of the rules and regulations we place on ourselves and group activities.

7. **Language can be used to monitor the process of communication.** Language is self-reflexive; it allows us to metacommunicate, to communicate about the communication process. We periodically ask ourselves if we are effectively communicating with one another; we share our thoughts and concerns about the group communication process. And we can *assess* its effectiveness.

Small-Group Communication Is Personal Communication

We speak with our colleagues, not at them or to them. We consider them to be our equals, and as such they deserve our respect. We coordinate, or synchronize, our verbal and nonverbal messages. If we didn't, we would be sending mixed messages, which would be confusing to the group members. Small-group communication involves content and relationship dimensions. We speak to group members as if we are speaking to each one individually. Remember, we speak *with* our colleagues.

INTERPERSONAL COMMUNICATION COMPETENCE

Interpersonal communication is also known as dyadic communication, communication between two people, generally in face-to-face interaction. When a third person enters the interaction, it ceases to be interpersonal and becomes **small group communication**. So how is it still interpersonal? The size of the group remains relatively small, so everyone can interact freely. Members are free to speak with other members, unlike when only two individuals are talking to one another. If one person stops, the connection between them is severed, and the interpersonal relationship ceases to exist. However, in small group discussion, when two members stop speaking, the link is not severed; members can still communicate in a variety of ways, thereby extending interpersonal communication.

How do we transform interpersonal communication into interpersonal communication competence? I wish it were as easy as it sounds. Competence means having the know-how, ability, skill, capability, or expertise to be able to accomplish something well. As we shall see when we read about Interpersonal Communication Skills for Leaders (Chapter 8), competently coordinating group interaction is a complex process. We can best describe the competence process by identifying its two basic components: the cognitive process (the internal state), which is how we take in or perceive, process, and store information; and our behavior (the external state), how we deliver verbal, nonverbal, and relational messages.

The first step in becoming competent is to self-monitor your thoughts before you speak and to understand your nonverbal cues. This is the most difficult step because we forget to remind ourselves of what we want to do. Many of us are not aware of our gestures when we speak. Some of us emote or exaggerate our nonverbal cues, while others rarely display any. Many times, we speak without really thinking of what we are saying until it is too late—oops, "I shouldn't have said that." We become aware through practice. Think about what you want to say before you speak. Don't let your emotions control you; you control your emotions. When we are fired up, we want to blurt it out, and fast. Ask yourself, "What's going on here?" If you do this or something similar, you switch from an emotional state to a cognitive state—you're now thinking instead of reacting. When you think, you can analyze; you can assess. It suppresses your emotions. Even if you are not emotional at the time you speak, just the fact that you pause to think about what you are going to say enables you to modify your statements. We do the same basic drill for our nonverbal cues. Once you are aware of your body movements, you can control them. The key is to control your verbal and nonverbal messages, to create messages that best represent your thoughts. When you are able to do this you have gained interpersonal communication competence. The next step is to transform this competence into relational competence, which is the ability to process and create messages that convey the type of relationships desired for effective group work.[15] As with any skill, the more you practice, the better you become.

Small group communication is a system designed to transfer information and meaning, or the exchange of information and meaning. How you frame and deliver your message, how you treat your colleagues, affects your place within the group. These communication skills will serve as potential power currencies when you become a group leader.

Dialectic versus Dialogue

According to Plato, there is but only one way to discover truth, and that is through the dialectical method.[16] Dialectics, during Plato's time, was a way to search for significant issues, identify alternatives, and generate standards or criteria for selection, all to be used to test proposals. As a way to find the truth, it occurred through a question–answer process that was designed for the participants to persuade one another.[17] Contemporary dialectics is often referred to as "a social dialogue in which people seek to come to understanding by opening themselves to the thinking of others with an interest in learning and changing."[18]

Dialectics has a theoretical basis for small group discussion. We use dialectics when we try to understand the relationship of propositions (an idea, offer, or plan put forward for consideration or discussion) to one another. For example, let's look at a problem-solving situation we'll call "Road Repair." A county board of supervisors agrees that a particular county road is in desperate need of repair. They are debating the method with which to repair it. One solution, or proposition, to the problem is to repair the road with macadam. Another solution, or proposition, is to use concrete. They will probably ask the county road superintendent a series of questions designed to compare and contrast the costs and benefits of each material. The supervisors will want to know which one is more beneficial, at what cost, and for how long. They will use the dialectical method for getting their answers. Dialectics in small group communication is useful and necessary when you want to get answers to questions regarding a central issue. It is a comprehensive examination of all positions relevant to the topic[19] and a way to test opinions. This is significant because dialectics helps the group stay focused by preventing disruptive or irrelevant questions that might sidetrack the problem-solving process. It is important to stay on track, to know what is being discussed, and to remain focused.

Once they have their answers, they will use a dialogue process—a conversation or discussion between themselves in which they will exchange ideas and opinions on the issue of road repair. Let's revisit the statement, "Small group communication is a system designed to transfer information and meaning, or the exchange of information and meaning." This is the dialogue process for problem-solving. It is an exchange of ideas in a discussion format. The supervisors will discuss not only the cost/benefit ratios of each type of material, but they will probably talk about other related topics, such as where they will find the money with which to repair the road, other county departments that will be required to participate, how long the road will be closed or have one-lane traffic accessibility. This totality of dialogue will be necessary for the board of supervisors to reach a well-thought-out solution to their problem.

CULTURE AND COMMUNICATION

Cultural Differences

 Culture
The dominant set of learned behaviors, values, beliefs, and thinking patterns we learn as we grow and develop in our social groups.

What is **culture**?

Globalization has presented us with many new issues for group participation and communication. Whether we travel to other countries and engage in group discussion or members of other cultures come to the United States, we must be able to effectively communicate with one another if we are to accomplish our tasks. Even if we never travel outside of the country, we live in the most diverse of all societies, which means that we are destined to have communication barriers, no matter where we go or what we do. You don't need to speak a second language in order to effectively communicate in a small group setting. However, you should know some of the basics that govern culture and communication.

What is culture? We can define culture as the dominant set of learned behaviors, values, beliefs, and thinking patterns we learn as we grow and develop in our social groups. Culture determines how we view ourselves and others, how we behave, and how we perceive the world around us.[20] Culture is basically a learned system of value-laden meanings that helps us to make sense of and explain what is going on in our everyday life[21] and determine how we fit into this life. It is the set of important understandings that members in a society have in common. Culture guides individual and collective behavior. We develop our cultural understanding from our parents, relatives, friends, teachers, primary groups, and many others who influence us or impart their dominant values, attitudes, beliefs, thinking patterns, and behaviors on us. Some cultural norms are so strongly ingrained into our daily lives that we may be unaware of certain behaviors. Sometimes it takes interacting with people from different cultures with different values and beliefs in order for us to recognize and modify our own. It is important to understand *how* and *why* cultural differences influence the communication process so we can effectively communicate in diverse group settings. Our goal is to develop cultural effectiveness, which is the ability to recognize cultural attributes and use related information to effectively interact with members of a given culture. Cultural attributes define a culture and distinguish it from other cultures.

Cultural Norms

Cultural norms refer to the collective expectations of what constitutes proper or improper behavior in a given interaction situation.[22] Each culture has explicit and implicit rules for behavior, which we call **normative rules**, or **cultural norms**. The following table represents communicative norms between the United States and other cultures.[23] (See Table 1.1.)

What Influences Thinking in Cultures?

The word **cognitive** or **cognition** refers to thought. **Cognitive style** refers to thought patterns, or the way we process information. Styles describe our typical mode of thinking, remembering, or problem-solving.[24] Cognitive styles influence attitudes, values, and social interaction, while **cognitive processes** refer to the relationship between thinking and language.

We take in data, or information, during every conscious moment. Some of this information is merely noise, and we ignore it. Some of it is of no interest, so we forget about it almost as quickly as we receive it. However, there are data that we consciously make an effort to accept or ignore. There are three aspects of cognitive styles that directly influence the communication process: (1) **open-mindedness** and **close-mindedness**—which refer to thought patterns; (2) **associative** and **abstract information processes**—how people process information; and (3) **particularistic versus universalistic thinkers**—how thinking and behavior are focused.

1. Open-mindedness. Open-minded people are just the opposite of those with minds like steel traps. Milton Rokeach (1960) believed that the basic characteristic that defined a person's open-mindedness is "the extent to which the person can receive, evaluate, and act on relevant information received from the outside on its own intrinsic merits, unencumbered by irrelevant factors in the situation, within the person, or from the outside."[25] Open-minded individuals tend to actively seek out more information before they make decisions. Also, they are more likely to see the relativity of issues.

   Close-mindedness. I'm sure you have heard the phrase, "His mind is like a steel trap." Another way of stating it is to say that he is close-minded. Close-minded people have tunnel vision—they see only a narrow range of data and ignore everything else when they make decisions. When compared to those who are open-minded, close-minded people tend to be less able to learn new information. They have more difficulty discriminating between pieces of information, so they tend to accept whatever authorities say is true. They also tend to have problems in resolving conflicts, and they generally refuse to compromise because they equate compromise with defeat.[26]

2. Associative information process. A person who thinks associatively filters new data, or sensory input, through the screen of personal experience. Genuinely new information is understood only by associating it with existing knowledge and experiences. If an associative thinker encounters something

Cultural norms
The collective expectations of what constitutes proper or improper behavior in a given interaction situation.

he or she has never experienced before, instead of creating a new cognitive category for it, he or she will attach it to something of similar construct and call it that, even though it isn't.[27]

TABLE 1.1	Comparing Cultural Norms	
Aspects of Culture	Mainstream American Culture Low-context communication	Other Cultures High-context communication
1. Communication and language	**Explicit, direct communication:** emphasis on how intention and meaning are best expressed through explicit verbal messages	**Implicit communication:** emphasis on how intention or meaning can best be conveyed through the context (e.g., social roles or positions) and nonverbal channels (e.g., pauses, silence, tone of voice) of the verbal message
2. Communication patterns	**Direct verbal mode:** straight talk, nonverbal immediacy, sender-oriented values (Sender assumes responsibility to communicate clearly. Speaker is responsible for constructing a clear, persuasive message that the listener can decode.)	**Indirect verbal mode:** self-humbling talk, nonverbal subtleties, interpretive values (Receiver of message assumes responsibility to infer hidden or contextual meanings of message.) Listener is expected to "read between the lines," to accurately infer the implicit intent of the verbal message and to decode the nonverbal subtleties that accompany the verbal message.
3. Direct and indirect verbal styles	Verbal statements tend to reveal speaker's intentions with clarity and are enunciated with tone of voice.	Verbal statements tend to camouflage speaker's actual intentions and are carried out with a softer tone.

Abstract information process. Unlike the associative thinker, the abstractive thinker can deal with something authentically new. When the abstractive person encounters new data, he or she doesn't have to lump it in with past experiences. The abstractive person is more able to extrapolate data and consider hypothetical situations

3. Particularistic versus universalistic thinkers. People are divided into particular versus universal thinkers. The particularist person feels that a personal relationship is more important than obeying rules or laws. The universalistic person tends to abide by rules and laws, while relationships are less important than one's duty to the company, society, and authority in general. These categories tend to cluster in certain patterns. Abstractive thinkers often display universalistic behavior: it requires abstractive thought to see beyond one's personal relationships and consider the good of society (which is a highly abstractive concept).[28]

What Influences Behavior in Cultures?

Value systems are the basis for behavior. Each cultural group has a well-developed value system. Because no two cultures share an exact value system, misunderstanding and conflict are often caused by differences in value orientations.[29] Values are our central, core ideals about how to live or conduct our lives. We define values as generalized evaluations of right and wrong that we learn from our culture and that we use to judge the behavior of ourselves and others. A value is simply a belief that some goals and paths to goal achievement are better than others. As a result, values are far more stable than attitudes and beliefs.[30]

In his value theory Milton Rokeach (1968) tells us that the self-concept is a powerful guide to behavior. Each of us has an identity we try to live up to. For Rokeach, the clearest reflection of people's identities is their values. Rokeach believes that people can be influenced by appeals to their value systems. If, for example, honesty is high on your hierarchy of values, you will return a lost wallet full of cash to its owner instead of keeping it. Values are key parts of our life scripts.[31]

There are two basic categories of values that we live by: **terminal values** and **instrumental values**. Terminal values are known as preferred end states of existence. These are values that we try to live life by and the ones we pass on from generation to generation. We see many terminal values in documents such as the Old Testament, the Torah, the Koran, and in many cultural religious beliefs. Some terminal values are:

1. Honesty (Honesty is the best policy.)
2. Truthfulness (It is always best to tell the truth.)
3. Salvation (eternal life)
4. Freedom (independence, free choice)
5. A world at peace (free of war and conflict)
6. Family security (taking care of loved ones)
7. Wisdom (a mature understanding of life)

Values
Our central, core ideals about how to live or conduct our lives.

Terminal values
Values that we try to live life by and the ones we pass on from generation to generation.

Instrumental values

Values we try to live life by on a daily basis.

Instrumental values are referred to as preferable modes of conduct. These are the values we try to live life by on a daily basis. Unlike terminal values, which may not be attainable, instrumental values are achievable. Some instrumental values are:

1. Ambition (hardworking, aspiring)
2. Cleanliness (neat, tidy)
3. Courage (standing up for your beliefs)
4. Politeness (courteous, well-mannered)
5. Helpfulness (working for the welfare of others)
6. Broad-mindedness (open-minded)
7. Responsibility (dependable, reliable)

We learn our values from our parents, teachers, government officials, religious leaders, and the judicial system; and in turn, we demand that these values be upheld by the very social institutions that taught us these values. That makes value transmission within a culture cyclical, self-perpetuating, and consequently very static and unchanging over time.[32] Values are key parts of our life scripts. One of our strongest motivations is to remain true to what we believe is right. Values play an integral part in small group communication.

Overcoming Language Barriers

Use Concrete Language

When we communicate in small group settings, we use less written language and more oral communication, which is informal language, characterized by shorter words and phrases and less complex sentence structures than written language. One of the most obvious signs of cultural difference is language difference. Language is the most important means by which a culture passes on its

Concrete language

Words that best describe or are most specific to tangible objects (people, places, and things.)

Abstract words

Those that refer to general ideas, attributes or qualities.

values and beliefs. When we say to use concrete language, we mean that you should use words that best describe or are most specific to tangible objects—people, places, and things. Words that are familiar to native speakers of English may not be familiar to non-native speakers. Also, speakers often use abstract words, which refer to general ideas, attributes, or qualities. Or they may use local or regional slang, colloquialisms, jargon, and contractions that may be understood only by those who are familiar with them. You may be familiar with the words in Table 1.2 that follows.

Of course, there aren't too many words that are completely abstract or concrete. Usually, the more specific a word, the more concrete it is. And the meaning of a word always lies in its context. The best words are often the simplest. Your words should be immediately understandable to your group members. Never try to impress them with jargon or long words. Your word choice is meant to articulate your thoughts and message with clarity so your colleagues can fully understand you the first time you speak. You should always use words carefully. This will help you communicate your intended message.

When we have a small group that is ethnically diverse, this has the potential to create problems in communication and understanding. We refer to this as **vocabulary equivalence**. Languages that are different often lack words that are directly translatable.[34] In small group communication, your language should be specific and concrete, simple and correct.

Abstract	Concrete	**TABLE 1.2**
vegetable	carrot	
tree	maple	
water	river	
clothing	dress shirt	
education	bachelor of arts degree	
car	corvette	
sports	soccer	
candy	lemon drops	
science	astronomy	
philosophy	Kantian ethics	
dessert	rocky road ice cream	

Jargon[33]

barrel full of monkeys	This term is used as a sarcastic description of something not being very much fun. *"Hey, Spense, how was Lisa's party last night?"* *"It was a barrel full of monkeys."*
phat	entertaining, intelligent, attractive, or otherwise to be admired. *"Hey, Spense, what do you think of Lisa?"* *"Man, she is P.H.A.T.!"*
sweet	awesome, amazing, nice *"Hey, Spense, how do you like that new guitar hero game?"* *"Man, it is sweet!"*
T-bone	to hit broadside *"I got t-boned by a drunk running a stop sign."*

Appropriate Behavior

When I refer to the term **self-monitoring**, I don't mean it in the context of being aware of images of the self and the ability to adapt these images to the situation at hand, as referred to by Sarah Trenholm and Arthur Jensen (1996). I mean it in the context that you should be aware of what you say and do before you say and do it. We self-monitor by thinking about what we will say and how we will say it, and by considering how our behavior will be perceived. If you take a moment to think about your message before you say it, which is proactive communication, chances are you will be selective in your word choice and delivery, or even change some of your language. Thinking—using your cognitive process—allows you to formulate a well-thought-out message rather than blurting out something random or reacting to someone else.

Nonverbal Cues

This also refers to nonverbal messages. Differences in verbal communication between cultures can be obvious, whereas nonverbal differences may be less obvious but equally important. The meaning assigned to body language and eye contact differs from culture to culture. As we have read, there are few, if any, nonverbal cues that have universal meaning. For example, when we are asked if everything is O.K., we give a thumbs up gesture. Just the opposite is true in Saudi Arabia, Denmark, Russia, Latin America, and Australia, where the thumbs up gesture is offensive or rude. Our O.K sign (thumb and forefinger curled in an O) means money to the Japanese. In the Netherlands, sucking one's thumb is a way of saying, "I don't believe you."

Here's another example. In the United States, to point, we use the index finger, although it is generally not polite to point at a person. However, in India, pointing with a finger is rude; Indians point with their chin. In South Korea, pointing is done using the middle finger. And finally, we make a victory gesture using the index and middle finger, but in New Zealand and Australia, the "V for victory" sign is considered obscene, especially when performed with the palm facing inward.

We can conclude that hand gestures are not universal: rather, they are culture-specific and often do not share the same meaning. The point is to be aware of your nonverbal cues when you are speaking in a diverse group. You may think that you are saying one thing, when in fact it may mean something totally different to someone else. One of the last things you want to do is offend a group member.

Conflict Management Differences

When we talk about conflict between group members, we often refer to dealing with it as **conflict management** instead of **conflict resolution**. Conflict is inevitable whenever two or more people interact. This conflict generally arises out of differences of opinion or disagreements about how to accomplish certain group tasks. As long as the group is actively pursuing a charge, there will be conflict and conflict management, seldom conflict resolution. Conflict has a definite role in the small group process, as we shall see in Chapter 11. When we speak about conflict and diversity in groups, we hold a basic principle in intercultural conflict management that people bring their **cultural assumptions** to that conflict. Cultural assumptions are a **cluster of beliefs** that govern behavior and are viewed as fundamental by those who hold them. Much of the way we manage conflict is a result of cultural programming, along with its implications. We discover that it is in conflict situations that it becomes apparent that we have strong preferences, predispositions, values, rules, and expectations of others that have all been shaped by culture.[35]

© Nebojsa Bobic, 2011. Under license from Shutterstock.

Competent intercultural conflict management depends on many factors. The first and foremost factor is to view conflict in small group settings as a positive thing, not negative and destructive. Conflict means that there are differences that need to be worked out, and these should be viewed as opportunities. These differences, when managed appropriately, bring clarity, strength, and understanding to the group. They facilitate the joint decision-making and agreement processes that are essential for joint decisions. The second factor is understanding that cultural differences can cause conflict, and once that occurs, cultural backgrounds and experiences influence how individuals deal with it. The third factor is to understand how you deal with conflict and to know that you can have a major influence on the conflict management process. The fourth is to understand that everybody doesn't approach conflict management in the same way. You need to know how individuals view conflict. Do they avoid conflict as much as possible? Do they accommodate rather than try to address conflict? Do they believe that something is wrong with people who get into conflicts? Do they enjoy conflict because it makes life more interesting for them? Or do they think that conflict should be resolved quickly and by any means necessary? And fifth, realize that conflict management in intercultural small groups can be a continuous process, and it will not end until the group completes its charge.

We have many different frameworks for thinking about culture and conflict—for example, high and low context, and individualist and collectivist. (See Table 1.3.) These starting points are relevant both in trying to understand differences and in trying to address them. We can generalize that people who value individualism tend to favor direct forms of communication and to support overt forms of conflict resolution, while people in collectivist societies may use less direct communication and more avoidance-style conflict resolution.[36]

Cultural assumptions

A cluster of beliefs that govern behavior and are viewed as fundamental by those who hold them.

TABLE 1.3	**High and Low Context Communication**

High Context Communication	Low Context Communication
1. High use of non-verbal signals.	High use of verbal messages.
2. Communications are indirect and seen as an art form.	Communication is direct and seen as instrumental.
3. Conflicts must be resolved before work can progress.	Conflicts can remain ongoing.
4. Conflict may be prolonged.	Conflict can aid creativity or be destructive.
5. Conflict may slow down change and innovation.	Conflict can be resolved relatively quickly.
6. Communication may be less precise.	Emphasis on facts and objectivity.

CULTURAL PROPOSITIONS

Collectivist	Individualist
1. Members use a greater degree of avoidance-oriented conflict style.	Members use a greater degree of solution-oriented conflict style.
2. Members tend to use more obliging or smoothing strategies to manage conflict.	Members tend to use more dominating or controlling strategies to manage conflict.
3. Members tend to use a greater degree of approval-seeking strategies in managing conflict.[37]	Members tend to use more autonomy-preserving strategies in managing conflict.

Stella Ting-toomey and Leeva C. Chung (2005)[38] have identified culture-based conflict lenses, which they call value patterns that color our conflict attitudes, expectations, and behaviors when we are involved in conflict. For example, for individualists or independent-self personality types, intercultural conflict management often follows an outcome-oriented model. Using an **independent-self-conflict lens**, a person often views conflict from (1) a content conflict goal lens, which emphasizes tangible conflict issues above and beyond relationship issues; (2) a clear win–lose conflict approach, in which one person comes out as a winner and the other person comes out as a loser; (3) a "doing" angle, in which something tangible in the conflict is broken and needs fixing;

and (4) an outcome-driven mode, in which a clear action plan or resolution is needed. Ting-toomey and Chung note that this type of person makes every effort to have his or her individual accomplishments brought to the attention of the entire group, and he or she wants to stand out and be recognized for all his or her task accomplishments.

In comparison, for collectivists or interdependent-self personality types, intercultural conflict management often follows a process-oriented model. Using an **interdependent-self conflict lens**, a person often perceives conflict from (1) a relational process lens, which emphasizes relationship and feeling issues; (2) a win–win relational approach, in which feelings and faces can both be saved; (3) a "being" angle, in which relational trust needs to be repaired and loyalty needs to be amended to preserve relational harmony; and (4) a long-term compromising negotiation mode that has a clear winner or loser in the ongoing conflict.

We can summarize their findings by saying that independent-self types are concerned with conflict outcome closure, whereas interdependent-self types are concerned with interpersonal and intragroup face-saving and face-honoring process issues. One group wants to have solution-based conflict management while the other is more interested in preserving face and the relationship. What is important to remember when engaging in small group conflict management is that everyone doesn't approach conflict the same way. Cultural differences play a major role in how we deal with conflict because conflict will differ from culture to culture. Each culture has very different styles and aspects of communicating, such as differences in language, meanings of facial expressions, and body language. These can become barriers to effective communication and conflict management.

ELEMENTS OF COMPETENCE

When conflict arises in a multicultural group setting and you want to intervene, you won't always know how to act, what to do, or what to say. The main thing to remember is to be yourself—don't try to fake it. Note in the box that follows that there are some things you should be aware of.[39]

Communication Knowledge

1. Spoken language. Consists of cultural dialects, words with special meaning and definition to the culture, often with blends of the native language with the dominant language.
2. Tone/inflection of voice. Both the denotative and connotative meanings of words change by raising or lowering the pitch of the voice on various key syllables or words in a sentence.
3. Eye contact/facial expression. Make a mental note about the duration of eye contact, how emotions are expressed, and feelings that are displayed through the face.

4. **Body language/gestures.** Observe the person's general body posture, his or her proximity to others, use of arms and hands to emphasize or illustrate the meaning of the words being spoken.
5. **Touch.** Frequency, force, and location of touching between individuals.

Skills for Bridging Barriers

1. **Listen effectively.** One of the most critical skills you can learn is to listen effectively. Listening skills must be developed because there are so many impeding factors such as:
   - Being more concerned with what we want to say than what is being said;
   - Hearing only what we want to hear;
   - Preconceived notions about what the others are saying or are going to say;
   - Assumptions and values that alter the meaning of the words between you and the speaker.
2. **Resist judgmental reactions.**
   - We should listen without subjecting the information to our own cultural biases.
   - When we communicate a value judgment, the speaker is put on the defensive.
3. **Monitor perception.**
   - Our perceptions are shaped by our cultural assumptions and values. We tend to filter communication and behavior through these lenses. You should be aware of this.
   - We should suspend our own assumptions and the values we normally attach to what we see or hear.
   - To do this, we should make a conscious effort to minimize cultural bias.
4. **Seek feedback.**
   - Ask those with whom you are speaking if you are being understood.
   - Clarify meanings that might be otherwise altered by cultural differences.
5. **Cultivate self-awareness.**
   - Monitoring perceptions requires self-awareness.
   - Be especially aware of your behavior patterns, communication style, and thinking patterns.
6. **Take risks.**
   - Be the first to open channels of communication.
   - Make yourself open to establishing initial trust.
   - Sufficient trust must be developed to permit some level of mutual exposure before communication can occur.

The strategies listed should help you develop your intercultural conflict management skills in a small group setting. They are but a few, but essential, elements that can get you to that goal. The more you know, the more competent you will become.

Some Differences Between Feminine and Masculine Communication[41]

TABLE 1.4

Feminine Talk	Masculine Talk
1. Use talk to build and sustain rapport with others.	1. Use talk to assert yourself and your ideas.
2. Share yourself, and learn about others through disclosing.	2. Personal disclosures can make you vulnerable.
3. Use talk to create symmetry or equality between people.	3. Use talk to establish your status and power.
4. Matching experiences with others shows understanding and empathy (e.g., "I know how you feel").	4. Matching experiences is a competitive strategy to command attention (e.g., "I can top that").
5. To support others, express understanding of their feelings.	5. To support others, do something helpful; give advice or solve a problem for them.
6. Include others in conversation by asking their opinions and encouraging them to elaborate. Wait your turn to speak so others can participate.	6. Don't share the talk stage with others; wrest it from them with communication. Interrupt others to make your own points.
7. Keep the conversation going by asking questions and showing interest in others.	7. Each person is on his or her own; it's not your job to help others join in.
8. Be responsive. Let others know you hear and care about what they say.	8. Use responses to make your own points and outshine the others.
9. Be attentive so that others feel free to add their ideas.	9. Be assertive so that others perceive you as confident and in command.
10. Talking is a human relationship in which details and interesting side comments enhance depths of connection.	10. Talking is a linear sequence that should convey information and accomplish goals. Extraneous details get in the way and achieve nothing.

GENDER AND COMMUNICATION

Gender Differences in Communication

As we noted earlier, culture is the foundation on which systems of communication are built. Culture also determines the roles we play in our everyday lives and the rules we must live by. We have been taught since early childhood that boys and girls should behave and speak in different ways. These expectations have been taught to us by our parents, relatives, teachers, friends, and so forth. In society, we distinguish between male and female roles, such as jobs. And in these roles we are taught that males speak a certain way and females speak a certain way. These are **sex-oriented** behaviors. They are a reference for a biological or anatomical designation. However, when we use the terms **feminine** and **masculine**, we are referring to gender, a type of personality orientation. When we describe someone as being feminine, we don't necessarily mean that the individual is female. The same holds for describing someone as masculine; it doesn't mean that the person is a male.

A person's psychological gender orientation is her or his level of self-identification, which includes both dominance (instrumentality) and submissiveness (expressiveness) when interacting with others.[40] A person with a well-developed feminine gender orientation will use mostly submissive communication behaviors. These behaviors will express helpfulness, affection, sympathy, compassion, warmth, and sensitivity to others' needs, tenderness, and gentleness. Conversely, a person who has a strong masculine gender orientation uses primarily dominant communication behaviors. This person will convey competitiveness, aggressiveness, self-sufficiency, forcefulness, assertiveness, a willingness to lead, and independence. In general, a masculine orientation expresses strong control needs while the feminine orientation expresses strong affection needs.

Differences Between Feminine and Masculine Communication

Have you ever noticed that there are distinct differences between male and female communication? Sometimes, it is like night and day. I remember a great example from a seminar I took many years ago. It goes something like this: Sally woke up with a terrible headache, and as she got dressed to go to work, she told her husband, Jim, about it. He immediately went to the medicine cabinet and got two aspirin and gave them to her. While at work, Sally remarked to one of her coworkers, Lupida, that she had had a headache all morning. Lupida replied, "Come here, honey, rest your head on my shoulder and tell me about it." One person tried to fix the headache problem for Sally by giving her aspirin, while the other recognized that Sally needed a little comfort.

Gendered Socialization in Conflict Situations

1. Women tend to defer and compromise.
2. Men often resort to bullying and unilateral fiats.
3. Men are more likely to adopt coercive stances.
4. Women are inclined to be affiliative.

Gendered Standpoints

1. Males typically play in large groups, engaging in competitive activities in which status, independence, and winning are prized.
2. Females usually play with two or three friends, and they favor games that require communication, cooperation, and attention to relationships.
3. For females, the **process of playing** is the focus, while **winning** is central in boys' games.
4. Individuals socialized into a feminine standpoint tend to see relationships as ongoing processes, and they perceive communication as a means to build and sustain connections.
5. Individuals with masculine standpoints generally see relationships as events and outcomes, and they regard communication as an instrument to assert status, solve problems, or convey information.
6. **Gendered standpoints** promote differences in feminine and masculine styles of creating and expressing intimacy.
7. Women view **personal talk** as the primary route to intimacy. Men generally regard doing things together as a means to **closeness**. Both women and men seek closeness, yet they select different paths to achieve it.
8. **From a feminine standpoint**, relationships are ongoing processes that are always evolving in ways that need to be talked through.
9. **From a masculine standpoint**, the emphasis on outcomes inclines men to see commitment as an event that is fixed at one time and doesn't require constant attention.

It is important to understand that there are many differences in the ways that males and females communicate, and group discussion is no exception. From information-gathering to conflict management, relationship-building to self-disclosure, there is no doubt that gender influences our communication.

ETHICS

Let's say, for example, that you're a member of the student council, and the council is trying to decide which vendor will be awarded the contract to provide all the food and beverage for Rush Week. The student president has been insisting that *Hearty Foods* get the contract, and he's even gone as far as to privately encourage a number of the other council members that *Hearty Foods* should be given the contract. After much debate, the council does award the contract to *Hearty Foods*. A few weeks after Rush, you hear that *Hearty Foods* promised

© Robert Kneschke, 2011. Under license from Shutterstock, Inc.

the student president a free vacation if he got them the contract. Should you care? I hope so. The student president had a **hidden agenda**, he secretly benefited from the choice the council made. Was this unethical? You bet!

What is ethics? Why should we care about ethical behavior in group discussion and interaction? Why do we consider ethics to be an integral component of small group work? The discussion about ethics is as old as mankind itself. Philosophers have studied ethics for centuries, and as we have discovered, there are no easy answers as to what constitutes good or right human behavior. Each culture, each generation within that culture, redefines proper human behavior. We can determine much about a culture by studying its established code of ethics.

Ethics Defined

The *Oxford University Press* defines ethics as the "study of the concepts involved in practical reasoning: good, right, duty, obligation, virtue, freedom, rationality, choice."[42] The *Columbia University Press*

Ethics

A code of conduct based on moral philosophy.

defines ethics as "the study and evaluation of human conduct in the light of moral principles. Moral principles may be viewed either as the standard of conduct that individuals have constructed for themselves or as the body of obligations and duties that a particular society requires of its members."[43]

Basically, ethics is a code of conduct based on moral philosophy. It involves systematizing, defending, and recommending concepts of right and wrong behavior. Ethical conduct defines how people should behave toward one another in a civil society, and it defines individual and group conduct in group discussion.

A Culture's Code of Ethics Defines That Culture

The ethical guidelines an individual or group holds are closely linked to their culture. It can be argued that a culture can be defined by its ethical code of conduct. Cultural values and expectations influence an individual's belief of what is right and wrong. Culture and ethical standards are intertwined; one influences the other. If a group continues long enough, it will develop its own culture; it will create codes of conduct for its members.

Philosophers today usually divide ethical theories into three general subject areas: metaethics, normative ethics, and applied ethics. Metaethics investigates where our ethical principles come from, and what they mean. The term meta means beyond or transcending. We can define metaethics as the study of the origin of ethical concepts. Although we will not be exploring metaethics, I mention it because normative and applied ethical conduct relate to small group work.

The primary branch of ethics that addresses moral behavior is **normative ethics**. Normative ethics involves arriving at moral standards that regulate right and wrong conduct. It is the yardstick for determining proper behavior. Normative theory establishes a single principle against which we judge all actions. Other normative theories focus on a *set* of foundational principles, or a set of good character traits.[44] The key assumption in normative ethics is that there is only one ultimate criterion of moral conduct, whether it is a single rule or a set of principles.

Normative ethics takes on a more practical task, which is to arrive at moral standards that regulate right and wrong conduct. The *Golden Rule* is a classic example of a normative principle: "We should do unto others what we would want others to do to us." Or, "Since I don't want my neighbor to steal my tools, then it is wrong for me to steal his." We call it a normative principle because it establishes a single principle against which we judge all actions. We use normative principles or normative ethics in small groups because they establish how we will interact with each other. These are the rules by which we conduct our business.

Applied ethics involves examining specific controversial issues, such as abortion, infanticide, animal rights, environmental concerns, capital punishment, euthanasia, and nuclear war. Recently, ethical issues have been subdivided into convenient groups such as medical ethics, business ethics, and environmental ethics, for example. When we refer to something as an issue, there must be two features that are necessary for an issue to be considered an applied ethical issue. First, the issue needs to be controversial in the sense that there are significant groups of people both for and against the issue at hand. For example, the issue of euthanasia would be an applied ethical issue since there are significant groups of people both for and against euthanasia. The second requirement for an issue to be an applied ethical issue is that it must be a distinctly moral issue. Universal health care can be considered to be a moral issue rather than a policy issue. Does the government have a moral directive to provide health care for everyone? Issues such as affirmative action policies, energy conservation, and immigration may be controversial and have an important impact on society, but they are not moral issues.

Normative Principles in Applied Ethics

1. **Personal benefit.** Acknowledge the extent to which an action produces beneficial consequences for the individual in question.
2. **Principle of harm.** Do not harm others. We don't mean it in a physical sense; rather, we mean that we should not intentionally set out to discredit our colleagues or damage their reputation, or take advantage of members' weaknesses.
3. **Principle of honesty.** Do not deceive others. Avoid a hidden agenda; avoid misleading the group; don't trick, cheat, or mislead. Refrain from making members believe things that are not true.
4. **Principle of autonomy.** Acknowledge a person's freedom over his or her actions or physical body. No one owns anyone else in the group, nor should one member have undue influence over another. People are free to make up their own minds.

Ethical Conduct in Groups

These principles represent a spectrum of traditional normative principles and are derived from both consequentialist and duty-based approaches. The first principle, personal benefit, is consequentialist because it appeals to the consequences of an action as it affects the individual or society. The principles of harm and honesty are duty-based because they are based on the duties we have toward others. And the principle of autonomy is based on moral rights.

GUIDELINES FOR GROUP DISCUSSION

It is an old cliché and used countless times, but it is still appropriate when speaking about guidelines for group discussion. There is an ancient Chinese proverb that says, "If you don't know where you are going, any road will take you there." In other words, without some kind of map directing you on how to get to where you're going, you'll wander aimlessly. This holds true for group discussion, too. Good group discussion *requires* guidelines. These guidelines help the group stay focused, and they foster effective discussion participation.[45]

Effective Discussion Participation

Effective Discussion Is Goal-Directed

When we say that effective group discussion is goal-directed, we mean that individuals have come together as a group to problem-solve, make decisions, declare policy, evaluate programs, gather facts, and so forth. Group discussion isn't about a group of people sitting around a table sharing ideas or socializing. It is purposeful discourse, which means that discussion must be goal-directed, and if it is goal-directed, there must be in place some relatively formal process. For example, your school is considering a campus-wide ban on smoking. You have been asked to participate in an *ad hoc committee* charged with determining whether a policy banning smoking campus-wide is really feasible—you are fact-finding—and the group's recommendation will weigh heavily on the decision makers. How do you plan on starting? What process will you use? Who will be responsible for what? The group has been formed because it would be impossible for one individual to accomplish all the fact-finding necessary in a timely manner, and too many people on campus have an interest in the outcome for one person to make the decision alone. Problem-solving, program evaluations, personnel hiring committees, and decision making, are all goal-directed behaviors in some form.

Effective Discussion Is Regulated by an Agenda

In order for group discussion to be effective, some method or procedure must exist that all members can follow and some rules of order in place that are meant to prevent or resolve conflict. Without procedural rules, there would be chaos, and the group would never be able to achieve its goal. Rules allow members to proceed efficiently in order to share information and work out solutions. Therefore, it is routine for members of a discussion group to follow some type of agenda that allows the leader to direct them from individual commitment to group solution. An agenda, then, is a formal list of things to be done in a specific order during group discussion.

Effective Discussion Requires That Every Member Be Responsible for the Group's Effectiveness

As a member of the university academic senate, I've witnessed too many faculty who have been nonparticipants, even though they volunteered to be there as representatives of their respective departments. They correct papers or do other chores while discussion occurs, and they always vote with the majority, yet they criticize everyone else for not doing their jobs. People who do not participate hurt the process; they don't help it. How so? Because they abdicate their responsibilities to others by not participating, they allow others to impose their own will or agenda. The process moves from democratic to totalitarian; a handful of individuals co-opt the process and make decisions for everyone else.

Whenever one group member decides to escape the responsibility of making choices by letting others judge the information, make procedural suggestions, or do the work, that person weakens the final product of the discussion. The quality of the decisions of a group discussion is only partly judged by their effect on the problem to be solved. The decisions are also judged against the question: Did the group process improve on what could have been done by an individual? If the answer to this question is "no," then the group process is a waste of time.[46]

The answer to this question should always be "yes" if every member assumes an obligation to participate. All members must be committed to listen, to think through, to reason, and to share results of their reasoning with the group. It is imperative that all members adopt a critical attitude toward the information they present and toward that presented by others. In order to do this, all members must know what is expected of them, what possibilities exist for behavior, and most important, how to separate personality from their own comments.[47]

Effective Discussion Presumes Cooperative Efforts and Attitudes

One of the positive features about having discussion regulated is that no one individual can monopolize the group's time or orate incessantly. Having an agenda means that discussion is an inherently cooperative endeavor in which the success or failure of the entire group depends on the labors and attitudes of each individual. For every member to be successful the entire group must be successful; and if the group fails, it is due to the fact that most of its members failed. Success occurs because most, if not all, members cooperated. This cooperation entails criticizing ideas, dissenting, and debating or arguing when it is legitimately required to do so; yet it also requires open-mindedness toward others' opinions that you may disagree with and determination to resolve any disagreement. Ideally, you should be able to speak your mind openly so the group can understand your reasoning, motives, interests, and so forth.

As a member of the discussion group, you are obligated to have ideas about the charge, topic, or question under discussion. You are obligated to present those ideas and to listen to the ideas of others. You are entitled, and at times urged, to be an advocate and to argue for those things you truly believe are right and justifiable. The group's goal is to come to common ground, and common ground can only be achieved if everyone is heard.[48]

Effective Discussion Requires Leadership

Because group discussion is complicated, someone needs to be able to manage it. We call that someone a **discussion leader**. Some groups allow for shared leadership responsibility, but at some point someone needs to make the tough decisions, follow protocols, and represent the group to others; and it is a good idea to have one person do this. Leadership occurs in a number of ways: it is appointed by a higher authority, elected, or privilege of rank; or it emerges from the group. Group discussion is more effective with a discussion leader than without one. We will be discussing various aspects of leadership in Chapters 4, 5, and 6.

SUMMARY

We have explored human communication and determined that it is a transactional process that is complex, dynamic, and contextual, and therefore irreversible, unique, and unrepeatable. We learned that communication is a result of shared meaning. It is symbolic in nature, and the meaning of symbols resides in the culture and individuals who create and share them. We share this meaning, in part, through verbal and nonverbal communication. Also, we see that cultures hold differing values in their communication and behavioral expectations, and these differences are also extended to gender differences and conflict management. We've studied what it means to be ethical and what normative group behavioral expectations are. And finally, we took a look at guidelines for group discussion and identified five general topic areas that help make effective group discussion possible. As you progress through this text, you will discover, we hope, that each chapter is designed to build upon the previous one, and ultimately you will have more than sufficient knowledge to effectively lead or be a member of any type of group discussion.

DISCUSSION

1. On page 8, **reasoning** is characterized as a "verbal communication skill" according to Berlo's research. Why would "reasoning" be a *part* of the communication process rather than *separate* from communication or *based on* communication? How does your understanding of such terms as "meaning" and "conception" help you account for Berlo's claim?

2. Using the five types of nonverbal communication described on pages 10–12, identify specific ways that members of a small group can send messages of positive commitment to the group without using words to do so. Then, identify specific ways that members of a small group can send messages of lack of commitment to, or suspicion of, the group without using words to do so.

3. In this class, you will probably do extensive academic work in small groups with other students. What are some potential ethical risks that might develop when you complete work, especially grade work, with other students? How can you help successfully highlight and negotiate ethical dilemmas in your small groups in this class?

4. When you experience a conflict brewing over something multiple people want or need (for instance, in your family or at work), what are the some of the first messages people send within these conflict settings? After you identify a working list of some common messages associated with brewing conflicts, discuss how these messages emphasize speakers' attempts to preserve autonomy, and/or how these messages emphasize speakers' attempts to seek approval. What do these different emphases suggest about culture?

5. This chapter acknowledges that small group communication is usually solution-directed, yet it also acknowledges that gendered communication patterns often involve contrasts between masculine styles that emphasize finding solutions and feminine styles that emphasize sharing experiences for their own sake. How can you reconcile these research findings so that small group contexts do not selectively favor masculine styles over feminine styles?

NOTES

1. Harris, T.E. (2002). *Applied organizational communication: Perspectives and pragmatics for future success.* Mahwah, NJ: Lawrence Erlbaum.

2. Borchers, T.A. (2002). *Persuasion in the media age.* Dubuque, IA: McGraw-Hill.

3. Woodward, G.C., & Denton, R.E., Jr. (2000). *Persuasion and influence in American life.* Prospect Heights, IL: Waveland Press.

4. Johnston, D.D. (1994). *The art and science of persuasion.* Dubuque, IA: Wm. C. Brown Communications.

5. Langer, Suzanne (1942). *Philosophy in a new key.* Cambridge, MA: Harvard University Press.

6. Johnston, D.D. (1994). *The art and science of persuasion.* Dubuque, IA: Wm. C. Brown Communications.

7. Johnston, D.D. (1994). *The art and science of persuasion.* Dubuque, IA: Wm. C. Brown Communications, Inc.

8. Berlo, David K. (1960). *The process of communication: An introduction to theory and practice.* USA: Holt, Rinehart and Winston.

9. Wood, J.T., Phillips, G.M., & Pedersen, D.J. (1986). *Group discussion: A practical guide to participation and leadership.* New York: Harper & Row.

10. Harper, N., & Asking, L. (1980). Group communication and quality of task solution in a media production organization. *Communication Monographs, 47,* 77–100.

11. Benne, K.D., & Sheats, P. (1948). Functional roles of group members. *Journal of Social Issues,* 41–49. Also see Wood, J.T., Phillips, G.M., & Pedersen, D.J. (1986). *Group discussion: A practical guide to participation and leadership.* New York: Harper & Row.

12. Trenholm, S., & Jensen, A. (1996). *Interpersonal communication.* Belmont, CA: Wadsworth.

13. Trenholm, S. (2008). *Thinking through communication: An introduction to the study of human communication* (5th ed.). New York: Pearson.

14. Trenholm, S., & Jensen, A. (1996). *Interpersonal communication*. Belmont, CA: Wadsworth.

15. Trenholm, S., & Jensen, A. (1996). *Interpersonal communication*. Belmont, CA: Wadsworth.

16. DeCaro, P.A. (2008). *Persuasíon*. Lima, Peru: Universidad Saint Martín de Porres.

17. Inch, E.S., Warnick, B., & Endres, D. (2006). *Critical thinking and communication*. New York: Pearson Education.

18. Rieke, R.D., Sillars, M.O., & Peteresen, T.R. (2005). *Argumentation and critical decision making*. New York: Pearson Education.

19. Inch, E.S., Warnick, B., & Endres, D. (2006). *Critical thinking and communication*. New York: Pearson Education.

20. Brake, T., Walker, D.M., & Walker, T. (1995). *Doing business internationally: The guide to cross-cultural success*. Dubuque, IA: McGraw-Hill.

21. Ting-Toomey, S., & Chung, L.C. (2005). *Understanding intercultural communication*. Los Angeles: Roxbury.

22. Ting-Toomey, S., & Chung, L.C. (2005). *Understanding intercultural communication*. Los Angeles: Roxbury.

23. Ting-Toomey, S., & Chung, L.C. (2005). *Understanding intercultural communication*. Los Angeles: Roxbury Publishing.

24. http://tip.psychology.org/styles.html. Retrieved February 27, 2008.

25. Rokeach, M. (1960). *The open and closed mind*. New York: Basic Books.

26. Trenholm, S., & Jensen, A. (1996). *Interpersonal communication*. Belmont, CA: Wadsworth.

27. Morrison, T., Conaway, W.A., & Borden, G.A. (1994). *Kiss, bow, or shake hands: How to do business in sixty countries*. Avon, MA: Adams Media Corp.

28. Harpaz, I. http://gsb.haifa.ac.il/dalia_files/4860.doc. Retrieved February 28, 2008.

29. Martin, J.N., & Nakayama, T.K. (2007). *Intercultural communication in contexts* (4th ed.). Dubuque, IA: McGraw-Hill.

30. Trenholm, S., & Jensen, A. (1996). *Interpersonal communication*. Belmont, CA: Wadsworth.

31. Rokeach, M. (1968). *Beliefs, attitudes, and values*. San Francisco: Jossey-Bass.

32. Johnston, D.D. (1994). *The art and science of persuasion*. Dubuque, IA: Brown and Benchmark.

33. http://www.urbandictionary.com. Retrieved March 1, 2008.

34. Jandt, F.E. (2004). *An introduction to intercultural communication* (4th ed.). Thousand Oaks, CA: Sage.

35. Hawkins, K. (1994). *Conflict analysis & resolution as education—Trainee materials*. San Francisco, CA: Community Board Program.

36. Martin, J.N., & Nakayama, T.K. (2007). *Intercultural communication in contexts* (4th ed.). Dubuque, IA: McGraw-Hill.

37. Ting-Toomey, S., & Kurogi, A. (1998). Facework competence in intercultural conflict: An updated face-negotiation theory. *International Journal of Intercultural Relations, 22*(1), 187–225.

38. Ting-Toomey, S., & Chung, L.C. (2005). *Understanding intercultural communication*. Los Angeles: Roxbury.

39. Adapted from the State of Florida Criminal Justice Standards and Training Commission. (n.d.). *Human diversity training manual*. Tallahassee, FL.

40. Wrench, J.S., McCroskey, J.C., & Richmond, V.P. (2008). *Human communication in everyday life*. New York: Pearson Education.

41. Author, source, and date unknown.

42. http://www.answers.com/topic/ethics-legal-term?cat=biz-fin. Retrieved December 14, 2007.

43. http://www.answers.com/topic/ethics-legal-term?cat=biz-fin. Retrieved December 14, 2007.

44. http://www.iep.utm.edu/e/ethics.htm. Retrieved December 19, 2007.

45. Adapted from Wood, J.T., Phillips G.M., & Pedersen, D. J. (1986). *Group discussion: A practical guide to participation and leadership* (2nd ed.). New York: Harper & Row.

46. Ibid.

47. Ibid.

48. Ibid.

2

Developing Effective Groups and Teams

CHAPTER OBJECTIVES

- Understand the role of performance in groups
- Know what constitutes a group or team
- Be familiar with the purpose of group work
- Explain when groups should be used
- Know how to team build
- Understand how theory explains group work
- Distinguish the various elements of a system
- Know the differing roles in groups
- Understand the Myers-Briggs Type Indicator

KEY TERMS

Goal interdependence

Behavioral interdependence

Context interdependence

Structure

Cohesiveness

Goals

Desired outcomes

Teamwork

Pinpointing

Value-added work

Field theory

Interaction process analysis

Task leader

Open system

Closed system

Static system

Dynamic system

Nonsummativity

Subsystem

Equilibrium

Group charge

Role

Formal role

Task role

Maintenance role

Self-centered role

CHAPTER OUTLINE

Before we explain what groups are, there are a few things we should discuss. Most students, and this probably includes you, have an aversion to group work—you despise working in groups, to put it mildly. And you know, I don't blame you for feeling this way. I did when I was a student too. Every time I was forced to work in a group, there was always that one person who didn't pull his or her own share of the work. These people let everybody else do it and then took the credit for something they didn't do. Or the student that never showed up when we had to meet outside of class—generally at the library or somewhere else on campus or close to campus. How about the student who has to take charge and dominate the group? What a turn-off. There's an old Chinese proverb that says, "The nail that sticks up gets hammered back down." In other words, there's no room for people who like to place themselves above the group.

Another thing I didn't like about group work was the grading system. It seemed that no matter how hard some of us worked, or the quality of our work, that one person who let us down also got us a lower grade. I used to argue with my professors that I shouldn't have been penalized with a lower grade because of someone else's poor performance. "That's the nature of group work," I was told. "You are graded on the effectiveness of the entire group, not just your performance. Too bad." It was too bad, for me. For a long time, I really avoided working in small groups. Once I entered graduate school, I refused to get trapped into group work. Looking back, I'm sorry I did. It wasn't until I began studying **performance management** in my Ph.D. program that I discovered the benefits and joys, if you can believe that, of small group work. My mentor, Dr. Daniel Montgomery, a professor of organizational communication and a licensed clinical psychologist, was a wizard at getting individuals in groups to work together effectively, and liking it. He quickly showed me the errors of my ways, and he did this by having me be his assistant on a consultancy he was contracted for to improve workplace productivity and communication at a hospice in Florida. At the end of the first day, I was hooked, lined, and sinkered. I was in awe at the ease with which he took a group of people who worked together, in the same building, but who rarely spoke or interacted with one another to the point where no one knew what the others were really doing, and he had them actually interacting, joking, and really enjoying themselves as they discussed the problems they had with each other. The morning session of the first day began with everyone suspicious of each other, but by late afternoon there was this transformative state—instead of department heads pointing fingers at other department heads and blaming them for their troubles, they were actually working out their differences. By the end of the three-day retreat, you would not have believed that this was the same group.

The world outside of school is primarily a world of group work. You cannot avoid it, and without groups we would not be where we are today—unquestionably. If you look at everything from the major advances in science to the construction of your parents' homes, these were not accomplished by individuals; no, they were all accomplished by groups working well together. The next time you go into a supermarket, observe the checkout counter. Is the cashier working alone, or is she or he being helped by a bagger, price checker, assistant manager, or even the manager? Why? To efficiently help you through the system. It takes group work—someone to scan the goods, someone else to bag and place those goods in the cart, and possibly someone else to help you take them to your car. It's all about performance. The better those store employees can make your experience there, the better you'll feel about returning to shop. I don't know about you, but I hate standing in the checkout line with a cashier who is slower than my ninety-five-year-old grandmother having some ridiculous conversation about nothing. Not good. What you should know before we discuss group work is that the final product or end result of group work is performance, period.

In class, you are forced to be in a group and work with people who don't want to work together, don't care to work together, or simply just don't care. It's an attitude thing. But in the work world, knowing how to lead a group, and doing it well, is a tremendous asset. There aren't too many people who can, and those who do generally get paid very well. Groups are unique. Groups can do just about anything they set their minds to. Because of groups, we've landed on the moon, sent spacecrafts beyond our solar system, and have explored the depths of our oceans. When you are asked to work in a group, it is your opportunity to learn, to share knowledge and experiences with others in order to accomplish a goal. This is a positive thing. You are rewarded in some way for this accomplishment. Whether that is a pay raise, award, acknowledgement, or simply ego gratification, an award is an award; and it feels good to earn one. We will learn more about the virtues of group work as we read through this text.

WHAT ARE GROUPS?

Goal interdependence

Groups share accomplishing a common goal.

Behavioral interdependence

Each member influences and is influenced by other members as they work together to achieve that common goal.

Groups are pervasive in any culture and any society. Groups are everywhere. The friends that you walk with between classes or study with in the library constitute a group. A sports team, a sorority, a fraternity, and your student board are all groups. Our government functions solely as a group. Business and industry operate as groups. As a matter of fact, little is really accomplished in society without the help of groups. Think about how long it would take one individual in a factory to produce one automobile—too long. And it would be too inefficient for one person alone to accomplish. That's why there are many people working together in groups or teams assembling automobiles; it is faster and more **efficient**.

Have you ever considered the power that groups have? A legislative body makes laws that regulate your behavior. For example, these laws determine when you can legally drive a car and under what conditions, how long you must attend school, and how much tax you will pay every week from your paycheck. A jury can send you to prison for the rest of your life—now that's a long time! And a group called OPEC determines how much money you will pay for your gasoline. All groups and teams are uniquely different; that is, the people who make them up, the conditions for which they exist, and the environment they exist in are all different from one another. However, many groups share similar distinctions and dynamics. When we study groups, we look for particular characteristics and common properties such as **interaction, interdependence, structure, cohesiveness,** and **goals**.

© J. McPhail, 2011. Under license from Shutterstock, Inc.

1. **Interaction.** This is the social actions that occur between individuals in a group. The interaction between group members also influences others who are either directly or indirectly associated with the group.
2. **Interdependence.** There are three criteria that mutually affect one another: (a) **goal interdependence**: groups share accomplishing a common goal; (b) **behavioral interdependence**: each member influences and is influenced by other members as they work together to achieve that common goal; (c) **context interdependence**: members work within a particular environment which they influence, and which also has an influence on them. This includes coworkers and those who may have an interest in the group's outcome.

Context interdependence

Members work within a particular environment which they influence, and which also has an influence on them.

3. **Structure.** The group creates and identifies individual roles, group behavioral norms, values, and so forth. These are the structural aspects of a group. They determine how the group will function.

4. **Cohesiveness.** After a group is formed, it develops a type of character all of its own. This character is a result of the individual members bonding to one another. They create a **synergy**, a dynamic state in which the team becomes greater than the individuals who make it up.

5. **Goals.** These are the broader, general outcomes you want to see as a result of the group's efforts. They are what the group plans on accomplishing. It is the level of performance that the group must attain.

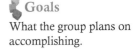

Structure
Determines how the group will function.

Cohesiveness
Individual members bonding to one another.

Goals
What the group plans on accomplishing.

This is a good time to discuss the differences between **goals** and **objectives**. Students often confuse goals and objectives and refer to them as the same thing; they are not. As stated above, goals are the broader, general outcomes you want to see as a result of the group's efforts. Generally, goals are not quantifiable; that is, we can't measure goal achievement. Goals are commonly described as the desired outcomes of a plan of action designed to solve a specific problem or policy that is the group's charge. Think of a goal as a directional statement,[1] such as planning to go to school. You can never arrive at planning to go to school because it is relative to where you are now, where you used to be, or where you will be some time in the future. You will need to supply a context if you want to turn the direction into some sort of destination. You will need to know where to go to school. This is your destination, otherwise known as the objective. Objectives are measurable outcomes; therefore, an objective is a measurable destination that represents the achievement of the group's goal.[2] It is a clear and measurable statement, written to point the way toward a particular level of awareness, acceptance, or action.[3] A stated objective should be evaluated by asking: (1) Does it really address the situation? (2) Is it realistic and achievable? (3) Can its achievement be measured in meaningful terms?[4] In other words, a goal tells you the direction you should go in, and an objective indicates when you've arrived there.

Desired outcomes
A plan of action designed to solve a specific problem or policy that is the group's charge.

In summary, when we talk about group dynamics, what we are really discussing is *human behavior.* In the study of groups and teams, we want to understand behavior; what motivates people; how to direct, change, and control individual and group behavior; and how leadership is facilitated by this understanding.

WHY GROUPS OR TEAMS?

For the purpose of this text, we will focus on the nature of **work-oriented groups**, which are **decision making** and **problem solving**. There are multiple functions for groups, but these are the two we concern ourselves with. Decision-making groups include such things as a board of supervisors or a board of education creating public policy. Another body of decision makers would be the U.S. Congress or your state legislature. A different type of decision-making body is the board of directors of a corporation, which determines policies for the directions of its company. Problem-solving groups tackle problem solving. These problems may range from how to increase worker productivity and how to develop a superior telecom system, to how to improve our educational system. Decision making is making a choice among two or more alternatives to solve a problem, whereas problem solving means that there is a gap between the current situation and a desired solution. Both processes end in an act of choice, even if the choice is not to make a choice.

Team Building

Teamwork

Cooperative behavior between group discussion members.

Working together and cooperating are better than working against one another. When we talk about groups or teams, what we really are referring to is creating an environment that fosters teamwork. Teamwork is always appropriate and desirable, and it is accomplished by making sure that cooperative behavior between group discussion members is **positively reinforced**.[5] (We will discuss reinforcement in Chapter 6). As we learned in Chapter 1, effective small group discussion requires tremendous effort on the part of the individual and the group as a whole. Unfortunately, for many groups, the **team process** has become more important than teamwork. Teamwork is the desired behavior. Team process is one way of facilitating that work; it should never replace it.

The First Question Should Be "What's the Problem?"

Pinpointing

Accurately identifying the problem.

The most important thing that any discussion group must do before it can determine who will do what, when, how, and for how long, is to accurately identify the problem. This is known as pinpointing the problem. The group cannot fact-find, set criteria and limitations, discover and select solutions, seek external resources, or move the group forward in any manner until the problem has been pinpointed. If the problem has not been accurately pinpointed, the group will have wasted its time, energy, and resources. You cannot produce a solution to something that doesn't exist, and if the group misidentifies the problem, that's exactly what they'll be trying to do.

The Second Question Should Be "What's the Best Way to Solve It?"

Value-added work

The activities that team members engage in that further the goal of the team by generating and delivering the appropriate solution or fulfilling the group's charge.

If, after answering these two questions, it is decided that a discussion group or team is the most appropriate method to solve the problem, then the group or team should be formed. By approaching problem solving in this manner, the group is doing value-added work right away. This is also known as **task interaction**. Since the problem has now been clearly identified, the group will know:

* Exactly what the charge is,
* When the charge is to be completed, and
* How well the discussion group should perform.

The Group or Team Provides Value-Added Work

Value-added work is the activities that team members engage in that further the goal of the team by generating and delivering the appropriate solution or fulfilling the group's charge. The key phrase is "further the goal of the team."

All team work is not value-added; only team work that adds to achieving the group's goal efficiently is considered value-added work.

THE NATURE OF GROUP DYNAMICS

The field of group dynamics combines theory, research, and practice.[6] The purpose of theory is to identify the characteristics of effective groups. Research either confirms or disconfirms the theory, and practical procedures based on sound theory are implemented in the real world to see if they work. The theory, research, and practical applications of group dynamics all interact and augment each other. Theory serves a two-fold purpose: it both guides and summarizes research. Research validates or disconfirms theory, and in so doing, can lead to its improvement and modification. Practice is guided by sound theory, and applications of the theory expose inadequacies that lead to refining of the theory, conducting new research studies, and modifying the application.

David Johnson and Frank Johnson (1997) define **group dynamics** as "the scientific study of behavior in groups to advance our knowledge about the nature of groups, group development, and the interrelations between groups and individuals, other groups, and larger entities" (p. 36). The interaction between group members is dynamic, not static. This interaction is "characterized by forces such as communication and leadership that are in constant motion and change" (p. 36). Social scientists who study groups analyze the dynamics within groups by creating theories and conducting research to test their theories. They then apply the validated theory to real-world situations to see if they work.

Understanding the **how's** of group and teamwork is good to know, but it is also essential to know the **why's**. We answer the why's through our understanding of the various theories that explain group behavior, psychology, and motivation. Theoretical knowledge gives us the foundation for understanding why groups function the way they do and why individuals think and behave the way they do. Theories (why's) and application, or practices, (how's) are inextricable—they are like salt and pepper, bread and butter, peanut butter and jelly. They complement one another in an effort to help us maximize our abilities to function in groups.

Interestingly, the first focus of researchers studying group dynamics was on the question "What change in an individual's normal solitary performance occurs when other people are present?"[7] We will explore three of the foundational theories about the nature of group interaction.

MACRO-THEORIES OF GROUP DYNAMICS

A Brief History

During the 1940s, Europe experienced the rise of dictatorships and the advent of World War II. During this period, most Americans were concerned about the fate of their country and the future of democracy. There was a general consensus that more needed to be known about how democratic organizations could be made to function more effectively. It was believed that the field of group dynamics could have significant potential for improving democracy. The health of a democratic society was seen as depending on the effectiveness of its component groups. Strengthening the family, the community, and the multitude of groups within our society was viewed as the primary means of ensuring the vitality of our democracy. People began to see that the scientific method could be applied to important social issues involving the functioning of groups—for example, leadership, decision making, and productivity. The belief that the solution to social problems could be facilitated by systematic research gained acceptance in both the scientific and general communities.[8]

Kurt Lewin's Field Theory

In order to understand the field of group dynamics, you need to understand the impact that Kurt Lewin had on social psychology. Kurt Lewin was a social scientist who, in 1946, started the Research Center for Group Dynamics at the Massachusetts Institute of Technology. Lewin considered himself to be allied in theory with Gestalt psychologists. He held a strong conviction for the importance of theory and practice and strove to apply laboratory techniques to social behavior in order to develop theories and continuously refine his theories with empirical evidence from these laboratory techniques. It was these principles that brought field theory, group dynamics, democracy and groups, and action research to be Kurt Lewin's most well-known and influential contributions.[9] His research in change theory, action research, and action learning earned him the title of the Father of Organizational Development.[10] Lewin is best known for his work in the field of organization behavior and the study of group dynamics, especially the study of leadership patterns and their influence on groups and group members. His interests were in the area of motivation, and his work was directed more toward practical application than to understanding for its own sake.[11]

General Observations of the Theory

Field theory

Also known as *force field analysis,* this theory comes from the idea that in order to explain behavior one must look at all dynamic interactions (behavior) between individuals and their environment; that all interactions influence outcomes.

Field theory, also known as force field analysis, comes from the idea that in order to explain behavior, one must look at all dynamic interactions (behavior) between individuals and their environment; it is the belief that all interactions influence outcomes. He wanted to identify those forces that drive a group or individual to make a certain decision and those forces that are preventing that decision from being made. Lewin believed that a group must know what the desired condition is and then must be able to identify what is preventing them from reaching that desired condition.[12]

Lewin tried to explain the why's of human behavior in group settings. His equation:[13]

$$B = f\,(P \longleftrightarrow E)$$

suggested that individual behavior (B) is a function (f) of something both inside the person (P) and outside the person in an environment (E). This something inside the person is motives or needs that are reflected in individual attitudes—the way individuals feel about things—and represented by personality—an individual's tendency to act.[14] The person and the environment are not independent of one another; rather, they are **interdependent**. People are influenced by the environment they are in, and the environment is influenced by the people.

Field theory of group dynamics assumes that groups are more than the sum of their parts. Lewin believed that behavior was determined by the totality of an individual's situation. In his field theory, a field is defined as "the totality of coexisting facts which are conceived of as mutually interdependent."[15] The field represents the complete environment of the individual. Individuals were seen to behave differently according to the way in which tensions between perceptions of the self and of the environment were worked through.

The entire psychological field, or lifespace, within which people acted, had to be viewed in order to understand behavior. Within this, individuals and groups could be seen in topological terms (using map-like representations). Lewin concluded that as individuals participate in a series of life spaces, such as family, work, school and recreational groups, behavior was represented as movements through life spaces that carry both positive and negative influences and are driven by people's perceptions based off their underlying psychological needs.[16]

Group dynamics resulted out of Lewin's work with field theory. Group dynamics are the interactions that influence the attitudes and behavior of people when they are grouped with others.[17] Lewin was particularly interested in the uniformity found in many group interactions and looked extensively at how field theory came into play in group settings and the roles that individuals take on when placed in a group setting.[18] Field theory emphasized the importance of individual personalities, interpersonal conflict, and situational variables.

Lewin believed that theorists and practitioners share a common interest in understanding reality and acting competently. He perceived them as having interdependent tasks: Practitioners identify significant problems to be solved; theorists develop a valid view of reality that contains the keys for solving the problems; and practitioners apply the theory. A great deal of Lewin's research emphasized the importance of active participation in groups in order to learn new skills, develop new attitudes, and gain new knowledge about groups. His research showed that learning is most productive in groups whose members can interact and then reflect on their mutual experiences.[19]

Robert F. Bales' Interaction Process Analysis

Robert Bales' interaction process analysis is one of the most prominent small group theories studied today. This theory aims to explain the pattern of responses in which groups work toward a goal of a group decision-making problem. Briefly stated, Bales suggests that under these conditions groups tend to transition in their interaction from a relative emphasis on problems of orientation, to problems of evaluation, and eventually to problems of control, and that simultaneous with these transitions, the relative frequencies of both negative reactions and positive reactions tend to increase.[20]

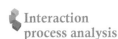 Interaction process analysis

Aims to explain the pattern of responses in which groups work toward a goal of a group decision-making problem.

Figure 2.1 illustrates the categories of interactions in Bales proposition.[21] Each is a type of statement that someone could make in a group. There are twelve categories grouped into four broader sets, which are identified by the brackets on the left and right of the list. In addition, the behavior types are paired, and each pair implies a particular problem area for groups. *Gives information* (6) is paired with *asks for information* (7); *gives opinion* (5) is paired with *asks for opinion* (8); *gives suggestion* (4) is paired with *asks for suggestion* (9); *agrees* (3) is paired with *disagrees* (10); *shows tension release* (2) is paired with *shows tension* (11); and *shows solidarity* (1) is paired with *shows antagonism* (12). Another way of looking at the model is to consider the four

FIGURE 2.1

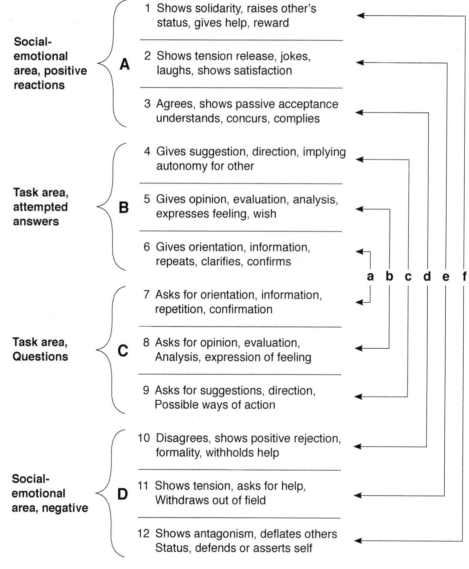

KEY: (A) problems of orientation (communication); (B) problems of evaluation; (C) problems of control; (D) problems of decision; (E) problems of tension-management; (F) problems of integration.

major problem groupings as: A = adaption to group work; B = development and maintenance of integration; C = expression and management of forces; and D = instrumental control.

There are two general classes of communication behavior. The first is **social-emotional**, represented by positive actions (A) such as *shows tension release, understands,* and *agrees,* and negative actions (D) such as *disagrees, shows tension,* and *shows antagonism.* The second is *task behavior* (B and C), represented by *gives suggestions, opinions,* and *information.*

Bales demonstrated how the perception of an individual's position in a group is a function of three dimensions. These include (1) dominant versus submissive, (2) friendly versus unfriendly, and (3) instrumental versus emotional. Bales' research allows us to predict the coalitions and networks of a group from the distribution of types, and he has shown that behavior type is related to the kinds of statements a person makes. The interaction that a group member initiates and receives depends in part on his or her behavior type.[22]

Within interaction process analysis research, Bales studied problems of tension management. He discovered that one of the ways that groups release tension is by telling stories, or dramatizing. Bales found that at moments of tension, groups will often behave dramatically and share stories, or fantasy themes, to reduce the stress.[23]

Bales also investigated leadership. He discovered that the same group will have two different leadership styles. The first is the task leader, who coordinates and facilitates the task-related discussions and directs energy toward achieving the task. The second, and equally important, is the **social-emotional leader**, who seeks to improve relations in the group, focusing on interactions in the positive and negative sectors. The task and social-emotional leaders are two different people. Leadership styles are discussed in detail in Chapter 5.

Task leader
Coordinates and facilitates the task-related discussions and directs energy toward achieving the task.

George C. Homans' Systems Theory of Informal Work Groups

George C. Homans contributed to the development of behavioral theories in large organizations, groups, and small groups. In his book, *The Human Group,* Homans (1950) sought to establish a general statement about human behavior that could be used to form increasingly more general sociological theories.[24] At this time, sociology had not been able to establish a general proposition about human behavior "of a kind sufficiently valid throughout for a general theory of sociology to be erected on it."[25] He wanted to devise more effective instruments for dealing with this problem. Homans viewed groups as social systems of interacting individuals and was interested in understanding how groups got their power to control individual behavior. Homans developed a model of social systems that helped him find the answer.[26] He scrutinizes three elements in a social system.[27] These elements are:

1. Activities. What members of a group do as members of it; they are the tasks that people perform; they are elements of social behavior.

2. **Interactions.** The relationships which the activity of one member of the group has to that of another; they are the communication behaviors that occur between people in performing those tasks. In Homans' text *Social Behavior: Its Elementary Forms,* he identified interactions as "the relation between the competence of the agents [group members] and their more purely 'social' behavior,"[28] thus labeling this as social interaction. Over a period of time, it has become known simply as interaction.

3. **Sentiments.** The sum of interior feelings, whether physical or mental, that a group member has in relation to what the group does; they are the attitudes, emotions, feelings, and affective states that develop between individuals and within groups.

Homans believed that although these concepts are separate, they are mutually dependent. Any change in one of these three elements will produce some change in the other two.[29]

The essence of his findings is that in all of the groups the forces which affect behavior are in a constant state of mutual dependence. Interaction and sentiment depend on each other. The more two members interact, the more they will like each other; the more they like each other, the more they will tend to interact. Both tendencies affect their behavior and that of the group.[30] Homans argues that each is also dependent on all the other elements, processes, and relationships that have been considered. He contends that "If either the liking of [member] A for [member] B or the way they do things together produces any considerable departure from what the group considers proper behavior, a reaction will be set up to bring them into line, and this too will affect other relationships and group behavior as a whole."[31] Homans calls this the external system in operation. Moreover, this group, or system of dependent relationships, which responds to its environment and may to some degree change it, can also be modified by the environment, and therefore is constantly adjusting and readjusting itself. In other words, a small group is a social system that reacts to its environment as a self-adjusting organization of response whose parts are mutually interdependent.[32] Whichever members act and react are not separate functions of the social system, or any combination of members or functions; rather, it is the system as a whole, a totality whose mutual interdependence is the system. Interdependence is a crucial key to Homans' research. It goes beyond merely describing the relations of variables within a group and also considers the relations of that group to its social environment.

GROUPS AND SYSTEMS

One of the most general theoretical approaches about human social behavior and group communication is system theory. System theory as we know it today was developed by biologist Ludwig von Bertalanffy in 1936. He established the field of study known as general system theory as a way to think about and study the multidisciplinary approaches to knowledge. Bertalanffy believed that there was a need for a theory to guide research in many fields because he saw strong similarities between them. His ideas have since been adopted by a number of social scientists and humanists who want to understand complicated interpersonal interaction.[33]

Bertalanffy's theory also offers us a broad perspective on how groups function. According to Berttalanffy's theory, an open system such as a group is defined as an organized set of interrelated and interacting parts that attempts to maintain its own balance amid the influences from its surrounding environment. Let's use a fictional restaurant, which we will call *Alyssa D's,* as an example of an open system. The restaurant employs cooks, dishwashers, bartenders, waitresses and waiters, each with his or her own personality and skills. When a cook is replaced, it affects all of the staff because there is now a new personality and a different skill-set. This new cook may bring new food ideas and get along with the other staff very well, or the new cook could be a disaster and disliked by everyone. The same holds for the other employees—a new dishwasher may not clean as well as the previous one, or a new waitress has more personality than the one she replaced. These interactions can be experienced by the restaurant's customers, especially those who frequent it. They notice how personnel changes can affect the service, quality of food, cleanliness, and so forth, for better or for worse. One change in personnel—the cook—influences one part of the system—the kitchen—which then influences another part of the system—the waiting staff—which may influence the entire system, until it eventually influences the experience of the restaurant's customers accordingly. A change in the kitchen has influence throughout the restaurant. This is a model of an open system. There are at least three other types of systems:

1. **Closed system.** This system has fixed and impervious boundaries that does not allow for much interaction between itself and its environment. Remote indigenous people live in a closed system. Rarely, if ever, can an outsider become a part of the communal system.
2. **Static system.** Neither system elements nor the system itself changes much over time in relation to the environment; for example, a professor who has been teaching the same response to student and community needs.
3. **Dynamic system.** The system constantly changes the environment and is changed by the environment. For example, a university influences the developmental changes of the community it is in, and the community influences curriculum changes within the university.

A new university nursing program may be instituted, which seeks support from the community. In return, a hospital may support that program and influence some of the curriculum that is offered by the new program.

Let's look at some **basic principles** of a systems approach to groups.[34]

Open system
A system that does not have fixed and impervious boundaries that allows for much interaction between itself and its environment.

Closed system
A system that has fixed and impervious boundaries that does not allow for much interaction between itself and its environment.

Static system
Neither system elements nor the system itself changes much over time in relation to the environment.

Dynamic system
A system constantly changes the environment and is changed by the environment.

Nonsummativity
When a system is greater than the sum of its parts.

1. **A system is greater than the sum of its parts, also known as nonsummativity.** Basically, a group is made up of individuals, with different backgrounds and communication patterns, in an environment, to achieve a common goal. These are the parts that make up a basic group; however, what it is missing are the dynamic interactions and interdependency that develop as the group works together. Once the group is formed and working, it engages in an ongoing process of defining and redefining itself, constantly changing to adapt and sustain itself against both internal and external forces. Over time, member relationships assume new qualities in response to the communication patterns. This transformative process reflects the dynamic interactions characteristic of an open system; thus, the system becomes greater than its parts.

2. **Though each subsystem is a self-contained unit, it is a part of a wider and higher order, and can be understood only within the context of the entire system.** Systems tend to be embedded within one another; that is, one system, or subsystem, is part of a larger system. A group may comprise a number of subgroups. It is impossible to understand one part of a group in isolation. You need to know its relationship to other subsystems and the group as a whole in order to understand its purpose. It can work parallel to other subsystems or in a series with them. For example, a student senate will have a number of subcommittees, such as a finance committee, activities committee, student organization regulatory committee, and so forth. They are independent from one another with each having its own function, but they are subsumed under a larger system called student senate.

3. **Groups are information systems.** Policy, decision-making, and advisory committees, for example, use information to produce a final report or achieve a goal. They rely on information as their primary resource.

4. **An open system and its environment are highly interrelated and mutually influential.** Systems do not work in a vacuum; they must exist within some type of environment or context. Many systems or groups are a part of a larger environment, such as an organization, company, community, or culture. The group becomes dependent upon this environment for a number of things, such as resources, meeting room availability, and personnel assistance. In turn, the environment is influenced by the group, perhaps by the impact of a policy or decision that affects the entire organization and its members.

5. **A system consists of a planned set of objectives and their relationships.** Objectives are *targets* that input, process, and output are directed to;[35] it is what the group plans on ultimately achieving. Objectives are directly related to each other, and they are generally sequential.

That is, certain objectives have to be met before others can be, until a goal has been achieved.

6. To be viable, a system must be strongly goal-directed, governed by feedback, and have the ability to adapt to change. A system is unified because it strives to achieve a common goal. A subsystem cannot have a separate agenda or goal-direction than that established by the system itself. Subsystems contribute to the overall mission of the system; if they didn't, either the subsystem or the system itself would cease to exist. Feedback is essential because it monitors the effectiveness and the efficiency of the various parts of the system. A system must also have the ability to adapt to changing internal and external forces in order to survive. If a system becomes static, it risks its own existence because it may not be able to positively respond to its environment.

> **Subsystem**
> A self-contained unit; that is, a part of a wider and higher order, and one which can be understood only within the context of the entire system.

7. Self-regulation and control. Groups are **goal-oriented** and **regulate** their behavior to achieve those goals. Group members must behave by certain rules and must respond to feedback. Rules govern or control the behavior and activities of members; if they didn't, we would have a group made up of unruly individuals doing their own thing.

8. Equilibrium. This is also referred to as **balance** or **homeostasis**. Equilibrium is self-maintenance.[36] The system should monitor itself to ensure that it is always in balance. Balance in group work refers to a myriad of elements and functions such as: (a) **Information overload:** Too much information to process in a given time period; (b) **Conflict:** There will always be conflict between group members and from external forces; however, there are times when conflict becomes destructive. (We will discuss conflict management in Chapter 11.) Self-monitoring helps identify conflict before it can become destructive. (c) **Members and member participation:** Sometimes, there aren't enough members to complete the charge in the time allotted, which generally becomes evident once it is determined what needs to be done after problem identification. The addition of new members may be sought. (d) **Resources:** Often, there aren't enough resources, such as access to experts, money, quality materials and supplies, personnel, and so forth. There should always be an adequate supply of resources with which to accomplish the group's goals. (e) **Environment:** This includes an easily accessible and comfortable room to work in, with adequate heat, air conditioning, and ventilation; freedom from noise and interruption; nearby restrooms; and refreshments.

> **Equilibrium**
> A system monitors itself to ensure that it is always in balance.

What is the function of a system? It is to **process energy, information,** or **materials** into a product or outcome for use within the system, or outside of the system (the environment), or both.[37]

All systems have **common elements.** These include **boundary, input, throughput, output, process, feedback, control, environment,** and **a goal.**

1. Boundary. The line or point where a system or subsystem can be differentiated from its environment or from other subsystems. The boundary can be rigid or permeable, or some point in between.

2. Input. The energy of group members and information used by the system.

3. **Throughput.** The processes used by the system to convert information from the environment into products that are usable by either the system or the environment. For example, thinking, planning, decision making, sharing information, and meeting in groups are throughputs.

4. **Output.** The product which results from the system's processing of information. For example, policy, solutions, rules, and decisions are outputs.

5. **Process.** The processes used to convert information into a final report that is usable by either the system itself or the environment. For example, problem solving, planning, thinking, and decision making are processes.

6. **Feedback.** Information about some aspect of data, members, environment, or the process that can be used to evaluate and monitor the system to guide it to more effective performance. For example, one member telling another member that his or her research was excellent is feedback.

7. **Control.** The activities and processes used to evaluate input, throughput, and output in order to make corrections. The group leader will evaluate members' roles and their effectiveness, timeliness of completion of tasks, and meeting attendance. This enables the leader to make corrections along the way so the group can remain dynamic and efficient.

8. **Environment.** The external conditions, resources, stimuli, people, and so forth that influence group function.

9. **Goals.** The broader, general outcomes you want to see as a result of the group's efforts. They are what the group plans on accomplishing. It is the level of **performance** that the group must attain.

Other terms related to small group communication include:

1. **Entropy.** The tendency for a system to develop order and energy over time.

2. **Equifinality.** The fact that there is more than one way that objectives can be achieved with varying inputs.

INITIAL ELEMENTS IN GROUP SYSTEMS[38]

Generally, there are four main features in a work-oriented (problem-solving or decision-making) group: **individual members, group size, group charge,** and **group record**.

1. **Individual members.** Groups are made of **individual members**. Each member is unique. They have their own personality, self-esteem, personal needs, abilities, values, attitudes, ethnicity, and socio-cultural-economic background. Often, group membership is determined by qualification or some type of entrance requirements. This can include anything from one's expertise in his or her field or specialty, to the ordinary citizen, depending upon the group and its charge. A committee investigating global warming may be comprised solely of experts in meteorology while a criminal prosecution jury requires broad representation from the community. Membership in a sorority or fraternity requires specific qualifications, as does graduating with the classification *summa cum laude*.

2. **Group size.** The size of the group can influence the process and outcomes of problem solving. Too many group members inhibit efficiency. A rule of thumb places the optimum group size between five and seven members.[39] Anything less than five inhibits diversity of opinion that is necessary when discussing broad perspectives and consideration of opinions. Also, members may feel intimidated or reluctant to disagree in groups of four or fewer for fear of alienating their colleagues. A sense of closeness has a tendency to impede critical, thoughtful analysis of issues and solutions.

Groups with more than seven members face equally serious problems. As with any large group, once status is assigned, members tend to develop hierarchies. The higher status members use their positions to affect the participation of lower status members. When this happens, we generally see the formation of subgroups within the larger group; problem-solving discussion becomes a futile exercise in politics rather than a deliberation about issues. This begins the group's spiral decent into ineffectiveness. Power plays negate group cohesion, which in turn leads to disgruntled and dissatisfied members, who may decide to permanently leave the group. One role of the group leader is to prevent this from happening. (We will discuss this in Chapter 8, Interpersonal Communication Skills for Leaders.) If you want to see an ineffectual group working hard at going nowhere and doing nothing, tune into CSPAN some time, and watch the U.S. Congress at work.

3. **Group charge.** Groups come together for a purpose. They are formed for reasons that provide a collective goal that should unify members. Understanding this purpose is crucial because it is not possible for a group to be effective unless all of its members understand precisely what the task is and what the final outcome is to be. We call this understanding the **group charge.** A group without a clear purpose or in which members disagree about the goal will be ineffectual, and this may eventually cause its demise. The first active step of any problem-solving group is to have clarification of purpose.

Group charge
The purpose or final outcome for group work.

4. **Group record.** A group record is the history of the past work by the group. This work may be from previous charges or the existing charge. The record may consist only of brief notes of member discussion or detailed accounts of current progress. However, not all groups keep records of what they do. You may find it advantageous to keep a record of member duties and actions, especially if a member fails to perform them. You eliminate a lot of bickering when you can remind people of what they were *supposed* to do, according to previous records, instead of what they *did* do, or failed to do.

ROLES IN GROUPS

Each member within the group must assume at least one type of role, and at times may perform multiple roles. The effectiveness of individuals', and ultimately the group's, efforts rests on the notion that they, alone, are responsible for their actions. We begin the study of roles with individual accountability.

Individual Accountability

A key factor mediating the effectiveness of group efforts is the members' sense of personal responsibility for contributing their efforts to accomplish the group's goals. This involves being responsible for (1) completing one's share of the work and (2) facilitating the work of other group members and minimally delaying or preventing their efforts. **Individual accountability** exists when the performance of each individual member is assessed and the results are returned to the group and the individual. It is important that the group know which members need more assistance, support, and encouragement in completing their work.

Types of Roles

Role
A name we give to a complex of many different kinds of behavioral observations.

Role is a name we give to a complex of many different kinds of behavioral observations. The word comes from the language of the stage: it is the part a person is given to play, and he or she may play it well or poorly.[40] Roles define expected relationships between group members, which are supported by group norms. There are two basic categories of roles: **formal** and **informal**. A formal role is a position either assigned by an organization or specifically designated by the group itself. A formal role can be associated with the position and status of a member, such as Speaker of the House in the U.S. Congress, where congressional members elect their leader. This implies certain rights and duties of that member toward other members of the group. An organization's position titles, such as chief executive officer (CEO), president, or secretary are generally considered to be formal roles. Behaviors for these roles are explicitly spelled out by the organization and are designated by the organization. As a rule, formal roles are independent of the person assuming the role.

Formal role
A position either assigned by an organization or specifically designated by the group itself.

In small groups, roles are usually informal and are a result of group transactions that emphasize functions, not positions like formal roles. And, unlike formal roles, such as leadership, a group member may fulfill leadership functions without formal designation; that is, the group determines which member leads them. In most groups, members fulfill a number of roles; that's because they perform more than one task. Informal roles are not explicitly defined by the group; rather, expectations regarding behavior and duties are implicitly relayed by members through degrees of approval and disapproval. There are typically three types of informal roles: task, maintenance, and self-centered.[41] The first two reflect George Homans' activities and interactions roles. **Task roles** (activities) are performative; they move the group toward goal achievement. They are meant to maximize member productivity; they are the *tasks* that people perform, the elements of social behavior. **Maintenance roles** (interactions) are the relationships which the activity of one member of the group has to that of another; they are the communication behaviors that occur between people in performing those tasks. Their function is to develop and maintain group cohesiveness. They are primarily the interpersonal relationships of members. The third role, the **self-centered role**, serves individual needs or goals while, at the same time, disrupting or impeding group goal achievement. This is an ego-centric role where the purpose of disruption is to divert attention to the individual instead of group tasks.

The type of group determines many of the roles that are assumed by its members, and there are literally countless types of groups and roles. It is impossible to list all of them. However, there are roles that seem to consistently reappear. See the following box.

Task role
The tasks that people perform; the elements of social behavior.

Maintenance role
The relationships which the activity of one member of the group has to that of another; they are the *communication behaviors* that occur between people in performing those tasks.

Self-centered role
Serves individual needs or goals while, at the same time, disrupting or impeding group goal achievement.

Task Roles

1. **Initiating-contributing (orienting).** Proposes new ideas or suggestions for rethinking the group goal or new directions on problem-solving techniques.
2. **Information giver.** Considers himself or herself a well-spring of information; offering facts and information, and personal experiences relevant to the group's charge.
3. **Information seeking.** Seeks clarifications; authoritative information and facts relevant to the problem, evidence; seeks suggestions and ideas from others.
4. **Opinion seeker.** Asks for viewpoints and opinions from others; states beliefs, values, judgments, and conclusions.
5. **Clarifier-elaborator.** Expands on suggestions made by others with examples and anecdotal evidence of his or her own; explains what others have said.
6. **Coordinator.** Indicates relationships between facts and ideas; tries to combine ideas and suggestions; organizes the group's work; promotes teamwork and cooperation.
7. **Recorder (summarizer).** Takes notes, prepares minutes, and reviews what has been previously said; serves as the group recorder of discussions.

8. **Leader-director.** Manages group process; keeps group on track and moving toward its goal; mediates problems within the group.
9. **Procedural assistant.** Facilitates group progress by performing incidental duties such as handing out materials, making sure that there are refreshments, etc.

Maintenance Roles

1. **Establishing norms.** Offers a behavioral code of conduct for members; challenges inappropriate and unproductive behavior; rebukes members when they violate those norms.
2. **Encourager-supporter.** The cheerleader for the group; a morale builder; provides praise and acceptance of members; encourages full member participation and tolerance of diverse thought; recognizes the value of others.
3. **Harmonizer.** Keeps the peace; mediates member differences; tries to reconcile disagreement; uses humor to reduce tension in times of conflict; suggests compromise or new alternatives; placates angry members.
4. **Gatekeeper.** Controls the flow of information and channels of communication; encourages or limits participation; promotes open discussion.
5. **Supporter.** Concurs with the position of another member; advocates ideas and proposals.

Self-centered Roles

1. **Aggressor.** Criticizes and attempts to diminish the contributions of others; minimizes the status of others; rejects or prevents others from voicing their proposals and ideas; seeks to demean others; tries to dominate the discussion; threatens other group members.
2. **Withdrawing.** The opposite of aggression. Avoids conflict; does not comment on others' proposals and ideas; will not commit to a position or opinion; refuses to express feelings; tries to act invisible when necessary.
3. **Blocking.** Prevents progress toward group goals by constantly raising objections, repeatedly brings up the same topic or issue after the group has considered or rejected it; will not cooperate; prevents the group from reaching consensus; refuses to accept a group decision, instead constantly resurrecting dead issues.
4. **Recognition seeker.** Dominates the discussion; boasts about self-achievements, expertise, or experience; changes subject matter to self; attempts to raise status or importance within the group.

Role Competence: Norms and Conformity

What is a **norm**? Norms are our ideas. They are not the behavior itself, but what people think behavior ought to be.[42] We assume that a norm is an expected behavior under particular circumstances. How do we know what is expected? Sometimes, the members of a group will articulate what the expected behavior is, but sometimes it is assumed or inferred, but never expressed. A norm, therefore, is the stated expression of behavior that defines an individual's role in the group. Norms describe how people should behave in a particular role. However, a norm is not the behavior itself; it is an idea. It is what people think behavior ought to be.[43] It is a statement specifying how one or more persons are expected to behave in given circumstances.[44]

Recognizing group norms is important to effective participation in group work. Once you know how to identify group norms, you will know how you respond to them. Group rules affect communication. Members will know when to respond, when not to, and when to question other members and rules. Those who do not conform to norms are usually punished. This can take the form of a censure, reprimand, privilege withdrawal, or even expulsion from the group. As such, norms are necessary for the group to get its work completed. They promote group cohesion and help maintain interaction.

BECOMING FAMILIAR WITH COLLEAGUES

Many groups begin with new members who generally don't know each other. This is a good opportunity to find out more about them.

1. **Getting to know the people you are working with.** It is important to know the people you are working with. The more familiar you are with them, the earlier the group will develop synergy; members will be able to manage conflict more effectively, develop good communication skills, and create an interdependence that will enable the group to achieve its goal.
2. **Why are they there?** Understanding why each member is there gives you insight as to their dedication to the group and its charge. People volunteer to become members because they want to engage the process and make a difference, whether that be on a school board, planning commission, student academic senate, or a community action committee.
3. **Does the group share a common interest?** Perhaps the group's charge is to decide whether their community should build a skate park. The interest is to provide a safe environment for children and teenagers. Do members share an interest in providing a safe place for people to skate? A skate park may not be the answer, but the interest should be shared by the group. Interest is an energizer.
4. **Is the problem related to your interests?** People tend to become active in group work when the problem is related to their personal interests. Interests

TABLE 2.1	Comparison of Effective and Ineffective Groups[45]

Effective Groups	Ineffective Groups
Goals are clarified and changed so that the best possible match between individual goals and the group's goals may be achieved; goals are cooperatively structured.	Members accept imposed goals; goals are competitively structured.
Communication is two-way, and the open and accurate expression of both ideas and feelings is emphasized.	Communication is one-way, and only ideas are expressed; feelings are suppressed or ignored.
Participation and leadership are distributed among all group members; goals accomplishment, maintenance, and developmental change are underscored.	Leadership is delegated and based upon authority; internal membership participation is unequal, with high-authority members dominating; only goal accomplishment is emphasized.
Ability and information determine influence and power; contracts are built to make sure individuals' goals and needs are fulfilled; power is equalized and shared.	Position determines influence and power; power is concentrated in the authority positions; obedience to authority is the rule.
Decision-making procedures are matched with the situation; different methods are used at different times; consensus is sought for important decisions; involvement and group discussions are encouraged.	Decisions are always made by the highest authority; there is little group discussion; members' involvement is minimal.
Controversy and conflict are seen as positive key to members' involvement, the quality and originality of decisions, and the continuance of the group in good working condition.	Controversy and conflict are ignored, denied, avoided, or suppressed.
Interpersonal, group, and intergroup behaviors are stressed; cohesion is advanced through high levels of inclusion, affection, acceptance, support, and trust. Individuality is endorsed.	The functions performed by members are emphasized; cohesion is ignored, and members are controlled by force. Rigid conformity is promoted.
Problem-solving adequacy is high.	Problem-solving adequacy is low.

Members evaluate the effectiveness of the group and decide how to improve its functioning; goal accomplishment, internal maintenance, and development are all considered important.	The highest authority evaluates the group's effectiveness and decides how goal accomplishment may be improved; internal maintenance and development are ignored as much as possible; stability is affirmed.
Interpersonal effectiveness, self-actualization, and innovation are encouraged.	Organizational persons who desire order, stability, and structure are encouraged.

are motivators, and individuals tend to care more about the problem and its potential solutions because of those interests.

5. **Do all group members share the same perspective about the problem?** This can be a double-edged sword. On the one hand, sharing the same perspective about the problem can minimize distractions and conflict, and keep the group focused. On the other hand, it can create groupthink and reject valid differences of opinion.

6. **Why did the group members choose this problem?** Generally speaking, people will choose what they want to work on based on **vested interest**. Similar interests have a tendency to influence group members in their choices.

7. **Identify the strengths that each member brings to the group.** Each person has at least one strength that no one else in the group has.

Probably the most frustrating part of group work is dealing with all of the different personality types and the differences members have in their approach to group work. You will not be able to modify or change these attributes, but knowing how to circumvent them and work with people who are very different from you will make you a more effective member or leader.

Myers-Briggs Type Indicator

The Myers–Briggs Type Indicator® (MBTI), developed by Isabel Myers and her mother, Katharine Briggs, in the 1940s, is an instrument for measuring people's preferences on how they relate to the world around them, based on the theory of psychological types described by psychologist Carl G. Jung. The theory basically states that what we observe as random variations in a person's behavior are actually quite orderly and consistent because of basic differences in the ways individuals make judgments based on their perceptions.[46] In developing the MBTI, the goal of Isabel Myers and Katharine Briggs was to make Jung's theory of psychological types understandable and useful in people's lives, and to make the insights of **type theory** they developed accessible to individuals and groups. The MBTI instrument addresses this goal.

Jung's theory, in part, identified four dichotomies, or **preferences**, which influence behavior:[47]

1. **Favorite world.** Do you prefer to focus on the outer world or on your own inner world?

   This is called **Extraversion (E)** or **Introversion (I)**.

2. **Information.** Do you prefer to focus on the basic information you take in, or do you prefer to interpret and add meaning?

   This is called **Sensing (S)** or **Intuition (N)**.

3. **Decisions.** When making decisions, do you prefer to first look at logic and consistency or first look at the people and special circumstances?

   This is called **Thinking (T)** or **Feeling (F)**.

4. **Structure.** In dealing with the outside world, do you prefer to get things decided, or do you prefer to stay open to new information and options?

   This is called **Judging (J)** or **Perceiving (P)**.

Myers and Briggs identified and described 16 distinctive personality types that result from the interactions among Jung's preferences. They are often shown in what is called a **type table**. (See Table 2.2.)

TABLE 2.2

ISTJ	ISFJ	INFJ	INTJ
ISTP	ISFP	INFP	INTP
ESTP	ESFP	ENFP	ENTP
ESTJ	ESFJ	ENFJ	ENTJ

The 16 MBTI Types® are described as:

- **ISTJ.** Quiet, serious, earn success by thoroughness and dependability. Practical, matter-of-fact, realistic, and responsible. Decide logically what should be done and work toward it steadily, regardless of distractions. Take pleasure in making everything orderly and organized—their work, their home, their life. Value traditions and loyalty.
- **ISFJ.** Quiet, friendly, responsible, and conscientious. Committed and steady in meeting their obligations. Thorough, painstaking, and accurate. Loyal, considerate, notice and remember specifics about people who are important to them, concerned with how others feel. Strive to create an orderly and harmonious environment at work and at home.
- **INFJ.** Seek meaning and connection in ideas, relationships, and material possessions. Want to understand what motivates people and are insightful about others. Conscientious and committed to their firm values. Develop a clear vision about how best to serve the common good. Organized and decisive in implementing their vision.
- **INTJ.** Have original minds and great drive for implementing their ideas and achieving their goals. Quickly see patterns in external events and develop long-range explanatory perspectives. When committed, organize a

job and carry it through. Skeptical and independent, have high standards of competence and performance—for themselves and others.

- **ISTP.** Tolerant and flexible, quiet observers until a problem appears, then act quickly to find workable solutions. Analyze what makes things work and readily get through large amounts of data to isolate the core of practical problems. Interested in cause, effect; organize facts using logical principles; value efficiency.

- **ISFP.** Quiet, friendly, sensitive, and kind. Enjoy the present moment, what's going on around them. Like to have their own space and to work within their own time frame. Loyal and committed to their values and to people who are important to them. Dislike disagreements and conflicts; do not force their opinions or values on others.

- **INFP.** Idealistic, loyal to their values and to people who are important to them. Want an external life that is congruent to their values. Curious, quick to see possibilities; can be catalysts for implementing ideas. Seek to understand people and to help them fulfill their potential. Adaptable, flexible, and accepting unless a value is threatened.

- **INTP.** Seek to develop logical explanations for everything that interests them. Theoretical and abstract, interested more in ideas than in social interaction. Quiet, contained, flexible, and adaptable. Have unusual ability to focus in depth to solve problems in their area of interest. Skeptical, sometimes critical, always analytical.

- **ESTP.** Flexible and tolerant, they take a pragmatic approach focused immediate results. Theories and conceptual explanations bore them; they want to act energetically to solve the problem. Focus on the here-and-now; spontaneous, enjoy each moment that they can be active with others. Enjoy material comforts and style. Learn best through doing.

- **ESFP.** Outgoing, friendly, and accepting. Exuberant lovers of life, people, and material comforts. Enjoy working with others to make things happen. Bring common sense and a realistic approach to their work, and make work fun. Flexible and spontaneous; adapt readily to new people and environments. Learn best by trying a new skill with other people.

- **ENFP.** Warmly enthusiastic and imaginative. See life as full of possibilities. Make connections between events and information very quickly, and confidently proceed based on the patterns they see. Want a lot of affirmation from others, and readily give appreciation and support. Spontaneous and flexible; often rely on their ability to improvise and their verbal fluency.

- **ENTP.** Quick, ingenious, stimulating, alert, and outspoken. Resourceful in solving new and challenging problems. Adept at generating conceptual possibilities and then analyzing them strategically. Good at reaching other people. Bored by routine; will seldom do the same thing the same way; apt to turn to one new interest after another.

- **ESTJ.** Practical, realistic, matter-of-fact. Decisive, quickly move to implement decisions. Organize projects and people to get things done; focus on getting results in the most efficient way possible. Take care of routine details. Have a clear set of logical standards, systematically follow them, and want others to also. Forceful in implementing their plans.

- **ESFJ.** Warmhearted, conscientious, and cooperative. Want harmony in their environment; work with determination to establish it. Like to work with others to complete tasks accurately and on time. Loyal, follow through even in small matters. Notice what others need in their day-by-day lives, and try to provide it. Want to be appreciated for who they are and for what they contribute.
- **ENFJ.** Warm, empathetic, responsive, and responsible. Highly attuned to the emotions, needs, and motivations of others. Find potential in everyone; want to help others fulfill their potential. May act as catalysts for individual and group growth. Loyal, responsive to praise and criticism. Sociable, facilitate others in a group, and provide inspiring leadership.
- **ENTJ.** Frank, decisive, assume leadership readily. Quickly see illogical and inefficient procedures and policies; develop and implement comprehensive systems to solve organizational problems. Enjoy long-term planning and goal-setting. Usually well informed, well read; enjoy expanding their knowledge and passing it on to others. Forceful in presenting their ideas.

Why would we want to know someone's type? Simple, it's a way of explaining why people behave the way they do; why humans act differently. We use personality typing to understand ourselves and others. Haven't you ever said about someone else in conversation, "Oh, Joe's the type of person who…" or "You know Cathy's type!?" No two individuals are the same; we are all unique in many ways, especially in our behaviors. The more type information a group leader has, the more efficiently he or she can achieve group goals. You certainly don't want to assign a critical task such as research to someone who adds meaning and likes to work within their own time frame. You may wind up with little information and a lot of useless interpretation.

Understanding types helps the group leader facilitate positive interaction between group members, which produces good performance, and aids in developing and maintaining synergy, among other things. Remember, the MBTI is a diagnostic tool that helps us understand who we are. It is useful in group work only if the information provided is used ethically and constructively to efficiently achieve the group's goal.

SUMMARY

We began this chapter by learning that groups and teams are performance-based, and that the final product or end result of group work is determined by that performance. We know that groups are inescapable in any culture, and that society is dependent on groups in order to function in an orderly manner. In our study of groups, we know to look for particular characteristics and common properties such as interaction, interdependence, structure, cohesiveness, and goals. These help us understand some of the dynamics of group functionality.

We've discovered that the nature of group dynamics is a combination of theory, research, and practice. These elements are never static, but interdependent and always improving upon each other. Four fundamental macro theories of group work—Kurt Lewin's field theory, Robert F. Bales' Interaction Process Analysis and George C. Homans' Systems Theory of Informal Work Groups, and System Theory—have given you some basic principles as to why groups function the way they do. Although it is impossible to identify all of the different types of roles related to group work, we were able to talk about the ones that consistently reappear. And finally, we learned that we will need to know who are colleagues are and who we are if we expect to work well together to achieve the group's goals. Understanding Chapter 2 gives you a solid foundation to build upon when you have to form your own group.

DISCUSSION

1. Concepts from this chapter such as **interdependence, nonsummativity** and **cohesiveness** indicate that a successful work–oriented small group can and does achieve goals together that its members could not achieve merely working on their own or working separately in sequence (like a factory production line). What examples of such "more than the sum of their parts" groups can you identify in your experience? Why are these groups important *as groups* in functioning in their respective fields?

2. On page 45, Bales' dimensions characterizing an individual's perception of her/his position in a group are identified as dominant/submissive, friendly/unfriendly and instrumental/emotional. Based on what you have learned so far, how would you expect norms of culture and gender to shape a person's responses along these dimensions?

3. What are some systems in our society that you believe are not effective because they are **closed** to outside influences or too **static** to evolve properly? Conversely, what are some systems in our society that you believe are effective because they are **open** to outside influence and/or **dynamic** in their evolution over time?

4. On page 53 the author suggests that the U.S. Congress is a good example of a group rendered ineffective by its size. Explore this idea in greater depth: What are the primary goals of the U.S. Congress? What elements of the system that is the U.S. Congress account for its ineffectiveness in achieving its goals? What elements of this system, if any, are well designed to help it achieve its goals?

5. Have each person in your group tentatively identify their Myers-Briggs type based on the descriptions on pages 59–62, then consider the various types present in your group. How would knowing these types help your group identify potential roles in which various members might flourish? How would they help your group identify potential roles in which various members might grow and change?

NOTES

1. Nager, N.R. & Allen, T.H. (1984). *Public relations: Management by objectives.* Lanham, MD: University Press of America.

2. Austin, E.W., & Pinkleton, B.E. (2006). *Strategic public relations management: Planning and managing effective communication programs* (2nd ed.). Mahwah, NJ: Lawrence Erlbaum Associates.

3. Smith, R.D. (2005). *Strategic planning for public relations* (2nd ed.). Mahwah, NJ: Lawrence Erlbaum Associates.

4. Wilcox, D.L., Cameron, G.T., Ault, P., & Agee, W.K. (2000). *Public relations strategies and tactics,* (8th ed.). New York: Pearson.

5. Daniels, A.C. (1989). *Performance management: Improving quality productivity through positive reinforcement.* Tucker, GA: Performance Management.

6. "The Nature of Group Dynamics" is adapted from Johnson, D.W., & Johnson, F.P. (1997). *Joining together: Group theory and group skills* (6th ed.). Boston: Allyn and Bacon.

7. Johnson, D.W., & Johnson, F.P. (1997). *Joining together: Group theory and group skills* (6th ed.). Boston: Allyn and Bacon.

8. Ibid.

9. http://psychology.about.com/od/profilesofmajorthinkers/p/bio_lewin.htm. Retrieved March 13, 2008.

10. http://www.nwlink.com/~donclark/hrd/history/lewin.html. Retrieved March 13, 2008.

11. Johnson, D.W., & Johnson, F.P. (1997). *Joining together: Group theory and group skills* (6th ed.). Boston: Allyn and Bacon.

12. DeWine, S. (1994). *The consultant's craft: Improving organizational communication.* New York: St. Martin's Press.

13. Lewin, K. (1946). Behavior and development as a function of the total situation. In Dorwin Cartwright (Ed.), (1951), *Field Theory in Social Science* (pp. 239–240). New York: Harper & Brothers.

14. Lewin, K. (1946). Behavior and development as a function of the total situation. In L. Carmichael (Ed.). *Manual of child development.* New York: Wiley. See also Hersey, P., Blanchard K.H., & Johnson, D.E. (2001). *Management of organizational behavior: Leading human resources* (8th ed.). Upper Saddle River: Prentice Hall.

15. Lewin, K. (1951) *Field theory in social science: Selected theoretical papers.* D. Cartwright (Ed.). New York: Harper & Row.

16. Daniels, V. (2003). *Kurt Lewin notes.* Sonoma State University. http://www.sonoma.edu/users/d/daniels/lewinnotes.html.

17. Webster's Unabridged Dictionary. (1996). New York: Random House Value Publishing.

18. http://www.psychology.sbc.edu/Kurt%20Lewin.htm. Retrieved March 17, 2008.

19. Johnson, D.W., & Johnson, F.P. (1997). *Joining together: Group theory and group skills* (6th ed.). Boston: Allyn and Bacon.

20. Amidon, E.J., & Hough, J.B. (Eds.). (1967). *Interaction analysis: Theory, research and application.* Reading, MA: Addison-Wesley.

21. For a more thorough explanation of Bales' interaction process model, see Amidon, E.J., & Hough, J.B. (Eds.). (1967). *Interaction analysis: Theory, research and application.* Reading, MA: Addison-Wesley.

22. Littlejohn, S. W. (1999). *Theories of human communication* (6th ed.). Belmont, CA: Wadsworth.

23. Ibid.

24. Homans, G.C. (1950). *The human group.* New York: Harcourt, Brace & World.

25. Ibid.

26. Roland S. Barth, Senior Lecturer, Harvard University, quoted in Harold J. Burbach, H.J. (1988, March) New ways of thinking for educators. *The Education Digest,* 3.

27. Homans, G.C. (1992). *The human group.* New Brunswick, NJ: Transaction Publishers.

28. Homans, G.C. (1974). *Social behavior: Its elementary forms.* New York: Harcourt Brace Jovanovich.

29. Hersey, P., Blanchard, K.H., & Johnson, D.E. (2001). *Management of organizational behavior.* Upper Saddle River, NJ: Prentice Hall. Also see Homans, G.C. (1992). *The human group.* New Brunswick, NJ: Transaction Publishers.

30. Homans, G.C. (1950). *The human group.* New York: Harcourt, Brace & World.

31. Ibid.

32. Ibid.

33. von Bertalanffy, L. (1968) *General systems theory.* New York: George Braziller.

34. Adapted from Gillies, D.A. (1982). *Nursing management: A systems approach.* Philadelphia: W.B. Saunders Company.

35. Certo, S. (1983). *Principles of modern management: Functions and systems.* Dubuque, IA: Brown.

36. Ashby, W.R. (1962). Principles of the self-organizing system. In H. von Foerster, & G. Zopf (Eds.), *Principles of self-organization* (pp. 255–278). New York: Pergamon.

37. Adapted from http://www.bsn-gn.eku.edu/BEGLEY/GSThand1.htm#top. Retrieved March 25, 2008.

38. "INITIAL ELEMENTS IN GROUP SYSTEMS" has been adapted and modified from Wood. J.T., Phillips, G.M.. & Pedersen, D.J. (1986). *Group discussion: A practical guide to participation and leadership* (2nd ed.). San Francisco: Harper & Row.

39. Bales, R.F., & Borgatta, E.F. (1995). Size of a group as a factor in the interaction profile. In A.P. Hare, E.F. Borgatta, & R.F. Bales (Eds.), *Small groups: Studies in social interaction* (pp. 129–139). New York: Knopf.

40. Homans, G.C. (1950). *The human group.* New York: Harcourt, Brace & World.

41. See Rothwell, J.D. (2004). *In mixed company: Communicating in small groups and teams* (5th ed.). United States: Thomson-Wadsworth.

42. Homans, G.C. (1950). *The human group.* New York: Harcourt, Brace & World.

43. Ibid.

44. Homans, G.C. (1974). *Social behavior: Its elementary forms.* New York: Harcourt Brace Jovanovich.

45. Adapted from Johnson, D.W., & Johnson, F.P. (1997). *Joining together: Group theory and group skills* (6th ed.). Boston: Allyn and Bacon.

46. http://www.myersbriggs.org/. Retrieved August 3, 2008.

47. Ibid.

Power Roles
Members, Leaders, and Ethics

CHAPTER OBJECTIVES

- Understand the power of groups
- Explain the types of power in groups
- Understand how members can influence group behavior
- Explain the structural process of individual power
- Introduce coercive forms of power
- Distinguish the two basic types of leadership in groups
- Comprehend the importance of power and ethics

CHAPTER OUTLINE

KEY TERMS

Power

Position power

Personal power

Bullying

Charisma

Agentic state

Fundamental attribution error

Identification

Internalization

DEFINING POWER

Group work cannot exist without some form of authoritative power structure. Power is an essential element to group life because it gives the group the ability to effectively complete its goals. Authorities use power to control the behaviors of others and to coordinate their activities. So what is power? How do we achieve power? Where does it come from? Does every member of the group have power? In this chapter, we will explore the concept of power and influence, and its application in group work. Let's begin by defining power. I'm sure you've heard people say that they have power over someone else because they can manipulate them or get them to do things they don't want to do. And they can do this in a number of ways. These people may define power as the ability to manipulate or control the activities of others. Others may say that they have power to get people to do things because of their charisma or charm—that they have a natural ability for power. Yet others may say that just the idea that they can make someone else do something is power. In some senses, they may all be correct.

Basically, power is simply the ability to get things done the way one wants them to be done. However, we need to define power, and there are many definitions of power, just as there are many types of power. One definition of power states that it is the ability to "influence and/or regulate and/or control outcomes."[1] Another source defines power as "… the ability to induce a person to do something he or she would not otherwise have done."[2] I like M.F. Rogers' simple definition of power as "the potential for influence"[3]; however, it falls short of one other concept—compliance. I prefer to view power as a form of influence and a means for compliance. I can influence someone to do something and get him or her to comply in many ways. It is a much broader concept for understanding power in group work. If we view power as a potential for influence and compliance, we can modify the way individuals think or behave. In group work, the concept of power is closely associated with the concept of leadership.

In order for any group to function, there must be distribution of power. Someone has to tell someone else what to do, and the person who is doing the telling must have some reinforcing means so that the other person will comply. Power is a resource that enables a person to bring about compliance from others or to influence them. It is a person's **influence potential**.[4] In organizations, we tend to see two kinds of power—position power and personal power. There are those individuals who can get others to comply because of their positions in the organization, such as the CEO or any of management's officers—they have position power. And then there are others who get their influence from their personality and behavior, such as individuals you admire—they have personal power.[5] Some people have both, while others seem to have no power at all. Must people who have power always exercise it? No, but they do have the capacity or potential to do so.

Power
A resource that enables a person to bring about compliance from others or to influence them.

Position power
Those who can get others to comply because of their positions.

Personal power
Those who get their influence from their personality and behavior.

Types of Power

There has been substantial research performed on the notion of power. What is considered to be the "classic among classics"[6] in power research was done by John R.P. French, Jr., and Bertram Raven, published in 1959.[7] They identified five different types of power in groups, organizations, or among individuals: **reward, coercive, legitimate, referent,** and **expert powers**.

1. Reward power is defined as power whose basis is the ability to reward. If your manager gives you a raise because he or she says that you've worked hard, then that is a reward—that person has reward power. The degree to which your manager has reward power is determined by his or her ability to provide that award. If your manager says that he or she will recommend you for a raise because you worked hard, that is still reward power, but it lacks the strength that the first example provides. You may or may not receive your raise. The raise is the incentive or reward for you to continue to work hard.

2. Coercive power is the opposite of reward power because it uses threatened punishment as a way to gain compliance. The strength of coercive power depends on the degree or magnitude of the punishment. If your manager tells you that the next time you're late for work you'll be docked two hours pay, that's coercive power. It is a punishment designed to get you to come to work on time. Similar to reward power, the degree of coercive power is determined by the manager's ability to provide the punishment. However, unlike with a reward, the employee threatened with punishment may quit, thus rendering the power useless.

3. Legitimate power is defined as that power that is inherent in an individual's position or office in which others have an obligation to accept his or her influence. In all forms of legitimate power, the notion of legitimacy involves some sort of established code or standard. Your teacher has a degree of legitimate power, as does a police officer or your employer because of the structure of the system each are in. Each one is granted a legitimate power as a result of an established code within that system. And that code also describes the general behaviors of those to whom it grants that power.

4. Referent power, unlike reward, coercive, or legitimate power; referent power, has its basis in the identification of one person with another. By identification, I mean the feeling of oneness that one person has for another or a desire for such an identity. It is the influence inherent in the respect and admiration others have for an individual. Individuals with referent power are perceived as credible, wise, and as role models, for example. Sports figures such as Michael Jordan, Brett Favre, Michael Phelps, and Eric Chavez are role models who have referent power.

© uremar, 2011. Under license from Shutterstock, Inc.

5. **Expert power** is a result of someone's knowledge, skill, and/or experience. The strength of the expert power that is given to someone varies with the knowledge or perception that others attribute to him or her. When you need legal advice, you generally accept an attorney's advice in legal matters. Or perhaps there is one auto mechanic who has a reputation for being the best in your area. You prefer to get your car fixed by this person because of his or her reputation as having the best skills. These are examples of expert power.

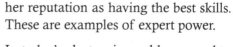

In today's electronic world, we need to identify a sixth power, although it can be argued that it belongs as a subheading of expert power according to the research performed by French and Raven:

6. **Informational power** derives its strength from individuals who know how to retrieve information. Today's electronic media (which includes the internet) make it virtually impossible for one individual to know how and where to retrieve all relevant information. Power is ascribed to those people who have this expertise.

There are three more powers that need to be recognized in group work:

7. **Earned power** results from effective performance that earns approval and respect from others.
8. **Political power** is derived from those activities that are not required as part of one's group role but that influence, or attempt to influence, the distribution of advantages and disadvantages within the group. It is political behavior that relates to the promotion of the self and group interests rather than being a part of the formal roles regulated by group norms and goals.[8]

9. **Social power** is the capacity to influence others, even when these others try to resist influence.[9] A powerful person can use and control others for his or her own ends.

In group work, because no two group members have exactly the same resources, each member operates from a different power base. People develop power in a group because they can provide or render service to that group through information, expertise, rewards, and punishment; or because they have been elected or appointed; or because they are well liked or have status in the group.

GROUP MEMBERS' INFLUENCE

When a group is newly formed, all members, save the leader, have equal influence. It is only through interaction and interpersonal communication that some members gain influence over others. There are two types of influence that have a tendency to be destructive to effective group work: bullying (a coercive influence) and charisma. Bullying, or aggressiveness, is a dysfunctional behavior because individuals ignore the rights of others by using offensive and hostile behaviors.[10] Bullying has a tendency to generate negative feelings such as guilt, fear of consequences, and alienation, which can inhibit or prevent effect group work. Aggression is a behavior employed to get one's way and stifle dissent or discussion. Unchecked, it can create groupthink and the possible extinction of the group. Bullying behavior should be challenged the moment it is first used.

The second type of influence is charisma. What is charisma? Good question! It is defined by such words as "charm, personality, appeal, personal magnetism, allure, and dynamic character," just to mention a few. Charisma is premised on individual perception. All of us know someone who we have said has charisma.

We'd do just about anything for the person if we were asked. And that's the problem with charismatic influence in group work—it has a tendency to replace substance with charm, especially when it comes to making decisions. Do we decide based upon the facts, or are we persuaded by a member's charisma? It's easy to spot bullying, but not so easy to identify charisma. What we want to achieve is **interpersonal influence**, which is a complex process that can take a great deal of awareness and sensitivity.[11]

© prodakszyn, 2011. Under license from Shutterstock, Inc.

Bullying

A dysfunctional behavior which ignores the rights of others.

Charisma

A trait called "charm, personality, appeal, or personal magnetism."

GROUP AND STRUCTURAL PROCESSES

As we noted, within every group there exists a power structure. A person's power in a group and a person's responsibility for what happens in that group generally go hand in hand. A structural process that addresses power and responsibility within group work is called the **superior/subordinate hierarchy**. A superior is someone who has authority over the group, usually the group leader, while a subordinate is someone who follows the directions of the superior, a group member. This structure relies on subordinate members to be obedient to the superior—to follow orders so to speak. Sometimes, members will follow orders even if they believe those orders to be questionable or wrong. There have been extensive studies in social psychology on interpersonal theories of behavior focusing on obedience in organizations and small groups. One of the most famous of these studies is Stanley Milgram's **Agency Theory** (1973). Milgram analyzed power by creating small groups in his laboratory at Yale University. He attempted to explain why obedience to authority, especially a malevolent authority, has such a strong hold on our behavior.[12] This theory suggests that at any particular time a person is in one of two distinct psychological states: the first is the **autonomous state**, in which behaviors are seen as self-directed. In this state, individuals make decisions based on their own ideas, beliefs, and experiences. The second or agentic state is a situation in which people see themselves as agents of a higher authority. In this state, individuals give up their own responsibility, deferring to those of higher status. When a person transitions from the autonomous state to the agentic state (the agentic shift), he or she follows orders without considering the consequences or whether the request is appropriate. This shift in responsibility means that the person no longer monitors his or her own behavior—he or she "just follows orders" and does not consider himself or herself responsible—"It's not my fault, the boss told me to do it." These individuals feel responsibility to the authority, but no responsibility for their behavior because some higher authority told them to do it. Individuals who have positions at the bottom of the hierarchy tend to do as they are told by those of higher status.[13]

Agentic state
When a group member or members exhibit undesirable, destructive, or evil behavior.

We learn to function in these two states from an early age. When you were growing up, your parents acted as agents, instructing you in ways of behaving and the importance of obeying others. This will be with you your entire life, with different people taking on the role of agent, for example, teachers, law enforcement officers, employers, and others who hold positions in the social hierarchy above your own.

Another interpersonal theory of social behavior suggests that group members are more likely to follow orders from authority rather than to rebel against them.[14] Forsyth (2006) says that "interpersonal theory assumes that each group member's action tends to evoke, or 'pull,' a predictable set of actions from the other group members... friendly behaviors are complimented by more friendly behaviors" (p. 266). However, if group members act in dominant, firm, directive ways—issuing orders or taking charge—then interpersonal theory suggests that other group members would behave submissively. The **interpersonal complementary hypothesis** predicts that (1) positive behaviors evoke positive behaviors, and negative behaviors evoke negative behaviors; and (2) dominant behaviors evoke submissive behaviors, and submissive behaviors evoke dominant behaviors.[15]

© michaeljung, 2011. Under license from Shutterstock, Inc.

One form of influence used to gain member commitment in group work is the **foot-in-the-door technique**. This is a classic sales technique for eliciting compliance by preceding a request for a large commitment with a request for a small one, the initial small request serving the function of softening up the target person.[16] The expression foot in the door comes from the days when door-to-door salesmen sold their merchandise on the doorstep. Each salesman knew that if he could just get through the door with his sales pitch, the client was likely to make a purchase. The foot-in-the-door technique works in small group work because the more a member goes along with small requests or commitments; the more likely that member will continue in a desired direction of attitude or behavioral change and feel obligated to go along with larger requests. The group member who starts up a casual conversation about philosophy or religion or who asks that you complete and discuss a survey on such topics may be employing the foot-in-the-door technique.[17]

COERCIVE METHODS CREATE DYSFUNCTIONAL GROUP PROCESSES

With some similarity to the agentic state, when a group member or members exhibit undesirable, destructive, or evil behavior, we tend to blame the person's character rather than the powerful group processes at work that forced him or her to behave that way in the first place. Social psychologists call this the fundamental attribution error.[18] We have a tendency to underestimate the importance of external group pressures and to overestimate the importance of the individual's internal motives and personality when we interpret behavior. Forsyth (2006) argues that "… obedience is not a reflection of the individuals in the group, but an indication of the power of the group itself. By controlling key bases of power, using power tactics, exploiting the nature of the subordinate–authority relationship, and prefacing large demands with minor ones, authorities exert great influence on group members" (p. 270).

As we have learned, there are numerous types of power and forms of influence in small group work. But once that power is used, how will members react? The exercise of power creates changes in both those it influences and those who use it.[19] The power holder can not only use power over group members, but can use it against group members. Forsyth (2006) says that in some cases, when the power holder only produces compliance, "… the group members do what they are told to do, but only because the power holder demands it" (p. 271). Members may yield to the pressure, even if they privately disagree with the power holder. This yielding to pressure only happens when the power holder closely watches the group. What happens when members admire the power holder? They begin to act like him or her; they create a nexus with that person called identification. When group members identify with the power holder, their self-image changes as they assume the behaviors, characteristics, and roles of the person with power.[20]

If a member or members maintain a prolonged period of identification, it can lead to internalization. When internalization occurs, group members are no longer carrying out the power holder's orders; rather, their behaviors reflect their own personal beliefs, opinions, and goals as conscious or subconscious guiding principles. The group members will perform the required actions even if the power holder isn't present; their actions reflect their private acceptance of the authority's value system.[21]

Not all group members acquiesce to these types of power tactics. Some members refuse to be coerced into obeying the power holder. They do this by either leaving the group or applying influence themselves. Forsyth (2006) says that "In many cases, members contend against those in power individually—particularly when they feel that others in the group have more power than they

Fundamental attribution error

The tendency to underestimate the importance of external group pressures and to overestimate the importance of the individual's internal motives and personality when we interpret his or her behavior.

Identification

When group members identify with the power holder. They begin to act like him or her; they create a nexus with that person.

Internalization

Group members are no longer carrying out the power holder's orders; rather, their behaviors reflect their own personal beliefs, opinions, and goals as conscious or subconscious guiding principles.

© Yuri Arcurs, 2011. Under license from Shutterstock, Inc.

do. But when members feel a sense of shared identity with the other low-power members of the group, they are more likely to join with them in a **revolutionary coalition** that opposes the power holder" (p. 272). A revolutionary coalition is defined as a subgroup formed within the larger group that seeks to disrupt or change the group's authority structure.[22] Members are more likely to rebel against a power holder if they believe that the power holder is responsible for decision making.

Another type of resistance to authority occurs by group members when an authority lacks referent power, but instead employs coercive influence methods and requires group members to carry out unpleasant assignments. This is called **reactance**—individual group members attempt to reassert their sense of freedom by affirming their individuality or autonomy. Group members undergo complex emotional and cognitive reactions when they feel that their freedom to make choices has been threatened or eliminated.[23]

Coercive tactics can produce negative emotions within group members, such as fear, anger, hostility, and depression.[24] Even when mildly coercive methods, such as threats, are used, members have a tendency to overreact and respond with even stronger threats. Over time, coercive power can cause group members to lose interest in their work, which eventually can cause a loss of member productivity when they are not monitored. The conflict created by coercive influence can disrupt the ability of the group to function.[25] Coercive tactics can also disrupt or undermine the quality of any interpersonal relationship members may have with each other or with the power holder.

Power can also compel those who have it to become more aggressive in dealing with members who are nonconforming or outspoken. When members work in a group for an extended period of time under the influence of powerful others, they tend to become inhibited. A member who initially is outspoken or nonconforming may be cajoled or ridiculed over a period of time to the point that he or she eventually becomes silent or conforms to the power holder's influence. In doing so, these changes are consistent with an **approach-inhibition model of power**.[26] Forsyth says that in this model there are two basic types of reactions to environmental events. "One reaction, approach, is associated with action, self-promotion, seeking awards and opportunities, increased energy, and movement. The second reaction, inhibition, is associated with reaction, self-protection, avoiding threats and danger, vigilance, loss of motivation, and an overall reduction in activity. Significantly, the approach-inhibition model suggests that power increases approach tendencies, whereas reductions in power trigger inhibition. In consequence, those with high and low power display contrasting emotions and actions across situations" (p. 275).

Generally speaking, then, when a person exercises power over others, the power holder gains the impression that the others do not control their own behavior, or, in other words, they are not autonomous. Therefore, they are seen as less worthy. In short, a person who successfully exercises power over others is more likely to believe that he or she is less deserving of respect. These people thus become good prospects to be exploited.[27]

LEADERSHIP POWER

What is leadership? We know that it is not the power to coerce others, or that we are born to be leaders as suggested by trait theories.[28] One definition of **leadership** is the process by which an individual guides others in their pursuits, often by organizing, directing, coordinating, supporting, and motivating their efforts.[29] This definition makes leadership a complex interdependency between a leader and group members, whereby cooperating individuals are allowed to influence and motivate others in order to advance the achievement of group and individual goals. Another definition of leadership is the process of influencing people to direct their efforts toward the attainment of particular goal(s).[30] By their very nature, both of these processes require the use of effective communication skills. In addition to effective communication skills, leaders must be both efficient and effective. **Efficiency** is the ability to do things right. **Effectiveness** is the ability to do the right things. Leaders who are efficient know how to utilize their resources. And leaders who are effective know how to maximize group member productivity and respond to both the internal and external environments in order to achieve group goals.

Designated Leader

Within the group context exists two basic types of leaders: the designated leader and the emerging leader. A **designated leader** is a person who is appointed by an authority outside the group to head the group or is elected by the group members. These types of leaders have the power to control the fate of others and thus have considerable power to coerce those under their leadership.[31] A designated leader has a special responsibility to maintain the group's perspective and to ensure that all of the necessary leadership services are performed. A designated leader may determine the group's goals, give directions that must be obeyed willingly or unwillingly, and in some cases, impose punishments on nonconforming members. A designated leader has the potential to reduce interpersonal interactions between him or herself and group members, thereby decreasing interdependency. This relationship enables the leader to influence group members while making the leader less susceptible to any influence from them.

Some people believe that it's necessary to designate a leader because it provides stability to the group. One argument for a designated leader is that someone must immediately organize meetings, obtain resources, represent the group, and facilitate participation. Another argument for this type of leadership is premised on the specific problems the group may encounter. That is, a designated leader may be important when member tasks are complex, or member personalities are so different that conflicts appear inevitable and someone has to take responsibility for managing them, or when the group needs a strong spokesperson.[32] Research shows that groups with designated leaders accepted by the members have fewer interpersonal problems and have a tendency to produce better outcomes than groups without designated leaders.[33]

Emerging Leader

The process of **leadership emergence** or **emerging leader** is determined by the group members themselves and not imposed by an authority outside the group, such as in a designated leader. One individual in the group begins as an equal with other members but emerges as the perceived leader. There are two kinds of emerging leaders: those who emerge from leaderless groups and those who emerge alongside an existing leader to meet particular needs. One benefit of this type of leadership is the fact that members get to know each other to some degree and the group has time to select the right person.

The difference between a designated leader and an emerging leader is not the amount of power but the basis from which the power is derived.[34] One common basis of power is the control of resources that are necessary or desired by others. The emerging leader may be the only member to have access to needed resources, such as money or materials, or the leader may possess organizational skills that other members don't have.

An emerging leader needs to maintain interpersonal relations with members because the relationship between an emerging leader and group members is reciprocal. The principle of interdependence permits the emerging leader to lead at the discretion of group members. In other words, the basis for an emerging leader's power is by the consent of the governed. If the group feels that the leader no longer leads effectively, or fails to satisfy the majority of members, his or her power is diminished. When this happens, the leader may be removed at any time.

Members respect and willingly comply with the leader because they perceive the leader to be helping them make progress toward their group goals. Aubrey Fisher (1980), known for his work on the communication dynamics of small group decision making, says that, "Perhaps more important than any other definitive characteristic, the leader is the person who consistently acts like a leader by performing leadership acts" (p. 193). A good leader, with good ideas, who gives directions well and who is goal-directed and self-assuring, can generate enthusiasm, support, and cohesion in a group.

POWER AND ETHICS

"Power tends to corrupt, absolute power corrupts absolutely." Lord Acton, historian and moralist, expressed this opinion in a letter to Bishop Mandell Creighton, Bishop of London, Church of England, in 1887 regarding the papacy of Rome.[35] He was referring to an observation that a person's sense of morality has a tendency to lessen as his or her power increases. Leaders have a responsibility to exercise their power ethically. Philosophers have studied ethics for centuries, and as they have discovered, there are no easy answers as to what constitutes good or right human behavior. Each culture, each generation within that culture, redefines proper human behavior. We can determine much about a culture by studying its established code of ethics.

Aristotle, an Athenian Greek philosopher in the fifth Century B.C., wrote extensively in *Nichomachean Ethics* regarding **moral virtues, the mean,** and **proper behavior**, that[36]

"Each moral virtue is a mean or lies between extremes of pleasure of action—doing or feeling too much or too little. The absolute mean is different from the mean as it is relative to the individual…. Morality, like art-work, requires that one neither under-do nor over-do. One must hit upon the right course (steering between too much and too little). This requires practice. Virtues are good habits or dispositions to do the right thing developed by means of particular virtuous acts. Means themselves do not admit of excess and deficiency (one cannot have too much courage, etc.)."

The Table 3.1 lists examples of the golden mean taken from Aristotle's *Nichomachean Ethics (Book II).*

The golden mean is important because it reinforces the balance necessary in life. Good judgment requires that one find the mean between extremes. Aristotle believed that moderation between two extremes was the key to acting virtuously.

When we speak about ethics, we are talking about a code of conduct that regulates human behavior. The *Encyclopedia*

Britannica defines ethics as the "branch of philosophy concerned with the nature of ultimate value and the standards by which human actions can be judged right or wrong. The term is also applied to any system or theory of moral values or principles."[37] The *Columbia University Press* defines ethics as "the study and evaluation of human conduct in the light of moral principles. Moral principles may be viewed either as the standard of conduct that individuals have constructed for themselves or as the body of obligations and duties that a particular society requires of its members."[38] D.D. Raphael (1981) says that "Moral philosophy is philosophical inquiry about norms or values, about ideas of right and wrong, good and bad, what should and what should not be done" (p. 8).[39] Moral philosophy addresses the question, "What ought I to do?" and an answer to that question requires much more than delivering the fundamental principle of morality.[40] The term moral philosophy has been used synonymously with ethics, the philosophical discussion of assumptions about right and wrong, good and bad, considered as general ideas and as applied in the private life of individuals.

It can be said, then, that ethics is the term we use to indicate the moral choices a person makes regarding his or her behavior. Ethical conduct defines how people should behave toward one another in a civil society. The ethical guidelines that an individual or group holds are closely linked to their culture. We can argue that a group can be defined by its ethical code of conduct. A group's values and expectations influence an individual's belief of what is right and wrong. The group and its ethical standards are intertwined; one influences the other.

TABLE 3.1

Vice (Defect)	Virtue (Mean)	Vice (Excess)
Cowardice (too little confidence)	Courage	Rashness (too much confidence)
Foolhardiness (too little fear)	Courage	Cowardice (too much fear)
Insensibility (too little pleasure)	Temperance	Self-indulgence (too much pleasure)
Meanness or Stinginess (too little giving)	Liberality	Prodigality or Wastefulness (too much giving)
Undue Humility (too little honor)	Proper Pride	Empty Vanity (too much honor)
Inirascibility (too little anger)	Good Temper	Irascibility (too much anger)
Shamelessness (too little shame)	Modesty	Bashfulness (too much shame)
Surliness	Friendliness	Flattery

Ethical Principles

There is an ancient Chinese proverb called the Wind-Grass Theory. It says that the will of the people bends to the will of the emperor, just like the blades of grass bend to the blowing wind. So it is in group work. A leader who unethically exerts his or her power will eventually influence those members who resisted that influence to change their personal ethics as exemplified in the agentic state. Leaders should serve as a model for members to follow—lead by example should be their motto. There are several **ethical principles** for leaders that are relevant for small groups:[41]

1. **Avoid deceptive or misleading messages.** The leader should always communicate the truth to members so they have all relevant information to act upon, especially in decision making, whether it supports the leader's position or not. This allows members an opportunity to evaluate all information in an unbiased and fair way.

2. **Maintain member autonomy in choice-making.** Do not impose choices on members. They have free will and the right to make their own choices.

3. **Practice fairness in work assignment.** Work assignments should be made with equity between all members as a primary consideration. Members should not be singled out and given too many or too few assignments.

4. **Treat all members fairly.** In dealing with members, the leader should always treat each one fairly and not show favoritism or dislike.

5. **Place concern for others above concern for personal gain.** A leader should not take advantage of the power of the leader position for personal gain or advantage. Hidden agendas, whether they are the leader's or member's, should not be allowed to interfere with the needs of the group.

6. **Maintain confidentiality.** A leader should always maintain confidentiality when communicating with a member or members outside of the group context, especially when caucusing with individual members. A leader will lose member trust if he or she breaks that confidentiality.

7. **Support members when they carry out policies and actions approved by the group.** Ethical leaders support members who carry out the plans of the group. They do not protect themselves by leaving group members to fend for themselves.

8. **Seek the greatest good for the group members.** The success or failure for completing the group charge is a collective effort. The leader should always seek what is best for group members.

9. **Impartiality—treat members consistently, regardless of sex, sexual orientation, ethnicity, or social background.** Members are valued for their contributions to the group. Ethical leaders minimize external status differences to encourage participation by all members.

10. **Establish clear policies that all group members are expected to follow.** Ensure that all members clearly understand group procedures and rules. The leader is expected to follow the same rules and procedures outlined for members.

11. **Participate in task assignments whenever possible.** The leader does more than lead. He or she should assist other members with task assignments whenever possible.

12. **Respect the opinions and attitudes of members, and allow members the freedom to consider the consequences of their actions.** This principle supports democratic, group-centered leadership that encourages equal opportunity for all members to participate.

13. **Avoid retaliatory tactics.** An ethical leader will never attempt to retaliate against members because they voted against the leader, disagreed with the leader's opinion, and so forth.

14. **Do the right thing.** When in doubt, the leader should always do the right thing for the welfare of the group.

SUMMARY

Power is an essential element to group life because it gives the group the ability to effectively complete its goals. While there are limitations to the amount and kinds of power in group work, it is necessary in order to control the behaviors of others and coordinate their activities. In order for any group to function, there must be distribution of power, whether that is given from an authoritative body to the group or by the group itself. Power is the resource that enables a person to bring about compliance from others or to influence them.

Underlying power are two types of influence that have a tendency to be destructive to effective group work: bullying (a coercive influence) and charisma. Bullying is a dysfunctional behavior while charisma is perceptual. Both can have negative influences on members.

Within the structural process that addresses power and responsibility is the principle of superior/subordinate hierarchy. A superior is someone who has authority over the group, usually the group leader, while a subordinate is someone who follows the directions of the superior, a group member. This structure relies on subordinate members to be obedient to the superior. Milgram's Agency Theory attempts to explain why obedience to authority, especially a malevolent authority, has such a strong hold on group behavior. Milgram suggests that at any particular time a person is in one of two distinct psychological states: the autonomous state, in which behaviors are seen as self directed; and the agentic state, a situation in which people see themselves as agents of a higher authority.

Leadership and power go hand in hand. Leadership is the process of influencing people to direct their efforts toward the attainment of particular goal(s), requiring the use of effective communication skills. In addition to effective communication skills, leaders must be both efficient and effective.

Ethics is a code of conduct that regulates human behavior. It is the branch of philosophy concerned with the nature of ultimate value and the standards by which human actions can be judged right or wrong. Ethical conduct defines how people should behave toward one another in a civil society. Small groups are guided by a code of conduct that members must follow if they are to function as a synergistic and cohesive body.

DISCUSSION

1. Two concepts related to power are **reward power** and **coercive power**. Are these merely two sides of the same coin, or are there aspects of reward power and coercive power that make them more complicated than just being mere "opposites" of each other? What relationships between people are necessary for reward power to function in their communication with one another? What relationships are necessary for coercive power to function?

2. **Referent power** is linked to role models and those we identify with. How significant do you believe role models are in our lives? How close a relationship do you have to have with a person for that person to have referent power? Could an athlete like Michael Jordan persuade you to change your behavior from a televised appearance, or would you only change your behavior based on the influence of someone closer to you?

3. What are some group contexts in your life (family, classes, teams, youth groups) where you have observed people (perhaps yourself)

engaging in **reactance** and trying to reassert autonomy and independence within a group? What conditions have led individuals to assert themselves in this way, in your experience?

4. As a member of a group, in most cases would you be *less* likely to trust the decisions and messages of a **designated leader** or an **emergent leader**? Why? Consider the answer you chose: what are some choices that type of leader (the one you would be *less* likely to trust) would need to make to effectively influence you and to gain your trust?

5. Recent years have seen an increasing focus on whistle-blowing in organizational settings, which happens when a member of an organization discloses secret information to those outside the organization because it reveals wrongdoing on the part of the organization. Consider the ethical principles on pages 79 and 80; which of these would discourage whistle-blowing, and which ones would encourage it?

NOTES

1. Lumsden, G., & Lumsden, D. (1997). *Communicating in groups* (2nd ed.). Belmont: Wadsworth.

2. Miner, J.B. (1988). *Organizational behavior.* New York: Random House.

3. Rogers, M.F. (1973). Instrumental and infra-resources: The bases of power. *American Journal of Sociology,* 79(6), 1418–1433.

4. Hersey, P., Blanchard, K.H., & Johnson, D.E. (2001). *Management of organizational behavior* (8th ed.). Upper Saddle River, NJ: Prentice Hall.

5. Ibid.

6. Matteson, M.T., & Ivancevich, J.M. (1996). *Management and organizational behavior classics* (6th ed.). Chicago: Irwin.

7. See French, R.P., Jr., & Raven, B. (1959). The bases of social power. In D.P. Cartwright (Ed.), *Studies in social power* (pp. 150–167). Ann Arbor: Institute for Social Research, The University of Michigan.

8. Schmidt, S.M. (1993) Organizational life: There is more to work than working. In S. C. Currall, D. Geddes, S. M. Schmidt, & A. Hochner (Eds.), *Power and negotiation.* Dubuque, IA: Kendall Hunt.

9. Forsyth, D.R. (2006). *Group Dynamics* (4th ed.). United States: Thomson-Wadsworth.

10. Trenholm, S., & Jensen, A. (1996). *Interpersonal communication* (3rd ed.). Belmont: Wadsworth.

11. Ibid.

12. http://www.stolaf.edu/people/huff/classes/handbook/Milgram.html. Retrieved Sept. 5, 2008. See also http://alevelpsychology.co.uk/social-psychology/social-influence/milgrams-agency-theory.html. and http://www.chssc.salford.ac.uk/healthSci/psych2000/psych2000/socialinfluence.htm. Retrieved Sept. 5, 2008.

13. Forsyth, D.R. (2006). *Group dynamics* (4th ed.). United States: Thomson-Wadsworth.

14. Carson, R.C. (1969). *Interaction concepts of personality.* Chicago: Aldine.

15. Forsyth, D.R. (2006). *Group Dynamics* (4th ed.). United States: Thomson-Wadsworth.

16. http://www.encyclopedia.com/doc/1O87-footinthedoortechnique.html. Retrieved Sept. 13, 2008.

17. http://www.studentaffairs.umd.edu/groups/foot.html. Retrieved Sept. 13, 2008.

18. http://www.sourcewatch.org/index.php?title=Fundamental_attribution_error. Retrieved Sept. 13, 2008.

19. Kipnis, D. (1976). *The powerholders.* Chicago: University of Chicago Press.

20. Forsyth, D.R. (2006). *Group dynamics* (4th ed.). United States: Thomson-Wadsworth.

21. Ibid.

22. Ibid.

23. Ibid.

24. Keltner, D., Young, R.C., Heerey, E.A. Oemig, C., & Monarch, N.D. (1998). Teasing in hierarchical and intimate relations. *Journal of Personality and Social Psychology,* 75, 1231–1247.

25. Forsyth, D.R. (2006). *Group dynamics* (4th ed.). United States: Thomson-Wadsworth.

26. Ibid.

27. Kipnis, D. (1976). *The powerholders.* Chicago: University of Chicago Press.

28. Johnson, D.W., & Johnson, F.P. (1997). *Joining together: Group theory and group skills* (6th ed.). Boston: Allyn and Bacon.

29. Forsyth, D.R. (2006). *Group dynamics* (4th ed.). United States: Thomson-Wadsworth.

30. Gibson, J.W. & Hodgetts, R.M. (1986). *Organizational communication: A managerial perspective.* New York: Harcourt Brace Jovanovich.

31. Fisher, B.A. (1980). *Small group decision making: Communication and the group processes* (2nd ed.). New York: McGraw-Hill.

32. Lumsden, G., & Lumsden, D. (1997). *Communicating in groups* (2nd ed.). Belmont: Wadsworth.

33. Hollander, E.P. (1978). *Leadership dynamics.* New York: Free Press.

34. Fisher, B.A. (1980). *Small group decision making: Communication and the group processes* (2nd ed.). New York: McGraw-Hill.

35. http://www.phrases.org.uk/meanings/288200.html. Retrieved September 29, 2008.

36. http://www.fred.net/tzaka/arismean.html. for a more complete explanation of Aristotle's Nichomachean Ethics. Retrieved December 16, 2007.

37. http://www.britannica.com. Retrieved December 14, 2007.

38. http://www.answers.com/topic/ethics-legal-term?cat=biz-fin. Retrieved December 14, 2007.

39. Raphael, D.D. (1981). *Moral philosophy.* London: Oxford University Press.

40. http://plato.stanford.edu/entries/kant-moral/. Retrieved December 28, 2007.

41. Galenes, G.J., Adams, K., & Brilhart, J.K. (2004). *Effective group discussion: Theory and practice* (11th ed.). New York: McGraw-Hill.

4

Member Roles and Responsibilities

CHAPTER OBJECTIVES

- Understand how roles affect individual and group performance
- Be familiar with the many types and functions of roles in group work
- Know how roles influence individual behavior
- Taking responsibility for one's behavior

CHAPTER OUTLINE

KEY TERMS

Status

Roles

Role

Formal role

Informal role

Task role

Relationship role
or socialemotional
role

Individual role

Role performance

Role conflict

Social loafing

Risk-averse

Risk-taker

Promotive interaction

ROLES AND STATUS

Members in small group work do not function independently of one another; that is, they do not choose what they want to do and when they want to do it. When you were growing up, I'm sure you were assigned chores or tasks to do. Everyone in the family did something to help out: someone took out the garbage on a regular basis; someone else did laundry; another person cleaned up after dinner, and so forth. Family members just didn't live together in the same house or apartment; they had different roles; they were expected to do certain things at particular times that kept the family together. The structure of a small group is similar in nature; that is, group members are not associated to one another at random; rather, they are connected in organized and predictable patterns. These patterns are often a complex mix of norms, roles, and interpersonal relations among and between group members.[1] Sociologist Erving Goffman (1961) says that a role is "the basic unit of socialization."[2] As with any group, culture, or society, each and every member of that social system identifies with and becomes

identified with that system when they assume a role in that system. Goffman argues that, "It is through roles that tasks in society are allocated and arrangements made to enforce their performance." Group roles come with a set of expectations that group members share concerning the behavior of an individual who has a certain role or roles within that group. A member's behavior is either consistent with or is inconsistent with group expectations.[3] In other words, if a person behaves within member expectations, we say that his or her behavior is considered to be role behavior. However, if a member did something that the group didn't expect, then they would describe that behavior as being out of character. The behavior was not consistent with the person's role expectations.

Synonymous with roles is status, and often these two terms are blended. However, there is a difference between someone's status and someone's role. What do they mean? Ralph Linton, one of the best-known American anthropologists of the mid-twentieth century, gave these concepts a significant place in social theory.[4] He said that a status is simply a collection of rights and duties, and a role represents the dynamic aspects of a status. In other words, **status** is the prominence or position someone has within the group, and **roles** specify the general behaviors expected of people who occupy different status positions within the group. When a person exercises the rights and duties which constitute the status, he or she is performing a role. A role and a status are inseparable; there are no roles without statuses or statuses without roles. For example, a group leader is a status in that the position may be occupied by a number of individuals in succession; the position doesn't disappear or change when the person leaves it; someone else takes his or her place.

Status

The prominence or position someone has within the group.

Roles

The general behaviors expected of people who occupy different status positions within the group.

When the group leader exercises his or her duties and responsibilities as a leader, such as assigning tasks to members or leading a group discussion, he or she now performs in the capacity of a role as group leader; that is, his or her behavior reflects what is expected of him or her.

Theodore Newcomb (1950) developed Linton's general point of view about roles and status and incorporated it into a broad theory of social psychology. He uses the concept of position rather than status and views position as the smallest element or construction block of societies and organized groups.[5] Dorwin Cartwright and Alvin Zander (1968) note that Linton views role as "the behavior of people 'as occupants of the position'... [that] every position which is recognized by the members of a group contributes in some way to the purposes of the group; this contribution represents its function."[6] However, B. Aubrey Fisher (1980) says that "To think of role solely in terms of 'position' in a group network of roles is to provide only a partial picture of a group's social structure."[7] He argues that there are more complex dynamics at work than simply a status or position. Roles define the formal structure of the group and differentiate one performance from another. A role may be defined as a set of expectations, or a pattern of appropriate behavior, of a person in a position toward other related positions. In the most general sense, we can categorize roles as formal and informal. A formal role is one that is assigned by the organization or specifically chosen by the group leader. Treasurer, secretary, and president are titles that reflect a formal role. Behavioral expectations for these roles are usually explicitly spelled out. You may have applied for a job where the prospective employer gave you a detailed job description. You knew what was expected of you if you were hired. This is an example of a formal role. An informal role is one that emerges from interactions between group members and is not appointed. It is a functional role rather an appointed position. A group member may take notes; that is, he or she performs the role of note taker, but without formal designation.

In small group work, there are three basic types of roles: **task role**, which relates to getting things done; **relationship role** (also known as a social-emotional role), which relates to the group climate and working relationships among members; and **individual role**, which refers to the idiosyncratic behavior of each individual member. Members who fulfill a task role focus on the group's goals and on the members' attempts to support one another as they work.[8] A task role can be defined as any position in a group occupied by a member who performs behaviors that promote completion of tasks and activities. A relationship role or social-emotional role can be defined as any position in a group occupied by a member who performs behaviors that improve the nature and quality of interpersonal relations among members, such as showing concern for feelings of others, reducing conflict, and enhancing feelings of satisfaction and trust in the group.[9] Often, groups have a tendency to develop both task roles and relationship roles. The individual role is an expressed behavior of an internal or psychological trait. It is impossible to list all of the types of roles in a group; however, Benne and Sheats (1948) have classified some roles common to groups.[10] The following examples in Table 4.1 are adapted from their classification:

Role
May be defined as a set of expectations, or a pattern of appropriate behavior, of a person in a position toward other related positions.

Formal role
A role that is assigned by the organization or specifically chosen by the group leader.

Informal role
A role that emerges from interactions between group members and is not appointed.

Task role
Any position in a group occupied by a member who performs behaviors that promote completion of tasks and activities.

Relationship role or social-emotional role
Relates to the group climate and working relationships among members.

Individual role
Refers to the idiosyncratic behavior of each individual member.

TABLE 4.1

Role	Function
Group Task Roles	
Initiator-contributor	Suggests new ways to approach a problem or offers possible solutions not yet considered by the group
Information seeker	Seeks facts and information; asks others for facts and information requests evaluations
Opinion seeker	Seeks more qualitative types of data such as attitudes, values, and feelings
Information giver	Presents data; offers facts and information for decision making
Elaborator	Clarifies ideas; gives additional information; expands ideas made by others; provides examples, illustrations, and explanations
Coordinator	Integrates; shows the relevance of each idea and its relationship to the problem; organizes the group's work; promotes teamwork and cooperation
Orienter	Gets members to refocus on topic when necessary
Evaluator-critic	Critiques ideas or suggestions; appraises the quality of the group's methods, logic, and results
Energizer	Encourages the group to continue working when discussion wanes
Procedural technician	Cares for operational details, such as materials, machinery, and so on
Recorder	Takes notes and maintains records; keeps track of the group's work; prepares reports and takes minutes
Group Building and Maintenance Roles	
Encourager	Praises others; expresses warmth and support; rewards others through agreement
Harmonizer	Mediates conflict among group members; helps relieve tension

Compromiser	Changes one's position on an issue in order to reduce conflict in the group
Gatekeeper and expediter	Sets up procedures and ensures equal participation from members by keeping communication channels open; manages communication flow
Group observer and commentator	Identifies positive and negative aspects of the group's dynamics and seeks change if necessary; makes comments on how the group is working
Follower	Accepts the ideas from other members and serves as an audience for the group

Individual Roles

Aggressor	Antagonizes the group by expressing disapproval of ideas, behaviors, and feelings. Verbally attacks group members
Blocker	Opposes the group unnecessarily; prevents progress toward group's goals; resists the group's influence; refuses to accept or support a group decision
Recognition seeker	Self-aggrandizer; stage hogger; calls attention to himself or herself; boasts of self-accomplishments, skills and abilities
Self-confessor	Expresses personal interests, feelings, and opinions unrelated to group goals
Playboy/girl	Cavalier, uninvolved in group; nonchalant
Dominator	Asserts authority or superiority; interrupts; refuses to accept others' conclusions, and imposes one's own
Help seeker	Relates insecurity, confusion, and negativity of one's self
Special interest pleader	Pleads special interests; demands time and resources for subgroup or special interest; stays apart from the group by advocating the interests of another group

Role Influence

Roles can influence group members in a number of ways. They can affect satisfaction and well-being—are they happy in their roles or do they find themselves frustrated and not wanting to perform their tasks? Some roles are more satisfying than others. People prefer high-status roles rather than low-status roles and roles that conform to their beliefs, attitudes, values, skills, and expectations. Once someone takes on a role, he or she begins to develop interdependence that is essential for group synergy, cohesion, and production, and with it, a potential for role conflict. We can identify at least four basic categories associated with role influence: (1) role ambiguity, (2) role fit, (3) role performance, and (4) role conflict.

Role Ambiguity

At times, the person who occupies the role, the **role-taker**, is not always clear as to the activities and responsibilities expected of him or her in that role, or to the rest of the group, the **role-senders**.[11] Forsythe (2006) says that "Even when a role has a long history in the group (e.g., many groups have always had a leader, a secretary, and a treasurer) or the group deliberately creates the role for some specific purpose (e.g., a note-taker is appointed) the responsibilities of the role may be ill-defined" (p. 184). When this happens, role-takers may experience **role ambiguity**—they aren't sure if they are acting appropriately or performing behaviors that others in the group should be doing, and they question their ability to complete their responsibilities.[12]

Role Fit

Role fit is the degree of shared characteristics between the expectations of a specific role and the belief, attitudes, values, skills, and other characteristics of the individual who holds the role. Generally speaking, a person can have a moderate-to-high role fit or a low role fit. For example, a person who is very personable and outgoing may have a high fit in a relationship role, or an individual who is good at mediating conflict would do well as a harmonizer. On the other hand, if an individual only saw himself or herself as a leader, the role of follower would be a low fit.

Role Performance

Role performance
The actual conduct of someone within a particular role.

Once someone has exercised a specific behavior, we call it role performance. It is the actual conduct of someone within a particular role. Each group member has an implicit notion of what that performance should be. For example, when I was the faculty representative to the university's academic senate, we had a leader (also known as the speaker) during one academic year who presided over each meeting with an authoritarian iron fist, dominating the discussions and cutting off anyone who disagreed with his positions. He became resented for his arrogant and overbearing approach to performing that leadership role, so much so that members refused to engage in spirited debate over issues and often left the meetings early. In his perspective, he was performing as he thought the role of speaker should be, while the members felt that his performance was inconsistent with their expectations. Very little was accomplished by the academic senate that year. This example demonstrates that each member's role belongs more to the group as a whole and less to the individual. Fisher (1980) claims that "Each person's role is a product of the entire group interaction—the combination of behaviors performed by the individual member and the behaviors performed by other members."[13]

Role Conflict

Occasionally, demands on a member's behavior may be more than he or she can perform (**role strain**), or the role behavior contradicts his or her role expectations with those of the group or other groups (role conflict).[14] **Role conflict** may be defined as a state of tension caused when an individual's behavioral expectations of that role conflict with the group's expectations associated with that role or is contradictory to his or her role performances in other groups. Or simply, the demands of one role are incompatible with the demands of another. As individual members create patterns of behavior based on their own personal set of expectations that are different from those of the group in general, the group's communicative behaviors serve to encourage or discourage these patterns based on the tensions they create.[15] The individual's unique behavior can be accepted or even rewarded by the group, thereby reducing or eliminating the state of tension; or it can be discouraged and possibly punished, generally increasing that tension.

Usually in small group work, members take on several roles at the same time. Each role demands time and skills, and not necessarily in equal amounts. **Interrole conflict** occurs when members discover that the behaviors associated with one or more of their roles are incompatible with those associated with other roles. Many of my students work full time and are single parents, yet they maintain a full-time status as a student. Often, these roles conflict with one another—getting a child to day care at the same time you are supposed to take an exam or having to attend a training session at work instead of making a class. If too much demand is placed on one role, then the other roles will be neglected.

> **Role conflict**
> A state of tension caused when an individual's behavioral expectations of that role conflict with the group's expectations associated with that role or is contradictory to his or her role performances in other groups.

© Rudyanto Wijaya, 2011. Under license from Shutterstock, Inc.

GUIDELINES FOR PRODUCTIVE PARTICIPATION

Individual Participation and Commitment

When a group is formed, or when individuals replace others in the group, it is an important point to keep in mind that individual need satisfaction may be quite different for each member of the group. This is often overlooked. It is assumed that group members have common goals and purposes; however, individuals may join a group for personal goals or purposes other than that of the group. For example, a person may join a group because he or she has a need for power, or another may have a need to interact with others, while yet another may have need for status or self-esteem. Individual group members do not necessarily have to share common needs, goals, and purposes with the group as a whole, but they do share one commonality, that of satisfaction. Each individual's needs are dependent upon the accomplishments of the group and achieving their goals. The degree to which an individual need satisfaction is achieved distinguishes effective from ineffective groups. When the needs are harmonious, the group is probably effective. But when they are not, the group is probably ineffective. Common, or at least harmonious, goals or purposes are, therefore, not criteria of groups, but of effective groups.[16] As a result, we have two contrasting positions: the group orientation and the individual orientation.

If a group is going to be productive, all members must do their fair share of the work. This means that individual participation must be governed by some sense of responsibility for contributing efforts to accomplishing the group's goals. Two necessary elements for responsibility are (1) completing one's share of the work, and (2) facilitating the work of other group members and accountability. **Individual accountability** occurs when the performance of each individual member is assessed and the results are given back to the group and individual.[17] Individual responsibility establishes a **minimum standard of performance** for each member. These standards set a floor by which members should not fall below, and not a ceiling that few can accomplish. (We will discuss performance standards in Chapters 7 and 8.)

One group phenomenon that is a problem of individual accountability is called social loafing—the tendency of individual group members to reduce their work effort as groups increase in size.[18] For example, a member who fails to show up for a group meeting, who is chronically late, performs the least amount of effort in his or her job, or fails to complete tasks, is considered a social loafer. Loafers exert little effort because of poor motivation,

Social loafing
The tendency of individual group members to reduce their work effort as groups increase in size.

© Sean Prior, 2011. Under license from Shutterstock, Inc.

disinterest, or a bad attitude. There may be many reasons for this. One reason that I've found to be consistent with loafers is that when they can't have their way in the group, instead of permanently leaving the group, they choose to loaf. This frequently occurs when there aren't substantive negative consequences or punishments. People will loaf and let others do their work because they know they can get away with it; at least they think they can get away with it. (More on this in upcoming chapters.)

There are at least five general factors to judge individual accountability by, and they are distinctly separate from criteria used for evaluating performance management (which we will discuss in Chapters 6, 7, and 8):

1. **Level of group development.** If the group is newly forming, then little, at first, can be expected of the individual. But as the group matures and roles and responsibilities are assumed, a standard of performance would have been established, along with performance expectations. If an individual enters or replaces a member in an established group, then performance standards would already have been established.

2. **Level of group performance.** Some groups have such low expectations of them that any level of performance other than low is the norm. However, problem-solving and decision-making groups have a relatively high level of performance expectations. Individual members work together to achieve a synergy that produces high performance levels.

3. **Number of members** (too many or too few). Too many group members can create a shortage of roles, or a redundancy of roles. When there are too many people and not enough jobs to go around, individual performance suffers. Members become idle; they look for things to do, and they become dissatisfied with the group very easily. It is difficult to judge performance when there is little for members to accomplish. Conversely, when there are too few members, performance expectations can be set too high. With too few people and too many tasks to perform, work product can be deficient, sloppy, or incomplete. Members often feel overworked and unappreciated.

4. **Degree of member turnover.** A group that has a high rate of member turnover means that there is something inherently wrong. A leader can be too authoritarian, or, depending on the group size, one member or a coalition of members makes it unbearable for anyone who doesn't fall in line with them to stay in the group.

5. **Member commitment.** Assuming that a member has the skills, knowledge, and abilities to perform his or her tasks, individual members must be committed to and accountable for their performance. Commitment is synonymous with dedication. Each member must be equally dedicated to fulfilling his or her obligations to the group and to himself or herself.

Obligations in Participation

1. Commitment doesn't mean just showing up for meetings. It means actively participating in group tasks and communicating with other members. The effective communicator in group work is a member who is committed to

© Yuri Arcurs, 2011. Under license from Shutterstock, Inc.

the group and its task. Members who are committed to the group tend to assume a very active verbal role in the group interaction. And in complementing true interdependence, very active participants usually exhibit a deep level of group commitment. If you have strong feelings about something, you will want to talk about it. Conversely, if you actively talk about it, you will come to feel strongly about it.[19]

2. Risk is essential to any commitment, to any development of the group, is the element of risk that is present in the situation. Fisher (1980) suggests that commitment to any group, to any loyalty, to any person, inherently and inevitably involves the risk of being wrong, of appearing foolish in the presence of others. We often take risks when we are alone, and if they turn out to be wrong, we don't embarrass ourselves in front of others. Becoming a part of group decision making requires the ability to risk, and if necessary, to endure frustration, disappointment, ridicule, or shame. Without that commitment by all or nearly all members of a group, especially decision-making or problem-solving groups, little will be accomplished; and decisions, if made, will be of predictably poor quality.

There are numerous people who are **risk-averse**; that is, people who refuse to take risk. And there are countless individuals who are **risk-takers**, people who aren't afraid of risk. In the group context, when we engage in **social risk**, we gamble that we will achieve a successful outcome. When a person hides his or her self and avoids risk, that individual is refusing to gamble. However, if committing oneself to a social situation risks the possibility of failure, avoiding that commitment positively assures the lack of success. Avoiding commitment and refusing to gamble guarantee failure. It is impossible for either the self or the group process to succeed.[20] The individual group member has a responsibility to engage in that element of risk if the group process is to survive. Anyone who communicates with another member, if that communication is to be effective and meaningful, must inevitably assume some risk of self. In order for communicators to be right, they must risk being wrong. The best compensations for risk-taking are positive results.[21]

3. Promotive (face-to-face) interaction[22]—members of productive groups who promote each other's success and well-being. We call this behavior **promotive interaction**. David Johnson and Frank Johnson (1997) define promotive interaction "as individuals encouraging and facilitating each other's efforts to complete tasks and achieve in order to reach the group's goals" (p. 28). Johnson and Johnson have identified nine behaviors that characterize promotive interaction. Members:

Risk-averse
People who refuse to take risk.

Risk-taker
People who aren't afraid of risk.

Promotive interaction
When members of productive groups promote each other's success and well-being.

a. provide other members with efficient and effective help and assistance;

b. exchange needed resources, such as information and materials and processing information, more efficiently and effectively;

c. provide each other with feedback in order to improve their performance on assigned tasks and responsibilities;

d. challenge each other's conclusions and reasoning in order to promote higher quality decision making and greater insight into the problems being considered;

e. advocate putting forth efforts to achieve mutual goals;

f. influence each other's efforts to achieve mutual goals;

g. act in trusting and trustworthy ways;

h. are motivated to work toward mutual benefit; and

i. feel less anxiety and stress.

Along with the nine behaviors that characterize promotive interaction, Johnson and Johnson (1997) have also identified at least seven effects that *promotive interaction* has on members:

1. There are cognitive insights and understandings that can only come from explaining one's conclusions and views to others.

2. It is within face-to-face interaction that the opportunity for a wide variety of social influences and patterns emerges.

3. The verbal and nonverbal responses of other group members provide important feedback concerning each other's performance.

4. Promotive interaction provides an opportunity for peers to hold each other accountable for doing their share.

5. Interaction among group members allows members to imitate the actions of more highly motivated members.

6. Interaction among group members allows members to compare their contributions with those of other members.

7. It is the interaction involved in completing the work that allows group members to get to know each other as persons, which in turn forms the basis for caring and committed relationships.

Responsibilities Each Member Has in Keeping the Vision and Accomplishing the Mission

The organizational context of the small group includes many aspects of the larger organization that influence the small group but that the group does not control. Two aspects that small groups should inherit from their larger organizational structures are a **shared vision** and a *clear mission*. Understanding these aspects of organizational context helps members identify how the larger organization is likely to help or hinder a group's efforts to improve its effectiveness.[23] Together, a shared vision and a clear mission provide meaning that can inspire and guide members' work.

Keeping the Vision

Vision plays a key role in small groups because it helps to direct, align, and inspire actions on the part of group members. A vision is the mental picture of the future that an organization seeks to create.[24] A vision identifies what the group should look like and how it should act as it seeks to accomplish its mission.[25] Without an appropriate vision, members' efforts can easily turn into a list of confusing, incompatible, and time-consuming projects that go in the wrong direction or nowhere at all. Without a vision to guide decision making, each and every choice group members face can become endless debate. The smallest of decisions can create heated conflict that saps energy and destroys morale. Insignificant tactical choices can dominate discussions and waste hours of precious time.[26]

© Andresr, 2011. Under license from Shutterstock, Inc.

Accomplishing the Mission

A mission is the purpose of the small group; it answers the question, "Why do we exist?"[27] A mission clarifies the group's purpose, its goals, and how to achieve them. The group tries to achieve its mission by accomplishing various goals, which in turn are achieved by accomplishing various tasks. The more efficient members are in achieving their tasks, the closer they are to realizing the group's mission.

Group members often have difficulty understanding the mission or vision of their organization and/or their group, either because they have never been explained to them or because different and powerful groups within the organization disagree about what the mission or vision should be. The value of the mission and vision lies in the shared commitment that members make to achieving them.[28]

Taking Responsibility for One's Behavior

Each individual group member has a responsibility to commit to the roles he or she takes and the responsibilities that accompany those roles. These commitments include, but are not limited to: (1) commitment to self, (2) commitment to people, (3) commitment to the task, and (4) commitment to the group.[29] For each commitment, every member should:

1. Commitment to Self
   Demonstrate autonomy

   a. Stand up for personal beliefs, even when they are in conflict with other group members, or the group as a whole
   b. Take responsibility and ownership for his or her decisions
   c. Take reasonable risks in trying out new ideas
   d. Be more concerned with achieving excellence than playing it safe

Build self as an effective team member

a. Show a high degree of integrity when interacting with others
b. Present self in a positive manner
c. Demonstrate confidence in self
d. Avoid destructive self-criticism

Accept constructive criticism

a. Be willing to admit to mistakes
b. Encourage and accept constructive criticism
c. Act on constructive advice in a timely manner.
d. Avoid discouraging people from giving constructive criticism

2. Commitment to People
Show positive concern and recognition

a. Consistently demonstrate concern and respect for members as individuals
b. Give positive recognition for others' achievements
c. Reinforce members' positive performance
d. Avoid destructive comments about group members

Encourage member participation

a. Encourage members to actively participate in group activities
b. Avoid taking credit for the ideas of others
c. Support members' positive ideas and suggestions in a timely manner

3. Commitment to the Task
Maintain the right focus

a. Understand and support the mission of the group and of the overall organization
b. Connect individual objectives to larger organizational goals
c. Concentrate on achieving what is most important to the group's goals
d. Place more importance on accomplishing the group's mission rather than following procedures

Keep it simple

a. Separate work into achievable components
b. Avoid unnecessary complications

Is action-oriented

a. Communicate a positive message to members about getting the job done
b. Emphasize the importance of regular progress
c. Encourage taking action to get tasks done
d. Concentrate on meeting deadlines

Build task importance

  a. Be committed to excellence in task achievement
  b. Make the task meaningful and relevant
  c. Encourage suggestions for improving productivity
  d. Do not diminish the importance of group work

4. Commitment to the Group

  a. Build the organization
  b. Know and support the mission of the group
  c. Discourage destructive comments about the group
  d. Inspire pride in the group

SUMMARY

This chapter has posed a number of considerations relative to individual performance. In this chapter, we have learned that roles in small group work come in many different types and functions. We have explored how roles affect and are affected by individual members and the group as a whole. Also, we have learned that being a member of a group requires certain obligations for individual participation. We see that the individual is responsible for his or her own behavior and realize that behavior can impact achieving a group's goals.

The most important consideration in small group effectiveness is the behavioral dimension—the role dimension. Member performance, and the ability for the group to achieve its goals, is dependent on role behavior and ultimately on performance. Human behavior is the single greatest cause of group failure. The individual's commitment to the group enables the group to survive and achieve its goals.

DISCUSSION

1. Which types of roles would you expect group members to be more fully committed to performing—**formal roles** assigned by a leader or **informal roles** that emerge in group interaction? Why? In your experience, which of these types does our society tend to place greater importance on, and what social values does this reflect?

2. Consider the list of **individual roles** in Table 4.1: Choose one of these roles at a time and discuss what kinds of messages groups might use to help a person who plays such a role to more effectively integrate her/himself into the group dynamic in a positive way. Assume that the person playing this individual role cannot be removed from the group (for instance, suppose that it is another student in this class working with your group for a group grade in the course): how can the group avoid frustrating this person and possibly enhancing the person's desire to play an individual role while still communicating the need for the person to more fully consider the group as a whole?

3. Suppose that your group suspects that one member is experiencing **role strain** when attempting to perform the role assigned to that person by the group leader. How should your group respond to this? Should the group leader take responsibility because s/he assigned the role, or should other group members reach out to the person experiencing role strain and offer help? Why? Should this role strain be discussed at a group meeting or in private, and why?

4. In what circumstances in your own life have you experienced **role conflict**? How do you assign differential importance to the roles in your life when one role in your life comes into conflict with another? When you experience role conflict, what standards or principles can you use to help you bring the various roles that are coming to conflict more in line with one another?

5. Suppose that a member of your group who was recently assigned a low-status role, such as a repetitive task that is necessary but that includes little creative work, begins to show weakening commitment to the group. What are some strategies your group could use to encourage that person to take more serious responsibility for her/his role?

NOTES

1. Homans, G.C. (1950). *The human group.* New York: Harcourt, Brace & World.

2. Goffman, E. (1961). *Encounters.* New York: Bobbs-Merrill.

3. Hare, A.P. (1976). *Handbook of small group research* (2nd ed.). New York: Free Press.

4. Homans, G.C. (1950). *The human group.* New York: Harcourt, Brace & World.

5. Newcomb, T.M. (1950). *Social psychology.* New York: Dryden.

6. Cartwright, D., & Zander, A. (1968). *Group dynamics: research and theory* (3rd ed.). New York: Harper & Row,

7. Fisher, B.A. (1980). *Small group decision making* (2nd ed.). New York: McGraw-Hill.

8. Forsyth, D.R. (2006). *Group dynamics* (4th ed.). U.S.: Thomson-Wadsworth.

9. Ibid.

10. Benne, K.D., & Sheats, P. (1948). Functional roles of group members. *Journal of Social Issues,* 4(2), 41–49. See also Forsyth, D.R. (2006). *Group dynamics* (4th ed.). U.S.: Thomson-Wadsworth.

11. Forsyth, D.R. (2006). *Group dynamics* (4th ed.). U.S.: Thomson-Wadsworth.

12. House, R.J., Schuler, R.S., & Levanoni, E. (1983). Role conflict and ambiguous scales: Realities or artifacts? *Journal of Applied Psychology,* 68, 334–337.

13. Fisher, B.A. (1980). *Small group decision making* (2nd ed.). New York: McGraw-Hill.

14. Ibid.

15. Frey, L.R., ed. (2002). *New directions in group communication.* Thousand Oaks: Sage Publications.

16. Hersey, P., Blanchard, K.H., & Johnson, D.E. (2001). *Management of organizational behavior.* Upper Saddle River, NJ: PrenticeHall.

17. Johnson, D.W., & Johnson, F.P (1997). *Joining together* (6th ed.). Needham Heights, MA: Allyn and Bacon.

18. Rothwell, J.D. (2004). *In mixed company* (5th ed.). Belmont, CA: Thomson-Wadsworth.

19. Fisher, B.A. (1980). *Small group decision making* (2nd ed.). New York: McGraw-Hill.

20. Ibid.

21. Ibid.

22. Promotive Interaction is adapted from Johnson, D.W., & Johnson, F.P (1997). *Joining together* (6th ed.). Needham Heights, MA: Allyn and Bacon.

23. Schwarz, R.M. (1994). *The skilled facilitator.* San Francisco: Josey-Bass Publishers.

24. Senge, P.M. (1990). *The fifth discipline: The art and practice of the learning organization.* New York: Doubleday.

25. Bryson, J.M. (1988). *Strategic planning for public and nonprofit organizations: A guide to strengthening and sustaining organizational achievement.* San Francisco: Josey-Bass Publishers.

26. Kotter, J.P. (1996). *Leading change.* Boston: Harvard Business School Press.

27. Senge, P.M. (1990). *The fifth discipline: The art and practice of the learning organization.* New York: Doubleday.

28. Schwarz, R.M. (1994). *The skilled facilitator.* San Francisco: Josey-Bass Publishers.

29. Adapted from Hersey, P., Blanchard, K.H., & Johnson, D.E. (2001). *Management of organizational behavior.* Upper Saddle River, NJ: PrenticeHall.

5

Leadership and Leadership Styles

CHAPTER OBJECTIVES

- Understand the meaning of leadership
- Be familiar with the three competencies of leadership
- Gain an understanding of the characteristics of leadership
- Know the various leadership styles

CHAPTER OUTLINE

Leadership
Defining Leadership

Competencies of Leadership
Communication Competence

Two Characteristics of Leaders
Vision
Credibility
Recognizing Leaders
Leadership as a Function in
a System
Leaders as Mediators

Leadership Styles
Classic Leadership Styles
The Managerial Leadership Grid
Determining Appropriate Styles
The Hersey-Blanchard Situational
Leadership Model
Four Basic Situational Leadership
Styles

Summary

LEADERSHIP

Everyone who participates in any type of group discussion should pay close attention to understanding leadership and leadership styles. Why? Because leadership affects every member and the group's ability to achieve its goals. You may find yourself in a position within the group where you may be called upon to act as leader, whether temporarily or permanently. Often, the group's leader

is replaced by someone from within the group, and at times a leader may come from outside of the group. Many groups choose to select a leader from their own ranks because of many factors, such as: the new leader knows each member; has worked with each member for a period of time; and knows their personality traits, knowledge, skills, and abilities. A new leader from within the group doesn't need to cultivate a relationship with each member; one already exists. But sometimes a group may seek a leader from outside of the group—for example, when members are unable to work together because of personality clashes, or one or more members seek the power of leadership for a personal agenda, or when a power struggle has divided the group, making it ineffectual. When group members are unable to effectively work together—that is, they become so dysfunctional that they are unable to achieve their goals—then an outside leader is sought who can bring new insight, energy, and authority to the group. For groups that engage in problem solving and decision making, this is essential.

Groups with designated leaders perform better than groups lacking a single leader. Research has shown that groups with single leaders work more efficiently, have fewer interpersonal conflicts or problems, and produce superior outcomes.[1] In addition, single leaders provide direction, coordination, and centralized authority, necessary elements for group progress and goal achievement.[2]

Defining Leadership

Leadership
Defines what the future should look like, aligns people with that vision, and inspires them to make it happen despite obstacles.

There are many definitions of leadership, just as there are types of leaders. And there is an age-old argument as to whether or not leaders are born or made—it's probably a combination of the two. Definitions of leadership range from the simple to the complex. Two of the simpler ones suggest that leadership is getting things done by influencing others, or a leader is a person whom someone will follow. A more complex definition is offered by George C. Homans (1950), who wrote that the leader is the person who comes closest to realizing the norms the group values highest. The leader's embodiment of the norms gives him or her high rank, and this rank attracts people: the leader is the person people come to; the scheme of interaction focuses on her or him. At the same time, a leader's high rank carries with it the implied right to assume control of the group, and the exercise of control itself helps maintain the leader's prestige. The high rank of the leader and the respect that is given to him or her are determined by the fact that the leader originates interaction for the group by giving orders that are in fact obeyed.[3] Donelson R. Forsyth (2006) defines leadership as "the process by which an individual guides others in their pursuits, often by organizing, directing, coordinating, supporting, and motivating their efforts" (p. 376).[4] A good working definition of leadership is offered by Paul Hersey, Kenneth H. Blanchard, and Dewey E. Johnson (2001), who observe that leadership "is the process of influencing the activities of an individual or a group in efforts toward goal achievement in a given situation" (p. 79).[5] I prefer John P. Kotter's (1996) simple definition: "Leadership defines what the future should look like, aligns people with that vision, and inspires them to make it happen despite obstacles."[6]

When we say that leadership is the process of something—whether that be guiding, directing, influencing, or what have you—it assumes that the person or persons being guided, directed, or influenced, obey what is ordered of them, as Homans suggested. This means that there must be some form of authority. But what is authority? We can answer that question with the following: "If an order given by a leader to a member of his group is accepted by the member and controls his activity in the group, then the order is said to carry authority."[7] This suggests that the authority of an order always relies on the willingness of the individuals to whom it is addressed to obey it. Authority is always a matter of individual decision.[8] As with any individual decision making in small group work, the individual must weigh any consequences that may be imposed by that authority for noncompliance.

This is a good time to distinguish the differences between leadership and management. Often, elements of one are mistaken for the other. When you, the student, enter the work world, you will probably be hired as an entry-level manager. As you will learn, there is a marked difference between a leader and a manager. A leader basically does four things: (1) Establishes direction: develops a vision of the future and strategies for producing the changes needed to achieve that vision; (2) Aligns people: communicates direction in words and deeds to all those whose cooperation may be needed so as to influence the creation of teams and coalitions that understand the vision and strategies and that accept their validity; (3) Motivates and inspires: energizes people to overcome major political, bureaucratic, and resource barriers to change by satisfying basic, but often unfulfilled, human needs; and (4) If successful, produces change, often to a dramatic degree, and has the potential to produce extremely useful change.

A manager also does four basic things: (1) Plans and budgets: establishes detailed steps and timetables for achieving needed results, then allocates the resources necessary to make it

© Monkey Business Images, 2011. Under license from Shutterstock, Inc.

happen; (2) Organizes and staffs: establishes some structure for accomplishing plan requirements, staffs that structure with individuals, delegates responsibility and authority for carrying out the plan, provides policies and procedures to help guide people, and creates methods or systems to monitor implementation; (3) Controls and problem solves: monitors results, identifies deviations from the plan, then plans and organizes to solve these problems; and (4) Produces a degree of predictability and order and has the potential to consistently produce the short-term results expected.[9] By the end of this chapter, you should come to realize that leadership in group communication is a combination of qualities from both management and leadership. This makes for an effective group leader.

COMPETENCIES OF LEADERSHIP

There are three general skills, or competencies, that leadership requires:[10] (1) Diagnosing: the ability to understand the current situation one is trying to influence; (2) Adapting: the leader's ability to alter his or her behavior and the other resources he or she has available to meet unexpected problems of the situation; and (3) Communicating: interacting with others in a way that people can easily understand and accept.

1. **Diagnosing** is a cognitive competency employing critical thinking. It is understanding what the current situation is and knowing what the leader can reasonably expect to make it in the future. The difference between the two is the problem that needs to be solved. This difference is what the other competencies are aimed at solving.
2. **Adapting** is a behavioral competency. The leader adapts his or her behavior and other resources in a way that helps close the gap between the current situation and that which the leader wants to achieve.
3. **Communicating** is a process competency. Having the abilities to diagnose a situation and adapt resources isn't enough. The leader must be able to effectively communicate these to the group. If the leader cannot communicate in such a way that members can understand and accept, then it is unlikely that he or she will meet stated goals.

Communication Competence

Communication competence

The extent to which a leader communicates in a personally effective and socially appropriate manner with group members and others outside of the group who are relevant

What we say doesn't always come out the way we mean it. This holds true for any form of communication. What does it mean to communicate competently in the context of group communication? **Communication competence** is the extent to which a leader communicates in a personally effective and socially appropriate manner with group members and others outside of the group who are relevant to achieving the group's goals. Some of the more important factors that constitute communication competence are: effective listening, rhetorical sensitivity, and appropriate language.

Effective Leaders Listen Well

Effective leaders listen well and are sensitive to the diverse and subtle influences on a group's ability to work together productively. Effective leaders employ **active listening** skills—a process of sending back to the speaker what the listener thinks the speaker meant, both literally and emotionally, which signals the leader's understanding of the speaker's total message—the verbal and nonverbal, the content and the feelings. (We will discuss listening in depth in Chapter 9).

Rhetorical Sensitivity

Effective leaders are **rhetorically sensitive**; that is, they think about the way group members communicate before, during, and after they interact with them. In doing so, they monitor situations, determine which self would be most appropriate for the occasion, enact an effective communicator style, and make necessary adjustments.[11] Effective leaders are empathetic, nonjudgmental, and objective when listening to group members.

Effective Leaders Use Appropriate Language

No matter how sensitive a leader may be, or how strong his or her ability to set a vision and goals, that leader will not be a competent communicator if he or she does not have the ability to express his or her thoughts into specific messages that others can understand and respond to. Effective leaders know when and how to use appropriate language; that is, language that is deemed suitable for a given situation that others will be able to comprehend.

Appropriate language

Language that is deemed suitable for a given situation that others will be able to comprehend.

TWO CHARACTERISTICS OF LEADERS

Regardless of leadership types, there are usually at least two characteristics we can expect leaders to demonstrate: **vision** and **credibility**.[12]

Vision

One of the most important characteristics of leadership is the ability to develop and maintain a sensible vision. Vision plays a key role by helping to direct, align, and inspire actions on the part of group members. Without an appropriate vision, members' efforts can easily dissolve into a list of confusing, incompatible, and time-consuming projects that may go in the wrong direction or nowhere at all. A sound vision guides the decision-making process; otherwise, the smallest of decisions can generate heated conflict that drains energy and destroys group morale. Within tactical group discussion, choices that are insignificant can dominate discussions and waste hours of the group's precious time.[13]

© BelleMedia, 2011. Under license from Shutterstock, Inc.

Credibility

A leader cannot be effective unless the group is willing to follow. This willingness is generally based on the group's perception of the leader's abilities and credibility. A leader needs the group's trust and confidence if he or she is going to direct the group toward the stated goals and vision.[14]

Credibility derives from some of the following factors:

1. **Competence:** knowledge and expertise in a topic
2. **Character:** honesty and trustworthiness
3. **Composure:** an ability to remain calm under stress
4. **Sociability:** likeableness
5. **Extroversion:** a degree of interest in others

Recognizing Leaders

A good leader serves as a catalyst for the group process. First and foremost, a good leader creates supportive conditions that enable members to facilitate goal achievement. These conditions are elements of the group process and include but are not limited to the list in Table 5.1.[15]

An effective leader enables and motivates the group to stay on track, to remain energized and empowered, to resolve conflicts constructively, and to make creative decisions, in order to reach desirable outcomes. The leader is the person the group looks to when it has reached an impasse, needs guidance in setting a new direction or staying on course, or needs order restored to an unruly group process. The most important aspect of leadership, after years of study, is that it is situational. Situational leadership means leaders must adapt to the particular environmental and individual needs of the moment.[16] We will discuss situational leadership later in this chapter.

Situational leadership

Leaders must adapt to the particular environmental and individual needs of the moment.

Leadership as a Function in a System

Leaders play keys roles in the systems in which they participate. They affect patterns of interaction within their groups, between their groups, and with the external environment; and they are influential in determining the outcome of the group process. Leaders must be able to bring in and process new information and new ways of approaching problems. Like a system, a leader must be flexible and able to respond to the environment in order for the group to be effective and successful. A **morphogenic** leader takes in, processes, and transforms information and procedures. This type of leader usually considers all of the possible consequences involved in a particular decision and takes considerable time to reach a conclusion. A **morphostatic** leader, however, is inflexible, resists change, and maintains the status quo. This type of leader follows a set of rules and seldom, if ever, deviates from those rules when making decisions.[17]

TABLE 5.1

Group Process	Leadership
Communication	Leader maintains open communication between and among group members. Group members initiate communication with anyone who has valid information or has an interest in the situation.
Conflict management	Leader teaches group members how to manage their own conflicts or provides the necessary means or training with which to do it.
Problem solving	Leader ensures that group members have access to relevant information to solve problems.
Decision making	Leader empowers group members to make many decisions on their own or as a group, or the leader and group members will jointly make appropriate decisions by consensus.
Sufficient time	Group members use relevant information and support from leader to set deadlines for their tasks.
Clearly defined roles	Group members use relevant information and support from leader to define and agree on their roles.
Motivating tasks	Leader helps members understand what makes a job motivating.
Clear goals	Leader helps group members learn how to set clear Goals; and, in turn, group members use relevant information and support from leader to discuss and set goals.

Leaders as Mediators

Leaders do more than just lead the group, assign tasks, and facilitate the group process. They also serve as mediators; that is, they serve as communication links between the group and its external environment, and between group members and the process in which they are engaged. In this type of environment, effective leaders must perform what we call object and action mediation. In **object mediation**, the leader must gather and form detailed impressions about the external environment. These include direct and indirect influences, or both positive and negative (negative influences are also referred to as environmental obstacles), on the group and group process. In **action mediation**, the leader determines which of those environmental obstacles must be removed, and does so through appropriate behaviors.

The leader as mediator assesses the situation, develops strategies for minimizing any possible negative effects on the group, and intervenes. The leader as mediator will help group members understand the situation so they can behave in appropriate ways. The leader depends on the group's cooperation and trust in his or her ability in order to be effective in this role. Good leadership is **interactive**.

In summary, leaders need to set long- and short-term goals, focus attention on relevant activities, manage conflict, and empower other group members to contribute to the process.

LEADERSHIP STYLES

The study of leaders and leadership in small group communication has historically been influenced by four conceptual approaches: **trait approach, style approach, situational approach,** and **functional approach**.[18] The research on trait approach was premised on the idea that leaders are people who have certain inherent personal characteristics that allow them to exercise leadership in a group. Researchers focused on identifying individual traits and characteristics that distinguish leaders from non-leaders.[19] The style approach is based on the belief that leaders exhibit different behavioral patterns while exercising leadership, which then directly affects group performance.[20] The situational approach to the study of small group communication assumes that leadership is a function of the interaction between the leader's personality and that of the followers' personalities, and of the social situation the group is in. And the functional

approach focuses on the duties or responsibilities performed by individuals who emerge as leaders.[21]

Leaders are sometimes perplexed because their associates do not react or respond as the leader wants. For example, the student group leader comes up with what she considers a good idea, and the student group is nonresponsive, listless. She asks for suggestions and in return receives mechanical replies or no reply at all. She assigns tasks, and nothing gets done. The leader is frustrated and doesn't understand why the group behaves the way it does. She decides that her ideas are no good or that her group members are just plain loafers and could care less about doing the work.

What can a leader do to get the response she wants from her group? She must first begin by recognizing that her group members respond less to what she says than to what she does. Implicit in the leader's relationship with her group is a set of expectations about how her group should act. She may not realize what her own expectations are, and the group may not consciously understand them, but they find themselves reacting as she expects.

The following examples explain some of the expectations implicit in various leadership styles.

Classic Leadership Styles

R.K. White and Ron Lippet (1960), two researchers who studied the styles approach to leadership, produced three different categories, which are still referred to today: **authoritarian**, *laissez-faire*, and **democratic**.[22]

Authoritarian

The authoritarian (also known as autocratic) type of leader has a great deal of power and authority, with an obsession for control. This type of leader determines all policies for group members. The authoritarian leader tries to control the direction and outcome of discussion, gives orders, and expects group members to follow those orders. This leadership style maintains a tight control on group member assignments and tasks. It is not uncommon for an authoritarian leader to use coercion and reward power to achieve goals. An effective authoritarian leader may get the work done, but she must not expect more than limited obedience, or she will be disappointed. Her attitude implies that followers or subordinates should obey commands and not think for themselves. The follower does not show initiative when commands cease.

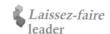

Authoritarian leader

Controls the direction and outcome of discussion, gives orders, and expects group members to follow those orders.

Laissez-faire

Laissez-faire is a French phrase that means to let people do as they want. The *laissez-faire* style of leadership is opposite to that of the authoritarian style. It is more of a neutral, hands-off style in which the leader refuses to help the group develop policies. A *laissez-faire* leader empowers the group to take control of all decisions and actions. Not only is there no concern for control, there is no direction for task accomplishment. This style of leadership is concerned with interpersonal relationships, and open communication is encouraged, and at times, rewarded. It's really a style of nonleadership. A mature and highly motivated and productive group may be a perfect match for the *laissez-faire* leader.

Laissez-faire **leader**

Empowers the group to take control of all decisions and actions.

Democratic

The democratic leadership style represents an attempt to find a reasonable compromise between the other two extremes. A democratic leader promotes the interests of group members and practices social equity. This style of leadership encourages the group to make its own decisions, but does help the group plan a course of action. The democratic leader performs both task and social leadership functions, but at the same time tries to avoid dominating the group with one person's views. The democratic leader shares power with the group and

Democratic leader

Promotes the interests of group members and practices social equity.

makes sure that all members are heard. Democratic leaders strive to develop referent and expert power as a means with which to motivate members and increase group productivity. They have the ability to promote collaboration, influence others, manage conflict, and listen effectively.[23]

The Managerial Leadership Grid™

The Managerial Leadership Grid, developed by Robert R. Blake and Jane S. Moulton, is a simple framework that identifies and defines a total of seven basic leadership styles that characterize workplace behavior and the resulting relationships. The seven Leadership Grid styles are premised on how two fundamental concerns (concern for people and concern for results) appear at varying levels whenever people interact. The grid places a concern for people on a vertical axis and a concern for task on a horizontal axis, which together define a two-dimensional space. Each of the seven leadership styles can be found on the grid and assigned a value of 1 (least) to 9 (most) on each of the two axes of concern for people and concern for task.[24]

The first five styles are team management (9,9), controlling (9,1), middle of the road (5,5), country club management (1,9), and impoverished management (1,1), according to the point along each of the axes at which a leader's behavior falls.[25]

The Seven Managerial Grid Styles:[26]

1. **9.9 Team Management (Contribute and Commit).** The leader initiates team action in a way that invites involvement and commitment. The leader explores all of the facts and alternative views in order to reach a shared understanding of the best solution. The leader shows a high degree of concern for both people (9) and task (9). The group works together with mutual respect and a strong goal orientation. Tasks are accomplished by committed people; interdependence through a common stake in organization purpose leads to relationships of trust and respect. This is a superior decision-making style.

2. **9.1 Controlling (Direct and Dominate).** (Controlling is also referred to as authority-obedience). The leader expects results and takes control by clearly stating a course of action. The leader enforces rules that sustain high results and does not permit deviation from those rules. The group may be highly efficient, but this style can create feelings of disenfranchisement in members. The leader is concerned with completing the task (9) but shows little interest or regard for relationships (1). Efficiency in operations results from arranging working conditions in such a way that minimizes human interaction. This style of leadership prevents creative decision making that results from group synergy.

3. **5.5 Status Quo (Balance and Compromise).** (Status Quo is also referred to as middle of the road). This leader endorses results that are popular but does not like to take unnecessary risks. Even though the leader is not strongly committed in either direction, the leader shows a moderate concern for

interpersonal relationships (5) and a moderate concern for the immediate task (5). The leader tests his or her opinions with others involved in order to assure ongoing acceptability. Adequate organization performance is achievable by balancing the need to produce work with maintaining group morale at a satisfactory level. The outcome is not likely to be optimal, but it may satisfy everyone to some degree.

4. **1,9 Accommodating (Yield and Comply).** (Accommodating is also known as country club management). This type of leader supports results that establish and reinforce harmony. The leader is known to generate enthusiasm by focusing on positive and pleasing aspects of work. Thoughtful attention to the needs of people for satisfying relationships produces a comfortable, friendly organization environment and work tempo. This is an inefficient style for finding a solution to a problem; however, if the group and the leader prefer to feel good about each other, and the leader assumes sole responsibility for decision making, then this is an appropriate style.

5. **1,1 Indifferent (Evade and Elude).** (Indifferent is also referred to as impoverished management). The leader in this style distances him or her from taking active responsibility for results in order to avoid getting entangled in problems. If compelled, the leader will assume a passive or supportive position. With a low concern for both people (1) and task (1), this leader does not attempt to influence group members and is indifferent as to whether or not they achieve their goals. This style is used by leaders who are overworked; don't care about the project, or who have retired on the job. The leader exerts minimum effort to get the required work accomplished sufficient to maintain organization membership. This style does not promote the group's interpersonal relationships or goal accomplishments.

6. **9 + 9 Paternalistic (Prescribe and Guide).** Leadership is provided by defining initiatives for the leader and others. The leader offers praise and appreciation for support, and discourages any challenges to his or her thinking. Similar to the team management style, the leader shows a high level of concern for both people (9) and task (9). However, instead of assuming the group has self-interest in the outcome and is working for intrinsic gratification, the leader assumes the group is burdened by the task and requires extrinsic rewards. The leader urges the group to complete its tasks, and then rewards the members in ways she or he has available—salaries, benefits,

or working conditions, for example. Some negative aspects are that group members may simply work for a price and never develop loyalty, commitment, or pride in the workplace.

7. **Opportunism.** The leader persuades others to support results that offer the leader private benefit. If members also benefit, that facilitates their support. The leader relies on whatever approach is needed to secure an advantage. The leader uses people, authority, and the environment as she or he sees fit. The leader has a 5,5 style toward group members considered equals; a 9,1 style toward those the leader views as less important; and a 1,9 behavior toward those in authority. The paternalistic style is viewed as self-serving, without genuine concern for the group's welfare.

There are two additional styles that are not a part of the Grid; however, they should be mentioned here: **situational style** and **problem-solving leadership**.

Situational

Situational leadership contends that strong direction (task behavior) with group members with low readiness is appropriate if they are to become productive. It also suggests that an increase in readiness on the part of the members who are somewhat unready should be rewarded by increased positive reinforcement and social-emotional support (relationship behavior). As group members reach

high levels of readiness, the leader responds by decreasing control over their activities and decreasing relationship behavior. The aim is to allow for individual autonomy tied to performance.[27]

Problem Solving

Problem-solving leadership is similar to the Grid's Team Management Style. This style of leadership is preferred by leaders who have strong confidence in their members and genuinely considers them their equals. These leaders believe that their colleagues can make valuable contributions toward the problem-solving process and are eager to get the group's brains working on the problem. The problem-solving leader presents the problem to the group to work out a joint solution. Once the problem has been presented, the leader becomes an active member of the group. All members are expected to participate throughout the planning and decision-making process. The solution is truly owned by the entire group.

Determining Appropriate Styles

What factors should be considered when deciding how to lead? Answering these questions should help you in determining the leadership style you should use.

1. **The leader's system and own leadership inclinations.**[28] How strongly does the leader believe that members should share in the decision-making

process? What is the relative importance she assigns to organizational efficiency, personal growth of subordinates, and of organizational goals?

2. **The leader's confidence in subordinates.** What is the level of trust that he/she has in other people in general? What is his/her personal view concerning the group's knowledge and competence with respect to the problem? Does the leader ask the question, "Who is best qualified to address this problem?"

3. **His/her feelings of security in an uncertain situation.** The leader who hands over control of the decision-making process to the group reduces the predictability of the outcome. Can he/she handle this tolerance for ambiguity?

One of the nagging dilemmas of leadership is often the difference between what the leader believes to be right and desirable and what he/she does in practice. Two questions that help determine any style of leadership are:[29]

1. How democratic can the leader be?
2. How authoritarian must the leader be?

Once you have addressed the questions listed above when deciding the style of leadership you want to assume, there are major conclusions you must reach in making these decisions, which are the answers to the following:[30]

1. **What type of organization or group am I leading?** This is an easy question to answer for the student leader; it is a college or university group communications course. If you are leading an organization, you need to know what type it is and what it does. On the surface, this sounds simple, but truly knowing the organization is much more difficult than you think. This will help determine the leadership style you will choose. If you are a group leader, then you need to know the type of group you are leading: problem solving, decision making, policy, and so forth.[31]

2. **How effective is this group's decision-making procedure?** Do group members continuously debate minor or insignificant issues and fail to address the ones that are important? Does the group rely on one or two individuals to decide for them? Does the group have a history of rushing through the decision-making process so they can conclude and move on to the next problem? As leader, you will need to observe how the group deals with decision making. It is their behavior, not yours, that will help you decide.

3. **What objective(s) do we want to accomplish?** You have to determine what areas of an individual's or group's activities you need to influence. Specifically, what objective(s) do you want to accomplish? Objectives are determined by the group's responsibility, problem solving, decision making, policy, and so forth; you must identify specific tasks that can be assigned to a group to accomplish their goal:[32]

   a. The goal is summarized using trigger words; e.g., improving the student lounge.

   b. Tasks to accomplish the goal are identified by the people involved:

    (1) conduct student surveys

    (2) research lounge history

    (3) contact gaming companies

4. **What is the group's readiness?** The leader diagnoses and determines the group's readiness to complete these tasks. The key issue is, "How ready is the group to accomplish these tasks?" If the group is at a high level of readiness, a minimum amount of leadership intervention will be needed. However, if the group is at a low level of readiness, considerable leadership intervention may be necessary.[33]

5. **What leadership action should be taken?** Now you have to decide which of the leadership styles would be appropriate for the group. The readiness of each member and the group as a whole has a primary influence on the choice.[34]

6. **What will be the consequences of my actions?** Have my assessments been accurate? Have I made the right leadership style choice? If not, then there may be a good chance that the group may not be able to complete their tasks and will fail to achieve their goal(s).[35]

The Hersey-Blanchard Situational Leadership Model

The Hersey-Blanchard Leadership Model (1985) suggests that successful leaders adjust their leadership styles. Hersey and Blanchard identify the key issue in making these adjustments— follower maturity—as indicated in leaders' readiness to perform in a given situation. Unlike many other models, the situational leadership model views leaders as altering their emphasis on tasks and relationship behaviors to best deal with different levels of follower maturity.

Four Basic Situational Leadership Styles[36]

The degree of individual or group readiness determines which style to choose.

Telling

The leader provides specific instructions and closely supervises performance— telling group members what to do, where to do it, and how to do it. The telling style is appropriate when the group or an individual member is low in ability and willingness, and needs leadership direction.

Appropriate behaviors for the delegating leader would be to:

- Directly state specific tasks,
- Positively reinforce small improvements,
- Consider consequences for nonperformance,
- Keep emotional level in check,
- Be sure not to overwhelm members,
- Reduce fear of making mistakes,
- Help step by step,
- Focus on instruction.

Selling

Explaining task directions in a supportive and persuasive way—explaining decisions and providing opportunity for clarification. Either the group or the individual is still unable, but at least they're trying. They are willing or confident. The selling style is different from telling because the leader is not only giving guidance but is also providing the opportunity for dialogue and clarification.

Appropriate behaviors for the delegating leader would be to:

- Seek buy-in through persuading,
- Check understanding of the task,
- Encourage questions,
- Discuss details,
- Explore related skills,
- Explain why,
- Give members small tasks (not run with it),
- Emphasize how to.

Participating

Here, the leader shares ideas and facilitates making decisions. The leader's primary role is one of encouraging and communicating. Appropriate leadership behavior would be high amounts of two-way communication and supportive behavior but low amounts of guidance.

Appropriate behaviors for the participating leader would be to:

- Share responsibility for the decision making with the group,
- Feed followers' need to know,
- Focus on results,
- Involve followers in consequences of task to increase commitment and motivation,
- Encourage and support,
- Discuss apprehension,
- Determine next step.

Delegating

The delegating leadership style allows the group to take responsibility for task decisions and implementation. It isn't necessary for the leader to provide direction about where, what, when, or how, because the group already has the ability to perform.

Appropriate behaviors for the delegating leader would be to:

- Listen to updates,
- Resist overloading.
- Encourage autonomy,
- Practice overall hands-off management,
- Reinforce member-led communications,
- Provide support and resources,
- Delegate activities,
- Encourage freedom for risk taking.

© Sean Prior, 2011. Under license from Shutterstock, Inc.

Once you have decided the type of leadership style you will assume, your task has only begun. It is you who will provide the vision, energy, and reinforcement that will be necessary for group cohesion, synergy, and task accomplishment. The following practical tips are designed to keep you on track:

- **Project energy.** When the group members seem to lack any enthusiasm or energy, it is you who will vitalize them. They will look to you for that spark.
- **Be involved.** An effective leader stays involved with the group, even if only to observe. Members exhibit more involvement, interest, and pride in their group when the leader is actively involved.
- **Assist evaluation and change for the group.** The group should be monitoring itself for opportunities to improve its performance. As leader, you should participate when possible, but resist dominating this process.
- **Persuade and persevere.** It will take a lot of persuasive discourse for you to get group members to see your point of view. It is easier to change behavior than it is to change someone's mind. That takes perseverance.
- **Maintain perspective.** It is easy for the group to get sidetracked. As noted earlier, a lot of meaningless and time-consuming discussion can be spent away from task achievement.
- **Target energy on success opportunities.** The group's task is to achieve its goal(s). This cannot be accomplished if energy and resources are directed toward unsuccessful opportunities.
- **Influence cooperative action.** This is called group communication for a reason; in order for the group to be successful, members must be able to work together. You, the leader, must foster this cooperative action.
- **Support creativity.** Just because you didn't think of it doesn't mean that it isn't as good, if not better, than what you've come up with. Creativity is brainstorming—great!!!!
- **Avoid the negative.** There is nothing worse in group work than to have one or two individuals who constantly focus on the negative. It is like a cancer that will eventually infect all of the group members. Your positive attitude, even when times look gloomy, will prevent this from happening.
- **Never be satisfied (seek continuous improvement).** Good is never good enough. You and the group can always improve. It is a sign of danger when you think that the group functions at its optimum. There is always room for improvement.

SUMMARY

In this chapter, we learned what constitutes leadership and leadership styles. There are three general skills, or competencies, that leadership requires: diagnosing, adapting, and communicating. We explored communication competence and what it means to be an effective listener and to be rhetorically sensitive, and the need to use appropriate language.

Two of the most important characteristics of leadership are: the ability to develop and maintain a sensible vision; and the need for the group's trust and confidence, which are products of the leader's credibility.

There are four conceptual approaches to leadership styles: **approach, situational approach, trait approach, style** and **functional approach**. Within the styles approach, we studied three of the classic styles: authoritarian, democratic, and *laissez-faire*. There are four basic situational leadership styles identified by Hersey and Blanchard: telling, selling, participating, and delegating.

Being a leader is no easy task; it takes considerable time, energy, and knowledge. As you should have now discovered, the leader in small group work is a combination of leader and manager. How you guide group members is as important, if not more important, than what you guide them to do. The following chapters will help you accomplish this.

DISCUSSION

1. Consider the importance of listening for the **communication competence** of an effective leader: What are some groups from your own life in which a leader has failed, even temporarily, to listen effectively? What were the consequences of this failure to listen—how did other people in the group react and respond?

2. Identify, through discussion, one specific leader that everyone in your group recognizes and agrees is ineffective (perhaps a government official, a famous sports figure, or a professor on your campus). Consider the five factors influencing a leader's **credibility** on page 104: How did the leader you chose fail to exhibit each of these factors?

3. For each of the following three leadership styles: **authoritarian, laissez–faire,** and **democratic,** work with your group to describe a specific group situation in which this leadership style might **negatively** affect group success, and an explanation of why this style might have this negative effect.

4. Use the **Managerial Leadership Grid** on page 108 to consider your own leadership inclinations: Which of these seven areas best fits, most of the time, your own values and communication style? Share your self–assessment with your group and discuss the leadership styles that span your group: Does your group have a variety of styles, or do many of you orient to the same one or two styles? How might this leadership style variety affect work in your group?

5. For each of the following four **situational leadership styles: telling, selling, participating** and **delegating,** work with your group to describe a specific group situation in which this leadership style would be a better fit for the group than the other two.

NOTES

1. Hollander, E.P. (1978). *Leadership dynamics.* New York: Free Press.

2. Larson, C.U. The Verbal response of groups to the absence or presence of leaders. *Speech Monographs, 38,* 177–181.

3. Homans, G.C. (1950). *The human group.* New York: Harcourt, Brace & World.

4. Forsyth, D.R. (2006). *Group dynamics* (4th ed.). Belmont, CA: Thomson-Wadsworth.

5. Hersey, P., Blanchard, K.H., & Johnson, D.E. (2001). *Management of organizational behavior* (8th ed.). Upper Saddle River, NJ: Prentice-Hall.

6. Kotter, J.P. (1996). *Leading change.* Boston: Harvard Business School Press.

7. See Homans, G.C. (1950). *The human group.* New York: Harcourt, Brace & World, Inc., p. 418. According to Homans, this definition was adapted from C.I. Barnard, The Functions of the Executive, 163, footnote 2.

8. Ibid.

9. Adapted from Kotter, J.P. (1996). *Leading change.* Boston: Harvard Business School Press.

10. The *Three Competencies of Leadership* have been adapted from Hersey, P., Blanchard, K.H., & Johnson, D.E. (2001). *Management of organizational behavior* (8th ed.). Upper Saddle River, NJ: Prentice-Hall.

11. Trenholm, S., & Jensen, A. (1996). *Interpersonal communication* (3rd ed.). Belmont, CA: Wadsworth.

12. Harris, T.E. & Sherblom, J.C. (2008). *Small group and team communication* (4th ed.). New York: Pearson.

13. Kotter, J.P. (1996). *Leading change.* Boston: Harvard Business School Press.

14. Harris, T.E., & Sherblom, J.C. (2008). *Small group and team communication* (4th ed.). New York: Pearson.

15. Adapted from Schwarz, R.M. (1994). *The skilled facilitator.* San Francisco: Jossey-Bass.

16. DeWine, S. (1994). *The consultant's craft: Improving organizational communication.* New York: St. Martin's Press.

17. Reeves, T., Duncan, W. J., & Ginter, P. M. (2000). Leading Change By Managing Paradoxes. *Journal of Leadership & Organizational Studies, 7*(1), 13–30.

18. Hirokawa, R.Y., Cathcart, R.S., Samovar, L.A., & Henman, L.D. (2003). *Small group communication: Theory and practice, an anthology* (8th ed.). Los Angeles: Roxbury.

19. Ibid.

20. Ibid.

21. Ibid.

22. White, R.K., & Lippet, R.O. (1960). *Autocracy and democracy.* New York: Harper & Row.

23. Engleberg, I.N., & Wynn, D.R. (2007). *Working in groups* (4th ed.). Boston: Houghton Mifflin.; Hirokawa, R.Y., Cathcart, R.S., Samovar, L.A., & Henman, L.D. (2003). *Small group communication: Theory and practice, an anthology* (8th ed.). Los Angeles: Roxbury.; Galenas, G.J., Adams, K., & Brilhart, J.K. (2004). *Effective group discussion: Theory and practice* (11th ed.). New York: McGraw-Hill.; Lumsden, G.L., & Lumsden, D. (1997). *Communicating in groups and teams: Sharing leadership* (2nd ed.). New York: Wadsworth.

24. Harris, T.E., & Sherblom, J.C. (2008). *Small group and team communication* (4th ed.). New York: Pearson.

25. http://www.gridinternational.com/gridtheory.html. Retrieved January 12, 2009.

26. Adapted from Hersey, P., Blanchard, K.H., & Johnson, D.E. (2001). *Management of organizational behavior,.* (8th ed.). Upper Saddle River, NJ: Prentice-Hall; and The Leadership Grid, http://www.gridinternational.com/gridtheory.html; and Harris, T.E., & Sherblom, J.C. (2008). *Small group and team communication* (4th ed.). New York: Pearson.

27. Hersey, P., Blanchard, K.H., & Johnson, D.E. (2001). *Management of organizational behavior* (8th ed.). Upper Saddle River, NJ: Prentice-Hall.

28. Zaleznik, A. (1966). *Human dilemmas of leadership.* New York: HarperCollins.

29. Ibid.

30. Adapted from Hersey, P., Blanchard, K.H., & Johnson, D.E. (2008). *Management of organizational behavior* (9th ed.). Upper Saddle River, NJ: Prentice-Hall.

31. Zaleznik, A. (1966). *Human dilemmas of leadership.* New York: HarperCollins.

32. Adapted from Hersey, P., Blanchard, K.H., & Johnson, D.E. (2008). *Management of organizational behavior* (9th ed.). Upper Saddle River, NJ: Prentice-Hall.

33. Ibid.

34. Ibid.

35. Wood, J.T., Phillips, G.M., & Pedersen, D.J. (1986). *Group discussion: A practical guide to participation and leadership.* New York: Harper & Row.

36. Adapted from Hersey, P., Blanchard, K.H., & Johnson, D.E. (2001). *Management of organizational behavior,* (8th ed.). Upper Saddle River, NJ: Prentice-Hall.

6

Leadership, Persuasion, and Motivation

KEY TERMS

Motives

Psychographics

Beliefs

Descriptive belief

Evaluative belief

Prescriptive belief

Attitude

Cognitions

Dissonance theory

Expectancy theory

Attribution theory

Theory of reasoned action

Anchors

Compliance gaining

Sanctions

Needs

CHAPTER OUTLINE

I'm certain that you have experienced what just about every person has experienced when first beginning any type of group work, whether that group is an athletic team-driven group, school theatre acting group, musical, community youth group, 4-H, and so forth. Initially, you are highly motivated to participate and perform your best. You want to show everyone that you are ready, willing, and able be a team player. For most people, after awhile the novelty wears off, and it becomes a challenge just to show up, let alone perform your duties and tasks. You discover that the leader has to cajole, prod, persuade, or even threaten you with some type of negative consequence or punishment in order for you to show up and do your best. For example, how many group activities have you

joined that have as a stipulation that if you miss X amount of meetings you will automatically be removed as a member? This is a punishment designed to do two things: (1) motivate you to show up when you are supposed to; and (2) act as a compliance-gaining technique that reinforces the punishment. It is really that simple: "Welcome to the team, John. We have practice three times a week. If you miss four or more practices, you will be dropped from the team." See, simple, isn't it? If you don't show up, you're out. The punishment of being dropped is designed to persuade you to show up. Group work is not much different because the motivating factors that got you involved in sports, etc., are the same as those in group work, unless you are assigned to a group and have no choice.

Okay, so you are now in a small group in your class, and you are the group leader. There are five of you in the group, you agree on a problem to solve and assign tasks. During the next class session, you ask each member how he or she is progressing. Three members say that the research is going well and show you their work to support the claim that they are doing well. Uh-oh, two members do not produce anything and say that they have better things to do with their time than to research. What is your response? What do you do versus what you would like to do? There is a big difference between the two.

© Nagel Photography, 2011. Under license from Shutterstock, Inc.

No two individuals have the ability to perform exactly in the same way. People differ, not only in their ability to perform, but also in their will to perform, or **motivation**. The degree of someone's motivation depends on the strength of their motives. Motives are often defined as needs, wants, desires, drives, or impulses within the individual. Motives are directed toward goals, which may be conscious or subconscious. If motives are directed toward goals, what is motivation? What does it mean to motivate someone? There are as many definitions of motivation as there are theories of motivation. Preferring the simple over the complex, we'll define motivation as "the internal force that drives individuals to accomplish personal, group, and organizational goals."

Motives
Needs, wants, desires, drives, or impulses within the individual; they are directed toward goals, which may be conscious or subconscious.

Motivation benefits the individual group member, the group, and the organization. It benefits the individual group member because it entrusts the individual member with new responsibilities (tasks) that allow the individual to achieve beyond what he or she previously thought he or she could. It releases their energy, creativity, and ability to think critically. It also promotes productivity because the individual performs efficiently and effectively. Motivation benefits the group because the group becomes more enthusiastic and active, which has a tendency to lead to success. Motivation also facilitates teamwork and group synergy. And motivation benefits the organization because it harnesses individual talents to the fullest and gives group leaders more time to engage in broad-based thinking, creating new visions, and developing group cohesion.

Motivation is a process of influencing or stimulating an individual to perform in such a way as to accomplish a desired goal or objective. Unfortunately, there isn't a single or simple way to stimulate motivation. Any degree of motivation must come from within each individual. This chapter focuses on leadership, persuasion, and motivation, which is followed by *Leadership and Performance Management* in Chapter 7. By the end of these two chapters, you should have a solid foundation as to *what* needs to be done to motivate people and how to do it.

PERSUASIVE THEORIES

Let me first begin by saying that I do not believe that a person actually persuades someone to do something; rather, I believe that someone influences the cognitive process of another individual. We do this is many ways. Saying that we persuaded someone is saying that we got into his or her mind and made him or her do something he or she either did not want to do, or was contemplating on doing, or just wasn't sure he or she wanted to do. We can persuade, or influence, someone to do something in two basic ways: first, we influence him or her psychologically, by creating messages that he or she can identify with; and secondly, by changing his or her environment, or the conditions that affect the way people behave. We can change human behavior without using the persuasive process by changing the conditions that affect or influence behavior. We will discuss this process in Chapter 7. Keep in mind that there is a general distinction between influencing behavior and motivating behavior. When we refer to motivation, we reference a subset of the persuasive processes; that is, once we have influenced someone's mind, we need to get him or her motivated to follow through behaviorally. There is a difference between the two. Your intent could be to merely change someone's belief about something; however, the overarching reason for doing that is to eventually change his or her behavior, too; to get him or her to behave in some manner. Motivational appeals are, at times, used to alter that behavior. They are a part of the persuasive process, and not the process itself.

Persuasive theorists like to use the word psychographics when referring to the internal, mental characteristics, and cognitive processes of a person. **Psychographics**, or the internal state of an individual, cannot be observed; rather, they must be inferred or generalized based on observation of behavior or lifestyle. I wouldn't know if a person was a racist unless I heard him or her speaking racial epithets or observed him or her congregating with a recognized racist group. As a rule, a person's behavior reflects his or her internal state; what he or she thinks is reflective in how he or she acts.

🪨 Psychographics
The internal state of an individual.

In marketing, psychographics are criteria for segmenting consumers by lifestyle, attitudes, beliefs, values, personality, buying motives, and/or extent of product usage. Psychographic analyses are used like **geographic** (place of residence or work) and **demographic** (age, income, occupation) criteria to describe and identify customers and prospective customers and to aid in developing promotion strategies designed to appeal to specific psychographic segments of the market for a product. Unlike demographics, psychographics delves deeper into people's lifestyles and behaviors, including their interests and values. Researchers collect information on needs, values, and attitudes, and, in the case of marketing, insights about consumer purchasing behavior.

© Maksim Toome, 2011. Under license from Shutterstock, Inc.

Communication cannot change an audience's demographic characteristics, but the change of a psychographic characteristic is frequently the specific purpose of persuasion. There are five different types of psychographics or internal states (cognitive characteristics) that are used to construct an audience profile: **beliefs**, **attitudes**, **values**, **needs**, and **ego-defense mechanisms**.

Beliefs

🪨 Beliefs
The hundreds of thousands of statements that we make about self and the world.

Depending on who is writing the definition, a belief is basically whatever an individual is willing to accept without direct verification by experience or without the support of evidence, resulting in assumption which is taken as a basis for action or nonaction. One of the most comprehensive theories on attitude and change is that of Milton Rokeach (1960, 1968, 1973).[1] He has developed an extensive explanation of human behavior based on beliefs, attitudes, and values.

Rokeach believes that each person has a highly organized system of beliefs, attitudes and values, which guides behavior. Beliefs are the hundreds of thousands of statements that we make about self and the world. Beliefs can be general or specific, and they are arranged within a system in terms of centrality or importance to the ego. At the center of the belief system are those well-established, relatively unchangeable beliefs that form the core of the belief system. At the periphery, or edges, of the system lie numerous insignificant beliefs that can change easily.[2]

Following Rokeach, we can say that "beliefs are simple propositions or statements that can be preceded by the phrase, 'I believe that...'"[3] There are three different belief structures, and each has its own basic distinctions between the others.

The first is called a **descriptive belief** because it describes to us the world around us; beliefs that focus on our judgments of what is good and bad are **evaluative beliefs**; and beliefs concerning how people should behave are called **prescriptive beliefs**. Examples of descriptive beliefs include:

I believe basketballs are round.
I believe birds have two wings.
I believe hats help keep the rain off our heads.
I believe the jungle is humid.

There are many descriptive beliefs created through our senses:

I believe that communication studies is a good major for getting a job when I graduate.
I believe that drinking one cup of coffee a day is good for me.
I believe that I should quit smoking.
I believe that saving for my retirement is a wise thing to do.

Evaluative beliefs link a behavior with a positive consequence or benefit, or a negative consequence or punishment. Proof or evidence for holding such a belief does not stem solely from direct observation of what our senses tell us, but rather from evidence accumulated over time (all of my friends in communication studies got jobs right after graduation; I heard experts say that coffee is good for the heart; family members who have smoked for a long time have emphysema; and, congress has been saying that Social Security might not be around when I retire).

And third, there are beliefs prescribing what people should do. Prescriptive beliefs commonly are linked to higher-order beliefs called values that focus on certain important consequences: a world at peace, equality, salvation, a comfortable life, a happy family life, and so on. Prescriptive beliefs deal with what people should and should not do, and these beliefs run a gamut of roles: male, female, minority member, supporter, sponsor, and citizen, for example.[4]

In addition, beliefs can be distinguished from one another on the basis of their origination. There are four major sources of beliefs:[5]

Descriptive belief
Describes to us the world around us.

Evaluative belief
Belief that focuses on our judgments of what is good and bad.

Prescriptive belief
Belief concerning how people should behave.

1. **Induction.** A person develops a generalized belief based on summation of past observations. Through repeated and confirmed experiences, a person may state, "I believe that red apples are good," "I believe that smoking has a negative effect on my breathing."

2. **Construction.** A person develops a belief concerning how two or more events are related to one another, and this construction may have little or nothing to do with reasoning or logic. Some constructions may be nothing more than conjecture based on limited observations: "I believe people who drive fast cars are mean and dangerous."

3. **Analogy.** A person develops a belief based on similarities among things or events. If two objects (a concord grape and a white seedless grape) are round, and both are have the same kind of covering, one may assume that the two are similar in taste. A person believes a concord grape would taste like a white seedless grape, until it is tasted and direct experience tells him otherwise.

4. **Authority.** A person develops and maintains a belief based on the authority of others. A great number of beliefs stem from authorities: The earth is warming; Simon Bolivar was a great leader; the oceans are polluted; and communism is a bad form of government, for example. These reflect only a few of the thousands of authority-related beliefs.

A third way of classifying beliefs is in terms of a central-peripheral dimension described by Milton Rokeach (1960). He identifies three areas: (1) the central belief, which entails primitive beliefs, the physical world, and the social world (rocks are harder than wood; it is better to give than receive); (2) the authority beliefs—beliefs about the nature of authority and source for information (obey your parents; July 4th is a national holiday); and (3) peripheral beliefs which are of two categories: those which are based on central beliefs (I believe brown coffee filters are better for me and the environment than the bleached white coffee filters) and those which are not. Many peripheral beliefs are concerned about the value of life (I believe that all life is sacred).

We construct **frames of reference** composed of our attitudes and beliefs. These reference frames can be used to make predictions about the effects of persuasion. Beliefs are formed along a set of central-peripheral dimensions, and this organization allows us to make predictions about the probable effects of persuasive messages.[6]

1. The more central the belief, the more individuals will resist to changes in that belief. You will find it very unlikely that the receiver will change his or her central belief, if that is your persuasive goal. The difficulty of changing a primitive belief through persuasion is greatly magnified if the belief is one that has consensus within the society.

2. Beliefs based on authority are also resistant to change, but not to the extent central beliefs are. The person who has long held a belief that doctors are always ethical, may have that belief weakened if he or she experiences a doctor who behaved unethically. Later, if that person accumulates more evidence about that doctor's conduct, he or she will change this authority belief.

3. Beliefs resulting from central beliefs are more resistant to change than those existing only as peripheral beliefs.

4. The more central the belief that is changed, the more widespread will be the changes in the remainder of the individual belief structure. The central beliefs we hold are connected to many peripheral beliefs. A change in a central belief may cause changes in peripheral beliefs. In other words, if one of your central beliefs changes, expect rather profound changes in how you think about many things.

Attitudes

An **attitude** is considered to be an accumulation of information about an object, person, situation, or experience, and it is often shaped very early in life. Attitudes are groups of beliefs organized around a focal object, and they predispose a person to behave in a particular way toward that object. Obviously, not everyone has the same attitudes; if that were so, we would have a monolithic human race. It is possible for a single experience with an object to shape an attitude. A child bitten at an early age by a dog might need only one such experience to develop highly negative attitudes toward dogs. But it usually takes more than one experience to create an attitude. Our brain operates in such a way that the information we receive is placed into belief structures containing related information. We develop structures about nature, people, education, churches, and governments, to name a few. By the time we are adults, these structures have become extremely complex.

Rokeach believes attitudes are of two important kinds that must always be viewed together. These are attitude toward object and attitude toward situation. A person's behavior in a particular situation is a function of these two in combination. Once we have formed our basic set of attitudes, we use these as a kind of filter that determines how new attitudes are going to be formed. This set of attitudes is called a frame of reference. It includes our internal state, past experiences, biases, and so forth. Reference frames are not composed of simple attitudes alone; for every attitude, there can be an overabundance of beliefs we hold concerning how the world operates. This frame of reference then affects which of the many messages in our environment we pay attention to. Researchers have shown that people can be primed to perceive ambiguous stimuli in ways that are consistent with the particular social cognition that was activated.[7]

The ability to communicate in an appropriate or effective manner also rests on the frame of reference we have in any given situation. Sarah Trenholm and Arthur Jensen (1996) assert that our actions are based on our perceptions. We produce messages that we think will be appropriate depending on how we see the situation: who the other person is, what she is doing, what we think her motives are, what are own goals and sense of self are, and what type of relationship we believe we have with her. Because perceptions channel action, our ability to exercise control over our own communication is directly linked to our awareness of social cognition processes. This awareness allows us to change our attitudes.[8]

Attitude
Considered to be an accumulation of information about an object, person, situation, or experience, often shaped very early in life.

Attitude change occurs because new information adds to the attitude or because it changes a person's judgments about the weight or valence of other information. Any one piece of information usually does not have too much influence on an attitude because the attitude consists of a number of things that could counteract the new information.[9] Attitudes differ from beliefs because they are evaluative; that is, our attitudes help us make decisions about people, events, objects, etc. because we use attitudes as reference points or anchors. Attitudes are correlated with beliefs and lead you to behave a certain way toward the attitude object or person. They are to a great extent the products of learning; they reflect the beliefs and feelings we have as individuals, the values of our culture, and our experiences in family, religious, educational, and general social life. As such, attitudes become those predispositions, those reaction tendencies we have either for or against people and objects in our environment. Attitudes, therefore, affect our perceptions, our judgments, our learning efficiency, indeed, our whole philosophy of life. They provide us with a relatively stable or fixed self-image.[10]

Some of the most important attitude change theories have been termed **consistency theories**[11] or tension-reduction theories.[12] Consistency theories were first written about for others to consider in the early 1940s, although the roots for such theories undoubtedly go back much farther.[13] Since World War II, various cognitive consistency theories have provided one of the most fruitful areas of study within communication and the behavioral sciences.

The term **cognitive consistency** refers to a number of specific theories which apply to different types of persuasive communication situations. Although the various consistency theories have unique aspects, all the theories are based on the common idea that inconsistency is somehow unpleasant or painful or distasteful, and that the tensions created by this unpleasant state will lead to attempts to reduce the tensions.[14] Leon Festinger is noted for his work on consonance and dissonance,[15] C.E. Osgood for theories explaining congruity and incongruity,[16] R.P Abelson and M.J. Rosenberg for consistency theory,[17] and Fritz Heider gave us balance and imbalance theories.[18]

Cognitions

The beliefs a person might have.

When we say that we have a theory of cognitive consistency, we are saying we have a theory about cognitions which deals with the consistency of those cognitions. **Cognitions** are the beliefs a person might have. Some theorists contend that internal contradictions in one or more beliefs can create problems for a person. For example, you hold the belief that it is wrong to steal; however, you find a paper bag with $50,000.00 in it. Your belief says that it doesn't belong to you, so keeping it would be stealing. But you desperately need the money. Do you keep it? When confusions and inconsistencies occur, people do their best to return to a state of cognitive consistency, where they feel most comfortable. Theorists believe that human beings want to reduce internal tension in their lives. They attempt to explain the need for humans to maintain cognitive consistency through thought and behavior.

Research demonstrates that the association among cognitions is at its best when bits of information are consistent. The simplest version of a cognitive consistency theory relevant to persuasion is **balance theory**. Larson (1995) claims that the earliest consistency theory was that proposed by Fritz Heider, balance theory (1946, 1958), and later elaborated by Theodore Newcomb (1953), who applied it to the simplest form of human communication: one person communicating interpersonally with another person about a single topic. A consistency theory indicates that when bits of information are inconsistent, there is a state of imbalance in the mind and a tension or uneasiness that calls for a return to cognitive consistency. Consider this simplified example. John is a junior in high school and works in his father's hardware store, where he must work every day after school, Friday nights, and all day Saturday. John is considered to be an excellent basketball player by his athletic coach and classmates. They are trying to persuade him to play basketball for the high school team. Although he really wants to play, he can't balance the time between working for his father and playing ball because game times generally fall on Fridays and Saturdays. John is experiencing cognitive dissonance.

The degree to which a person can tolerate cognitive inconsistency is dependent upon the strength of the activation of related cognitions. If two bits of inconsistent information are not associated by a strong mental pathway, the inconsistent beliefs or attitudes may linger for a long time before they are simultaneously brought to consciousness. If, for example, John has a stronger need to honor the bond and his duty to his father than playing basketball, the inconsistency will be short-lived and eventually disappear. However, if the need to play basketball is as great as his duty to his father, then the inconsistency will co-exist until he is forced to make a decision between the two. Internally, John will have to achieve cognitive consistency, a mental balance. There are three ways by which a person can achieve this consistency:

1. John and his father can have a negative attitude toward basketball and a positive attitude toward one another. (John and his father can both dislike basketball and like each other, so they experience comfort and balance.)
2. John and his father can have a positive attitude toward basketball and can have good feelings toward one another. (John and his father can both like basketball and like each other, thus achieving comfort and balance.)
3. John and his father can disagree about basketball and can dislike each other. (John and his father are not alike, and they dislike each other, so it is comforting to know that they disagree about the value of basketball.)

Hopefully, for John, number 2 is achieved.

Clearly, the greater extent to which a persuader understands the association between an audience's cognitions and existing or potential inconsistencies among these cognitions, the greater is the persuader's chance of changing cognitions. The persuader who tries to strengthen preexisting beliefs in an audience can do so by creating a balanced, or comfortable, situation for the audience. One of the most important rules of making a situation balanced is that the less important element (belief, attitude, or value) is usually the one which is changed.

Cognitive Dissonance

Dissonance theory

Predicts that when two things do not follow from each other, we will experience psychological tension, which we will try to reduce in some way.

Leon Festinger's theory of cognitive dissonance (1957) is one of the most important theories in the history of social psychology, and it probably has encouraged the most discussion (favorable and unfavorable) and research (in excess of 300 studies) in the area of attitude change. Unlike the balance theory, which predicts a change in attitudes, judgments, or evaluations, **dissonance theory** predicts that when two things do not follow from each other, we will experience psychological tension, which we will try to reduce in some way. He suggests that these psychological tensions, or cognitive elements, are knowledge about facts, objects, behaviors, circumstances, and the like. It is believed that Festinger includes beliefs, opinions, and attitudes in this general category. He holds that people tend to resolve or reduce any inconsistency between their attitudes and their behaviors. Festinger argues that any two cognitive elements, including attitudes, perceptions, knowledge, and behaviors, will have one of three kinds of relationships. The first of these is null, or irrelevant; the second is consistent, or *consonant*; and the third is inconsistent, or dissonant. Dissonance occurs when one element would not be expected to follow from the other. Therefore, any two cognitions may either be relevant or irrelevant to each other. Any relevant relationships may be of two types: consonant or dissonant. For example, for the diet-conscious individual, reports by The American Heart Association attribute clogged arties leading to a heart attack to eating foods saturated with transfats create no dissonance, because his or her behavior and the heart attack information are in consonance. To the person who indulges in fast-food greasy French fries and hamburgers, the heart attack reports and his or her decision to continue eating these foods can produce considerable dissonance because consistency is absent. The dissonance will be great when the relevant elements involved are of great importance to the individual, such as one's health. The dissonance will increase with the number of cognitive elements that are in dissonance, such as more reasons why a person should not have a steady diet of fast food. What is consonant or dissonant for one person, however, may not be for another; therefore, we must always ask what is consistent or inconsistent within a person's own psychological system.

It is assumed that cognitive dissonance occurs after some decision or choice; that isn't the case. Festinger makes the following distinction:

> The person is in a conflict situation before making the decision. After having made the decision, he is no longer in conflict; he has made his choice; he has, so to speak, resolved the conflict; he is no longer being pushed in two or more directions simultaneously. He is now committed to the chosen course of action. It is only here that dissonance exists, and the pressure to reduce this dissonance is *not* pushing the person in two directions simultaneously.[19]

This theory explains that cognitive dissonance is a tension state varying in accordance with the significance or centrality of the elements involved and the degree of conflict present. The degree of tension resulting from the dissonance provides the motivational power to seek the elimination or reduction of the dissonance. Tension reduction involves more than change; it has a quantitative as well as a qualitative dimension. More specifically, we can change our evaluations or judgments a little, a moderate amount, quite a bit, or not at all.[20] Griffin (1997) notes that there are three different hypotheses that show ways to reduce dissonance between attitudes and actions.[21]

> Hypothesis 1: Selective Exposure Prevents Dissonance. Festinger claims that people avoid information that is likely to increase dissonance. We tend to stick to our own kind by associating with people who are like us, and we select things to read and watch on TV that are consistent with what we believe. People who are like us will keep those things away that make us uncomfortable.
>
> Hypothesis 2: Postdecision Dissonance Creates a Need for Reassurance. Close-call decisions can result in a tremendous amount of internal tension after the decision has been made. Three conditions can heighten the dissonance: (1) how important the issue; (2) the longer it takes to make a decision between two equally desired options; and (3) how difficult it is to reverse the decision once it has been made. These factors make a person uncomfortable wondering whether or not he or she has made the right choice. Once this difficult choice has been made, he or she is motivated to seek support and reassurance for his or her decision.
>
> Hypothesis 3: Minimal Justification for Action Induces a Shift in Attitude. Originally, people thought that inner attitude and outward behavior were the beginning and end of a cause-and-effect sequence. In other words, what the person thinks about the behavior is what he or she does. But this hypothesis states the opposite. The minimum incentive should be offered to make a change in attitude.

Much of the theory and research on cognitive dissonance has centered on the various situations in which dissonance is likely to result. These include such situations as decision making, forced compliance, initiation, social support, and effort. Decision making has received a considerable amount of research attention. The amount of dissonance an individual experiences as a result of a decision depends on four variables, the first of which is the importance of the decision. Certain decisions, such as skipping lunch to get office work done, may be unimportant and produce little dissonance, but buying a fishing boat can result in considerable dissonance.

The second variable is the attractiveness of the chosen alternative. Other considerations being about equal, the less attractive the chosen alternative, the greater the dissonance. Chances are you will experience more dissonance from buying a fishing boat that was more a skiing boat (that your wife wanted) than a fishing boat (that you wanted).

Third, the greater the perceived attractiveness of the unchosen alternative, the stronger one feels the dissonance. If you really wanted to purchase an RV instead of the boat, you will experience dissonance.

Finally, the greater the degree of similarity or overlap between alternatives, the less the dissonance. If you are debating between two similar boats, making a decision in favor of one will not result in much dissonance, but if you are deciding between a boat and an RV, you will experience dissonance.

How does a persuader use dissonance to his or her advantage? This can occur when he or she wants to create change in his or her audience. For example, in political persuasion, a challenger will attempt to create dissonance in the minds of the voters by challenging one or more existing beliefs held about a popular incumbent. If the incumbent is perceived as being honest, the challenger may suggest evidence to the contrary, even if that evidence is not verifiable. The goal is to place doubt in the audience's mind about the incumbent's reputation, and not to prove that the incumbent actually is dishonest. If the message is repeated often enough, or if other claims of dishonesty are made to support the initial claim, then there is a strong possibility that the audience will accept the challenger's message. When this occurs, the audience suffers dissonance. Eventually, the audience will have to decide which candidate holds their trust, and that will happen on Election Day.

The persuader should consider the opportunities in using cognitive dissonance as a motivating principle. It is difficult to create dissonance when: (1) the belief is held with strong conviction, and (2) there is public commitment to the belief; but it is not impossible. Beliefs that are more easily disconfirmed tend to be those that do not require real physical proof or evidence. The key for the persuader who seeks to create dissonance is to create conflicting beliefs that the audience has, or conflicting beliefs with actions that the audience must take. This dissonance creates a tension, and tension reduction is sought by changing existing evaluations. This then leads to alternative choices.

Expectancy Theory

Victor H. Vroom, a professor and trained psychologist from the Yale School of Organization and Management, researched the behavior of groups and formal organizations. He gained a particular interest in the work behaviors of the individual—for example, behaviors which affect or are otherwise relevant to the workplace that people perform. This included the phenomenon of occupational choice as well as job satisfaction and job performance. From this research, he developed what he called the Concept of Expectancy (1964),[22] also known today as **expectancy theory**. Vroom states that the specific outcomes, or rewards, achieved by a person are dependent not only on the choices that he or she makes but also on the events which are beyond his or her control. For example, a person who decides to buy a lottery ticket is not certain that his or her ticket is the one that will win the lottery. Whether or not he or she does win the lottery is a function of many chance events. Similarly, the person who seeks political office is seldom certain that he or she will win the election; the student who submits an application for a scholarship can't be assured that he or she will be awarded one; and the worker who goes up for promotion isn't guaranteed that he or she will get it. Vroom says that most decision-making situations involve some element of risk, and the theories of choice behavior must be reconciled with

Expectancy theory

The specific outcomes, or rewards, achieved by a person are dependent not only on the choices that he or she makes but also on the events which are beyond his or her control.

the role of these risks in determining choices that people do make.[23]

Whenever a person chooses between alternatives which involve uncertain outcomes, it is apparent that his or her behavior is affected not only by his or her preferences among these outcomes but also by the degree to which he or she believes these outcomes are probable. Psychologists may refer to these beliefs as expectancies. Expectancy is defined as a momentary belief concerning the likelihood that a particular act will be followed by a particular outcome. Vroom adds that "Expectancies may be described in terms of their strength. Maximal strength is indicated by subjective certainty that the act will be followed by the outcome while minimal (or zero) strength is indicated by subjective certainty that the act will not be followed by the outcome" (p. 17).

Basically, according to Vroom, there are two types of conditions that affect the likelihood that people will work. The first is economic in nature. If people are going to work, then there must be some opportunity to work. Producers must have a demand for their goods and services, and employers must have a demand for people to produce these goods and perform these services. The second type of conditional, says Vroom, is motivational. A person would rather work than not work. Expectancy theory leads us to predict that, given the opportunity, a person will choose to work when the strength of the outcomes (rewards) which he or she expects to achieve from working are more positive than the strength of the outcomes which he or she expects to achieve from not working. For example, a person loses his or her job and collects unemployment. Is the motivation to take another job that pays about the same amount as unemployment stronger than the motivation to remain on unemployment? There may be events that will influence the decision-making process, such as the person's unemployment may expire in two weeks; or the job has a promise of a substantial pay increase within 30 days of hire.

These two types of conditions—economic and motivational—may vary independently of one another. It is the motivational aspect of this that small group communications is interested in. We want to understand the motivational significance of outcomes which group members attain through task achievement. In other words, does each member meet or exceed his or her expectations at the end of each task? If so, what motivated him or her to perform well; if not, why not? Expectancy theory emphasizes self-interest in the alignment of awards (outcomes) with group member wants, needs, or desires. It also addresses why members view certain outcomes as attractive or unattractive. It emphasizes the connections among expected behaviors, rewards, and group goals. And it is concerned with individual perceptions and provision for feedback.

Expectancy Violations Theory

Expectancy violations theory, developed by Judee Burgoon (1978),[24] proposes that emotional experience and expression (verbal and nonverbal) can be understood according to what experiences and expressions are expected in interpersonal relationships, the extent to which expressions that have been displayed deviate positively or negatively from expectancies, the degree to which other types of expectancy violations create emotional expressions, and the effects of deviating from firmly held patterns of emotional expression. According to the theory, we have expectations about the behavior of another person based on social norms as well as our previous experience with that other person and the context in which the behavior occurs. In other words, this means that individuals anticipate people they interact with to behave in certain ways. When our expectations are violated, we will respond in specific ways. If an act is unexpected and we interpret it favorably, and it is evaluated positively, it will produce more favorable outcomes than an expected act with the same interpretation and evaluation. These expectations can involve virtually any verbal or nonverbal behavior, including, for example, eye contact, distance, and haptics (touching). For example, has a stranger in a crowd ever stared at you? No matter how hard you attempted to avoid eye contact, didn't it make you feel uncomfortable? This type of aggressive behavior from a stranger generally causes a heightened sense of arousal and discomfort because you do not expect an unfamiliar individual to stare at you.

Stephen Littlejohn[25] (1999) states that the common assumption is that when expectancies are met, the other person's behaviors are judged as positive; and when they are violated, the behaviors are judged as negative; however, Burgoon has found that this is not always the case.[26] Violations are often judged favorably. Let's use the above example with the stranger staring at you. Not only does the stranger stare at you, he begins to move toward you. How do you now feel—uneasy? The expectancy violation theory explains this feeling of uneasiness. Before you have a chance to move away, he yells out your name, "Hey, aren't you so and so? Don't you remember me? We met at the John's party a few weeks ago." You feel relieved. The expectancy violation is now viewed favorably.

Whether judged as good or bad, violations cause the perceiver to be aroused. A stranger staring at you, or standing too close to you, can trigger feelings that your expectations are being violated. In some cases, you may feel comfortable with the violation; in others, you may feel discomfort. What is key is that a generally unnoticed behavior now becomes noticeable. Interpretation depends upon the perception of the individual whose expectations are being violated.

When your expectations are met, the behavior goes unnoticed; but when your expectations are violated, you become aware of that violation. Your inclination is to interpret, then evaluate the behavior. An important variable in the evaluation process is reward valence, or the degree to which you find the interaction rewarding. Conversely, valence may be negative, depending upon the cost/benefit ratio. We can identify six propositions of expectancy violation theory:[27]

1. Interactants develop expectations about the nonverbal communication of others.
2. Violations of communication expectations are arousing and distracting, causing an intentional shift to the communicator, relationships, and violation characteristics and meanings.
3. Communicator reward valence moderates the interpretation of ambiguous communicative behaviors.
4. Communicator reward valence moderates evaluation of communicative behaviors.
5. Enacted behaviors that are more favorably evaluated than expected behaviors constitute positive violations; enacted behaviors that are less favorably evaluated than expected are negative violations.
6. Positive violations produce more favorable outcomes, and negative violations produce more unfavorable ones relative to expectancy confirmation.

In summary, the expectations violation theory can be used to explain both non-verbal and verbal expectations. We know that individuals react differently to communicative behaviors. Violations can be positive or negative, depending on the person's opinion of the individual interacting with him or her. If a violation is positive and communicated by a high-valence source, then the outcome will be viewed more favorably and vice-versa. Our behavioral expectations of others will either be confirmed or violated, and the people who interact and the context they are interacting in will determine the valence.

How can we use expectancy violation theory in group work? There are times when members expect certain behaviors from the leader. As a means of augmenting a particular point in an argument, one may do the opposite of what is expected. When this is used as a stimulus-response tactic, the act becomes memorable. Group members correlate the behavior with a particular proposition of the argument. If the leader has high-valence with the group, then the behavior becomes remembered favorably. If repeated, the act then replaces the proposition in the minds of the members, and the leader merely has to recreate the act in order to initiate recall.

Attribution Theory

Another behavioral theory of persuasion is the attribution theory. **Attribution theory** focuses on causal inferences. It attempts to explain how people account for the actions of others. Unlike scientific psychology, which attempts to determine the actual causes of behavior, naïve psychology, as attribution theory

Attribution theory

Attempts to explain how people account for the actions of others.

is sometimes called, centers on the perceived causes of behavior by ordinary people every day in life. Fritz Heider, founder of attribution theory, drew attention to the fact that it was valuable to understand and appreciate the average person's naïve or commonsense explanations for the surrounding external environment (the world at large). He was the first to draw upon the kinds of distinctions people generate when making attributions. Heider differentiated between the scientific community's explaining the world at large—through the creation of hypotheses, engaging in systematic observations, completing statistical analyses to test hypotheses, and refuting any competing or alternative explanation for a relationship—and the naïve explanations of the average layperson who is not scientifically trained. However, Heider was the first to recognize that people (laypersons) do, in fact, make inferences in a basically logical and analytical manner.

It is basic human nature to want to understand and make sense of the world and the behavior of others. By analyzing the context of an action or situation, we attribute a motive, cause, or reason for someone's behavior. We form impressions of others based on those observations. In evaluating this behavior, we must ask to what extent the behavior we observe is a reflection of the person's personality or to what extent it is a circumstance of a situation. Attribution theorists have studied how we decide whether to attribute an observed behavior to internal (personality) or external (situational) causes.

Heider outlines several causal attributions that people commonly make. These include situational causes (being affected by the environment), personal effects (influencing things personally), ability (being able to do something), effort (trying to do something), desire (wanting to do it), sentiment (feeling like it), belonging (going along with something), obligation (feeling you ought to), and permission (being permitted to). A one-to-one relationship does not exist between the observed behavior and the cause. Many types of behaviors may be perceived as originating from a single cause, or one behavior may be the result of several causes.

© Andresr, 2011. Under license from Shutterstock, Inc.

An important consideration based on attribution theory is that we actively infer reasons for our own behavior; that is, we try to rationalize our behavior so we can justify it. We also infer reasons for the behavior of others. Examining how we analyze ourselves provides insight into developing arguments for persuading people to act in a certain way. A persuader can provide reasons to justify desired behavior. Listing positive consequences of desired behavior can increase commitment to that particular behavior. There are problems with this approach. There is no certainty of correct or precise interpretation of individual motives, and such an approach encourages oversimplification of human behavior.

So what does this mean for the source of a persuasive message in group work? As a source, you should realize that your audience is likely to make internal attributions for your behavior; they are likely to ignore situational circumstances that may have dictated your behavior; they will hold you accountable for your failures and misfortunes; and if you have the good fortune to have a positive reputation, this may overshadow negative interpretations of your future actions.

For group members who are the recipients of persuasive messages, attribution errors can result in misperceptions. A member may prematurely discredit a source, or members may be led to form an unsubstantiated positive impression of a persuader. To accurately compare the merits of competing persuasive messages, the member must be careful of prematurely discrediting a persuader or creating an invalid positive impression.

The task for the persuader is to figure out how certain messages or behaviors will be interpreted. What makes the process complex is that human perception plays a major role in interpreting the messages of others.[28] Because no two people process information the same way, attributions of intent can vary within members exposed to the same persuasion. One member may praise the leader for defending a controversial policy; another may condemn the very same effort as a collection of cleverly worded half-truths.

It is important to remember that although attribution theory appears to be less than precise, the fact is that an analysis of our own behavior or the behavior of others provides useful information about how persuasion and motivation work.

MODELS OF BELIEF CHANGE

Behavior is almost never caused or influenced by only one or two beliefs or by a single attitude. Behaviors we engage in are shaped by beliefs about behavior and its consequences, our attitudes (likes and dislikes), and the pressure to behave in a normative manner (the pressure to behave in ways others expect us to behave). In this part of the chapter, we will look at ways in which receivers combine information in order to form attitudes and to make decisions about behavior.

Theory of Reasoned Action

Icek Ajzen and Martin Fishbein[29] have developed a **theory of reasoned action**, a theory that helps explain how attitudes guide behavior. According to the theory, the most important influence or cause of a person's behavior is **behavior intent**. The individual's intention to perform a behavior is a combination of attitude toward performing the behavior and subjective norm. It is clear in the way it treats the link between beliefs and attitude. The theory makes the assumptions that: (1) human beings are rational and make systematic use of information available to them; and (2) that people consider the implications of their actions before they decide to engage or not engage in certain behaviors. A person's attitude is a function of one's salient beliefs about behavior. Ajzen and Fishbein argue:

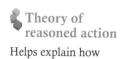

Theory of reasoned action

Helps explain how attitudes guide behavior.

People consider the implications of their actions before they decide to engage or not engage in a given behavior. For this reason we refer to our approach as a theory of reasoned action.... We make the assumption that most actions of social relevance are under volitional control and, consistent with this assumption, our theory views a person's intention to perform (or to not perform) a behavior as the immediate determinant of action.[30]

The theory of reasoned action looks at behavioral intentions as being the immediate antecedent to behavior. It is believed that the stronger a person's intention to perform a particular behavior, the more successful he or she is expected to be. Intentions are a function of salient beliefs and/or information about the likelihood that performing a particular behavior will lead to a specific outcome. Intentions can also change over time. The longer the time period between intention and behavior, the greater the likelihood that unforeseen events will produce changes in intentions. Ajzen and Fishbein theorize that intentions are a function of two basic determinants: (1) attitude toward behavior, and (2) subjective norms of behavior.[31]

An attitude is the first antecedent of behavioral intention. The attitude component refers to the specific action under consideration (e.g., to buy an automobile or not). It is a person's positive or negative belief about performing a specific behavior. These beliefs are called **behavioral beliefs**. A person will intend to perform a certain behavior when he or she evaluates it positively. Attitudes are determined by the individual's beliefs about the consequences of performing the behavior (behavioral beliefs), weighted by his or her evaluation of those consequences (outcome evaluations). Those attitudes are believed to have a direct effect on behavioral intention and are linked with subjective norm and perceived behavioral control.

People's intentions are affected by both their attitude toward a possible behavior and the subjective norms regarding that behavior. The norm component considers the expectations of other people about behavior. According to the theory, the individual constructs this attitude toward the behavior by a careful analysis of available information. This attitude is a function of the person's beliefs concerning the likely outcomes to result from performing the behavior and the person's positive or negative feelings about those outcomes.[32]

Subjective norms are also assumed to be a function of beliefs that specific individuals approve or disapprove of performing the behavior. Beliefs that underlie subjective norms are termed **normative beliefs**. An individual will intend to perform a certain behavior when he or she perceives that others who are important to them think he or she should. Those important to them might be a person's spouse, close friends, physician, and so forth. This is assessed by asking individuals to judge how likely it is that most people who are important to them would approve or disapprove of their performing a given behavior. Essentially, individuals calculate the costs and benefits associated with social behavior.

Ajzen modified the Theory of Reasoned Action by adding a third antecedent of intention called **perceived behavioral control** and renamed this the Theory of Planned Behavior, also referred to as a conscious deliberation of factors. There are four components to the theory:

1. Attitude toward the behavior is the first determinant of behavioral intention. It is the degree to which the person has a favorable or unfavorable evaluation of the behavior in question. Our attitudes toward a behavior result from our general beliefs about the potential consequences of the behavior and our evaluation of the likelihood of such consequences or outcomes of the behavior.

2. Subjective norm is considered the second predictor of behavioral intention. This is the influence of social pressure that is perceived by the individual (normative beliefs) to perform or not to perform a certain behavior. Each referent exerting that social pressure is evaluated in terms of the extent to which the individual is motivated to comply with the referent's opinion or pressure.

3. Perceived behavioral control is the third antecedent of behavioral intention. This construct is defined as the individual's belief concerning how easy or difficult performing the behavior will be. It often reflects actual behavioral control.

4. Behavioral intention is an indication of how hard people are willing to try and of how much an effort they are planning to exert, in order to perform the behavior. This is influenced by three components: a person's attitude toward performing the behavior, the perceived social pressure, called subjective norm, and perceived behavioral control.[33]

There are a number of implications for persuasion that can be inferred from this theory.[34] The first four stem from altering components in the attitude construct:[35]

1. **Change the total number of beliefs to be considered by the individual.** Persuaders can increase the number of beliefs which are related to the targeted behavior. For example, everyone knows that chewing tobacco leads to oral cancer. Persuasive messages can add additional health risks or beliefs concerning chewing tobacco, including the fact that it causes stomach cancer and throat cancer, and that it permanently stains your teeth.

2. **Change the belief strength of the receiver's held beliefs.** Despite years of public service announcements and warnings about chewing tobacco, especially directed toward young athletes in school, many people still question the link between chewing tobacco and various health risks. They have the attitude that it won't happen to them or any harm derived is years away. Therefore, one way of influencing them is to provide plenty of messages aimed at convincing the receivers that they personally are susceptible to various health risks and consequences of oral cancer.

3. **Change the evaluations by which receivers rate the consequences of the beliefs.** Persuaders want to increase the positive evaluations of beliefs which support

© Gemenacom, 2011. Under license from Shutterstock, Inc.

adherence to their message, while increasing the negative evaluations of beliefs which oppose the action advocated or desired by the persuader. One can easily emphasize the undesirability of any of the negative consequences associated with chewing tobacco, such as asking those who chew if they would like to "lick a spittoon," for example, thus making sure that there are plenty of highly negative evaluations of the various beliefs associated with chewing tobacco.

4. **Change the configuration of beliefs in order to make certain beliefs more salient.** The best way of actually adopting this plan of action is to group beliefs into several types, link the beliefs to an overarching goal or value, and have the individual decide between two divergent viewpoints. For example, if an individual had thoroughly studied all aspects of buying a new car, a salesperson (the persuader) may group together all beliefs concerning safety (for example, how safe the car is in an accident, how it protects children, what the car's record is for repairs, whether air bags afford protection, and how it performs in rain and snow), and then group together all the beliefs dealing with saving money. Ultimately, the persuader (salesman) wants to raise the fundamental question: Which is more important, safety of one's family members or saving a few dollars?

The theory of planned behavior may explain how attitudes guide behavior; it also suggests why attitudes may not predict behavior. For example, while we may think that the excessive drinking of alcoholic beverages is not healthy for us, peer pressure and the act of binging by well-liked heroes and celebrities may influence the decision to binge drink.

Social Judgment Theory

Social Judgment theory comes from the work of psychologist Muzafer Sherif and his associates, and addresses the way people make judgments about messages.[36] This study challenged a long-standing view that a person could compare two statements on a given issue and judge which of the two statements was more favorable (or unfavorable) to that issue.[37] Does the individual's view on an issue influence his ability to identify the differences among positions taken in regard to an issue? Does an individual's attitude toward an issue act as an *anchor* point from which he or she evaluates other views toward the issue? The theory suggests that any attempt at persuasion must focus on the receiver of the message. Basically, this principle argues that we have categories of judgment by which we evaluate persuasive positions.

Anchors
Reference points, are the beliefs, attitudes, and biases of the individual; they are key elements in deciding what type of message will be most effective.

Individuals make judgments on the basis of **anchors**, or reference points. These anchors are the beliefs, attitudes, and biases of the individual, and they are key elements in deciding what type of message will be most effective. Sherif argues that people do not evaluate messages based on merit alone. In social perception, anchors are internal and based on past experience. The internal anchor, or reference point, is always present and influences the way a person responds to a message. They compare arguments with their current attitudes and decide if they should accept one of the argued positions.[38]

Sherif included one more critical element to social judgment theory—**ego involvement**. The more important the issue is to one's ego, the stronger the anchor will influence what is understood. This additional theory treats attitudes and beliefs as a continuum in which there is a range of acceptable positions, a range of neutral feelings, and a range of unacceptable positions. Individuals judge messages based on both internal anchors and ego involvement. The more relevant the issue is to one's self-image, the stronger the anchoring position.[39]

In order to understand how our internal anchors (or reference points) function in relation to attitude change, we must consider three important concepts: latitudes of acceptance, rejection, and noncommitment. The first, **latitudes of acceptance**, consists of all the attitudinal positions around the anchor on a particular topic that we find acceptable. On many issues, there is a range of positions that people can accept. Persuasive messages that fall within this latitude of acceptance generally tend to be more successful.

Between the latitudes of acceptance and rejection is the latitude of **noncommitment**. In this level, there is little issue involvement by the individual. An individual no longer accepts some positions, but he or she doesn't reject them either. Situational considerations become more of a concern—such as the character of the speaker, nonverbal attributions, and so forth.

In contrast, the **latitude of rejection** consists of those options that a person would not choose. They would be the least tolerable, sometimes bordering on the repugnant. Messages that fall within this range will not encourage attitude change.

The most important factor determining latitude size is issue involvement. Therefore, it is important to know where the latitude of acceptance ends and the latitude of rejection begins. There are many persuasive implications for this theory. Assimilation constitutes persuasion, but assimilation and persuasion are not the same; contrast effect represents failure to persuade.[40] Judgment is crucial to persuasion. If you offer positions that people judge as reject, you are not going to persuade. According to the theory, judgment occurs very rapidly. People do not passively assimilate information; then make judgments. Rather, they make these judgments as they receive the information (transactional communication):[41]

A change in attitude, therefore, implies change in his categories for evaluation, which amounts to changing a part of himself; and it implies manifest change in the patterned behaviors from which they are inferred. The frame of reference for studying attitude change, therefore, includes the individual's stand and his degree of involvement in it, which affects the extent to which it is the major anchor in a communication situation. It includes the communication itself, its form, and the order of arguments. It includes the communicator and the source, both of which affect the extent to which the position presented in communication anchors the individual's subsequent appraisals of the issue. This, a source and speaker with high standing or prestige in the person's eyes, in effect, enhances the anchoring function of the advocated position. Similarly, any event or procedure that successfully involves the individual in a position presented to him, such as the necessity of doing a good job of presenting it or defending it himself, increases the salience of that position as an anchor when he subsequently evaluates the issue.[42]

From the perspective of *Social Judgment Theory,* it explains: (1) the process of information evaluation, (2) distortions in evaluation, and (3) how the task of the persuader changes as a result of issue involvement. The issue of anchor points helps us to understand how positions or persuasive arguments are compared and contrasted. Assimilation and contrast effects demonstrate misleading alterations in the evaluation process, which we, as message receivers, should attempt to avoid. Finally, the scope of our ability to make judgments visually demonstrates how difficult the persuasion task is, under conditions of low and high issue involvement. If our audience is known to favor an idea similar to ours or is at least noncommittal, it may take only one or two attempts to have messages assimilated into the scope of acceptance.[43] If the audience is highly ego-involved and opposed to a particular position, a single message will more than likely be rejected. Persuasion would require many messages over a long period of time, each gradually expanding the latitude of acceptance and slowly moving the favorite position (another belief).[44]

Compliance Gaining

 **Compliance gaining**

Trying to get people to do what you want them to do, or to stop doing something you don't like.

Compliance gaining, trying to get people to do what you want them to do, or to stop doing something you don't like, is a controversial theory for many researchers. Compliance gaining is one of several types of communication that have been studied from a person-centered perspective.[45] Compliance-gaining messages are among the most researched in the field of communication. We will focus on the three most influential.[46]

Gerald Marwell and David Schmitt[47] introduced compliance-gaining research and strategies to the field of communication in 1967. They isolated sixteen strategies commonly used in gaining the compliance of other people (a completely satisfactory list has yet to be developed).

Compliance-gaining strategies, according to Marwell and Schmitt, use an exchange-theory approach. This approach, which is often used in social theory, is based on the assumption that individuals basically act to gain something from other individuals in exchange for something else. This model is inherently power-oriented; you can gain the compliance of others if you have sufficient resources to give them what they want.

Marwell and Schmitt's Compliance-Gaining Strategies

1. **Promising.** Promising a reward for compliance.
2. **Threatening.** Indicating that punishment will be applied for noncompliance.
3. **Showing expertise about positive outcomes.** Showing how good things will happen to those who comply.
4. **Showing expertise about negative outcomes.** Showing how bad things will happen to those who will not comply.
5. **Liking.** Displaying friendliness.

6. **Pregiving.** Giving a reward before asking for compliance.
7. **Applying averse stimulation.** Applying punishment until compliance is achieved.
8. **Calling in a debt.** Saying the person owes something for past favors.
9. **Making moral appeals.** Describing compliance as the morally right thing to do.
10. **Attributing positive feelings.** Telling the other person how good he or she will feel if there is compliance.
11. **Attributing negative feelings.** Telling the other person how bad he or she will feel if there is noncompliance.
12. **Positive altercasting.** Associating compliance with people with good qualities.
13. **Negative altercasting.** Associating noncompliance with people with bad qualities.
14. **Seeking altruistic compliance.** Seeking compliance strictly as a favor.
15. **Showing positive esteem.** Saying that the person will be liked by others more if he or she complies.
16. **Showing negative esteem.** Saying that the person will be liked less by others if he or she does not comply.

One of the most important theoretical questions about compliance-gaining tactics has been how to reduce the list of all possible tactics to a manageable set of general strategies or dimensions. A long list of how to persuade others does not tell you much more than you already know. A shorter list would crystallize the tactics into essential qualities, functions, goals, or some other set of dimensions that would help explain what people are actually accomplishing when they try to persuade other people.[48]

Marwell and Schmitt asked subjects to apply the sixteen strategies to various compliance-gaining situations in an attempt to create such a set of principles. From analysis of these data, five general strategies, or clusters of tactics emerged: rewarding (for example, promising something in return for compliance), punishing (threatening a negative consequence), expertise (as in displaying knowledge of rewards), impersonal commitments (appeals to morality), and personal commitments (calling in a debt owed).

Schenck-Hamlin, Wiseman, and Georgacarakos (1982) produced a much more complicated means with which to classify compliance-gaining strategies.[49] This research group developed a scheme based on strategies that subjects indicated they actually used because they were concerned about the lack of a theoretical basis for taxonomies such as those created by Marwell and Schmitt. Schenk-Hamlin, et al., suggest that we should distinguish between appeals and the manner in which the appeal is presented. They isolated four factors in their model. The first is the degree to which the persuader reveals the compliance-gaining goals. Does the persuader reveal the objective(s) of the message? A persuader may use strategies that are direct. The directness of a strategy concerns the degree to which the persuader's intent is obvious. For example, a cosmetics clerk may say, "I'm going to sell you makeup that will make you sexy." A more subtle strategy for the cosmetics clerk would be indirectness. This is a tricky approach: "I'm not really the cosmetics clerk, but I can tell you what types of makeup would make you sexy." And other approaches may be purposely mis-leading: "I couldn't help noticing you trying on that makeup while shopping. May I show you some that would definitely make you sexier?" Choices of strat-egies are contextually dependent.

The second factor of compliance gaining is based on sanctions, needs, and reasons and explanations. **Sanctions** motivate individuals through the use of punishments and rewards. Sanctions are messages that illustrate how receivers will benefit by modifying an attitude, belief, or action, or how receivers may be punished by maintaining their existing attitude, belief, or action. **Needs** are appeals to human motivations and values. People are often motivated to satisfy belonging, self-esteem, self-awareness, or self-improvement needs. A receiver may act on a needs-based persuasive message because it may be associated with affirming values important to the receiver, such as patriotism, religious belief, or family ideals. Reasons and explanations are rationales that appeal to evidence or support. A persuader may introduce rationales that provide reasons in sup-port of his or her argument.

The third factor of compliance gaining is whether the rationale for the ac-tion required is stated or implied. A simple request such as "Please close the door" implies a reason, but does not state it. "Would you please close the door because bugs are flying in" offers an explanation that provides a rationale for the request.

The fourth factor of compliance gaining addresses who controls the situa-tion; that is, the extent to which the persuader is dominant, passive, or equal. In the event that a persuader employs rewards or punishments, the persuader controls the outcome. When control is dominant, the receiver is restricted in his or her freedom to respond to the message and his or her choice of action. Conversely, guilt appeals place control with the other person.

Lawrence Wheeless, Robert Barraclough, and Robert Stewart (1983) per-formed one of the most comprehensive analyses of compliance-gaining litera-ture to produce a variety of compliance-gaining schemes.[50] These researchers believe that compliance-gaining messages are best classified according to the kinds of power employed by communicators when attempting to gain the com-pliance of another individual.[51] Power is access to influential resources. It is a result of interpersonal perception, since people have as much power as others perceive that they have.

The Wheeless group isolated three general types of power. The first is an individual's perceived ability to manipulate the consequences of a particular course of action. Parents often use this type of power when rewarding or pun-ishing children. In a compliance-gaining situation, parents may tell children that they will take them to the movies (a reward consequence) if they clean their rooms.

The second type of power is the perceived ability to determine one's re-lational position with the other person. Here, the person with the power can identify particular elements of the relationship that will induce the compliance. For example, if one person has more vested in a relationship than the other, that person may concede more to that other person for fear of losing the relationship.

Sanctions

Motivate individuals through the use of punishments and rewards.

Needs

Appeals to human motivations and values.

Examples of Sanctions, Needs, and Rationales

TABLE 6.1

Types of Appeals

Sanctions	Examples
fear	If you don't obey, terrible things will happen to you.
promise	If you do this, I will buy you a present.
ingratiation	I have done so many nice things for you that you should do what I ask.[52]
debt	You owe me for the last favor.
allurement	Other people will reward you for doing this.
aversive stimulation	I will make your life miserable until you do it.
warning	Other people will make you miserable if you don't do this.

Needs	
belonging	Other people will like you if you do this.
security	You will be safe if you do this.
esteem (positive)	You will be valued by others if you comply.
esteem (negative)	People will not think highly of you if you don't comply.

Rationales	
direct request	Please do this.
explanation	This is the logical thing to do (evidence provided).

The third type of power employs the perceived ability to define values or obligations or both. In this compliance scenario, one individual has the credibility to tell the other person what norms of behavior are accepted or necessary. Returning a favor is an example of this. One communicator defines what is right and acceptable, and the other individual complies by behaving in accordance with this standard.[53]

In a compliance-gaining situation, an individual assesses his or her power and chooses tactics that invoke that power. Attitude change expressed from compliance pressures represents an observable adoption of the persuader's position without personal acceptance of it. The opinions may not be adopted because the individual that the compliance-gaining tactics are directed toward believes in their content; rather, he or she adopts simply to acquire some external or internal incentives.[54]

What we have discussed in explaining compliance gaining addresses primarily short-term goal achievement. Enlisting long-term compliance, especially long-term lifestyle change compliance, is a significant problem. A persuader will need to reassess his or her communication strategies in order to achieve this. A review of language expectancy and reinforcement principles necessary to advance a propositional framework relating communication strategies for long-term compliance that will motivate and guide an individual's future actions will be challenging.

MOTIVATIONAL RESEARCH

Motives Are the "Why's" of Behavior

All humans have needs, and needs are the fundamental building blocks to understanding the persuasive process. Human needs are what drive us to action and what motivate our behavior.[55] Working to satisfy needs gives us pleasure; they motivate achievement and progress. Sometimes their influence on us is so strong that we do things we normally wouldn't do. We can appeal to someone's needs if we understand them. We can influence his or her behavior. We can persuade him or her to do something that he or she normally would not do. We will look at three general approaches to motivational research: Maslow's Inventory of Needs, Murray's Inventory of Psychogenic Needs, and Alderfer's ERG theory.

MOTIVATIONAL THEORIES

Maslow's Hierarchy of Needs

Abraham Maslow was a humanistic psychologist who developed a hierarchic theory of needs that focuses on the well-adjusted, emotionally healthy individual. Humanists do not believe that human beings are pushed and pulled by mechanical forces—either stimuli and reinforcements (behaviorism) or of unconscious instinctual impulses (psychoanalysis). Humanists focus on an individual's potentials. They believe that humans strive for higher level capabilities; that they seek to test the boundaries of creativity, the highest areas of consciousness and wisdom. Without denying the importance of a person's innate needs, Maslow stresses the urge toward self-actualization (peak experiences of happiness and fulfillment), and asserts that a general motivational hierarchy exists where the needs of certain lower or deficiency motives must be satisfied before the needs of the higher or *being* motives can be met. Individuals who achieve this consciousness—the higher or being motives—are labeled fully functioning person, healthy personality, or the self-actualizing person.[56]

All of these needs Maslow considers to be instinctive, with the very basic ones equivalent to that of animals. One of the many interesting things Maslow noticed while he worked with monkeys early in his career was that some needs take precedence over others. For example, if you are hungry and thirsty, you will tend to try to take care of the thirst first. After all, you can do without food for weeks, but you can only do without water for a couple of days. Thirst is a stronger need than hunger. Similarly, if you are very, very thirsty, but someone has put a choke hold on you and you can't breathe, which is more important? The need to breathe, of course. On the other hand, sex is less powerful than any of these. Maslow took this idea and created his now famous hierarchy of needs.

Aside from the particulars of air, water, food, and sex, he described five broader layers: the physiological needs (health, food, sleep), the needs for safety and security (shelter, removal from danger), the needs for love and belonging (love, affection, being part of groups), the needs for esteem (self-esteem and esteem of others), and the need to actualize the self (achieving individual potential), in that order. Beyond these five basic needs are higher levels of needs. These include the needs for understanding, aesthetic appreciation and spiritual needs. In the levels of the five basic needs, the person does not elevate himself or herself to the second need until the first need has been met or satisfied. Once that happens, the person strives to achieve the next level, then the next, until he or she has satisfied all levels.

© tonobalaguerf, 2011. Under license from Shutterstock, In.

Physiological Needs

These are biological needs—the maintenance of the human body. They include the needs we have for oxygen, water, protein, salt, sugar, minerals, vitamins, and so forth. Also, there are the needs to be active, to rest, to sleep, to get rid of bodily wastes, to avoid pain, and to have sex. They are the strongest needs because if a person were deprived of all needs, the physiological ones would come first in the person's search for satisfaction. If we are not well, then anything else really doesn't matter. Without question, these are the most powerful of all needs. If survival needs are not met, all of a person's mental and physical energy is focused on getting food, water, and shelter. All other needs are forgotten.

Safety Needs

After we have satisfied all of our physiological needs, the needs for safety come next. Safety needs include our need for security, freedom from harm, anxiety, and fear. A peaceful and stable society generally makes people feel safe from wild animals, criminal assault, murder, chaos, tyranny, and the like. Adults usually have little awareness of their security needs, except in times of emergency or when they are faced with social uncertainties. The satisfaction of this needs category provides us with a stable world.[57]

Needs of Love, Affection, and Belongingness

When we have satisfied our needs for safety and physiological well-being, the next class of needs is for love, affection, and belongingness. Maslow states that people seek to overcome feelings of loneliness and alienation. There is a need

to be with others, both giving and receiving love, affection, and a desire for social cohesion. In our day-to-day life, we exhibit these needs in our desires to marry, have a family, be a part of a community, a member of a church, a brother in the fraternity, a part of a gang or a bowling club. It is also a part of what we look for in a career. We have a strong desire to achieve these goals.

Needs for Esteem

After the first three classes of needs have been satisfied, the needs for a little self-esteem now become foremost. Esteem needs may be characterized by achievement, adequacy, mastery, competence, independence, and freedom. Maslow notes two versions of esteem needs, a lower one and a higher one. The lower one is the need for the respect of others—the need for status, prestige, fame, glory, social recognition, attention, reputation, appreciation, dignity, even dominance. The higher form involves the need for self-respect, including such feelings as confidence, competence, achievement, mastery, independence, and freedom. When these needs are satisfied, the person feels self-confident and valuable as a person. The negative version of these needs is low self-esteem, weakness, a sense of helplessness, feelings of being worthless, and development of inferiority complexes.

FIGURE 6.1
Maslow's
Hierarchy
of Needs

All of the preceding four levels Maslow calls deficit needs, or D-needs. If you don't have enough of something—i.e., you have a deficit—you feel the need. But if you get all you need, you feel nothing at all. In other words, they cease to be motivating. Maslow sees all these needs as essentially survival needs. Even love and esteem are needed for the maintenance of health. He says we all have these needs built in to us genetically, like instincts. In fact, he calls them instinct-like needs.

Needs for Self-Actualization

The last level is a bit different. Maslow has used a variety of terms to refer to this level: He has called it growth motivation (in contrast to deficit motivation), being needs (or B-needs, in contrast to D-needs), and self-actualization. As a person progresses from deficiency needs to growth needs, extrinsic rewards, such as money and status (which are so important at level four), are replaced by intrinsic rewards. Now, the person is motivated to excel for the sheer joy of the task or activity. An intrinsic reward is an intense satisfaction that comes from within the individual. Once this level of needs is engaged, they continue to be felt. In fact, they are likely to become stronger as we feed them. They involve the continuous desire to fulfill potentials, to "be all that you can be," like the Army recruitment slogan. They are a matter of becoming the most complete, the fullest you—hence the term, self-actualization.[58]

Murray's Inventory of Psychogenic Needs

The second approach to identifying and classifying human needs is Murray's Inventory of Psychogenic Needs. Like Maslow, Murray attempts to catalogue motives; however, it is impossible to make an adequate inventory because the motivational complexity of humans and the disagreement between scholars regarding what energy states can properly be called motives make any list impossible. Murray identifies twelve physiological needs and 28 psychogenic needs, which may be said to be our social-psychological needs or motives. The following reflects Murray's list as reproduced by Hilgard, Atkinson, and Atkinson.[59]

A. Needs associated chiefly with inanimate objects

1. Acquisition: the need to gain possessions and property.
2. Conservation: the need to collect, repair, clean, and preserve things.
3. Orderliness: the need to arrange, organize, put away objects; to be tidy and clean; to be precise.
4. Retention: the need to retain possession of things; to be heard; to hoard; to be frugal, economical, and miserly.
5. Construction: the need to organize and build.

B. Needs expressing ambition, will power, desire for accomplishment and prestige

6. Superiority: the need to excel, a composite of achievement and recognition.
7. Achievement: the need to overcome obstacles, to exercise power, to strive to do something difficult as well as quickly as possible.
8. Recognition: the need to excite praise and commendation; to command respect.
9. Exhibition: the need for self-dramatization; to excite, amuse, stir, shock, thrill others.
10. Inviolacy: the need remain inviolate, to prevent a depreciation of self-respect, to preserve one's good name.
11. Avoidance of inferiority: the need to avoid failure, shame, humiliation, ridicule.
12. Defensiveness: the need to defend oneself against blame or belittlement; to justify one's actions.
13. Counteraction: the need to overcome defeat by striving again and retaliating.

C. Needs having to do with human power exerted, resisted, or yielded to

14. Dominance: the need to influence or control others.
15. Deference: the need to admire and willingly follow a superior; to serve gladly.
16. Similance: the need to imitate or emulate others; to agree and believe.
17. Autonomy: the need to resist influence, to strive for independence.
18. Contrariness: the need to act differently from others; to be unique; to take the opposite side.

D. Needs having to do with injuring others or oneself

19. Aggression: the need to assault or injure another; to belittle, harm, or maliciously ridicule a person.
20. Abasement: the need to comply and accept punishment; self-depreciation.
21. Avoidance of blame: the need to avoid blame, ostracism, or punishment by inhibiting unconventional impulses; to be well behaved and obey the law.

E. Needs having to do with affection between people

22. Affiliation: the need to form friendships and associations.
23. Rejection: the need to be discriminating; to snub, ignore, or exclude another.
24. Nurturance: the need to nourish, aid, or protect another.
25. Succorance: the need to seek aid, protection, or sympathy; to be dependent.

F. Additional socially relevant needs

26. Play: the need to relax, amuse oneself, seek diversion and entertainment.
27. Cognizance: the need to explore, ask questions, satisfy curiosity.
28. Exposition: the need to point and demonstrate; to give information, explain, interpret, lecture.[60]

Alderfer's ERG Theory

Clayton Alderfer of Yale University[61] took Maslow's work on hierarchy of needs and revised and realigned it. He identified three core needs: existence, relatedness, and growth. If you compare Alderfer's groupings, they are similar to Maslow's hierarchy of needs: growth corresponds to self-actualization and esteem needs; existence grouping is similar to basic safety and physiological needs; and relatedness corresponds to social needs.

What does Alderfer's ERG theory add to our understanding of needs? Paul Hersey, et al. (2001) answer that by referring to Stephen Robbins'[62] comparative analysis of Alderfer's work to that of Maslow's. They suggest that Alderfer's work is a more valid description of the need hierarchy than is Maslow's theory for two principle reasons:[63] Table 6.2 illustrates these relationships.

Comparison of Maslow's and Alderfer's Categories of Needs	**TABLE 6.2**

Maslow	Alderfer
Self-Actualization/Esteem	Growth
Social	Relatedness
Safety/Physiological	Existence

"What's my motivation?"

Dan Piraro

1. Maslow's step-by-step hierarchy assumes that only one of the five categories of needs will be predominant at a given time. ERG theory allows for more than one need—for example, safety and social—to be operating more or less equally at one time.

2. Maslow's theory asserts that a person will remain at a need level until it is adequately satisfied. ERG theory suggests that a person frustrated or blocked at a need level will regress to a lower level.

Group leaders should be aware of some of the motivating factors that compel members to behave the way they do. Some may become obvious in the early stages of getting to know one another; others may take a bit of time to find out; some may never be discovered. If group members work together for a relatively long period of time, then some motivational needs become apparent. The primary way of determining needs is through observation and listening; we observe member behavior to a particular stimulus (usually an assigned task), and we listen for feedback from that member or other members. There are many influences for motivation—psychological, physical, and environmental. You cannot be expected to know all or most of them. But you should recognize that people do things for a reason. You may not identify it at the time, but it still exists. Once you have identified motivational needs, you can use them to your advantage in group work. For example, if you know that a particular member is a high achiever, that the more complex the task is, the greater he or she produces, then you assign complex tasks to that individual. You don't have to understand the psychological dynamics as to why he or she has such a high need; suffice to know that he or she thrives on such work. This is to your advantage. You might want to pair this person up with a member who is a low achiever.

In Chapter 5, we said that a good leader creates supportive conditions that enable members to facilitate goal achievement. And we identified one of those conditions as motivating tasks, in which the leader helps members understand what makes a job motivating. Motives arouse and maintain activity and determine the general direction of the behavior of an individual. **Motives**, or needs, are the catalysts of action. The need with the greatest strength at a particular moment determines behavior. We call these high-strength motives.[64]

A motive tends to decrease in strength if it is either satisfied or blocked from being satisfied. Generally speaking, satisfied or blocked needs normally do not motivate individuals to continue a behavior. People have many needs, all of which are continually competing. No one person has exactly the same mixture of strength of these needs as another. Some people are driven mainly by achievement; others are concerned primarily with security, and so on. Although you must recognize individual differences, leaders cannot presume to decide which motives are most important to group members. If you are to understand, predict, and control behavior, you must know what members really want from their assigned tasks. Leaders have to know their people to understand what motivates them; they cannot just make assumptions.[65]

Increasing Motive Strength

- **High-strength motive.** If an existing need increases in strength to the point that it now becomes the high-strength motive, it has the potential to change that behavior.
- **Cyclical patterns.** The strength of some needs tends to appear in a cyclical pattern. For example, you can eat a satisfying breakfast in the morning, but as the day passes you find yourself wanting to eat again. You've learned that the need for food recurs on a regular basis, no matter how much or little you ate previously. However, you can increase or delay the speed of this cyclical pattern affecting the environment. For example, a person's need for food may not be high-strength unless the immediate environment is changed such that the senses are exposed to the sight and aroma of tempting food.[66]

We can generally classify activities that are a result of high-strength needs into two categories: goal-directed activity and goal activity.

- **Goal-directed activity.** When a person is motivated to reach a particular goal, we call that a goal-directed activity. If a person's strongest need at a given moment is sleep, various activities such as looking for a place to nap, grab forty-winks, find a motel, or go to bed, would be considered goal-directed activities.
- **Goal activity.** A goal activity is the process of achieving the goal itself. With regard to sleep, a bed is the goal, and sleeping is the goal activity. Paul Hersey, et al. (2001, p. 29) aptly summarize the differences between the two:

An important distinction between these two classes of activities is their effect on the strength of the need. In goal-directed activity, the strength of the need tends to increase as one engages in the activity until the goal is reached or frustration sets in. Remember, frustration develops when one is continually blocked from reaching a goal. If the frustration becomes intense enough, the strength of the need may decrease until it is no longer potent enough to affect behavior—a person gives up. The strength of the need tends to increase as one engages in goal-directed activity; however, once goal activity begins, the strength of the need tends to decrease as one engages in it.

The question leaders must ask themselves before they attempt to motivate people is, "What do I want to influence?" The answer should be behavior. A word we will substitute for behavior is **performance**. Leaders motivate members' performance—their behavior. If we look at motivating people, we must **pinpoint** (being concise) behaviors, or performances that need to be improved.

The next question that a leader should ask when thinking about developing group performance is:

> "What area of my group's work or individual members' work do I need to influence?"

As leader, you need to identify areas that you believe need motivating. Does each member know specifically what his or her responsibilities are, or the goals and objectives? Have they been identified and understood by each member? Once the objectives or responsibilities are identified and understood, you must clearly specify what constitutes good performance in each area, so that you, the leader, and group members know when performance is approaching the desired level. It is the sole responsibility of the leader to specify what good performance looks like. (We'll discuss this in much more depth in Chapter 10—Goal Setting). It is improbable to motivate behavior in areas that are unclear. It is extremely important to remember that motivational needs, like positive reinforcement, must have value to the performer—each group member. This cannot be stressed enough. The value of the reinforcer/motivator lies with the performer. For example, "What are their needs?" or "What do they want from the group?"

© Atmostfear, 2011. Under license from Shutterstock, Inc.

Each individual member requires a different motivator to complete a specific task successfully—but the GOALS always remain the same. We'll conclude this chapter by identifying the Four R's that are typically used as motivators.

- **Recognition.** This occurs when a member is recognized by the group (and at times the organization) for the consistent, and sometimes outstanding, behaviors (task performance) that support group goals. It is as a symbolic means for showing appreciation for a particular accomplishment, usually in the form of a gold watch, plaque, or trophy.
- **Reinforcement.** This is the strengthening of behavior by following it with positive (R+) or negative (R-) reinforcers.[67]
- **Reward.** This is usually given for some outstanding accomplishment. A reward is a tangible item; and it can take the form of money, gifts, a trip, or time off, for example, that is intended to influence behavior toward a specific direction. Rewards are often confused with reinforcers, but they are not the same. Rewards are typically not immediate, frequent, or personal, but accomplishment driven.
- **Relationships.** This is the relationship between one or more of the members and/or the leader. Relationships identify who and what members are to each other. This is a type of identification that answers the question: "Who are we to one another?"

The goal of every leader is to have all group members performing their best. In such a diverse society as ours, flexibility is the key to motivating group members. As leader, you need to:

1. Recognize the different personal needs and goals of each individual.
2. Provide a diversity of motivators to match the varied needs of group members.
3. Be flexible in accommodating the cultural differences within a diverse group when attempting to motivate members.

SUMMARY

We have reviewed leadership, persuasion, and motivation. We have attempted to integrate concepts of leadership with persuasive theories, such as balance theory, cognitive dissonance theory, expectancy violation theory, attribution theory, theory of reasoned action, and social judgment theory. Persuasion is an integral component of motivation and leadership. At times, persuasion itself is the key motivating factor.

We also learned about compliance gaining and compliance-gaining techniques. These techniques are directed toward the needs, wants and desires of individuals as a way to get them to perform or behave accordingly. A drawback to compliance-gaining strategies is that they generally aren't long-term, nor do they last beyond the immediacy of their use.

Last but definitely not least, we explored motivational theories, more specifically, Maslow's Hierarchy of Needs, Murray's Inventory of Psychogenic Needs, and Alderfer's ERG theory. This group of theories focuses on basic human needs as motivation. People will do just about anything if the right need or set of needs is identified.

DISCUSSION

1. What motives might an in–class small group identify among its members that can be used to motivate performance? Probably the easiest and most common answer to this question is "to get a good grade," but how does a focus on grades alone as a motivating factor potentially hinder an in–class group's success? How can such a group motivate its members through other means?

2. For each of the four major sources on belief on page 6, **induction, construction, analogy,** and **authority**, work with your group to identify one advertisement everyone is familiar with that attempts to build belief using this particular source.

3. Identify some specific behaviors that a group member might exhibit suggesting that s/he is experiencing some form of **cognitive inconsistency** while working in a group. Based on your list of these behaviors, describe some specific strategies than an effective leader might use to help this group member resolve the inconsistency without resorting to behaviors that are destructive to the group, such as leaving the group or refusing to perform.

4. Consider the following situation: A group member has recently been seriously under-performing because, years ago, she had a very negative interpersonal experience with a person who has been newly assigned to her group. Discuss some ways the group's leader might use each of the four strategies under the **Theory of Planned Behavior** on pages 19 and 20 to encourage her to change her behavior.

5. Consider the five clusters of **compliance–gaining** strategies described on page 23: rewarding, punishing, expertise, impersonal commitments, and personal commitments. Work with your group to identify a specific small group situation for each of these five clusters in which this cluster of strategies would be likely to be *ineffective* as a way of gaining compliance.

NOTES

1. Rokeach, M. (1960). *The open and closed mind.* New York: Basic Books, Inc.Rokeach, M. (1968). *Beliefs, attitudes, and values.* San Francisco: Jossey-Bass. Rokeach, M. (1973). *The nature of human values.* New York: Free Press.

2. Littlejohn, S.W. (1999). *Theories of human communication.* Belmont, CA: Wadsworth.

3. Bettinghaus, E.P., & Cody, M.J. (1994). *Persuasive communication* (5th ed.). New York: Harcourt Brace College, p.34.

4. Ibid.

5. Bettinghaus, E.P., & Cody, M.J. (1994). *Persuasive communication* (5th ed.). New York: Harcourt Brace College. See also Scheibe, K.E. (1970). *Beliefs and values.* New York: Holt, Rinehart, and Winston.

6. Ibid.

7. Fisk, S.T., & Taylor, S.E. (1984). *Social cognition.* Reading, MA: Addison-Wesley.

8. Trenholm, S., & Jensen, A. (1996). *Interpersonal communication* (3rd ed.). Belmont, CA: Wadsworth.

9. Littlejohn, S.W. (1999). *Theories of human communication.* Belmont, CA: Wadsworth.

10. Brembeck, W.L., & Howell, W.S. (1976). *Persuasion: A means of social influence* (2nd ed.). Englewood Cliffs, N.J.: Prentice-Hall.

11. For an overview of consistency theories, see Petty, R.E., & Cacioppo, J.T. (1981). *Attitudes and persuasion: Classic and contemporary approaches.* Dubuque, Iowa: Brown.

12. Larson, C.U. (1995). *Persuasion: Reception and responsibility* (7th ed.). New York: Wadsworth.

13. For discussion of early work on consistency theories, see McGuire, W. (1966). The current status of cognitive theories. In S. Feldman (Ed.), *Cognitive consistency* (pp. 2–4). New York: Academic Press.

14. Bettinghaus, E.P., & Cody, M.J. (1994). *Persuasive communication* (5th ed.). New York: Harcourt Brace College.

15. Festinger, L. (1957). *The theory of cognitive dissonance.* New York: Harper and Row.

16. Osgood, C.E., Tannenbaum, P., & Suci, G. (1957). *The measurement of meaning.* Urbana: Ill.: The University of Illinois Press, pp. 189–216; also see: Osgood, C.E., & and Tannenbaum, P. (1955). The principle of congruity in the prediction of attitude change. *Psychological Review, 62,* 2–55.

17. Abelson, R.P., & Rosenberg, M.J. (1958). Symbolic psycho-logic: A model of attitudinal cognition. *Behavioral Science, 3,* 1–13.

18. Heider, F. (1946). Attitudes and cognitive organization. *Journal of Psychology, 21,* 107–112.

19. Festinger, L., p. 39.

20. Larson, C.U. (1995). *Persuasion: Reception and responsibility* (7th ed.). New York: Wadsworth.

21. Griffin, E. (1997). *A first look at communication theory.* New York: McGraw-Hill.

22. Vroom, V.H. (1964). *Work and motivation.* Malabar, FL: Robert E. Krieger.

23. Ibid.

24. Burgoon, J. (1978). A communication model of personal space violation: Explication and an initial test. *Human Communication Research, 4,* 129–142.

25. Littlejohn, S.W. (1999). *Theories of human communication.* Belmont, CA: Wadsworth.

26. Burgoon, Hunsaker, & Dawson. (1994). *Human communication* (3rd ed.). Thousand Oaks, CA: Sage.

27. Ibid.

28. Woodward, G.C., & Denton, Jr., R.E. (2000). *Persuasion & influence in American life* (4th ed.). Prospect Heights, IL: Waveland Press.

29. Fishbein, M. A. (1980). Theory of reasoned action: Some applications and implications. In H. Howe & M. Page (Eds.), *Nebraska symposium on motivation* (vol. 27) (pp. 65–116). Lincoln: University of Nebraska Press; Fishbein, M., & Ajzen, I. (1981). *Belief, attitude, intention, and behavior: An introduction to theory and research.* Reading, MA: Addison-Wesley.

30. Ajzen, I., & Fishbein, M. (1980). *Understanding attitudes and predicting social behavior.* Englewood Cliffs, NJ: Prentice Hall, p. 8.

31. Woodward, G.C., & Denton, R.E., Jr. (2000). *Persuasion & influence in American life* (4th ed.). Prospect Heights, IL: Waveland.

32. Fazio, R., & Roskos-Ewoldsen, D. (1984). Acting as we feel. In C. Arnold & J.W. Bowers (Eds.), *Handbook of rhetorical and communication theory* (p. 83). Boston: Allyn and Bacon.

33. For a more complete explanation of Ajzen and Fishbein's theory see http://hsc.usf.edu/~kmbrown/TRA_TPB.htm.

34. Bettinghaus, E.P., & Cody, M.J. (1994). *Persuasive communication* (5th ed.). New York: Harcourt Brace College.

35. Ibid.

36. Sherif, C.W., Sherif, M., & Nebergall, R. (1965). *Attitude and attitude change: The social judgment-involvement approach.* Philadelphia: W.B. Saunders.

37. Bettinghaus, E.P., & Cody, M.J. (1994). *Persuasive communication* (5th ed.). New York: Harcourt Brace College.

38. Littlejohn, S.W. (1999). *Theories of human communication.* Belmont, CA: Wadsworth.

39. Woodward, G.C., & Denton, Jr., R.E. (2000). *Persuasion & influence in American life* (4th ed.). Prospect Heights, IL: Waveland.

40. Infante, et al. (1997). *Building communication theory* (3rd ed.). Prospect Heights, IL: Waveland.

41. Sherif, C.W., Sherif, M., & Nebergall, R. (1965). *Attitude and attitude change: The social judgment-involvement approach.* Philadelphia: W.B. Saunders.

42. Ibid.

43. Johnston, D.D. (1994). *The art and science of persuasion.* Dubuque, IA: Brown and Benchmark.

44. Infante.

45. Applegate, J.L. (1982). The impact of construct system development in communication and impression formation in persuasive messages. *Communication Monographs, 49,* 277–289.

46. Marwell, G., & Schmitt, D. (1967). Dimensions of compliance-gaining strategies: A dimensional analysis. *Sociometry 30,* 350–364.

47. Marwell, G., & Schmitt, D. (1967). Dimensions of compliance-gaining strategies: A dimensional analysis. *Sociometry, 30,* 350–364.

48. Littlejohn, S.W. (1999). *Theories of human communication.* Belmont, CA: Wadsworth.

49. Schenck-Hamlin, W.J., Wiseman, R.L., & Georgacarakos, G.N. A model of properties of compliance-gaining strategies. *Communication Quarterly, 30,* 92–100.

50. Wheeless, W.J., Barraclough, R. & Stewart, R. Compliance gaining and power in persuasion. In R.N. Bostrom (Ed.), *Communication Yearbook* (7th ed.) (pp. 105–145). Beverly Hills, CA: Sage.

51. Littlejohn, S.W. (1999). *Theories of human communication.* Belmont, CA: Wadsworth.

52. The classic study by Kipnis, D., & Vanderveer, R. (1971). Ingratiation and the use of power. *Journal of Personality and Social Psychology, 17,* 280–286, explains how well ingratiation tactics work.

53. Littlejohn, S.W. (1999). *Theories of human communication*. Belmont, CA: Wadsworth.

54. Hass, G.R., (1981). Effects of source characteristics on cognitive responses and persuasion. In R.E. Petty, T.M. Ostrom, & T.C. Brock (Eds.), *Cognitive responses in persuasion*. Hillsdale, N.J.: Lawrence Erlbaum Associates.

55. Johnston, D.D. (1994). *The art and science of persuasion*. Dubuque, IA: Brown and Benchmark.

56. Simons, J.A., Irwin, D.B., & Drinnien, B.A. (1987). *Psychology: The search for understanding*. New York: West.

57. For a more concise explanation of Maslow's Hierarchy of Needs see http://www.xenodochy.org/ex/lists/maslow.html#level2.

58. Johnston, D.D. (1994). *The art and science of persuasion*. Dubuque, IA: Brown and Benchmark.

59. Brembeck, W.L., & Howell, W.S. (1976). P*ersuasion: A means of social influence* (2nd ed.). Englewood Cliffs, N.J.: Prentice-Hall, Inc. See also Hilgard, E.R., Atkinson, R.C., & Atkinson, R.L. (1971). *Introduction to psychology* (5th ed.). New York: Harcourt Brace Jovanovich.

60. Murray, H.A., (Ed.) (1938). *Explorations in personality*. Oxford: Oxford University Press.

61. Alderfer, C. (May, 1969). An empirical test of a new theory of human needs. *Organizational Behavior and Human Performance,* 142–175.

62. Robbins, S.P. (1993). *Organizational behavior* (6th ed.). Englewood Cliffs, NJ:

63. Hersey, P., Blanchard, K.H., & Johnson, D.E. (2001). *Management of organizational behavior* (8th ed.). Upper Saddle River, NJ: Prentice-Hall.

64. Ibid.

65. Ibid.

66. Ibid.

67. Daniels, A.C., & Daniels, J.E. (2004). *Performance management: Changing behavior that drives organizational effectiveness*. Atlanta, GA: Performance Management Publications.

7

Leadership and Performance Management

CHAPTER OBJECTIVES

- Understand the principles of performance management
- Know how the ABC model of behavior change works
- Gain an understanding of reinforcement strategies

CHAPTER OUTLINE

What do you think is the most difficult obstacle a group or team leader has to overcome? Is it getting members to follow orders? Persuading members that they really to need to work together? Compelling them to do things that they don't want to do? Or, perhaps, making sure that members even show up? Do we cajole, bribe, or threaten members with negative consequences, sanctions, or even punishments, in order to get them to comply? No, none of the above. The most difficult obstacle a team leader has is to have all members perform their best, their optimum, and do it with the same interest, energy, and enthusiasm they would typically put into a labor of love. And if I used a sports metaphor, I would include the word teamwork. You'll notice that I used the word performance instead of behavior.

Thomas Gilbert (1978), considered to be the father of contemporary performance management, wrote in his book *Human Competence* that "Behavior is a necessary and integral part of performance, but we must not confuse the two. Unfortunately, we often do. To equate behavior and performance is like confusing a sale with the seller. Naturally, we cannot have one without the other. But the sale is a unitary transaction, with properties all of its own, and we can know a great deal about it even though we know little—perhaps nothing at all—about the seller."[1] This chapter is all about managing performance.

WHAT IS PERFORMANCE MANAGEMENT?

We can define performance management (PM) as a systematic and data-oriented approach to managing people at work that relies on positive reinforcement as the major way to maximize performance. The essential words in this definition are systematic and data-oriented. Systematic means that in order to determine if any particular management procedure is effective, you must specify the behaviors and results to be affected. Furthermore, you must develop a way to measure these behaviors and results and a way to determine the methods for changing current performance. The final steps are to use those methods and evaluate results. Data-oriented means that we use data to evaluate the effectiveness of motivational strategies. This assumes that all performance can be measured.[2] Measuring or measurement refers to the assessment of performance and results achieved by both the group as a whole and individual members. Measurement gives us a way to determine what has been accomplished and can also serve as a basis for deciding when those accomplishments need special recognition. This process of measurement means determining the level of performance by judging the quality, quantity, timeliness, and cost effectiveness of group work against a set of predetermined standards. Performance management is derived from the field of study called Applied Behavior Analysis.[3]

When we apply PM to groups, it is called **group** or **team performance management**. In this context, performance management includes activities designed to ensure that goals are consistently being met effectively and efficiently. Here, PM focuses on group or team behaviors as they relate to performance. This is quite different from team building, which consists of activities that are believed to indirectly lead to improvements in team or group performance. Group

Systematic

Means that in order to determine if any particular management procedure is effective, you must specify the behaviors and results to be affected.

Data-oriented

Means that we use data to evaluate the effectiveness of motivational strategies.

Measurement

Refers to the assessment of performance and results achieved by both the group as a whole and individual members.

performance management, however, identifies the group behaviors that will lead to the group successfully achieving its stated goals and objectives, and it uses a systematic process to change those behaviors accordingly in order to improve performance. Basically, the overall goal of performance management is to make sure that group members work optimally to achieve the results desired by the organization. Group success is defined by the group's ability to produce results. All group results are the product of individual behavior. A good group leader will define the results that are needed and then decide the behaviors that will deliver those results.

Does PM offer value to small groups and teams? The answer unquestionably is "Yes!" There are a number of reasons why organizations and groups use PM. The following six, adapted from Aubrey C. Daniels' (1989) text *Performance Management,* highlight the value PM has to groups:[4]

1. **PM works.** Performance management is **practical**. It is not a generalized abstract theory that suggests ways to think about problems; it is a set of specific actions for increasing desired performance and decreasing undesired performance.

2. **PM produces short-term as well as long-term results.** Once you implement your PM program, you should see some measurable success. No miracles at first, no program can claim results that quickly. As you progress, you will see what works and what doesn't work, and take the necessary steps to correct the problem.

3. **PM requires no psychological background.** PM rejects the belief that in order to work effectively with people you must first understand their deep-seated anxieties, feelings, and motives. For the group or team, we take the position that the only way you can know people is by observing how they behave (what they do or say). PM accepts people as they are, not as they were or how we ideally would like them to be. Because it deals with the here and now, group leaders do not need to pry into people's private lives or their history in order to lead them effectively.

4. **PM is a system for measuring many types of performance.** Since PM is based on knowledge acquired through a scientific study of behavior, the principles can be applied to behavior wherever it occurs. PM applies to people, wherever they work and no matter what they do. However, it may be easier to see how PM applies to group work rather than to jobs where the main outcome is creativity. PM assures that if people are involved in any activity, PM can enable them to work consistently at their full potential.

© Yuri Arcurs, 2011. Under license from Shutterstock, Inc.

5. **PM creates an enjoyable place in which to work.** It is commonly held that if you are doing something you enjoy, you are more likely to perform well than if you don't like what you are doing. Unfortunately, some leaders have the notion that fun and work don't mix. If, however, the fun comes from doing the work, then leadership should be preoccupied with how to increase fun rather than eliminate it. When you have fun that is directly related to your task mission, enthusiasm, quality, and productivity can be dramatically improved.

6. **PM is an open system.** PM does not include motivational tricks. Just as leaders influence the performance of the people they lead, group members influence the performance of leaders by the same process. There is nothing about the principles that says reinforcement only works down the organization. PM works equally well up and down the organization. In the final analysis, changing performance with PM will result in everybody getting more of what they want from group work. Who could complain about that?

THE ABC MODEL OF BEHAVIOR CHANGE (ANTECEDENTS, BEHAVIOR, AND CONSEQUENCES)

The ABC Model of Behavior Change is not a complex abstraction that requires an engineering degree to figure it out. One of the benefits of this model is that it is simple, which makes it easy to put into operation. It works on the basic premise that in order to change performance, which is the combination of behaviors and their accomplishments; you must first change what people do—their behavior. We define behavior as any observable and measurable act—or simply—anything you can see a person do.[5]

When we think about **performance**, most of the time we see it as composed of a number, or series, of behaviors directed toward some **outcome** or **goal**. In groups, performance may consist of the behaviors of researching a particular aspect of an issue, writing a summary report, printing copies for the group, and making an oral presentation explaining your findings. The goal might be to provide a timely report so other members can follow up on your research. A change in any of your behaviors changes the performance. For example, if you fail to write a summary report, you cannot make the oral presentation on time.

So the question should be: how do we design a group environment in which people know what to do and do it consistently?

Behavior can be changed in two main ways—by what comes *before* it and by what comes *after* it. Let me repeat that...Behavior can be changed in two main ways—by what comes before it and by what comes after it.

A condition that precedes and is associated with a specific outcome but does not necessarily cause the outcome is an antecedent. When you try to influence behavior before it occurs, you are using antecedents. A **consequence** is the effect, result, or outcome of something that occurred earlier. When you attempt to influence behavior by doing something after it occurs, you are using consequences. Consequences unquestionably are the most important part of the

Behavior

Any observable and measurable act—or simply—anything you can see a person do.

Antecedent

A condition that precedes and is associated with a specific outcome—but does not necessarily cause the outcome.

ABC model if we want to manage behavior effectively. We use consequences to steer behavior in the direction we want it to go.

Performance management combines the systematic use of antecedents and consequences to improve group-related performance. The three elements—**antecedents, behavior, and consequences**—unite to form the ABC model of behavior change.

An antecedent stimulates a behavior, which is followed by a consequence. When we understand the way these two elements interact, it allows us the ability to analyze group performance problems, develop plans to correct those problems, and design group environments and management systems that will induce a greater degree of performance.

What are antecedents? They can be any number of things: a person, a place, a thing, an object, or an event, which occurs before a behavior that encourages the group or individual members to perform a particular behavior. There are many similar and familiar words that we use in everyday language that represent an antecedent. The words provoke, incite, stimulate, signal, remind, cue, prompt, induce, cause, trigger, and encourage are all similar to the concept of antecedent.

In group work, we design the environment to cause or stimulate the correct or desirable responses and performances from members. Some of the more common antecedents used in group work are such things as **goals, objectives, priorities, roles, policies, procedures, standards,** and **rules**. These are intended to communicate to group members what is expected of them. Probably the most common of all used antecedents communicated in group work is the word "meeting." Predetermined meetings are, by their very nature, designed to influence your behavior. You know when to show up at a particular time, date, and location. And if you fail to show, then you can expect some type of negative consequence. If you haven't discovered it already, you will once you enter the work force, that training and education are probably the most common antecedents used by business to change or improve performance.

There are other types of antecedents. The behavior of other people is also an antecedent. **Social Learning Theory** emphasizes indirect learning; that is, learning that involves anticipation and imagination.[6] One of the most important ways we learn is by watching other people being rewarded or punished. This is called **modeling** or **vicarious learning**.[7] The actions of fellow group members and the group leader influence the actions of other members. When we see what happens to someone else, this illustrates that it may happen to us. If you see a fellow member rebuked by the group leader for coming late to a meeting, you learn that such behavior is unacceptable. A rebuke is a type of punishment. This is known as vicarious learning. When we see a member rewarded for doing an outstanding job and we attempt to duplicate that behavior, we call that modeling. Social learning theory is based on the belief that people learn through observing others' behavior and attitudes, and the outcomes (consequences) of those behaviors. Most human behavior is learned through modeling; by observing others, we form an idea of how new behaviors are performed, and on later occasions this serves as a guide for our own behavior.

ANTECEDENTS

What Are the Characteristics of Antecedents?

Antecedents always come before the behavior they influence. They are intended only to set the conditions for the behavior or performance; they don't control it. The primary function of the antecedent is to communicate information about behavior and its consequences. Antecedents may tell someone what to do, when to do it, and often, how to do it. For example, a checkout sign in a grocery store that says, "Cash or debit cards only" states the desired behavior. Another sign in the same store may say, "Take a number for service." This antecedent communicates information about the desired behavior and its consequences.

Antecedents work because they have been paired with consequences. The antecedent "Take a number" tells you what you need to do if you want service, which is the consequence. Without taking a number, chances are you won't get service. Do an experiment the next time you are required to take a number prior to getting the service. It doesn't matter if it is in the bakery, doctor's office, or any service that you wait for in which you need to take a number. Don't take the number, and see if you get the service anyway. I'll bet that you won't. We learn that the reason antecedents influence behavior at all is that they have been associated with particular past consequences. The most influential antecedents are those that are consistently paired with a particular consequence (an ear infection always hurts). The effectiveness of antecedents is also determined by **consistency**. The less consistently antecedents are paired; the less effective they will

be in triggering the behavior. For example, you were told by your instructor at the beginning of the semester that coming late to class would not be tolerated. If you come to class late, you will not be allowed in, your instructor told you. The first time a student came to class late, she was not allowed in, but the second time another student came to class late, he was allowed in. This happened quite often during the semester. Eventually, most of the students didn't believe that the instructor meant what he said. They didn't believe the antecedent, "If you come to class late, you will not be allowed in." The instructor lacked consistency between the antecedent and the consequence. The effectiveness of an antecedent may be measured by the degree of correlation between the antecedent and the behavior consequence that is associated with it.[8]

In this case, the antecedent, "If you come to class late you will not be allowed in," became ineffectual because the degree of correlation between the antecedent and the behavior consequence is low. When the correlation is low, the desired behavior (coming to class on time) will often seem to be unaffected by that particular antecedent (won't be allowed in class). There was little consistency between the antecedent and the consequence. When the correlation is high (every student who came to class late wasn't allowed in), the desired behavior (all students come to class on time) consistently occurs in the presence of the antecedent.

© Anya Ponti, 2011. Under license from Shutterstock, Inc.

Consistency in maintaining the correlation between antecedents and consequences develops something we call **trust**. Leaders develop members' trust; it just doesn't happen merely because the person is a leader. If people always do what they say they're going to do, we learn to trust them; those who do not are not trusted. If the group leader fails to keep promises, you quickly learn that that person cannot be trusted, which not only affects you, but the entire group as well.

There are times when consequences may also be antecedents. What may be a consequence to one person may be an antecedent to another. It's similar to the saying, "What may be one person's junk is another person's treasure." For example, when we see someone do something that leads to a positive consequence, this may increase the likelihood that we will behave similarly under the same circumstances. Group performance is constantly affected by what people see being rewarded and punished. If members see hard work rewarded, there probably will be more hard work (modeling). Conversely, if one member is continually late to meetings without consequences, others will tend to be less punctual (also modeling). Unfortunately, antecedents that do not have consequences have short-term effects. When an antecedent generates a behavior and the anticipated consequence does not occur, the antecedent will quickly lose its power as a prompt to the behavior. Antecedents get a behavior started, but only consequences maintain behavior.[9]

When I was a graduate student, I attended a performance management seminar featuring Aubrey C. Daniels as the keynote speaker. I distinctly remember him saying that the classic error people make regarding antecedents and compliance gaining is that if other people don't do what they are told the first time, leaders tell them again. But the second time they'll tell them louder, longer, or meaner until such time as they may be yelling or threatening some type of punishment. If a group leader gets members to commit to performing a task right the first time, then he or she must plan and deliver positive consequences to those members when they do it.

How Do We Select the Right Antecedent?

It is important to remember that antecedents must be paired with appropriate consequences. Let's look at the three most powerful classes of antecedents for insight as to how we might plan the right antecedent: The first class of antecedents is those that clearly describe the desired performance and expectations of individual group members and the group as a whole. For example, the group leader or the organization may articulate established objectives, task descriptions, task specifications, standards, or priorities. These detail what members will do and how they are expected to do it.

The second class of antecedents is those that have a history of being associated with a specific consequence. For example, running a red light or a stop sign almost always will get you a ticket if a police officer sees you do it. Or tanning too long in the hot sun will give you a sun burn that you know will hurt. In these examples, the antecedents and their inevitable consequences share a history of association—lie out in the sun too long, and you'll get a sunburn; run a red light, and you'll get a ticket.

The third class of antecedents is those in which the behaviors occur just prior to the desired performance. For example, a group member is setting up an audio/visual display for a meeting, and she asks for help. Or you are walking between classes, and someone asks you for directions to the library. Reflecting on these three classes of antecedents will help you determine types of consequences to pair with each.

What Are the Most Common Types of Antecedents Used in Small Groups?

There are numerous antecedents used in small group work, too many to mention here. Instead, we will discuss some of the more common types. I would have to say that probably the most common type of antecedent used in small groups is the provision of policies and procedures that govern group work. Policies and procedures fall under the first class of antecedents because they clearly describe the desired performance and expectations of group members. Policies and procedures are rules that members should live by; they govern behavior. Task assignment is another common antecedent because it describes specific member behavior. Task assignment precludes members from doing whatever they want; it is descriptive by nature. Holding a meeting, which includes establishing specific meeting times and dates, is also a common antecedent. Meetings are generally governed by an agenda. Providing adequate task aid is a common antecedent that has a tendency to be overlooked. This may include current expectations, clear and understandable instructions or directions, adequate materials and tools, handout materials or flow charts, etc. Too often, I have found that expectations or instructions that are not clear and precise result in poor performance. People can't do their jobs to their best ability if they don't clearly understand what that job is. That isn't their fault, but they often get the blame. The consequence doesn't fit the antecedent. Objectives, tasks, standards, and priorities should be clearly specified in writing. The last common antecedent we'll discuss is the environment where the group conducts its meetings. Is the room appropriate? Is there adequate lighting? Is the room temperature comfortable for members? Are there enough chairs? Is the table big enough? Are there visual aids? Is the room quiet or noisy? Are there refreshments? An uncomfortable, noisy, and either too hot or too cold a room creates poor conditions for group work.

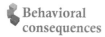 **Consequence**

The effect, result, or outcome of something that occurred earlier.

Behavioral consequences

Can be explained as events that follow behaviors and change the probability that those behaviors will recur in the future.

CONSEQUENCES

What Are Behavioral Consequences?

When we talk about consequences, we mean behavioral consequences. B.F. Skinner (1953), a behavioral psychologist, used the term to describe the effects of the consequences of a particular behavior on the future occurrence of that behavior. Behavioral consequences can be explained as events that follow behaviors and change the probability that those behaviors will recur in the future.[10] You know what consequences are; you've known them since you were a little baby. Remember the first time you were told not to touch a burning match? It burned, didn't it? The behavior was touching the match; the consequence was burning your finger. Ouch! You quickly learned not to do that again. And that's what consequences are meant to do, either prevent you from repeating a behavior or reinforce a behavior. Consequences are the single most effective tool a group leader has for increasing both individual member and collective group performance, and improving group morale. The leader must understand that there is only one direct answer to the problems of poor performance, poor quality of work-product, low productivity, and disgruntled members—consequences. But it must be an appropriate matchup between antecedents and consequences. The ineffective use of consequences creates and maintains poor performance and low morale. The key to using consequences is to provide appropriate consequences.

One thing you should know about consequences—they don't always work. Consequences only work if the person or persons they are applied to care about the consequences. If the person doesn't care what happens as a result of his or her behavior, then all of the consequences in the world won't help you. For example, if an employer threatens to fire an employee whenever that person is late for work, that employee will get to the point that he or she won't care about the job anymore and will more than likely quit the next time he or she is threatened. However, if that employee truly wants and needs the job, that person will probably change his or her behavior and come to work on time. Or, we often read that our prison systems are overcrowded. Why would anyone want to go to prison? Prison is a consequence of a behavior. Unfortunately, many people in prison didn't care about the consequences before they did whatever it was that put them there in the first place. The point is the person whom the consequence is directed at must care about that consequence in order for it to be effective.

Effects of Consequences

Some consequences can increase or maintain the probability that a desired behavior will occur while some consequences may decrease it. Making behavioral choices, which are followed by consequences, is a pattern that repeats itself many, many times in the course of a day. Sometimes we consciously think about them, sometimes we don't. And seldom, if ever, do we view behavior as a function of its consequences. Consequences do not simply influence what someone does; they control what someone does. Every behavior has a consequence. This doesn't just apply to group work, but to every human behavior.

If you want to understand why members do what they do, instead of asking, "Why did they do that?" ask, "What happens to them when they do that?" When you understand the consequences, you are able to understand the behavior. This is similar to understanding an argument. If you want to know the purpose of someone's argument, look for his or her conclusion. The conclusion will tell you what that person wants you to think or do. Consequences are like conclusions. If you understand what happened to a person, you'll understand why he or she behaved the way he or she did. Just like antecedents, consequences come in many forms and countless types. What people do, what they say, what they give us, and even what they don't give us can all be consequences that will affect our behavior. That is why, as a leader, you need to understand consequences.

There are four basic reasons that explain why people don't do what we want them to do in the group: (1) they don't know what to do; (2) they don't know how to do it; (3) there are obstacles in the environment; and (4) they don't want to do it.[11] If a group member doesn't know what to do or how to do it, or he or she is held back because of obstacles in the environment, these are problems caused by **antecedents**. However, if a member or members don't want to do it, this is a problem of **consequences**. As we mentioned earlier, consequences provide the key to performance; understand the consequences, and you are able to understand the behavior. There is nothing more irritating than group members who don't do what we want them to do. As leaders, we say things like, "You should do it; you ought to do it; that's what you're here to do; it's your job." I acknowledge that in class it is often difficult getting members to do what they're supposed to do. And it is unfortunate that classmates don't do all that they should. People do what they do because the consequences support what they're doing. I can think of two excellent examples that illustrate this. Let's imagine that there are two managers whose jobs are in jeopardy; one we'll call Norman, the other Paul. Norman has heard a rumor that his job is in jeopardy, so he chooses to perform non-risky decision making. If the rumor is true, he wants to play it safe; if it isn't, he wants to look good to upper management. Norman adopts decision making as consensus-driven, or will only make decisions that he feels are safe, or will defer any risky decisions to his colleagues. Whenever Norm is confronted with a controversial decision, he finds a way in which to avoid it. He feels that the consequences of making a risky decision, which may be losing his job, outweigh his authority to make one. Paul, on the other hand, is the store manager for a supermarket chain who is currently under performance review, which is not looking too good for him at the moment. His superiors have told him that employee performance needed improvement. Paul is a really nice guy who genuinely cares about his employees. Paul's problem is that he doesn't know how to increase employee performance or have employees

improve on poorly rated performance. He holds regular motivational meetings, provides ice cream bars or donuts during the meetings, and pats everybody on the back who he thinks is doing a good job. He also attempts to increase productivity in each department as a way to show his superiors that he can do the job. The problem Paul encounters with attempting to increase productivity is that the employees see it as more work, more pressure, more stress, and they don't want to participate. In this example, the immediate consequences to all store employees for increasing productivity are negative. Paul believes that the problem is motivational; his mini-meetings are designed to motivate.

Paul's problem isn't one of motivation; it's one of consequences. Once we understand the consequences people experience when they do or don't do something, motivation becomes clear. When people fail to perform the way we would like them to, we say it is a motivation problem, and we explain their behavior as "He doesn't care," "She's just putting her time in," "He's got a bad attitude," or "She's lazy." All of these explanations are used when the real problem is consequences.[12]

How We Experience Consequences Determines Their Effect

Consequences don't affect everyone the same way; people are different, and they will respond to the same consequence differently. Every individual has unique likes and dislikes, and they determine the particular consequence that will be effective in changing a person's behavior.

In order to be effective as a group leader, you must know how members experience various consequences. A consequence that one member may wish for or like very much may be one that another member has no interest in or may even dislike. It is not uncommon for leaders to view consequences from the perspective of the organization, not of the performer. Effective leaders know how members experience consequences, not just how they themselves experience them. This helps them when they need to pair antecedents with consequences.

Immediate Consequences Are Most Effective

Consequences have their greatest impact on behavior when they are immediate. The longer you wait to implement a consequence, the weaker it will become. For example, if a child misbehaves in the morning, the parent doesn't wait until late afternoon or the next day to discipline. If a group member does an outstanding job, that person should be recognized during the earliest part of the meeting. The most immediate consequences are those that occur while the member is engaged in some group activity. The longer you wait, the weaker the consequence becomes.

Types of Consequences

There are four types of operant conditioning: positive reinforcement, negative reinforcement, punishment, and extinction.

1. **Positive reinforcement.** A positive reinforcer is defined as any consequence that increases the chance that the behavior that came before the reinforcement will be repeated more often in the future. For example, if you study very hard for your exams, you will probably get an A in each course. The grade is the positive reinforcer for you to study hard.

2. **Negative reinforcement.** A negative reinforcer is defined as any consequence that decreases the chance that the behavior that came before it will occur less often in the future. This is similar to the concept of a reward. Basically, this occurs when something negative is removed from a person's experience as a way to increase the chance of a particular behavior happening again. For example, if your roommate sees you studying hard for a test, he or she may do your chores so you can continue studying. It is likely that this good studying behavior will recur when it's time for you to do your chores again. A good deal of our behavior is regulated by negative reinforcers. We often do things to avoid something else, such as going to the dentist.

3. **Punishment.** Sometimes our behavior gets us a consequence that we don't like or don't want. When we do, we are less likely to do it again. It weakens

the behavior because we experience it as a negative consequence of the behavior. Getting something we don't like is called punishment.

4. **Extinction.** This is no longer reinforcing a previously reinforced response. It is defined as failure to get what you want. When people do something and as a result get no reinforcement, they will be less likely to repeat that behavior in the future. Reducing or eliminating behavior in this way is called extinction. For example, if a member throws a temper tantrum and is ignored, that person will likely not do it again.

ABC ANALYSIS: A PROBLEM-SOLVING PROCESS

An ABC Analysis is a problem-solving process in which the antecedents and consequences currently in use for both the problem and the correct behaviors are identified and classified. An ABC analysis involves much more than finding an antecedent or consequence for a specific behavior. Because it is very difficult to discover exactly which antecedent triggers a particular behavior, or which consequence maintains it, the ABC analysis helps us discover **patterns** among the many possible antecedents and consequences that are associated with the behavior.

The 7-Step ABC Analysis[13]

Step 1: Describe the problem performance and the performer(s). The first thing you need to is identify a problem and describe it in terms of behaviors that

---

TABLE 7.1   Overview of an ABC Analysis

Problem Behavior: Student group member not showing up for meetings

Antecedents	Consequences
Doesn't have the time	Less of an assigned work load
Busy with friends on campus	Gets yelled at by group members
Schedules other things to do	Does other things
Relies on members to do work	Other members do work

Desired Behavior: Student group member shows up for meetings

Antecedents	Consequences
Maintains assigned work load	May be rebuked if work not done properly
Members refuse to carry student	Less time to do other things
Poor report to instructor	Poor grade

are taking place or not taking place. This is not for a group of people who exhibit the same or similar behavior; an ABC analysis is only accurate when done from the perspective of the **individual**. When identifying behaviors for an ABC analysis, you need to avoid statements such as "Doesn't care," or "Bad attitude" or "Just lazy"; these are too vague for completing an analysis.

How do you specifically describe a problem, and especially the behaviors that cause the problem? One way is to ask the question, "What did I see the person do (or hear that she did) that led me to conclude that she doesn't care, is just lazy, or has a bad attitude?" Rephrase what you see and hear so you can clearly convey those behavioral problems, such as:

Seldom shows up for meetings
Rarely, if ever, volunteers for task assignments
Constantly complains about group members
Shows little, if any, interest in working with members
Speaks badly about members to people outside of the group

By identifying the specific behaviors, such as seldom shows up for meetings, you replace the vague statement of "Doesn't care" with one that can be analyzed. Finding the behaviors that precisely define the problem is called **pinpointing**. Aubrey C. Daniels (1989, p. 43) notes that "the most effective ABC analyses are those in which the behaviors and/or the performance have been pinpointed."

Step 2: Describe the correct or desired performance. In Step 1, we identified the problem behavior. In Step 2, we state what we want the person to do differently from the behavior described in the first step.

The question we ask in this step is: "If the individual was not doing the problem behavior, what would I want her to be doing?"

You'll discover that many of the correct or desired behaviors are easily defined because they are the opposite of the problem. For example, "Shows up for all meetings" is the opposite of the problem behavior "Seldom shows up for meetings," or "Shows enthusiasm in working with members" is the opposite of "shows little, if any, interest in working with members." However, not all of the problem behaviors are so obvious; there are those that are more subtle, such as "Takes poor meeting notes." This should be replaced with "Improves meeting notes." Areas for improvement can be specifically identified.

Step 3: Determine the severity of the problem. In most cases, the severity of the problem is determined by its frequency. How often does it happen? If the person who is complaining about other group members seldom does it, then you can say that person is having a bad hair day. But if that person complains at just about every meeting, then the frequency is high and you know that the problem is severe. It is difficult to perform an ABC Analysis when the problem behavior occurs infrequently. An ABC Analysis is most appropriate when the behavior you don't want occurs frequently. Once you have pinpointed the behavior, you will need to determine if it requires the time and energy necessary to solve it. You should focus on frequent behavioral problems that negatively impact group performance and synergy.

| TABLE 7.2 | PROBLEM AND CORRECT BEHAVIORS FOR AN ABC ANALYSIS |

Problem Behavior	Correct Behavior
1. Submitting task assignments late	1. Submitting task assignments on time
2. Poorly developed research materials	2. Well-developed research materials
3. Constantly arguing with members	3. Not arguing with members
4. Always interrupting members	4. Not interrupting members
5. Coming late to meetings	5. Coming on time to meetings
6. Regularly deviating from agenda	6. Focusing on agenda
7. Is disrespectful to one or more members	7. Is respectful of all members
8. Seldom comes to meetings prepared	8. Always comes to meetings prepared
9. Prefers working independently	9. Works cooperatively with members

Step 4: Complete an ABC Analysis for problem performance.

Step 4a: This is the easy step: write the problem performance and the name of the performer on a form—like the one in Figure 7.1.

Step 4b: This step is more difficult. Brainstorm and list all the antecedents and consequences you can think of for the problem behavior. This list is the heart of the ABC Analysis, so try to identify as many as possible, even if you think they are trivial.

Figure 7.1 shows the completed portion of the ABC Analysis form for the problem performance, "does poor research." Let's assume that, as group leader, you have a member who resists doing academic research. She knows how to use search engines such as Google or Yahoo, but she refuses to use the more academic search engines and data bases such as ERIC, Communication and Mass Media Complete, or ICPSR data sets. As group leader, you know that your grade is premised, in part, on producing an academic report based upon reliable and valid sources, and Yahoo or Google may not always produce these sources. Your instructor has said that any nonacademic source will result in a poor grade.

Step 4c: Cross out any antecedents and consequences that are not relevant to the performer. You will need to review each consequence on the form and ask: "Does this consequence have a payoff for the group member?" Remember, the group member must view this consequence as being important to himself or herself, not to you or the group. Too often, only those that have a payoff for the group are listed, such as:

FIGURE 7.1

ABC ANALYSIS
Performer(s): Marcella

Problem Performance	Antecedents	Consequences	P/N	I/F	C/U
Poor research	Needs training seminar from library.	Avoids hassles of training.	P	I	C
	Thinks academic research is a waste of time.	Peers may ridicule	N	F	U
	Likes using Google or Yahoo.	More time for other things	P	I	C
	Thinks other members do research better.	Members might disagree.	N	I	U
	Doesn't care about grade.	Poor grade	N	F	C
	Spends more time with boyfriend.	Enjoys self	P	I	C
	Works more hours.	Earns more money.	P	I	C
	Doesn't like confusing websites.	Can't take advantage of academic sources.	N	I	U
	Takes the class credit/no credit.	Spends less time on assignments	P	I	C

- Other members repeat research
- Delayed reports
- More time needed to produce reports
- Increased anxiety

These are group payoffs, not member payoffs. Consequences that are significant to the group may not be significant to the problem performer.

After you have listed all of the consequences you can think of, cross out any of them that you believe may be considered unimportant to the problem performer. Figure 7.2 shows the list from Figure 7.1 with one consequence crossed out, a consequence the problem performer in our example would probably find unimportant.

Step 4d: After you have crossed out any consequences, for each remaining consequence indicate whether it is **P/N**, **I/F**, or **C/U**. The consequences are categorized according to three criteria:

- Type of consequence—positive or negative, **P/N**
- Its immediacy—immediate or future, **I/F**
- The probability of occurrence—certain or uncertain, **C/U**

FIGURE 7.2

ABC ANALYSIS
Performer(s): Marcella

Problem Performance	Antecedents	Consequences	P/N	I/F	C/U
Poor research	Needs training seminar from library.	Avoids hassles of training.	P	I	C
	Thinks academic research is a waste of time.	Peers may ridicule	N	F	U
	Likes using Google or Yahoo.	More time for other things	P	I	C
	Thinks other members do research better.	Members might disagree.	N	I	U
	Doesn't care about grade.	Poor grade	N	F	C
	Spends more time with boyfriend.	Enjoys self	P	I	C
	Works more hours.	Earns more money.	P	I	C
	Doesn't like confusing websites.	Can't take advantage of academic sources.	N	I	U
	Takes the class credit/no credit.	Spends less time on assignments	P	I	C

Remember that the consequences are categorized from the perspective of the person in question, the problem performer.

- **Positive or negative.** To decide whether the consequence is positive or negative, you just need to determine if this is something the person wants or doesn't want. In Figure 7.2, there are five positives and four negatives, but one of the negatives has been crossed out as unimportant to the performer. As leader, you will get to know each member, and this will help you make your determination as to whether a particular consequence will have a positive or negative impact.
- **Immediate or future.** An immediate consequence is one that occurs during the behavior or on its completion. Any consequence after the fact is considered Future. Many consequences in group work occur days, if not weeks, after the performance has occurred. As a rule, the longer the delay between behavior and consequence, the less effectiveness that consequence will have on the problem behavior.
- **Certain or uncertain.** This is the likelihood or probability that the consequence will actually occur. Again, this is from the problem performer's

FIGURE 7.3

ABC ANALYSIS
Performer(s): Marcella

Problem Performance	Antecedents	Consequences	P/N	I/F	C/U
Poor research	Needs training seminar from library.	Avoids hassles of training.	P	I	C
	Thinks academic research is a waste of time.	Peers may ridicule	N	F	U
	Likes using Google or Yahoo.	More time for other things	P	I	C
	Thinks other members do research better.	Members might disagree.	N	I	U
	Doesn't care about grade.	Poor grade	N	F	C
	Spends more time with boyfriend.	Enjoys self	P	I	C
	Works more hours.	Earns more money.	P	I	C
	Doesn't like confusing websites.	Can't take advantage of academic sources.	N	I	U
	Takes the class credit/no credit.	Spends less time on assignments	P	I	C

perspective. Does the person really believe that he or she will experience the consequence? The question you need to ask is: "Has the person experienced the consequence as certain to happen, or not very likely to happen?"

As group leader, you may warn a member that he or she will receive a poor performance grade if he or she refuses to participate in group discussion. The member, however, knows that some of the other members had been told the same thing when they didn't participate, and they didn't get poor performance grades. As a result, the member may see this consequence as uncertain. You, however, believe that you will write a poor performance report, even though you rarely do so. The fact that you said you would makes you believe that it is a certain consequence. Regardless of this, your warning will have little effect because in the member's experience the consequence is uncertain.

Step 5: Complete an ABC Analysis for the correct or desired performance.

Step 5a: Once you have determined the undesired performance, you write the **correct** performance of the form. In Figure 7.3, the performance we want is written in the correct space.

Step 5b is the same as in Step 4. It provides additional guidelines you may want to consider when you perform an ABC Analysis. All you need to do is ask the same questions about the correct behavior that were asked about the problem behavior.

1. What is the payoff to the problem group member to do good research?
2. What consequences have value to her?
3. Does she see the consequences as P/N, I/F, C/U?

Step 5b: As simple as it may sound, training is usually an antecedent for the correct or desired behavior. In our example, perhaps the underlying reason Marcella doesn't perform good research is that she has never been taught how to do academic research; therefore, she finds excuses in order to avoid it. Aca-

demic research training would be a good antecedent for the correct or desired behavior. Too often, instructors take it for granted that students know how to research. I have a policy of scheduling my lower-division classes two days in the library at the beginning of each semester with a research librarian specifically to teach freshman and sophomore students how to use university resources; that way, I know that they have been trained in the basics. It also helps them as they transit through upper-division courses that demand good research skills, such as a Communication Research course in quantitative and qualitative analysis. As a leader, you need to assume that people don't have the necessary training to complete the project—simply ask. It may save you much contention in the group.

Step 6: The diagnosis: Summarize the antecedents and consequences that are occurring now. By the completion of Step 5, you should have been able to identify the antecedents and consequences causing the performance problem. In Step 6, we need to summarize and review this information. This process produces five conclusions:

1. **Antecedents.** We find that the problem behavior will have many antecedents and the correct behavior will have just a few. There could be a multitude of conditions that prompt the behavior, but only a few that trigger the correct or desired behavior.
2. **Positives and negatives.** The number of positives and negatives are basically the same for both the problem behavior and the correct behavior. However, based solely on this, it is difficult to predict what the person would do; therefore, we continue our analysis.
3. **Impact of positives and negatives.** Although the positives and negatives are about the same for the unwanted behavior, the negatives appear to be

FIGURE 7.4

ABC ANALYSIS
Performer(s): Marcella

Desired Performance	Antecedents	Consequences	P/N	I/F	C/U
Good research	Pressure from classmates	Takes time from other things.	N	I	C
	Produces better work	Grade improves.	P	F	U
	Sees boyfriend less.	Enjoys self less.	N	F	U
	Enjoys a challenge.	Makes research easier.	P	F	U
	Classmates acknowledge improved research.	Feels good about self.	P	I	C

more powerful than the positives. Spending less time with her boyfriend seems to be a stronger negative than the positive consequence of "Feels good about self." The difference here is that the negative of "Sees boyfriend less" is future and uncertain, even though it is more powerful than the positive "Feels good about self." We prefer positives that are immediate and certain, even though they don't seem to be significant in the long term for the simple reason that they tend to be immediate and certain (PIC) while negatives are future and uncertain.

4. **PICs.** Aubrey Daniels says that this is perhaps the most important one. The problem behavior has more PICs than the desired behavior. While it is true that NICs are as powerful as PICs, you must remember that NICs stop behavior rather than keep it going. Therefore, PICs are the most effective consequence for maintaining or increasing performance.

5. **Future/uncertain consequences.** As a general rule, the more delayed the consequence, the less impact it will have on the behavior or performance. Therefore, consequences that are uncertain and delayed have a limited effect on the performer. Also, there is a correlation between the number of times a consequence is associated with a behavior and the effects they have on behavior. The fewer times a consequence is associated with a behavior, the weaker effect it has on the behavior. An ABC Analysis often reveals that for the problem performance, the future/uncertain consequences tend to be negative. The opposite is typically true for the desired behavior. The future/uncertain consequences tend to be positive.[14] This means that consequences for both desired and unwanted behaviors are weak. In other words, consequences—either negative or positive—that are uncertain or delayed have limited impact on the behavior. You should always consider using consequences that are immediate and certain.

Step 7: The solution. A completed ABC Analysis for our problem performer suggests two possible ways we can increase the correct or desired behavior:

1. Add positive/immediate consequences for the correct or desired behavior;
2. Add antecedents for the correct or desired behavior.

The best way to get Marcella to change her undesired behavior to productive behavior is to make sure that she gets some form of payoff for doing it; the more immediate that payoff, the better. Sometimes, it can be something as simple as a pat on the back; other times, it may be acknowledging her efforts in front of the group, or perhaps giving her extended time to complete a project.

An effective leader will monitor each member's performance on an individual basis and record it on a graph. This graph is a real time history of the performer's behaviors. It is a good tool to have when you want to praise a member for improving himself or herself, such as Marcella.

Aubrey Daniels (1989, p. 49) maintains that "If the graph has a daily goal on it and goal attainment has been paired consistently with praise, the graph will become an effective antecedent for improved performance." Group leaders will need to monitor members' performance in order to provide positive/immediate consequences. Part of that process includes speaking with individual members about the things they did to improve their performance. It is up to you to observe proper work habits, cooperative behavior, and other desirable actions. Also, if you develop a reinforcement system where each member knows precisely what is expected of the group, they will then be able to participate in providing reinforcement (P/I) for each other. Usually, P/I reinforcers are in short supply. We have a tendency to tell people what they're doing wrong, but generally refrain from praising people when they do things correctly.

PM is all about observation and employing positive/immediate reinforcers or consequences. Eventually, you'll be able to introduce positive/future reinforcement. After some experience, you'll be able to introduce new antecedents that will have positive effects on both desired behaviors and consequences.

Does an ABC Analysis Have Value?

We can answer that with an emphatic YES! The ABC analysis can be applied to any individual or group behavior or performance problem. There may be times when you won't understand why a problem performance exists; in these cases, the ABC analysis will be helpful. When conducted correctly, the analysis will show that there are logical reasons why people do what they do. And more importantly, it usually will suggest a solution.

As a leadership tool, the ABC analysis helps us to create an environment that will promote those behaviors in order to benefit the individual and the group in both the short and long term. The ABC analysis is a good leadership tool for planning any performance change. To use it effectively, an in-depth understanding of reinforcement is essential. That's the next part of this chapter.

REINFORCEMENT

Up to this point, you should have a fairly good understanding of what antecedents and consequences are, and how to conduct an ABC Analysis. Let's go back to our example. We have analyzed Marcella's performance and have a pretty good idea as to what the desired behavior should be. The question becomes, "How do we get her to do what we want her to do?" You merely can't tell her what to do; you need to reinforce the desired behavior. The process in which a person receives a reinforcer is called reinforcement.[15] A reinforcer is generally considered to be an object or event. Reinforcers and reinforcement are the most important concepts to understand in managing performance because reinforcement increases behavior. Everybody needs positive reinforcement from time to time, no matter who you are.

> **Reinforcement**
> The process in which a person receives a reinforcer.

Abraham Maslow was a humanistic psychologist who developed a hierarchic theory of needs that focuses on the well-adjusted, emotionally healthy individual.[16] He believed that human needs are what drive us to action and what motivates our behavior. Working to satisfy needs gives us pleasure; needs motivate achievement and progress.[17] Sometimes, their influence on us is so strong that we do things that we normally wouldn't do. We can appeal to someone's needs if we understand them. We can influence his or her behavior. We can persuade him or her to do something that he or she normally would not do. It helps us to look at these needs as a general description of reinforcers.

- **Physiological needs.** These are biological needs—the maintenance of the human body. They include the needs we have for oxygen, water, protein, salt, sugar, calcium, and other minerals and vitamins.
- **Safety needs.** When all physiological needs are satisfied, the needs for security come next. Safety needs include our need for security, freedom from harm, anxiety, and fear. The peaceful, smoothly running, stable, good society ordinarily makes people feel safe enough from wild animals, extremes of temperature, criminal assault, murder, chaos, tyranny, and the like.

  Humans try to predict the future in order to gain control over their environment. The popularity of psychics and fortune tellers, our addiction to weather forecasts, calendars, scheduling, and daily routines all attest to our need for security. The satisfaction of this needs category provides us with the stability in living and living in a stable world.
- **Needs of love, affection, and belongingness.** When the needs for safety and physiological well-being

© Golden Pixels LLC 2011. Under license from Shutterstock, Inc.

are satisfied, the next class of needs for love, affection, and belongingness emerge. Maslow states that people seek to overcome feelings of loneliness and alienation. There is a need for affiliation with others, both giving and receiving love, affection, and a desire for social cohesion. In our day-to-day life, we exhibit these needs in our desires to marry, have a family, be a part of a community, a member of a church, a brother in the fraternity, a part of a gang or a bowling club. It is also a part of what we look for in a career. We strive intensely to achieve these goals.

- **Needs for esteem.** After the first three classes of needs have been satisfied, the needs for a little self-esteem now become foremost. Esteem needs may be characterized by achievement, adequacy, mastery, competence, independence, and freedom. Maslow noted two versions of esteem needs, a lower one and a higher one. The lower one is the need for the respect of others, the need for status, prestige, fame, glory, social recognition, attention, reputation, appreciation, dignity, even dominance. The higher form involves the need for self-respect, including such feelings as confidence, competence, achievement, mastery, independence, and freedom. When these needs are satisfied, the individual feels self-confident and valuable as a person.

- **Needs for self-actualization.** The last level is a bit different. Maslow has used a variety of terms to refer to this level: He has called it growth motivation (in contrast to deficit motivation), being needs (or B-needs, in contrast to D-needs), and self-actualization. These are needs that do not involve balance or homeostasis. As a person progresses from deficiency needs to growth needs, extrinsic rewards, such as money and status (which are so important at level four), are replaced by intrinsic rewards. Now, the person is motivated to excel for the sheer joy of the task or activity. An intrinsic reward is an intense satisfaction that comes from within the individual. Once this level of needs is engaged, they continue to be felt. In fact, they are likely to become stronger as we feed them! They involve the continuous desire to fulfill potentials, to be all that you can be. They are a matter of becoming the most complete, the fullest, you—hence the term, self-actualization.

Just as people need food, air, and water—the most basic needs—they also need social recognition, praise, and challenge—the higher needs. These higher needs can be used as positive reinforcers. Positive reinforcement has a way to make members feel good about themselves and, in turn, about the group leader. This increases morale, which, in turn, improves the quality of group work and creates a positive climate for the group.

We've talked about reinforcement and reinforcers; so what is a reinforcer? There are two types of reinforcers: **positive** and **negative**. A reinforcer is anything that follows a behavior and causes it either to maintain or increase the frequency or likelihood of a response.[18] Reinforcers have a least three distinctive features:[19]

1. A reinforcer always follows a behavior; it can never **precede** it. Remember, anything that comes before the behavior is an **antecedent**. As group leader, if you promise a member that you will give him or her less work on the next project if he or she works harder on this one, that is a bribe—a

compliance-gaining technique—not a reinforcer. A reinforcer always comes after the behavior.

The first thing you need to do before you can analyze a behavior is to decide on the behavior that troubles you and then observe what follows it. This is the only way you will discover reinforcers.

2. Reinforcers usually increase the frequency of a behavior. We can say that something is a reinforcer if, and only if, it increases the frequency of behavior. Reinforcers have a tendency to change. There may be times when reinforcers no longer produce an increase in the desired behavior, or there may be a decrease in the desired behavior. When this occurs, the consequence may no longer be reinforcing, and you will need to perform another ABC analysis. It is not the fault of the reinforcer. People tire of the best reinforcers simply because they're over exposed to them. For example, your favorite ice cream is rocky road. You love rocky road, but seldom eat it. If you ate rocky road ice cream every day, you would soon tire of it. Reinforcers are the same way. If you get too much of something, you eventually will no longer respond positively to it. Your group members may respond to your reinforcers in similar fashion. You will need to constantly keep an eye on individual performance to make sure that the consequences are still working.

3. A reinforcer can be anything material or social. **Material reinforcers** include, but are not limited to, such things as a $10.00 Starbucks or Jamba Juice card, a free lunch, or an achievement award. **Social reinforcers** are usually interpersonal interactions between the leader and members, such as a pat on the back, recognition for a job well done, or inclusion in conversations. Whatever reinforcer you choose to use, remember that you may need to use it or something similar with other members. What's good for one is good for the entire group. The last thing you want to do is to create a perception that you are playing favorites with members.

Now that you know what reinforcers are, where can you find them? There are a number of places. Remember Maslow's hierarchy of needs? This is a good starting point. All humans have needs, wants, and desires. As we mentioned earlier, needs motivate us to action, as do wants and desires. Although these aren't reinforcers, knowing what a person wants will help you discover effective reinforcers. Fortunately, many of us share similar needs, wants, and desires; but none of us share them exactly the same. One of the most common mistakes leaders make in choosing reinforcers for group members is that they assume members want what they want, even when there are major differences in values, education, social

© karen roach, 2011. Under license from Shutterstock, Inc.

status, and culture. Each member is different with his or her own unique set of reinforcers. Performance management will not work effectively unless the member's reinforcers are offered.

I have found an excellent way to discover effective reinforcers. I privately talk to each member and ask each to speak about his or her likes, dislikes, hobbies; what he or she finds most satisfying about group work, and what he or she most dislikes about it. Basically, I ask them to talk about themselves. Given the opportunity, people love to speak about themselves; however, you will need to guide the discussion. This is where good interpersonal communication skills come in hand, which we will discuss in Chapter 9. Once you have decided on which reinforcers to use, make certain that they are under your control. The last thing you want to happen is that you are overruled by a superior. Every group leader has limitations in power; what they can and can't do. Always do things that you know are within those limits. This will help you maintain, and even build, your leadership position and credibility.

Another way to discover reinforcers that will work with a particular member is to observe what that member chooses to do voluntarily. What people do may be an indication as to what is reinforcing to them. Generally speaking, preferred behaviors can be used to reinforce unpreferred behaviors. This is called the **Premack Principle**, after psychologist David Premack, who initially proposed the rule. It states that high-probability behaviors (those performed frequently under conditions of free choice) can be used to reinforce low-probability behaviors.

🔖 Premack Principle
States that high-probability behaviors (those performed frequently under conditions of free choice) can be used to reinforce low-probability behaviors.

Parents often use a variation of the Premack Principle on their children: "If you eat your vegetables (sometimes a nonpreferred behavior), you can have dessert (usually a preferred behavior)." Or, "If you do your homework by 5:00 p.m. (a nonpreferred behavior), you can watch *The Simpsons* tonight or you can play a video game (a preferred behavior)." The Premack Principle allows leaders to find reinforcers that occur naturally in the group setting. It relies on a contingency contract, explicit or implied: If a member does X, then he or she can do Y. The Premack Principle also is one of the best time-management techniques you can use for group work. List all of the tasks the group has to do, and rank them in the following order: top of the list—the thing each member would most like to do; bottom of the list—the thing each member would most not like to do. Then reverse the list, and start with the one at the bottom, the least-favored task. Every time you complete a task, the next one becomes more reinforcing.

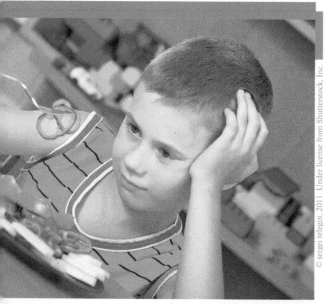

© sergei telegin, 2011. Under license from Shutterstock, Inc.

Finding effective reinforcers at first is a trial-and-error method. Don't be discouraged if you are not successful at first. You may want to speak with other group leaders who may have used reinforcers. The best reinforcers are those that are always available to you. A readily available reinforcer is a **WHIP**—**W**hat you **H**ave **I**n your **P**ossession. Social reinforces are the ones that are most available and usually the easiest to implement. You don't have to ask permission or have a budget to pat someone on the back, write a note on performance, or praise in some way. The more you do it, the more reinforcers you will find.[21]

So far, we have talked about positive reinforcers. What about negative reinforcers? **Negative reinforcement** strengthens a behavior because a negative condition is stopped or avoided as a consequence of the behavior.[22] Negative reinforcement has a way of making people do things in order to escape or avoid something they don't want to do. However, negative reinforcement is still reinforcement, nonetheless. Generally, it will increase or maintain a performance. Human nature dictates that people will perform to avoid something negative. For example, let's say that Marcella always comes late to group meetings. You, the leader, begin assigning her research tasks, knowing that she dislikes them. You tell her that she can avoid research assignments if she comes to meetings on time. This is a negative reinforcer. There is a tendency to confuse negative reinforcement with punishment. **Punishment** weakens a behavior because a negative condition is introduced or experienced as a consequence of the behavior. Punishment decreases performance, and negative reinforcement increases performance, at least in the short term. All group work behavior is the product of reinforcement—either positive or negative. And it's important to know which kind of reinforcement is generating the behavior in the group environment. Positive and negative reinforcement produces very different kinds of performance. With positive reinforcement, members do things because they want to. With negative reinforcement, they do things because they have to. The most you can hope for with negative reinforcement will be just enough work to escape or avoid punishment. If all you are seeking is compliance, then negative reinforcers can be effective. Negative reinforcers are ineffective if fear is not present to some degree. If negative reinforcers are used to get a performance started, positive reinforcement should be used to keep it going.[23]

The following is a rule of thumb when using reinforcers:[24]

> **Punishment**
> Weakens a behavior because a negative condition is introduced or experienced as a consequence of the behavior.

1. **Personalize your reinforcement.** Your reinforcers should reflect your interpersonal communication style. If you use tangible or social reinforcers that you are not comfortable with, the group will notice, and they typically will not be accepted as reinforcing.

    When acknowledging your appreciation for efforts or accomplishments, express your praise in terms of how you feel. Describe in a few well-chosen words what the person did that you liked and why you liked it. Above all, personalize your reinforcers.

2. **Make your reinforcement sincere.** Your reinforcement should be both personalized and sincere. The sincerity of your reinforcement is very important. Sincerity is expressed by what you say and how you say it. If you are not sincere, then it is unlikely that what you say will be reinforcing. Never tell a person something you do not mean. If a member is not doing a good job, don't tell him or her that he or she is—be sincere; that's a part of good leadership.

3. **Reinforce immediately.** The best time to reinforce is when you observe the behavior. Reinforcement works best when members are doing what you want them to do.

Reinforcers lose their effectiveness over time. The longer you delay between the performance and the reinforcer, the less impact the reinforcer will have on the performance.

Reinforcement is meant to reinforce whatever is happening at the time it occurs.

4. **Make your reinforcement specific.** Specific reinforcement generally refers to some form of praise. Tell members exactly what they did that you liked. Identify their behavior or behaviors in specific terms.

One way of being specific with a group is to develop a feedback system. Ask members to tell the group what they did to accomplish their task or how they improved their performance.

5. **Reinforce frequently.** As a rule, the more frequently a person is reinforced for a desired performance, the stronger that performance will be. How many reinforcers are enough? That depends on the situation and the individual. Some people need lots of reinforcement while others tend to shy away from it. After working with your group, you should be able to determine the frequency of reinforcement with each individual.

6. **Don't reinforce and punish at the same time.** Often, when we deliver reinforcement, we have a tendency to express both what we did and didn't like about the performance. On one hand, we praise them; then on the other hand, we say something negative about their behavior. Here's the problem: if reinforcement is frequently followed by a negative, then reinforcement becomes an antecedent for punishment. The reaction to reinforcement soon becomes, "What have I done wrong?" I call it the but syndrome. "You do this well, but…" Separate the two. First, reinforce the behavior; then let a little time go by before you point out something that you think needs to be changed. Don't confuse people by mixing reinforcement and punishment. Deliver them on separate occasions.

7. **Don't mix goal setting and reinforcement.** Does this sound familiar? "Marcella, you did a great job with your research. Thank you. But in the future, could you get it to me sooner than you did this time and could you include a cover page?" Sometimes, when we reinforce a behavior, we ask the member for something else.

This request now becomes a punisher. We are telling people that they did great, but didn't do great. We are repeating number 6. "Don't reinforce and punish at the same time." You can set whatever goal you want for the group and each member; however, you must reinforce improvement toward that goal, not the goal itself. Reinforcement modifies the behavior—it is a positive consequence. One important key to remember to The ABC Model is consistency when it comes to consequences: "Do what you say you're going to do." Eventually, your consequences will become the antecedents.

SUMMARY

In this chapter, we explained performance management and the differences between it and team building. We learned that PM is systematic, data-oriented, and measured, and we examined the value that PM brings to group work. We explored the ABC Model of Behavior Change, and learned about antecedents, behavior, and consequences—both positive and negative. Along with these, we studied the 7-Step ABC Analysis Model and reviewed Maslow's Hierarchy of Needs and its importance in identifying reinforcers. We concluded with seven tips to help ensure that you will be effective when using reinforcers in your leadership role.

DISCUSSION

1. Why is it so important within **Performance Management** that evaluations of performance be **data–driven** and supported by consistent **measurement**? What situations can you identify from your own experience in which leaders seems to have expectations of some sort but were not connecting these expectations clearly to measurement and data? How did this lack of connection to data affect people's relationship to the leader?

2. Identify as many as possible of the **antecedents** associated with your performance within this course in small group communication. Devote special attention to those that are not explicitly stated, such as on the syllabus: How do you know that these antecedents matter, even though they are not explicitly stated?

3. Consider again the fact that "getting a good grade" is probably the most common **consequence** associated with performance in your small group communication course. Based on what you read in this chapter about consequences, what drawbacks might grades have as the primary consequence guiding behavior among students in this course?

4. Consider again the consequence of "getting a good grade" as you imagine that one of your group members does not seem to mind that the group's grades will suffer if he submits assignments late, misses meetings, and so on. Discuss what your answers might be, as a leader, to the question posed in Step 4b of the ABC analysis (page 14) about why he does not seem to relate to lower grades in the same ways other group members do. Based on your responses and on your understanding of the process of ABC analysis, what choices might you have to encourage him to change his performance?

5. Use the **Premack principle** to work with your group, generating a list in order of the tasks from the least rewarding to the most rewarding. How are you able to confidently determine this rank order? What qualities tend to make a given task unrewarding, and what qualities tend to make a given task rewarding?

NOTES

1. Gilbert, T.F. (1978). *Human competence: Engineering worthy performance*. New York: McGraw-Hill.

2. Daniels, A.C. (2000). *Bringing out the best in people*. New York: McGraw-Hill.

3. Ibid.

4. Daniels, A.C. (1989). P*erformance management: Improving quality productivity through positive reinforcement* (3rd ed.). Tucker, GA: Performance Management.

5. Ibid.

6. Bandura, A. (1977). *Social learning theory*. Englewood Cliffs, N.J.: Prentice-Hall.

7. Trenholm, S., & Jensen, A. (1996). *Interpersonal communication*. Belmont, CA: Wadsworth.

8. Gilbert, T.F. (1978). *Human competence: Engineering worthy performance*. New York: McGraw-Hill.

9. Daniels, A.C., & Daniels, J.E. (2004). *Performance management: Changing behavior that drives organizational effectiveness* (4th ed.). Atlanta, GA: Performance Management.

10. Kotter, J.P. (1996). *Leading change*. Boston: Harvard Business School Press.

11. Daniels, A.C. (1989). *Performance management: Improving quality productivity through positive reinforcement* (3rd ed.). Tucker, GA: Performance Management.

12. Fournies, F. (1978). *Coaching for improved work performance*. New York: Van Nostrand.

13. Adapted from Daniels, A.C. (1989). *Performance management: Improving quality productivity through positive reinforcement* (3rd ed.). Tucker, GA: Performance Management.

14. Ibid.

15. Gilbert, T.F. (1978). *Human competence: Engineering worthy performance*. New York: McGraw-Hill.

16. Simons, J.A., Irwin, D.B., & Drinnien, B.A. (1987). *Psychology: The search for understanding*. New York: West.

17. Johnston, D.D. (1994). *The art and science of persuasion*. Dubuque, IA: Brown and Benchmark.

18. http://science.jrank.org/pages/5785/Reinforcement-Positive-Negative.html. Retrieved August 13, 2009.

19. Lecture notes from Dr. Daniel Montgomery, The Florida State University, Tallahassee, Fl, 1995–1996.

20. http://www.psywww.com/intropsych/ch05_conditioning/premack_principle.html. Retrieved August 16, 2009.

21. Daniels, A.C. (1989). *Performance management: Improving quality productivity through positive reinforcement* (3rd ed.). Tucker, GA: Performance Management.

22. http://www.mcli.dist.maricopa.edu/proj/nru/nr.html. Retrieved August 22, 2009.

23. Gilbert, T.F. (1978). *Human competence: Engineering worthy performance*. New York: McGraw-Hill.

24. Adapted from Daniels, A.C. (1989). *Performance management: Improving quality productivity through positive reinforcement* (3rd ed.). Tucker, GA: Performance Management.

8

Leadership and Team Building

CHAPTER OBJECTIVES

- Understand the purpose of leadership
- Be familiar with roles of leadership
- Be able to explain the decision-making process
- Be able to explain the problem-solving process
- Know how teams and groups work with a leader
- Be familiar with modeling behavior and leadership

KEY TERMS

Dependability
Competence
Credibility
ACORN test
Proactive behavior
Process

CHAPTER OUTLINE

Leadership
    Decision-Making Process
    Problem-Solving Process

Making Teams Work
    Behavior Is the Key
    Creating the Proper Environment

Managing Teams
    Modeling: What to Model

Reinforcement: Know What You
    Want to Reinforce
Process versus Content
How to Support the Process
Reinforcing

Summary

LEADERSHIP

"A leader is best when people barely knows he exists,
Not so good when people obey and acclaim him,
Worse when they despise him.
But of a good leader, who talks little,
When his work is done, his aim fulfilled,
They will say: We did it ourselves."

Lao-tzu

It is said that leaders are people with managerial skills and personal power who can influence others to perform actions beyond those that could be dictated by those persons' formal (position) authority alone. In Chapter 2, we said that working together and cooperating are better than working against one another. We work in groups and teams for many goal-oriented reasons, but primarily because we can't achieve organizational goals most effectively by ourselves. And most effective groups aren't self-directed; instead, they have a leader who provides guidance and resources individual members cannot match. Team building is, in part, effective communication consisting of the leader, the group or team members, and the environment in which the work is performed.

- **The leader.** It is the leader's job to build an environment in which teamwork can be achieved. One of the first things a leader has to do is to create and maintain credibility with the group. There are four factors that influence this effort: drive, dependability, competence, and credibility. **Drive** is the physical and mental effort used by the leader. Dependability is the reliance people have in the leader's word—can they trust what he says? Competence is the leader's ability to get a job done effectively and efficiently. Credibility is the degree to which a leader is believable. An effective leader enables and motivates the group to stay on track, to remain energized and empowered, to resolve conflicts constructively, and to make creative decisions, in order to reach desirable outcomes.
- **The group or team.** It doesn't matter how hard the leader tries to develop group teamwork; the leader cannot do it without the support of individual members. Members must have positive group norms and feelings toward the leader and the organization.
- **The environment.** The environment must be conducive for maximum performance. Too often, organizations impose operating philosophies that create teamwork problems. Effective teamwork is achieved by positively changing the internal environment.

Dependability
The reliance people have in the leader's word.

Competence
The leader's ability to get a job done effectively and efficiently.

Credibility
The degree to which a leader is believable.

It is the leader's responsibility to make sure that group or team members clearly understand what team building is and what it is not. Effective leadership is a complex endeavor. Leaders not only lead, they facilitate the group or team. This is accomplished in a number of ways, but most importantly leaders empower members and create an environment where: (1) members feel significant, feel that they are valued and can positively contribute to the group charge; (2) members are part of a team; they develop a sense of community that fosters synergy; (3) members view tasks as challenging, stimulating, fun, and at times, exciting; (4) members feel that they are pulled or drawn to a goal rather than pushed to a goal; (5) members are energized through positive reinforcement. Leadership is leading others to lead themselves.

Team leadership is challenging. Becoming an effective team leader requires that you:[2]

1. **Develop the ability to trust others.** You cannot do all of the work yourself. Once a task has been delegated, you trust that the member will, at the very least, satisfactorily complete that task on time.

2. **Learn to share information.** Communicate well. Group work can only be achieved if there is a constant flow of information between all members. It is imperative that the leader provide any and all information relevant for the group to achieve its charge.

3. **Learn to give up authority.** Members need to be empowered. Empowerment means that members have a degree of autonomy with which to complete their tasks.

4. **Intercede only when necessary.** An effective leader knows when he or she should intercede and when to leave the group alone. Too much interference on the part of the leader has a tendency to create an atmosphere of distrust amongst members; too little intercession may cause the group to lose direction.

In Chapter 2, we also said that the primary functions of **work-oriented groups** are **decision making** and **problem solving**. Decision making is making a choice among two or more alternatives to solve a problem, whereas problem solving means that there is a gap between the current situation and a desired solution. Both processes require clear-cut objectives. A group without clear-cut objectives lacks behavioral guidelines for its members.[3]

Decision-Making Process

The decision-making process generally requires six phases: (1) identify a goal and a problem preventing goal achievement; (2) examine constraints; (3) develop and analyze alternative ways of responding; (4) make the decision; (5) plan action and implement the decision; and (6) evaluate the results or consequences.[4]

1. **Identify a goal and a problem preventing goal achievement.** Identify a goal that needs to be achieved and a problem or a set of problems that stand in the way of achieving that goal. The team needs to know where it is going. Unfocused members sometimes go beyond their authority, do

© StockLite, 2011. Under license from Shutterstock, Inc.

sloppy work, solve problems that do not exist, or fail to solve the assigned problem. Once the team understands what it is supposed to accomplish, it can examine any constraints imposed on them and then generate potential options for accomplishing that goal. For example, your local board of education and board of supervisors agree that a new elementary school needs to be built to accommodate a growing student population. The goal is to build a new school; however two problems emerge: where to build the new school and how to pay for it. The boards must determine if there is land available, and if so, whether they can generate the funds necessary to build it.

2. **Examine constraints.** The decision-making process has two types of constraints: internal and external. External constraints are those imposed on the decision-making process, such as the time, money, resources, energy, knowledge base, or other resources that the group or individual has to use for the process. Internal constraints are those integral to the problem. They may have instigated the initial problem, or they may have to do with limitations on the implementation, such as government regulations, the physical location, technical or design difficulties, etc. Continuing with our example, each board may have constraints as to its legal authority—that has the power to do what. Other constraints may surface, such as, disagreement among members of each board as to the location of the new school, its design, choosing general contractors; the list of constraints can be extensive. Usually, the more complex the decision, the more complex the constraints. For the classroom, always try to keep decision-making projects as simple as possible. Your goal is to learn about the process, not get bogged down in the process.

3. **Develop and analyze alternative ways of responding.** We need to develop and analyze alternative ways of responding to the problem and constraints. Avoid accepting an either-or response—it is either this or it is that. Good decision making requires the exploration of multiple viable solutions to the problem. In negotiations, we call it expanding the pie or brainstorming.[5] The goal is to broaden the possible options or alternatives for the decision-making process.

4. **Make the decision.** When we have considered all of the possible alternatives, we finally have to make a choice. This is a critical phase of the process. By the time this phase of discussion is reached, the team is often fatigued. There is a tendency to jump to conclusions with the slogan, "Well, it's obvious what we ought to do is..." Statements like this subvert the team's work. It is in this phase that all of the alternatives should be discussed and the merits of each debated. The team has spent considerable time and energy researching and developing alternatives. Now is not the time to make hasty decisions.

5. **Plan action and implement the decision.** Develop a plan of action and implement the decision we have made. A proposal for implementing the plan of action should be as specific as possible. It should detail the group's charge, the criteria and limitations used for fact-finding, how it discovered and selected potential solutions, and the reasoning process used in choosing an appropriate solution. Then the plan of action is implemented by the appropriate authority.

6. **Evaluate the results or consequences.** Evaluate the results, or consequences, of our decision and of the process itself. Evaluation is an ongoing process once we implement the plan. It is a way for measuring the plan's effectiveness. We use the results from our evaluation as a feedback loop, which informs our decision making the next time.

Problem-Solving Process

The problem-solving process is similar to the decision-making process in many aspects; however, their purposes are quite different. The purpose of a problem-solving group is to find the best solution to a problem, which includes a solution that is cost-effective, easy to implement, and has short-, medium-, and long-term benefits.[6] Leaders must be able to bring in and process new information and new ways of approaching problems.

1. **Define the problem.** This is where the group gets to diagnose the problem. What makes it a problem? Who is affected by the problem? Why should we care about the problem? What makes the current situation untenable? Once we have defined the problem, we clearly define our goals and the criteria we will use to recognize and evaluate our achievement of those goals. After we have established our goals, we need to understand what it is that stands between us and them. Accurately identifying the problem may not be an easy task. What at first appears to be the problem may simply be a symptom. All of your research, plan of action, and decision making regarding solutions are premised on accurately identifying and defining the problem. If your group misdiagnoses the problem, then you will endeavor to solve something that doesn't exist.[7]

2. **Examine constraints in the context of goals.** The problem-solving process shares the same constraints with the decision-making process. The specifics of the constraints may vary, but the criteria remain the same.

3. **Search out alternatives.** Developing alternatives or options is often the most creative and exciting part of the problem-solving process. It involves researching and gathering as much information from as many sources as possible, processing, and synthesizing that information, and forming it into recommendations that respond to the problem.

4. **Make the decision.** This is where the group decides which of the recommendations best meets the goals they have set out to achieve. Their choice must take into account the costs and consequences of their best long-term solution in comparison to their more practical, more affordable, and more easily implemented and maintained solutions.

5. **Implement the decision.** In classroom group work, the group will produce a proposal that should be implemented, and that's as far as it will go. In the practical world, a separate body or authority generally implements the decision.

6. **Evaluate the decision.** We will not know if the decision making/problem solving process is complete until it has been determined whether or not it has accomplished its goals/objectives or whether the consequences are better or worse than we expected. How do we know this? Any effective evaluation has a procedure for measuring the success of the outcome as it relates to the definition of the original problem. This measurement tool is created when we define our goals and objectives. At the beginning of the process, we identify a given desired outcome, which becomes apparent if it meets certain specific criteria. These criteria become the basis for the evaluation.

Leadership requires that the leader truly understands the power of teamwork.[8] What makes teams so powerful? Two things: first, teams are diverse. Diversity increases the quality of wisdom that each member brings, and diversity brings new information and experiences. These are valued qualities. Second, teams improve work product and productivity. Do you remember the example about teamwork in the supermarket? Teams improve customer service, quality, innovation, and cost-effectiveness, just a name a few things.

MAKING TEAMS WORK

A primary role of leadership is to bring people together to solve problems. This increases the opportunities for members to receive positive reinforcement. Each team member has the potential to positively reinforce every other team member. Peers have the potential to exert tremendous influence on the behavior of peers, whether for better or worse. Team members have more contact with each other than do their group leaders, so reinforcement can be more frequent; and, since they are together while the work is occurring, reinforcement is likely to be immediate.[9] If the purpose of team building is to produce effective teams, then it is important to have some criteria for determining what constitutes effectiveness. Effective leadership depends on the group's willingness to follow. This willingness is generally based on the group's perception of the leader's abilities and credibility. A leader needs the group's trust and confidence if he or she is going to direct the group toward the stated goals and vision.

Behavior Is the Key

Teams or groups are composed of individuals. As leader, it is important to note that you cannot reinforce a team—only the behaviors of team members. The most important consideration in team effectiveness is the behavioral dimension. The requirement for team work to change is of much less importance than the need for people to change their behaviors and performances.

The way people behave is the single greatest cause of team-implementation failure.[10]

> You cannot reinforce a team. You can only reinforce the behaviors of team members.

The inability of team leaders to change the behaviors of team members can lead to resistance and discontent, and may eventually lead to the leader abandoning the process of reinforcement. You can reward a team, but it works best when *all* members are contributing equally. It's the leader's responsibility to apply consequences to team members in such a way that everybody is reinforced appropriately for their contributions to the team.[11]

> The best way to break an old habit is to replace it with a new one ... and reinforce it a lot.

Assuming that you can stop individual members from performing undesirable behaviors, which is difficult if not impossible in classroom groups, there's no guarantee that they'll begin performing in ways that are consistent with the team concept. You want to avoid forcing or coercing people into change because it works only as long as you are able to maintain very stringent controls and when you are prepared to dole out effective punishment for noncompliance. The alternative approach is to be ready to reinforce the new behaviors immediately. Any positive behavior change, as little as it may be, should be reinforced.

Creating the Proper Environment

One of the keys to successful group leadership is having an environment that fosters effective group work. When we talk about group environment, it is more than just where we are— the physical setting—when we communicate. Effective leadership requires that the leader create a particular environment that facilitates team work. This includes **information**, **confirmation**, and **instrumentation**.[12]

Information

1. **Provide clear and timely direction.** Sometimes, nothing is worse than not knowing specifically what you need to do and when you need to have it done. Clearly communicate whatever task you have assigned to each member, and provide timely directions. One way of checking that there is clear communication is to ask each member to repeat back to you when and how you expect them to perform their tasks.[13]
2. **Provide clear job descriptions.** The task structure must be clearly defined. The leader should describe this in such a way that there is only one way of performing a task, or communicate the degree to which the leader can clearly specify how something is to be accomplished. Clear job descriptions help keep the member focused on the assigned task and also allows for clear and timely evaluation of the member's performance.[14]
3. **Make certain the job descriptions pass the ACORN test.** The **ACORN** test is an acronym for five qualifications of every good description of the mission or charge of the group (at the policy level). Once the leader identifies the mission, it is much easier to describe the accomplishments at other levels correctly.[15] They are:

ACORN test
An acronym for five qualifications of every good description of the mission or charge of the group (at the policy level).

- **Accomplishment.** Is it an accomplishment that has been achieved and not just a description of a behavior? If the mission has been identified in behavioral terms; that is, if it is not a task toward achieving a goal, then it has not been identified. Distinguishing between accomplishments and behavior is not such an easy thing to do as it may sound at first. One way to make certain that we are describing accomplishments is to ask the question: Can we observe this thing we have described when we are not actually observing the performer, or when the performer is not there? Descriptions such as a list of research data bases are accomplishments because we can see them if the group member is not there. If we are not describing behavior, then the member responsible for an accomplishment doesn't need to be there at the time.

- **Control.** Do the members who have been assigned the task or charge have primary control over it, or does good performance principally depend on others? Members must have control over their task; otherwise, it cannot reasonably be described as their task. If one member has the charge of researching data bases, then that one person has control over that research. However, if other members engage in the same task, then researching data bases can't be described as one member's charge because that member lacks control.

- **Objective.** Is it a true overall objective or simply a subgoal? A task or charge is an overriding objective or goal of any role. If we can assign more than one goal to a role, chances are all but one (and maybe all of them) are subgoals. If this happens, then we have either failed to identify the charge altogether, or we have not distinguished it from a subgoal. A key question to ask is, "If this accomplishment were perfectly achieved, would performance be perfect? Would anything more be expected of the performer?" If the answer is no, then the charge or task has been accomplished.

- **Reliability.** Can this mission or charge be reconciled with other goals of the group, or is it incompatible with them? Usually, when the tasks or charges of two roles within the same group appear to be in conflict, one (or both) of them is poorly conceived. For example, one member is given the charge of note-taking. If a second member is given the same charge, and that person's notes are different than the other member's, there is a conflict. One or both roles have been ill-conceived.

- **Numbers.** Can a number be assigned to it; that is, can the performance be measured? We must be able to measure the performance, especially at the level of the task; otherwise, we have not described the task. The ultimate test of whether we have really identified a measurable accomplishment is to determine whether that task is observable and measurable after the performer has left.

The ACORN rule, and the five tests it represents, is very useful for evaluating the descriptions of a charge or task. Once we have identified the charge, it then becomes easier to develop the subgoals or the accomplishments that comprise the responsibilities and duties of the role.

4. **Provide good behavioral models.** "Do as I say and not as I do" doesn't apply here. There are good behavioral models available to you. If it is not yourself, then there are colleagues or others who you know who are good models. We use models for social learning, for directing others as to how they should perform. If you want good performance from your members, then identify one or two good models that they can mirror.

5. **Provide clear measurable performance standards.** This is a key to PM and getting members to perform well. People have to know prior to performing how they are going to be measured or evaluated. A performance standard is a statement of the expectations or requirements that you establish for each particular rating level.

   Earlier, we said that when we develop our performance goals and objectives, it is at that time that we also create the evaluation standards we will use to measure that performance. Whatever standards you use, make sure that they are attainable, objective, measurable, realistic, and clearly stated in writing.

6. **Provide an environment that rewards members for being responsible team players.** This is where you can be very creative. "I brought the doughnuts; who has the coffee?" When I teach an early morning small groups communication class, I bring the doughnuts. Sugar rushes are good for students, they energize them to work. But more importantly, it helps me create a rewarding environment and an environment in which students know that those doughnuts will be gone within 15 minutes. Most students *want* to show up on time rather than *have* to show up on time. You don't have to bring food; you can do other things that are equally creative. You get to decide what the meaning of responsible is and how responsible behavior will be rewarded.

7. **Provide an environment that allows members to feel safe to take responsibility and act independently, even at the risk of making a mistake.**

As leader, you should consider the following characteristics of effective teams: (a) Goals and values are clearly stated; they are understood and accepted by everyone. Members are oriented to goals and results; (b) Members clearly understand their assignments and tasks, and how their role contributes to the group charge overall; (c) The basic climate is one of trust and support among members; (d) Communications are open; members have an opportunity to share all information relevant to the goals of the team; (e) Decision making is open to all members. They make free, informed decisions, and not decisions that they think the leader wants;

© Nikola Bilic, 2011. Under license from Shutterstock, Inc.

(f) Leaders are supportive of each member and maintain high personal performance standards; (g) The team structure and procedures are consistent with the tasks, goals, and members involved.[16]

Confirmation

Confirmation is a feedback process. Feedback is similar to reinforcers; they are best when used right after a behavior. Group and member motivation can increase performance and member satisfaction when the team receives useful and positive feedback about its progress.[17] In simple terms, feedback tells people how they are doing. Follow these three principles:[18]

1. **Provide immediate, frequent, feedback.** You want to do this very frequently in the beginning of the group process. Members aren't sure how they should perform or what your expectations of them are. Immediate and frequent feedback provides direction, helps build trust, and reinforces members' performances, all of which contribute to group synergy.

2. **Provide positive, educational feedback.** Remember the difference between can't do and won't do? Positive, educational feedback is designed to help members who can't do become members who can do. One way to do this is to provide instructional feedback that educates a member as to how he or she should be able to perform. Too often, leaders tell members what they want them to do, but many times those members don't know how to do it. Providing positive, educational feedback teaches members how to perform.

3. **Provide only the necessary feedback.** Feedback encourages members to perform and provides evidence of their progress. Too much feedback can diminish its purpose; too little can be harmful. Offer feedback when it is necessary, when it is warranted to do so. Your feedback will have more strength and meaning to members.

Instrumentation

Instrumentation is the tangible support that a leader provides to the group. There are four general areas for consideration:

1. **Tools.** Tools refers to any and all equipment that may be necessary for each member to fulfill his or her task. In classroom group work, you will probably have your own laptop computer, or you will be able to use one in the school library or computer center. However, outside of the academic world, the organization you work for should provide all of the tools necessary for the group to achieve its goal. It is incumbent upon the leader to ensure that those tools are safe, reliable, and necessary.

2. **Procedures.** Group work can, at times, become somewhat boring. Design procedures that combat boredom and/or fatigue. Avoid the rote and mundane of everyday meetings if possible. Try to make the atmosphere enjoyable and lively. Periodically, do the unexpected. Also, you will want to provide simple and clear job aids, especially handouts, overheads, and power point presentations. The simpler, the better.

3. **Resources.** Chances are you will not be responsible for resources in classroom group work. However, organizations are responsible to provide members with quality materials and supplies, and a comfortable work environment.

4. **Incentives.** It is your responsibility to make individual and team performance matter; that's a part of being a leader. You should also eliminate hidden obstacles and competing incentives that may impede performance. In classroom group work, hidden obstacles may include having access to meeting rooms for your group to meet outside of class or access to computers. Try to schedule outside-of-class meetings ahead of time; this enables you to reserve a campus room once the group has agreed on times and days to meet.

© Tyler Olson, 2011. Under license from Shutterstock, Inc.

MANAGING TEAMS

When we talk about managing teams, we are really saying that we are managing individuals whose performance is viewed as a team performance. It is important to keep in mind that individual need satisfaction is going to be different for each member of the group (think about Maslow's Hierarchy of Needs). We often assume that group members have common goals and purposes. For example, your group may have four students who have very different needs. The only commonality you may share is the fact that you are taking a small groups course. Other than that, the only need you may share is the accomplishment of your group's charge so you can pass the class. The same basic principle applies in organizational settings; that is, each individual in a team may not share common needs except to achieve the group's charge.

As a leader, you are challenged on multiple fronts. How do you manage a team of individuals who are diverse in needs, save one? We will explore five general criteria:

Modeling: What to Model

1. **Proactive behavior.** This can be a combination of behaviors designed to facilitate and enhance group synergy. As leader, you may want to be aware of how individual needs affect the group's dynamics. Group members generally assume roles early in the establishment of group dynamics. Leaders provide group-building opportunities that move members from an "I" to a "We" orientation. Once individual members use the we term, they then consider themselves a part of the team and not just an individual

 Proactive behavior

Can be a combination of behaviors designed to facilitate and enhance group synergy.

functioning in a team setting. Always be prepared to adjust schedules to accommodate all members, and provide a balance between highly structured periods and more stimulating activities. Show empathy at all times, especially when members are in a state of crisis. Empathy demonstrates a genuine caring for members' well-being. Choose an environment that is suitable and comfortable for all members. And encourage members to share information, interact with one another, and develop interpersonal communication.[19] These are some examples of proactive behavior. As you get to know the members of your group, you will be able to discern the types of proactive behaviors you should use.

- **Accountability.** Everyone is equally accountable for their behavior, performance, and duties, including the leader. Avoid making exceptions whenever possible; this shows a degree of favoritism and has the propensity to discourage other members from accepting responsibilities or fulfilling their tasks. Teamwork means that everyone is accountable for his or her behavior.
- **Clarity about what is or is not under your control.** Leaders have limited control over much of the group process. One way of building trust is to let members know early what you have the authority to do and what you don't. Never embellish your position or authority.

2. **A focus on tasks and results.** Maintain group focus on tasks and results. It's easy to get sidetracked; discussions have a way of meandering all over the place. The leader directs and guides members in group discussion.

3. **Optimism and commitment.** Teams and/or groups in an organization may be permanent, ongoing, or they may be chartered for the long term, unlike your class group which meets only for one semester or term. After awhile, optimism may be replaced with indifference or pessimism. When this happens, members lose their commitment to their task or even to the group. A part of leadership is to renew that optimism that the group once felt when they first got together. This, in turn, reinforces their commitment to complete their goals and objectives.

4. **Giving and receiving constructive criticism.** Giving constructive criticism can be another way of picking out members' faults. Constructive criticism is designed to be instructional in nature; in other words, not to point a finger at someone and say, "You did this well, but…," instead, to identify a particular unwanted behavior that needs to be modified into a wanted behavior. "You did this well, but…" should be replaced with "Perhaps another way of approaching it may be," or, "May I suggest a different approach." And expect members to do the same to you. As leader, you will experience more constructive criticism than you will ever imagine; take my word for it. It is an inherent part of leadership.

5. **A focus on solutions, not blame.** Never point a finger at a member and blame him or her for not completing a task. It's a natural thing to do. Don't assign blame; rather, find alternative solutions. If a member has a habit of not completing an assignment, find a solution that will help him or her finish it. For example, if Marcella's report lacks material from an academic

data base but the rest of her research assignment is complete, it may be because she doesn't know how to perform academic research. Remember the difference between can't and won't? Marcella needs to be tutored as to how to research academic databases. Once she learns it, she'll produce a complete assignment, which will result in positive consequences. The leader creates antecedents that are catalysts for positive consequences.

Reinforcement: Know What You Want to Reinforce

You will want to design a reinforcement system that ensures the effective delivery of reinforcement to all group members, not just to some of them. The most important consideration in designing a reinforcement system is to make sure that one person's reinforcement does not limit another's. You cannot substitute one member's success by reducing the likelihood that another member will succeed. Do the opposite; create a system that is designed so that one member's success increases the likelihood that other members will also be successful.[20]

The following four general areas should be considered in order to maximize performance:

1. **Member expectations.** Members need to know what is expected of them. If they don't have knowledge of what is expected, then they will not be able to perform appropriately. It is one of the differences between can't and won't. If members don't know, then they can't perform.
2. **Task-centered behavior.** We reinforce behavior that is centered on performing tasks. These include: (a) a willingness for members to accept responsibility for their behavior, even for making mistakes; (b) taking the initiative and not waiting to be told what to do when they already have that knowledge; (c) and self-reflection.
3. **Creativity and integration.** This is one of the most critical parts of group work that is not reinforced as well as it should be. How often have you been encouraged to think critically, to come up with new and innovative ways of doing things, and when you do, you get little or no recognition? After awhile, you say to yourself, "Why bother?" Good leadership demands that you encourage all members to think creatively and integrate that creativity.
4. **Cooperation.** There is no group work without cooperation. However, it's more than just telling members to cooperate. It is a part of your charge to create an environment that fosters cooperative behavior. Remember, again, the difference between want to and have to. Reinforce want to behavior rather than have to.

Process versus Content

Fundamentally, group work consists of a process (usually referred to as a meeting) and it's content. A **process** is generally a prescriptive set of guidelines on how to conduct or manage group behavior toward achieving objectives and goals. Standing committees and subcommittees, those that are considered to be permanent in nature, all follow some process. Robert's Rules of Order is an

 Process

Generally a prescriptive set of guidelines on how to conduct or manage group behavior toward achieving objectives and goals.

example of a process used in formal group work. A process also includes how leadership manages individual member communication; that is, what is said, what is not said, how it is said, and when it is said. And at times, it involves the nonverbal behavior that accompanies the spoken message.

- **What is said.** This is generally determined by an agenda and the agenda items. In small group and team work, the leader creates an agenda, which is a road map for what needs to be accomplished during that meeting. Discussion usually centers on items as they appear on the agenda. Some leaders allow for new discussions as a part of the overall agenda; some do not. Leaders request that members stay focused and not deviate discussion from the agenda.

- **What is not said.** If it is not on the agenda, it probably will not be discussed. That being said, there is another dimension to what is not said. What is not said includes disparaging and derogatory remarks of other members and the leader. Civility in discourse is always the rule. That doesn't mean you can't say something negative about another member's behavior. How members conduct themselves is always open to criticism and discussion, whether positive or negative. But a leader should never allow abusive or hurtful language.

- **How it is said.** Meaning not only resides in the content of what is said—the **denotative** meaning (the public, conventional meaning)—but also in the way it is said—the **connotative** meaning (often the emotionally charged meaning).[21] As leader, you will want to temper how your members deliver their reports and how they speak to one another, especially during debate, which we will cover in Chapter 12, Conflict Management.

- **When it is said.** You have heard the saying, "There is a time and place for everything." Well, that applies here, too. If the group is not too informal; that is, if there aren't restrictions as to who can speak and when, then there are generally two times when a member is heard: (1) when it is his or her time to speak according to the agenda; or (2) when the leader recognizes him or her to speak. This is an important part of the process. The leader controls the flow of discussion and determines who can speak and when. If not, then there would be a lot of shouting and pandemonium, and nothing would be accomplished.

How to Support the Process

The process would be useless if it were not reinforced. The following six recommendations should be used as a guide for supporting the process, but they certainly are not the only guides you may want to adopt. Those you will learn through experience.

1. **Maintain ground rules.** Once you have established the rules to live by, you will need to follow those rules. You cannot make exceptions. It will create a number of problems for you as leader. It sets a precedence once you fail to maintain ground rules; some member will seek to take advantage of

rule-breaking. Making exceptions also has the appearance of favoritism. One key to Performance Management is, "Do what you say you are going to do." **Be consistent.** If you have ground rules, adhere to them.

2. **Intervene only when necessary.** As leader, you are also a facilitator. Effective facilitators intervene only when necessary. They do not attempt to dominate the process; they help move it along when it gets bogged down, off direction, or when there is destructive conflict. A facilitative leader empowers members and increases their responsibilities and ownership of the group's charge and tasks, and at the same time reduces member dependence on the leader.[22]

3. **Intervene using the rules.** When the leader does intervene, he or she does so in accordance to the rules that govern the group. This established process acts as both a sword and a shield. It acts as a sword by bringing members who transgress the rules back to the process, and it acts as a shield by protecting the process from going astray.

4. **Use the plural we or collective group.** This is **inclusive** language, and it is very important to group cohesion. This reinforces the concept of group and deemphasizes a member as an individual. When you refer to we, us, or group, it tells members that they are a part of something bigger than themselves—that they are there to work together as a team.

5. **Avoid rescuing.** Rescuing behavior occurs when a leader tries to save a member when he or she has done something not acceptable to the group. For example, a member did not complete an assigned task on time, and the leader intervenes by making an excuse for that behavior; or a leader will give extra time to have something competed when he or she really shouldn't. Rescuing behavior sends a destructive signal to the other members of the group.

6. **Modify ground rules when necessary.** The key phrase here is "when necessary." All rules have the potential to be modified according to the group's needs, and sometimes they need a higher authority to be changed. However, avoid changing them just because you or someone else doesn't like them. Before long, you may discover that there aren't any real rules to live by. When this happens, your leadership authority diminishes, and group cohesion decays.

Examples of Ground Rules

You will need to establish ground rules if you are going to be a successful leader. I don't know of any structured group, whether a family, sports team, business, or a corporation, that doesn't operate by some form of ground rules. You will need to consider the following:

1. **No gossiping.** If there is one thing that will turn one member against another, it is gossiping—talking about other members when they aren't there. This rule is a must; adhere to it at all times. And when you do hear gossip, nip it in the bud as quickly as you can. You want all members to feel that they are safe with you, that you can be trusted.

2. **Stick to tasks and objectives.** Stay focused and keep the group on track. As leader, it is your responsibility to maintain progress toward the group's end. They are there for a purpose.

3. **Be specific; use examples.** Avoid speaking in generalities. Use examples that members are familiar with to clarify your points. People tend to *see* in their minds what you mean and understand what you are saying when you connect with them. Examples are a great way to do this.

4. **Use statements and not questions.** Using statements or declarative sentences removes ambiguity, especially when you or other members are presenting information, or when you give members directions. Questions are used when you seek information.

5. **Include everyone in the discussion.** Inclusivity gives everyone a sense of contribution, which leads to continued group cohesion. Every member's voice should be heard as long as they contribute positively toward achieving group goals. Members may feel as though they are not a part of the group if they are ignored, especially when they have something to say.

6. **Share all relevant information.** Groups work best when they are fully informed by the leader. In order to make informed decisions, members need all relevant information.

7. **Observe time limits.** Time limits are set so the agenda can be covered in a reasonable amount of time. Each agenda item has an approximate time limit. The more complex or controversial the agenda item, the more time required. Remember, as leader, you have a certain amount of time to address a number of items. You want to avoid carrying over items to the next meeting; you'll discover that you will not get much done.

8. **What goes on in the group stays in the group.** All too often, one or more members will gossip to friends, colleagues, or to anyone who will listen to them, about other group members, or the way the meeting was conducted, or about things they didn't like about the group. If a conflict occurs between members, any discussion about behavior should remain within the group and end when the meeting adjourns. Bad mouthing members to others shows disrespect, not only for that person, but for the group as a whole. It has a way of interfering with group synergy, cohesion, and morale.

9. **End each group with a self-critique and a group critique.** Self-critiques are also referred to as self-reflection. There is a difference between our self-perception, how we see ourselves, and how others see us. I like to do the group critique at the conclusion of each meeting, not just at the completion of the group's charge. What is a critique? It is an assessment of how you, each member and the group as a whole, perform. I view a self-critique differently than I do a group critique. At the conclusion of the group work, I ask each member to critique himself or herself on his or her overall performance. I generate my list of questions for members from my observations of, and experiences with, them. However, the group critique has a different purpose; that's why I do it after each meeting. I call it my Target Balance Sheet (TBS). I prepare this on a flip chart prior to each meeting, and I keep each flip chart as a way to demonstrate the progress being made by each member and the group as a whole.

On the top of the flip chart, I write "What we want to accomplish" by the meeting. Then I draw a line down the center of the page, almost to the end, but not quite; and on the left side of the page I write "Identify specific accomplishments"; on the right side of the page, I write "Identify what still needs to be done." Once we have determined both sides of the page, we then identify how each member will accomplish the next round of objectives. Figure 8.1 identifies how a TBS should be constructed.

10. **Establish procedures for dealing with uncooperative or unproductive members.** This is difficult for student groups. How do you deal with someone who fails to show up for group meetings, or doesn't do their share of the work? Ground rules that address these types of behavior should be established and discussed when the group first meets, this way each member knows what to expect if they transgress those rules. These rules should be supported by your instructor, considering that they are reasonable.

FIGURE 8.1
Sample target balance sheet.

TARGET BALANCE SHEET
DATE: March 3, 2010

WHAT WE WANT TO ACCOMPLISH

Today's Accomplishments
1. Determined the problem.
2. Selected areas for research: What are the evidences and symptoms of the problems?
3. Assigned research areas to members
4. Established objectives

Still Needs to Be Done
1. Find what caused the conditions.
2. Determine what the effects of the symptoms are.
3. Has the problem happened before; if so, how was it handled?

Still Needs to Be Done
1. John will research what caused conditions.
2. Malina will research effects of symptoms.
3. LaTisha will research if problem has happened before.

Reinforcing

Up until this point you've read about what you need to reinforce. The companion to the what's are the how's. All too often we are told what we need to do but seldom taught how we need to do it. How do we deliver reinforcement? The following are guidelines for the effective delivery of reinforcement:[23]

• **Personalize your reinforcement.** When you deliver your reinforcement, express your praise in terms of how you feel. For example, use "I appreciate," or "The group appreciates." If you write a note to the member whose performance you are reinforcing, go beyond writing, "You did a good job today"; you should also include in a few well-chosen words about what he or she did that you liked and why you liked it. This makes the reinforcement personal.

- **Reinforce immediately.** The moment when you actually observe someone in the act is the best time to reinforce. Reinforce while he or she is doing what you want. You do not want to wait between observing the performance and delivering the reinforcer. The longer you delay the less impact the reinforcer will have on the performance. However, there will be times when there will be a delay between the behavior and reinforcement. When this happens, you run the risk of inadvertently reinforcing the wrong behavior because the behavior you wanted to reinforce may not be occurring at that time. The general rule on delivering reinforcement is: better late than never, but best immediately. If you have no choice but to reinforce late, then the recognition has to be very specific. You will want to pinpoint the behavior so the person knows precisely what he or she did to earn the reinforcer.

- **Make your reinforcement specific.** Praise is a specific reinforcer to most people. It doesn't hurt to be praised at times, and it is a great reinforcer for a leader. When we refer to praise, we mean that being specific means telling members exactly what they did that you liked or helped the group toward achieving its objectives. This is especially important when delivering reinforcement in groups. As leader, you observe more than one person working in the group. Many different behaviors occur at the same time. Many individual behaviors are productive for the group while some may not be. If the reinforcer is not specific, you may inadvertently reinforce the bad behaviors as well as the good behaviors. One way of being specific in a group setting is to ask each member what he or she did to accomplish the goal or objective, or how he or she helped move the group process forward. If you have a good feedback system in place, you'll find that it will not always be necessary to be specific.

- **Make your reinforcement sincere.** If your reinforcement isn't delivered with sincerity, members will know it immediately. It is extremely important that you deliver your reinforcer with sincerity, and this applies to both what you say and how you say it. You should never tell a member something you don't mean; you will lose credibility not only with them, but with the entire group because it will raise suspicion that you've not meant what you've said. Avoid telling members the same thing, such as, "You've been fantastic," or "You are unbelievable." Overusing a reinforcer makes people feel uncomfortable and diminishes its effectiveness. Refrain from using flattery, humor, and sarcasm. As we've noted before, what you say may not be received in the way you intended. State your social reinforcer first; that will get their attention; then note what they did that you liked—the tangible behavior. People generally regard specific reinforcement as sincere.

- **Reinforce frequently.** It takes many reinforcers to develop a habit; one or two just won't do it. Generally speaking, the more frequently a member is reinforced for his or her desired performance, the stronger that performance will become. How much is too much? How much is enough? Well, that depends on the person. Some people require a lot of reinforcement; some don't. Aubrey C. Daniels (1989) recommends the 4:1 rule. This means that every time a leader applies a negative consequence to a member's behavior, he or she should find at least four opportunities somewhere in the group process to reinforce the desired performance. However, this is only a guide to reinforcement. The most important reason for using the 4:1 rule is to increase the amount of reinforcement you use. As leader, you will find that there will be times when you must say, "No!", set limits, ignore certain responses, or use consequences someone won't like. That's a part of leadership, like it or not.

Good leadership requires that the leader be **interactive** with all members of the group. An interactive leader assesses the situation and develops strategies for ameliorating the possible negative effects on the group, helping members understand the situation and behave in appropriate ways. For the leader to be effective in this role, he or she depends on the group's cooperation and trust in his or her ability. This ability is proven over time by the leader's actions; cooperation and trust are earned.

In Chapter 5, we discussed leadership styles. But how do you determine which type of style to adopt with your group? Answering these questions should help you in determining the leadership style you should use.[24]

- **What objective(s) do we want to accomplish?** First, you must decide what areas of an individual's or group's activities you would like to influence. Specifically, what objective(s) do you want to accomplish? In group work, these areas will vary according to the group's responsibility.
- **What specific tasks can be assigned to a group to accomplish the goal?** The tasks required to accomplish the goal are identified by the people who make up the group, for example:

  - Someone to take notes of the meeting
  - Group observer
  - Leader
  - Fact-finders
  - Someone(s) to present the plan

- **What is the group's readiness?** It is the leader's responsibility to diagnose the readiness of the group that will accomplish these tasks. The key issue is how ready or receptive is the group to accomplish these tasks? If the group is at a high level of readiness; that is, they have the knowledge and skills to perform those tasks, only a low amount of leadership intervention will be required. If, on the other hand, the group is at a low level of readiness; that is, members need to be instructed or trained in order to perform the tasks, then considerable leadership intervention may be required.

© Brenda Carsson, 2011. Under license from Shutterstock, Inc.

- **What leadership action should be taken?** Once the leader has made these assessments, then it should be obvious as to the necessary actions the leader will take. They can range from doing nothing to requesting that members receive some type of training in order to perform effectively. The purpose here is to ensure that member roles and tasks can be achieved. The last thing a leader wants to do is assign a task, such as statistical research, to someone who lacks a working understanding of statistics. Or assign someone as a note-taker who has a difficult time taking accurate notes.

The next step is deciding which of the leadership styles would be appropriate for the group. The readiness of each member and the group as a whole has a primary influence on the choice. Leaders who choose a *laissez-faire* style of leadership are somewhat assured that each member has the ability to perform their tasks, so little intervention is required. However, if it appears as though members may not be up to performing their tasks, a more authoritarian leadership style may be required.

Once a leadership style has been adopted, the leader will need to answer the question, "What was the result of the leadership intervention?" This step requires assessment to determine if results match expectations. It is during this period of development—beginning with leadership intervention and ending with results—that the leader must positively reinforce each member's performance as he or she approaches the desired level of performance that the leader seeks.

Therefore, after intervention, the leader must assess the result through rechecking the objectives, rediagnosing readiness, and ascertaining if further leadership intervention may be needed.

And finally, what follow-up, if any, is required? If there is a gap between current performance and desired performance of the individual or group, then follow-up is required in the form of additional leadership interventions, and the cycle starts again.

We can summarize the basic dimensions of leadership task and relationship behavior as:

Task Dimensions

1. **Goal setting.** The leader specifies the goals members are to accomplish.
2. **Organizing.** The leader organizes the work situation for members.
3. **Setting timelines.** The leader sets timelines for individual and group task accomplishment.
4. **Directing.** The leader provides specific directions for accomplishing tasks and objectives.
5. **Controlling.** The leader specifies and requires regular reporting on individual and group progress.

Relationship Dimensions

1. Giving support. The leader provides support and encouragement for individual members and the group as a whole.
2. Communicating. The leader engages in interactive give and take discussions about task activities.
3. Facilitating interactions. The leader acts as a facilitator, and at times, a mediator, between members' interactions.
4. Active listening. The leader seeks out and listens to members' opinions and concerns.
5. Providing feedback. The leader provides feedback on members' accomplishments.

You may discover that you wish you had a list of practical tips to help you out at times, especially when you question yourself as an effective leader or when things don't look like they're going too well. The following are practical tips to lead by:

- Project energy. Members always look to the leader when they need to be energized. Project energy; it'll rub off on those members who need it, and it will revitalize the others.
- Target energy on success opportunities. Not only should you project energy, you should target it on those things that will foster success for members. Don't waste your time on unproductive behaviors or unproductive tasks; focus your energy toward those things that will help the group be successful.
- Take the initiative. Members look to you to volunteer first. This is an example of leadership by example. Be the first to step forward and take the initiative.
- Be involved. One sure way to earn the respect of members and to know what is going on at all times is to be actively involved with the group. Know what and how each member is doing. By being involved, you will be able to spot behaviors that may need to be modified before they become a problem. Also, it will do wonders for group morale and synergy.
- Influence cooperative action. By being involved, you will automatically influence cooperative action. This is group or team work, remember? Individual members work together— they cooperate to achieve a goal.
- Persuade and persevere. Use your power of persuasion to nudge members in the direction you want them to go or to resist going in the

wrong direction. Never use coercion. You will have some not-so-good days and some great days; hang in there; don't be discouraged. Tomorrow is another day.

- **Utilize pyramid learning (teach others).** If you teach one member something, he or she, in turn, will teach the others. This is one way members learn in a group setting.
- **Support creativity.** Allow the brilliance to shine through. You may not think someone's suggestion is a good idea at the time, but let him or her try. Premature judgment is a leader's number one nemesis. Avoid prejudging.
- **Maintain perspective.** Stay on track; keep your perspective. You had a vision when the group first formed. The last thing you want to do is alter your perspective when you know it's right. It will make you look wishy-washy or weak.
- **Avoid the negative.** Nothing discourages a group quicker than a leader who dwells on the negative. Stay positive. Keep a positive attitude. Discuss the negative only when you are making a comparative analysis—something is positive or negative. Negativity is like a cancer in group work. It will eat away at creativity, morale, synergy, enthusiasm, energy, and cohesion.
- **Never be satisfied (seek continuous improvement).** At no point, until you have completed your charge, should you be satisfied with the group's work. Always seek to improve, even if it appears that there isn't room for improvement.

SUMMARY

In this chapter, we began with an overview of leadership and team building. We explored the decision-making process, which required six phases: (1) identify a goal and a problem preventing goal achievement; (2) examine constraints; (3) develop and analyze alternative ways of responding; (4) make the decision; (5) implement the decision; and (6) evaluate the decision.

We found that the problem-solving process is similar to the decision-making process in many aspects, although their purposes are quite different. We learned that the purpose of a problem-solving group is to find the best solution to a problem, which includes a solution that is cost-effective, easy to implement, and has short-, medium-, and long-term benefits.

We noted that it is important that you as a leader cannot reinforce a team—only the behaviors of team members; and that the most important consideration in team effectiveness is the behavioral dimension. In addition, we found that one of the keys to successful group leadership is having an environment that fosters effective group work, which includes information, confirmation, and instrumentation.

And finally, in understanding how to manage a team of individuals who are diverse in needs, we explored six general criteria: appropriate behavior to model, knowing what you want to reinforce, the differences between process and content, how to support the process, and how to reinforce.

DISCUSSION

1. Consider the four choices described on page 3 that an effective team leader should make. In your experience, what might cause leaders to not trust members of the group, to withhold information, or to attempt to maintain authority by controlling as much of the work as possible? What contextual or environmental factors might encourage a leader to make these choices, even though they are destructive to the building of a team? How can a leader effectively negotiate these factors?

2. Why does diversity among group membership promote high quality group decision making? Conversely, why would having a group that features a great deal of similarity across its members' perspectives and skills inhibit high quality group decision making?

3. Much of the political discourse in the United States implies that the President is ultimately responsible for the course of this country's history during that President's administration. Try to clarify *one* specific charge that should be the responsibility of the President by using the **ACORN test**. How close can you come to passing all five elements of the test? What obstacles prevent passing all five elements of the test as you define one specific charge/task for the President?

4. Consider one hypothetical student in your in–class group who is habitually late or absent, who does not complete assignments, and who does not show commitment to the group. How could your group provide feedback about these behaviors that is positive and constructive? How could modeling play a role in this effort to avoid focusing on negative behaviors?

5. This chapter includes the claim that creativity is useful to group effectiveness and is not positively reinforced as much as it should be. Why might this be the case? What demands might a leader be orienting to when s/he is not encouraging member creativity?

NOTES

1. Kiessling, T.S. (2006) *Power point lecture notes.* California State University, Turlock, CA.

2. Schwarz, R.M. (1994). *The skilled facilitator: Practical wisdom for developing effective groups.* San Francisco: Jossey-Bass.

3. Hersey, P., Blanchard, K. H., & Johnson, D.E. (2001). *Management of organizational behavior.* Upper Saddle River, N.J.: Prentice Hall.

4. Fisher, B.A. (1980). *Small group decision making* (2nd ed.). New York: McGraw-Hill. Wood, J.T., Phillips, G.M., & Pedersen, D.J. (1986). *Group discussion: A practical guide to participation and leadership.* New York: Harper & Row.

5. Fisher, R., & Ury, W. (1981). *Getting to yes.* New York: Penguin.

6. DeWine, S. (1994). *The consultant's craft: Improving organizational communication.* New York: St. Martin's.

7. Galanes, G.J., Adams, K., & Brilhart, J.K. (2004). *Effective group discussion* (11th ed.). New York: McGraw-Hill.

8. Hirokawa, R.Y., Cathcart, R.S., Samovar, L.A., & Henman, L.D. (2003). *Small group communication theory and practice.* Los Angeles: Roxbury.

9. Daniels, A.C. (1989). *Performance management: Improving quality productivity through positive reinforcement* (3rd ed.). Tucker, GA: Performance Management.

10. Daniels, A.C., & Daniels, J.E. (2004). *Performance management: Changing behavior that drives organizational effectiveness* (4th ed.). Atlanta, GA: Performance Management.

11. Ibid.

12. Gilbert, T.F. (1996). *Human competence: Engineering worthy performance.* Library of Congress, Wash., D.C.: International Society for Performance Improvement.

13. DeWine, S. (1994). *The consultant's craft: Improving organizational communication.* New York: St. Martin's.

14. Ross, R.S. (1989). *Small groups in organizational settings.* Englewood Cliffs, NJ: Prentice-Hall.

15. Gilbert, T.F. (1996). *Human competence: Engineering worthy performance.* Library of Congress, Wash., D.C.: International Society for Performance Improvement.

16. Bennis, W., & Nanus, B. (1985). *Leaders.* New York: Harper and Row.

17. Engleberg, I.N., & Wynn, D.R. (2007). *Working in groups.* New York: Houghton Mifflin.

18. Daniels, A.C. (1989). *Performance management: Improving quality productivity through positive reinforcement* (3rd ed.). Tucker, GA: Performance Management.

19. Adapted from http://www.teachervision.fen.com/teaching-methods/classroom-management/7235.html. Retrieved September 7, 2009.

20. Daniels, A.C. (1989). *Performance management: Improving quality productivity through positive reinforcement* (3rd ed.). Tucker, GA: Performance Management.

21. Trenholm, S., & Jensen, A. (1992). *Interpersonal communication* (2nd ed.). Belmont, CA: Wadsworth.

22. Schwarz, R.M. (1994). *The skilled facilitator: Practical wisdom for developing effective groups.* San Francisco: Jossey-Bass.

23. Adapted from Daniels, A.C. (1989). *Performance management: Improving quality productivity through positive reinforcement* (3rd ed.). Tucker, GA: Performance Management.

24. Adapted from Hersey, P., Blanchard, K. H., & Johnson, D.E. (2001). *Management of organizational behavior.* Upper Saddle River, N.J.: Prentice Hall.

9

Interpersonal Communication for Leaders

CHAPTER OBJECTIVES

- Describe the role that relationships play within group settings
- Explain the model of dialectical tensions in group interaction
- Identify the factors affecting individual responses and motivations to share information
- Explain the symbolic constitution of meaning and its role in organizations
- Describe the critical listening process as well as the barriers and behaviors that can compromise it
- Identify the factors that shape communication climates
- Describe the role of social and cultural factors on group interaction

KEY TERMS

Particular other

Response styles

Self-disclosure

Uncertainty

Symbolic interaction

Face

Facework

Active listening

Critical listening

Empathy

Pseudolistening

Communication apprehension

CHAPTER OUTLINE

Interpersonal Communication in Groups
    Relational Communication
    Relational Dialectics and Group
        Leadership

Beginning with the Self
    Response Styles
    Self-disclosure and the Johari
        Window
    Uncertainty Reduction

The Self with Others
    Symbolic Interaction
    Facework

Listening
    Active Listening
    Critical Listening
    Barriers to Listening
    Nonlistening

Communication Climate
    Supportive/Defensive Climates
    Race, Gender, and Language
    Assessing Your Interpersonal
        Leadership Style

Summary

Communication, even in groups, begins with interpersonal communication. Effective small groups work together to create shared meaning, and they listen and speak with one another while making decisions. The more effectively group members are prepared for these interpersonal interactions, the better their decisions will be.

Effective small group leaders rely on shared group meanings to inspire member commitment and to move groups through stages of the decision-making process. Effective leaders also rely on their own interpersonal abilities to establish and maintain supportive communication climates.

This chapter, therefore, focuses on interpersonal relationships. The goal of the chapter is to enhance your understanding of several elements of interpersonal communication that are crucial in small group interaction: self disclosure, individual needs within the group, response styles, shared meanings, public face, listening, and communication climates.

INTERPERSONAL COMMUNICATION IN GROUPS

Relational Communication

Leaders who understand interpersonal communication in small groups recognize three distinct relational levels that, together, affect group discussion: (1) the **self,** (2) others with **particular significance,** and (3) the **society.**

> The individualist self is correlated with personal agency and goal–directed behavior; a relational self is more oriented toward maintaining relationships with particular significant others; and a collective self is subsumed within the context of a larger group or community.[1]

The subject of this section is relational meanings and their relevance for small group communication; the following two sections treat the two remaining levels, the self and the society.

The idea of **particular others** is important because when working in groups, members often communicate in ways that reflect unique commitment to the group (see Chapter 11, specifically the section on groupthink).

Particular others matter because they help us to create shared meanings, which are the foundation of all relationships, including small groups. Through creating shared meanings, we develop agreement about the world around us. These change from relationship to relationship; indeed, shared meanings are what distinguish one relationship from another. A single small group might have a shared meaning for an idea like timeliness that differs from other groups' sense of the same idea. Shared meanings provide a communication context that enables us to set goals and act on those goals with the confidence that others will support us rather than thwart us.

In some groups, members may feel committed to their relationships with particular others in the group. This is often the case with professional groups that persist over long periods of time, such as departments or expertise-based workgroups. In other groups, the relationship orientation is less significant than members' commitment to taking part in making a specific decision. This is often the case with professional groups that are formed to accomplish a task and then dissolve once the task is accomplished, such as ad hoc teams or temporary committees (see also Chapter 5, specifically the section on situational leadership). Indeed, recent research suggests that group personality, which is more than the sum of individual personality traits, can be psychologically measured.[2]

It is critical for a leader to understand the extent to which members orient to one another as particular others because particular others have a major impact on how we see ourselves. We also look to particular others for cues for interacting with a wide range of people—from those we also consider part of our inner circle to those we only know as acquaintances to those we meet for the first time. Within a large organization, for example, members of a group who have a strong commitment to one another as particular others may communicate with external members of the organization in remarkably similar ways because of their high regard for one another and/or for the group itself. Leaders must be aware of this orientation and respond accordingly—perhaps by carefully modeling communication for the group, or perhaps by taking group members' relationships into account when delegating tasks or assigning roles. Here are some good questions to ask, in order to respond effectively to the role of members as particular others in one another's lives:

> **Particular other**
> A person who influences our communication because we expect to, or choose to, continue and deepen our relationship with this person over time.

© wanitszka, 2011. Under license from Shutterstock, Inc.

- Does my group include members who will continue to relate to one another, inside or outside of the group, for a long period of time after our task is completed?
- Do the members of my group mirror my attitudes, or one another's attitudes, toward external groups or individuals?
- Do members of my group, including me, socialize outside of group meetings?
- Do the members of my group, including me, interact in group discussion in ways that reflect our relationships outside group meetings?

Relational Dialectics and Group Leadership

What an effective leader must appreciate is that such member orientations will shift even within the same group, depending on several group development and leadership factors. Thus, an effective way to understand relational influences on group communication is the dialectics approach; this approach, derived from the work of Leslie Baxter and applied to group settings, is an increasingly important scholarly approach to group leadership.[3] Remember that dialectics involves people moving between two opposing ideals, or poles, within an interaction (see Chapter 1 for a definition of dialectics). Barge proposed six sets of dialectical tensions that operate within groups[4]:

1. **Task behavior ⟷ Social–emotional behavior.** Members' shifting emphasis on communicating about tasks (task behavior) and communicating regard for one another (social–emotional behavior).
2. **Symbolic roles ⟷ Substantive roles.** Members' shifting emphasis on communication that legitimizes leadership and role differentiation (symbolic roles) and communication that move toward completing tasks, regardless of existing roles (substantive roles).
3. **Group stability ⟷ Group adaptability.** Members' shifting emphasis on communication that enhances existing group boundaries and structure (group stability) and communication that enhances group flexibility and permeability (group adaptability).
4. **Centralized power ⟷ Decentralized power.** Members' shifting emphasis on communication that defers to existing authority (centralized power) and communication that shifts power across the group (decentralized power)
5. **Short-term goals ⟷ Long-term goals.** Members' shifting emphasis on communicating within limited time periods (short-term goals) and communicating within extended time periods (long-term goals).
6. **Internal focus ⟷ External focus.** Members' shifting emphasis on communicating about the needs and development of the group as a unit (internal focus) and communicating about the needs and development of the larger organization (external focus).

Group leaders who strive to identify these tensions and recognize their impact on interpersonal communication within the group can benefit in two distinct ways:

1. Leaders can respond flexibly as members' orientations shift. Such shifts will likely occur as tasks and roles change, as the group develops, and as external conditions evolve over time; an effective leader can prepare for these shifts by using dialectical tensions as a framework.[5]
2. Leaders can better support the personal and interpersonal development of each group member by better understanding each member's effort to negotiate tensions between her or his own needs and those of the group itself. A hallmark of interpersonal communication is that it involves this ongoing process of negotiation between the individual person and the social world. The two dialectical poles of this negotiation process, self and society, are the subjects of the next two sections.

BEGINNING WITH THE SELF

Nearly all models of interpersonal communication include concepts such as goal-directedness, individual intention, and internal cognitive and emotional states.[6] Small group leaders, therefore, must understand that communication is not merely transparent at the level of verbal and nonverbal behaviors among the group. Members' individual differences and personal histories will strongly influence group discussion, no matter what the nature of the group or its leadership.

Response Styles

One way individual members shape group communication is through their varied **response styles** when change occurs.[7] Such change might be new tasks or externally directed goals; new leadership, authority, or group roles; time pressure; or contentious discussions.

Response styles
Cognitive-behavioral responses to cope with stressful events; divided into two types: **ruminative** and **distractive**.

Members whose responses are **ruminative** will tend to focus more intently on how they feel about a stressor; in group communication, this might include seeking opportunities to confront other members or have one's feelings explicitly validated. Such members will tend to emphasize the factors that led to their experience of stress. These responses may translate into positive group roles such as opinion-giver or orienter; they may also translate into negative group roles such as aggressor or dominator.

Members whose responses are **distractive** will tend to focus more on opportunities to escape from the stressful situation; in group communication, this

© Lev Olkha, 2011. Under license from Shutterstock, Inc.

© EDHAR, 2011. Under license from Shutterstock, Inc.

might include seeking opportunities to end meetings or avoid conflict. These responses may translate into positive group roles such as harmonizer or follower; they may also translate into negative group roles such as joker or withdrawer.

Effective small group leaders will acknowledge the response styles that may vary across group members. Members who tend toward ruminative responses may need leaders to help them focus on the overall picture: group goals, the inevitability of differing opinions, and the improved vantage point that often comes from taking time to reflect—perhaps when an issue is revisited at a later meeting, for example. Members who tend toward distractive responses may need leaders to help draw them back into group discussion safely, perhaps by focusing on a specific task or issue that requires their expertise or direct attention.

Other more or less stable interpersonal styles can affect members' participation in group discussion; two among these are argumentativeness and verbal aggressiveness.[8] Group members will also vary in their desire for intimacy and self-disclosure, which is the subject of the next section, and in their tolerance for uncertainty, which is the subject of the final section treating the self in communication.

Self-disclosure and the Johari Window

Another important way that group members will vary is in their willingness to self-disclose and, by self-disclosing, to become more intimately connected to other group members. Two influential theories of interpersonal communication, Social Penetration Theory and Communication Privacy Management Theory, hold that managing self-disclosure is the primary means through which individuals negotiate relationships with others.

Self-disclosure
Voluntarily sharing information about oneself that is not otherwise available to others.

According to the Social Penetration Model, self-disclosure tends to be reciprocated: the more an individual chooses to disclose, the more his or her relational partner will likely do the same, extending the relationship into more complex stages of development.[9] According to the Privacy Management Model, individuals choose whether or not to disclose for the purposes of maintaining boundaries of privacy that protect the self and shape identity within groups; it need not be reciprocated and does not necessarily deepen relationships.[10]

These contrasting perspectives on self-disclosure suggest that group members may choose to disclose voluntarily, or to avoid disclosure, for reasons that vary with the individual. Interestingly, disclosure of private information may not even necessarily be voluntary in all cases, as indicated by a widely used model for understanding the self and private information, called the **Johari Window**.[11] (See Figure 9.1.)

FIGURE 9.1
The Johari Window

	Known to Self	Unknown to Self
Known to Others	Public	Blind
Unknown to Others	Private	Unknown

The four quadrants of the Johari Window show how what we know about ourselves intersects with what others know about us:

1. **Open area.** Information in this section is known to ourselves and also known to others; in a small group setting, this is likely to include our names, physical features such as height and artifacts of appearance (clothing, hair, etc.), and—in some groups—occupational expertise and roles within organizations.
2. **Blind area.** Information in this section is unknown to ourselves but known to others; in a small group setting, this might include nonverbal habits like fidgeting with a pen when an unpleasant topic is discussed, nonverbal responses like resentful facial expressions when a competitor within the group is speaking, unusually long turns at talk, and so on.
3. **Hidden area.** Information in this section is known to ourselves but unknown to others; in a small group setting, this might include a personal history that affects your work in a group, such as if you have been the victim of sexual harassment and are assigned to a workgroup with sexually competitive and open people.
4. **Unknown area.** Information in this section is unknown to us and also unknown to others; in a small group setting, this might include your aptitude for a new task that no one in the group has been asked to perform before, including you.

Effective group leaders appreciate the role that self-disclosure, whether voluntary or not, whether reciprocal or not, plays in group affiliation. As a group develops socially, in both short-term and long-term goal contexts, members will also change their orientations toward boundaries between private and shared information. Some relationships among members, and the group's relational context as a unit, may deepen in terms of members' feelings of closeness, while other relationships may weaken.

Some specific benefits for group members of revealing personal information include:

- Enhanced feelings of trust
- Relief of stress
- Enhanced group cohesiveness

Some specific drawbacks for group members of revealing personal information include:

- Negative responses from group members
- Weakening of useful boundaries between the self and the group[12]

Uncertainty Reduction

Uncertainty
An inability to predict and/or explain others' behavioral choices; divided into two types: **cognitive** and **behavioral**.

Another factor complicating group members' participation in group interaction is that communicators vary according to their tolerance for uncertainty, which is the central concept in a major theory of interpersonal and intercultural communication called Uncertainty Reduction Theory.[13] The central assumption of this theory is that we experience uncertainty as unpleasant, and we will strive to communicate in ways that reduce our uncertainty within a given situation.

We experience **cognitive uncertainty** when what others do or say conflicts with our beliefs, attitudes, or values. In a small group setting, if our group proposes a solution to a problem that requires diverting organizational resources that were previously earmarked for another project, we might experience cognitive uncertainty. Role conflict, discussed in Chapter 4, is another good example of cognitive uncertainty in small groups.

We experience **behavioral uncertainty** when we do not have a way to predict what others will do or say. In a small group setting, if a sudden, highly vocal and demonstrative conflict emerges between two members who have previously been quiet followers in the group, we might experience behavioral uncertainty. Groups that do not have an established history but are, instead, formed on an ad hoc basis among members who do not typically work together are good examples of contexts marked by behavioral uncertainty.

Scholars studying uncertainty reduction argue that certain predictable connections exist between levels of uncertainty (Remember, we want to reduce uncertainty; it is unpleasant.) and other relational conditions. These include the ideas that we have high levels of uncertainty when we first meet people, especially people who are not similar to us, and this means that we will tend to seek information and to act reciprocally in ways that mirror others; as we decrease our uncertainty, we will tend to like people better, to feel more intimate, and to show these feelings more in nonverbal ways.[14]

Small group leaders should, for these reasons, act to reduce uncertainty in order to foster productive social relationships within the group, and also recognize when group members may be acting to reduce their own uncertainty. Three types of strategies communicators use to reduce uncertainty have been identified[15]:

1. **Passive strategies.** Communicators reduce uncertainty through passive observation; in a small group, this might include listening to a new member participate in discussion before directly addressing that person.

2. **Active strategies.** Communicators reduce uncertainty through taking action, but not by directly interacting with the person creating the uncertainty; in a small group, this might include asking another member of a large organization whom you already know about his or her department members who are a new part of your group.

3. **Interactive strategies.** Communicators reduce uncertainty through directly interacting with the person creating the uncertainty; in a small group setting, this might mean offering to share a meal after a meeting with a new member of a group.

© shyshak roman, 2011. Under license from Shutterstock, Inc.

An element of Uncertainty Reduction Theory that is especially useful for group leaders is the presence of antecedent conditions, which are situational factors that make relational uncertainty more likely, even before an interaction takes place.[16] One of these is the potential of one communicator to reward or punish another, causing high uncertainty; such potential is common in professional small groups, especially when group members do not share equal status within the group. But status is not the only factor affecting reward potential: even among peer-based small groups, members may vary in their access to outside channels or resources, which could also enhance uncertainty.

© Monkey Business Images, 2011. Under license from Shutterstock, Inc.

A second antecedent condition pertinent in small groups is the expectation of future interactions; if members expect to continue interacting with one another, it will be much more important for them to predict and explain one another's behavior. This is why the social development of a small group is essential to its ability to succeed over the long term on tasks; if members remain uncertain for too long, they will be less able to focus their communication on tasks because they will be orienting to reducing uncertainty instead.

Group dynamics include more than individuals building relationships and developing social structures within the group, however. Social structures that are much broader and more enduring than the group also have a significant impact on interpersonal communication.

THE SELF WITH OTHERS

Symbolic Interaction

Symbolic interaction

Creating the meanings, through interacting with others and reflecting on ourselves, that motivate all of our actions.

The theorist who has had the widest influence on how we understand the relationship of the individual to society is Mead. Mead and others associated with what came to be known as the Chicago School (from the University of Chicago) of humanistic research developed a perspective called symbolic interaction.

For the Chicago School, meaning is not fixed permanently by language when we use a word to refer to something. Instead, meanings are actively negotiated, and they change how we understand ourselves and how we act toward others. This idea is similar to the concept of shared meanings discussed earlier in the chapter; but to show how it relates to broader society, we need to understand three key concepts:

1. **Mind.** The human ability to use symbols that we share with other people. Language is a central aspect of mind. In a small group, this indicates that we constitute meanings together when we work as a group, and we cannot accomplish anything—from directing tasks to adopting roles to sharing ideas—if we do not honor the importance of language held in common and understood in common by every person in the group.

2. **Self.** Our reflection on ourselves, including reflecting on ourselves the way others see us. In a small group, this indicates that we are changed by our interaction with the group, and we also change others. When we adopt leadership roles, for instance, we begin to see ourselves as leaders. But this view is simultaneously affected by the view others in the group have of us, and our view of ourselves as leaders cannot survive unless it is consistent with the views of the group.

3. **Society.** The entire web of human relationships that connect us to one another. In a small group, there is no such thing as complete autonomy for the group, no matter how much freedom it has within an organization and no matter how many resources it can capitalize on. The expectations that shaped members' lives prior to the group, and that shape members' lives outside the group, will always constrain the values, beliefs, and ideas offered within the group. The recent struggles of financial corporations are a good example of the impact of society on the group.

The three concepts mind, self, and society collectively present a model of communication in which we live through language; language is not a tool that we pick up when we need it and drop down again but is instead the very means through which we understand who we are, what we want and need, and how we relate to the communities we live in.[17] Two prominent theories of organizational processes depend on this assumption that meaning is constituted in interaction: **organizational culture** and **structuration**:

1. **Organizational culture.** Organization culture focuses on the ways that organizations create and sustain organizational culture through shared rituals and symbols.[18] Examples might include company picnics, shirts with company logos, special terminology for staff members that is used only within the organization, and so on. Leaders must be uniquely attuned to the ways that such culture is passed on throughout the organization; an effective leader is able to work within the symbol system that prevails in her or his organization as if it is another language. The leader cannot overlook the importance of rituals in sustaining group identity and member commitment; a particular group meeting might be less important than full group participation in an organizational event, for example.

2. **Structuration.** Structuration offers a model of organizations that shows how, through developing rules, policies, procedures, traditions, and networks, organizational structures take on a life of their own and become self-sustaining.[19] From this perspective, the actions of individual members, especially leaders, can only be understood within the context of these structures; we have already discussed examples of this in earlier chapters by considering organizations as systems (Chapter 3) and roles and norms (Chapter 4).

The idea that organizational structures have a life of their own becomes particularly important when a leader examines constraints on goal-setting or the availability of feedback cycles outside the group, for example.

Facework

Another way that our immersion in the larger society plays a crucial role in group discussion is our engaging in facework.[20] This process is dependent on the concept of face, which refers to the public image we have for and with others.

The central construct of **facework** is the sense that each one of us has a reputation or impression that we carry with us from interaction to interaction. This is our face, and it is something that we feel a powerful pressure to uphold. The primary impetus for our recognizing that we care about our face, or public image, is that we feel it is threatened by something someone else does—this is called, by Ting–Toomey, a face threatening act. An example in a small group might be one member ridiculing an unconventional solution offered by another member.

Typically, when our face is threatened, we might take one of two actions in response: face-saving, which means trying to avoid embarrassment, and face-restoring, which means trying to preserve our autonomy.[21] If a group member whose proposal has been ridiculed engages in face-saving, he or she might join in, ridiculing the idea himself or herself, or suggesting that it was just offered

Face
The public image we have for and with others.

Facework
Actions that we take to negotiate the public image we want or that another person wants.

as a lark. Notice that the group member is not concerned with status in this response, but simply with reducing his or her vulnerability to further ridicule. If the same group member instead engages in face-restoring, he or she might defend the proposal vigorously or call into question the group process that resulted in ridiculing the proposal before it was carefully examined. Notice that the group member's concern in this example is maintaining power, even at the risk of sustaining potentially unwelcome attention on him or herself.

Another component of facework relevant to small group leadership is the relationship of culture to facework.[22] This depends on the distinction between individualist and collectivist cultures (see Chapter 1). A person from an individualist culture will often focus on protecting his or her face and on maintaining autonomy, even at the expense of group harmony, while a person from a collectivist culture will often focus on preserving the face of all parties involved and maintaining social harmony, even at the expense of individual autonomy.

LISTENING

There is perhaps no interpersonal set of skills more vital for effective group decision making than listening skills. Yet listening skills are typically not directly taught nor explicitly practiced in educational or training sessions;[23] so leaders must model listening skills themselves and actively help to develop them across the group if they hope to foster effective decision making.

Active Listening

Listening begins with intention; a person cannot listen without choosing to focus his or her attention in a conscious way. This requires a deliberate behavior—tuning the physiological channel that includes the ear and the brain (both parts of the hearing ability) to the audible speech of another person. Active listening should also include the eye-brain channel in order to consider nonverbal elements of the message.

Once verbal and nonverbal messages are received, they must also be interpreted, a process that engages memory (what we have learned) as well as perception (what we expect from the speaker). Memory and perception affect all communication, whether we are conscious of it our not, but the more conscious we become of memory and perception, the more we have the chance to successfully evaluate the messages and our own understanding of them. The ears, eyes, and mind must all be as clear as possible of distractions that focus attention elsewhere. These factors, collectively, require active listeners to engage physically and cognitively.

A summary of these aspects of active listening can be encapsulated in a list of guidelines for leaders who wish to model active listening within the group:

Guidelines for Active Listening

- Choose to listen.
- Attend fully to the speaker.
- Avoid focusing on distractions.
- Face the speaker, including turning the body if necessary.
- Do not listen passively—actively engage your memory.
- Do not listen passively—actively engage your perceptions.

If you always follow these guidelines in interactions, you will be surprised how quickly you can distinguish yourself as a listener; these behaviors are disappointingly uncommon.

Critical Listening

The next step in the listening process is to develop and model the skills necessary to listen critically. This means more than active listening; it involves using the listening process to contextualize and evaluate messages within the decision-making process. This process is critical, not in the sense of negatively judgmental, but in the sense of facilitating productive critique or close examination of the evidence for claims as well as the beliefs, attitudes, and values that support those claims. Such critical listening enables all members to think critically about group ideas and experiences and, thereby, to make better decisions. (See Chapter 11 for the relationship of critical thinking to decision-making.)

Two principles are foundational in the critical listening process: First, each of us has a unique experience of the world that is shared with no other person. Second, as a result of this uniqueness, perceptions vary from person to person, and thus even in a sustained interaction with shared meanings, there is always a slight difference in understanding from communicator to communicator.

Each of these two principles, unique experience and varying perception, will be examined more closely in connection with the critical listening process.

Given that each of us has a unique experience of the world, we cannot ever quite put ourselves in another's shoes. Yet the critical listening process demands that we attempt to do exactly this. Such an attempt is called empathy, which means voluntarily adopting the perspective of the other person within an interaction. When we listen with empathy, we accomplish two goals that aid the interaction: First, we show care for the other person, giving that person much greater motivation to clarify his or her meaning for us and to take the time to make sure that we get it. Second, we shift out of our own perspective, even if only hypothetically, giving ourselves a heightened opportunity to examine the other person's claims in terms of what they mean for that person. This makes our evaluation of claims much more robust and well rounded. Showing care and improving our understanding of claims are both exceptionally valuable for leaders in small group settings.

Given that each of us has different perceptions rooted in our unique experience, shaped by our personal histories and the physiological and psychological dimensions of ourselves that we share with no one else, we cannot ever quite be sure that the messages we get are precisely the messages the other person

Active listening
Choosing to focus attention in a conscious way.

Critical listening
Using the listening process to contextualize and evaluate messages within the decision-making process.

Empathy
Voluntarily adopting the perspective of the other person within an interaction.

FIGURE 9.2
Transactional
Communication
Model

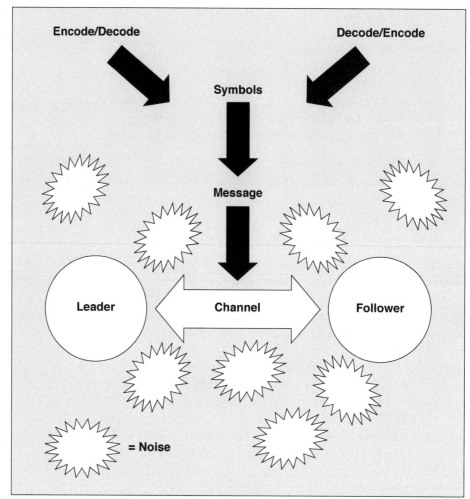

intended to give us. We can, however, engage in a series of voluntary behaviors that can help us clarify our own perceptions as much as possible in listening situations. These behaviors include: encouraging speakers to extend their turns at talk and, thereby, clarify ideas; asking questions when appropriate to explicitly identify our own perceptions and to check their validity within a given context; requesting evidence from speakers to support their claims; offering feedback in both verbal and nonverbal ways so that we play a role in shaping the speaker's message and helping it fit the interaction; and remembering messages so that meanings can be created and sustained in common over time. Engaging in these behaviors will help ensure that shared meanings within groups, while—again—never perfectly shared among all members, are as close as the group can manage. As with empathetic listening, these listening behaviors foster both group commitment and critical thinking—commitment because they engage all speakers and listeners in creating and sustaining shared meaning, and understanding because they center meaning-making within the interaction.

Again, a summary of these aspects of the critical listening process can be encapsulated in a set of guidelines for leaders:

Guidelines for Critical Listening

* Listen with empathy.
* Remember what is said.
* Respond to what is said.
* Encourage speakers.
* Ask clarifying questions.
* Name and check your own perceptions.
* Seek evidence for claims.

Barriers to Listening

Effective leaders acknowledge, as they model both active and critical listening within their groups, that barriers to listening will consistently arise. Listening requires that we be vigilant about the emergence of these barriers, and effective leaders will strive to minimize them within the group.

Barriers to Effective Listening

* **Mental distractions.** Thinking about other issues or needs while trying to listen. These can especially occur in small groups in instances of role conflict (Chapter 4) or overly aggressive leadership (Chapter 5).
* **Physical distractions.** Some listening environments are not physically conducive to listening—for example, when members cannot fully see one another, when unwanted noises are prevalent, or when facilities prevent audible interaction. These can especially affect groups working in organizations with limited resources.
* **Prejudgment or bias.** Listening with the expectation of our prejudices merely being confirmed can prevent us from appreciating the nuances of a message or from being open to its ability to change us for the better. This can especially affect heterogeneous groups.[24]
* **Message barriers.** These might include overly complex or overly long messages. This can especially affect small groups that are highly permeable to outside feedback or that require extensive information in order to make decisions.

Nonlistening

The barriers described above can hinder the efforts of a dedicated group member to listen, despite his or her best intentions. However, just as listening itself is an active, consciously controlled behavior, certain other active, consciously controlled behaviors can be destructive to listening environments, especially within small group settings in which the actions of each group member have a great impact. For this reason, effective leaders must prepare to recognize the following types of **nonlistening**, and to refocus group discussion on building positive listening orientations using the strategies for active and critical listening listed previously.[25]

Pseudolistening
When a member merely pretends to listen but is not actually listening.

- **Pseudolistening** happens when a member merely pretends to listen but is not actually listening. It is easiest to identify when a listener does not offer meaningful feedback; a leader can discourage pseudolistening by requesting feedback directly from members, requiring them to address what is said.
- **Monopolizing** happens when a supposed listener repeatedly shifts the focus from the ideas offered by a speaker to the interests of the supposed listener—or even to the subject of the supposed listener himself or herself. A leader can discourage monopolizing by developing and using a consistent procedure for group discussions, which might include democratically shared responsibility for topic generation and/or the emergence or assigning of group maintenance roles that redirect communication back to task elements.
- **Selective listening** happens when a member only listens to some part of a message but not all. This is easiest to identify when a member cannot consistently recall certain parts of a message; a leader can discourage selective listening by building redundancy into the discussion process through clarifying questions, summaries, and so on.
- **Defensive listening** happens when a member treats communication as hostile or aggressive when it is not intended in these ways. A leader can discourage defensive listening through modeling and normalizing perception checking in group discussion, with statements such as, "What I hear you saying is …"
- **Ambushing** happens when a member listens for specific ammunition designed to attack a speaker on response. As with defensive listening, a leader can discourage ambushing by modeling and normalizing perception checking.
- **Literal listening** happens when a member listens for information while ignoring relational messages. This is easiest to identify when a listener does not demonstrate empathy for the speaker; a leader can discourage literal listening by modeling empathy and by normalizing relational talk within the group.

COMMUNICATION CLIMATE

Supportive/Defensive Climates

Leaders who model the active and critical listening styles described in the section above will provide a strong foundation for supportive communication within the group. Similarly, leaders who identify and redirect the nonlistening behaviors described in the section above will help prevent a defensive communication climate within the group.

A **supportive** communication climate includes the following characteristics:

- Group members feel positive regard for one another as people.
- Group members value their identity as part of the group.
- Group members value the time they spend with the group.

- Group members value the opportunity to contribute to the group.
- Group members understand and feel capable of performing their roles and responsibilities within the group.
- Group members understand the roles and responsibilities of other members, and show confidence in others' performance of these roles and responsibilities.
- Group members are willing to share divergent ideas.
- Group members are willing to analyze and evaluate their own and others' ideas.
- Group members are open to clarifying or modifying their own ideas.
- Group members expect the group to accomplish its goals.

Conversely, a **defensive** communication climate includes the following characteristics:

- Group members treat one another as functionaries rather than people.
- Group members feel disparagingly toward the group as a whole unit.
- Group members feel uncomfortable about being a member of this group.
- Group members expect group discussion to be tedious and look forward to adjourning meetings.
- Group members feel uncomfortable about their own roles or responsibilities.
- Group members lack confidence in others' performance of their roles or responsibilities.
- Group members are unwilling to share ideas.
- Group members are unwilling to examine or recombine ideas.
- Group members demonstrate hostility toward one another.
- Group members expect the group to fail to meet its goals.

Much of this textbook is devoted to helping leaders make choices that foster supportive climates and that prevent defensive climates. Additional factors relating to communication climate will be examined in the following section; one of these is treated here.

A factor that can significantly influence communication climate by minimizing robust group discussion is communication apprehension. This is a feeling of discomfort that some people have when asked to participate in communication settings, and for some people, it is particularly acute in small group settings compared with other contexts. Members who experience apprehension within small group interaction will be much less willing than others to offer ideas, to examine others' ideas, or to show positive regard for the group.[26]

Communication apprehension

A feeling of discomfort that some people have when asked to participate in communication settings.

Leaders can support apprehensive group members by using some of the strategies described in the following section on language, as well as by using some of the strategies detailed in earlier chapters. However, understanding communication apprehension means understanding that it will not necessarily go away simply because of positive actions by leaders or group members. Instead, support for apprehensive group members means treating their experiences developmentally—being patient in supporting the apprehensive members. A useful strategy for supporting apprehensive group members is giving the member very specific, localizable tasks; this enables the person to focus his or her attention on the task rather than on the social dynamic of the group, and also enhances self-worth and a sense of belonging because it integrates the member into the group process in a nonthreatening way.[27]

Race, Gender, and Language

The cultural influences addressed in Chapter 1 are not the only ways that diversity affects small group discussion. Scholars have shown that race[28] and gender[29] also influence member participation in groups as well roles, response styles, and shared meanings.

One way to understand how and why groups are shaped by race and gender is to consider how dominant white men have been, historically, in organizational settings. This means two things: First, white perspectives and men's perspectives have been normalized, and as a result it is sometimes difficult for group members of color, or for women group members, to find ways to share ideas, adopt roles, and—especially—take on leadership positions, given the way such members' perspectives may differ from the norm. Second, group members of color and women members have been required to understand multiple ways of communicating because they have had to adopt the communication styles of white people and/or men in order to succeed professionally.[30]

How can effective leaders integrate the perspectives of members of color and women in the group setting? For the reasons stated above, this means more than simply being more inclusive in group composition or group participation—it means finding ways to utilize the distinctive resources available to increasingly diverse groups. From an interpersonal perspective, explicit communication that acknowledges and questions dominant procedures, norms, and meanings is the best way to help all members of a diverse group to maximize their individual potential and fully collaborate in shaping the group.[31]

Again, there are two reasons that explicitly marking and questioning dominant modes of communication are effective in diverse groups: First, it ensures that all members have an equitable opportunity to understand what the group expects of them; implicit communication where members are assumed to know the right way to participate, in contrast, will merely benefit those who have already established traditions of success within the dominant system. Explicit communication puts all members, even those who bring fresh perspectives to the group, on a more equal footing. Second, calling the dominant modes of communication into question enables the group to valorize alternative ways of doing things; the value of this will be discussed at greater length in Chapter 11, but it is especially important in a diverse group because it means that dominant modes of communication will only continue to be normalized if they are the most effective for all members of the group—not just because they are best for some members, or because they are "how things have always been done."

The most successful approach to making dominant modes of communication explicit is to consider how the group, and leaders in particular, use language. Effective ways to use language in all groups, but especially in groups with meaningful diversity include the following:

- Make expectations of members as **explicit** as possible—including times of meetings, lengths of turns at talk, group deliberation and decision-making procedures, and so on. Take nothing for granted in terms of what all members should know.
- Make descriptions of goals, responsibilities, and roles as **concrete** as possible, including lists, labels, signs, and examples. Take nothing for granted in terms of what all members should know.
- Use **gender-inclusive** language. Avoid referring to mankind or using words such as man, guys, he, and him as if they refer to all people.
- Avoid **exceptionalism**. Do not refer to a person's race or gender, especially if the race of white people or the gender of men is not marked in parallel (these are almost never marked in communication, whereas the race of people of color or the gender of women are very often marked).
- Avoid **tokenizing**. Do not assume that a person can or should speak on behalf of his or her entire race, or that a woman can or should speak on behalf of all women.

Assessing Your Interpersonal Leadership Style

One successful model for assessing how interpersonal styles influence leadership was developed by Bass and is called transformational and transactional leadership. In its present form, it includes the following six factors:

1. Charisma/inspirational

- Provides followers with a clear sense of purpose that energizes the group;
- Is a role model for ethical conduct;
- Builds identification with the leader and his or her stated vision.

2. Intellectual stimulation

- Gets followers to question tried and true problem-solving methods;
- Encourages followers to question and improve upon new methods.

3. Individualized consideration

- Focuses on understanding the needs of each follower;
- Works continuously to get followers to fulfill their potential.

4. Contingent reward

- Clarifies what is expected from followers;
- Clarifies what followers will receive if they meet performance expectations.

5. Active management by exception

- Monitors task execution for potential problems;
- Corrects problems to maintain current performance levels.

6. Passive–avoidant leadership

- Reacts correctively and only after problems become serious;
- Avoids making decisions.[32]

Notice that each of these six factors involves a relational component—how the leader chooses to orient to interactions with followers—and a shared meaning component—how the leader creates and sustains key symbols together with followers. This model thus encapsulates the core interpersonal elements discussed throughout this chapter, and it provides a useful basis for examining your own interpersonal orientations and their effect on your leadership style.

SUMMARY

We began this chapter by learning how interpersonal relationships in groups are an outgrowth of relational communication between individual group members. We know that relational dialectics and group leadership are integral for effective communication, and that self-disclosure is the voluntary sharing of information about oneself that is not otherwise available to others. In accordance with self-disclosure, we learned about the Johari Window.

We discovered the self in society, how symbolic interaction creates meaning for us through our interactions with others, and how that meaning motivates us. Through the concepts of face and facework, we understand how the larger society plays a critical role in group discussion. And we now know that there is, perhaps, no interpersonal set of skills more vital for effective group decision-making than listening skills. We explored the many barriers to listening, and examined behaviors such as nonlistening and pseudolistening.

A factor that can significantly influence communication climate by minimizing robust group discussion is communication apprehension, something that a good leader looks for. We explored how race and gender affect language and, therefore, individual participation. And finally, we assessed our interpersonal leadership styles.

DISCUSSION

1. Consider the contrasting perspectives on **self disclosure** discussed on page 6: What are some of your own experiences with self disclosure and its effect on developing relationships? Do you find that self disclosure tends to be reciprocated and deepens relationships in most cases, or do you find that this is not necessarily a reliable prediction of how self disclosure will affect us?

2. Suppose that a new member of your group is trying an **active strategy** of reducing dissonance by having separate one-to-one conversations, asking each group member how they feel about other members and about the group. What are some responses to these interactions that might help the new member reduce dissonant feelings without harming the cohesiveness of the group?

3. What are some specific features of the **organizational culture** shaping your group in this class? How are the cultures of your school, your class, your major, etc. affecting your small group's work?

4. You are in a group discussion: One member directly criticizes another member's idea; the member whose idea was criticized, however, then quickly moves to save **face** and preserve **harmony** by seeking points of agreement with the other group member. You are concerned that the idea is getting lost in the effort to save face; what are some responses you could choose that would respect the idea generator's need to save face but that would also recover group interest in the idea?

5. Given that race and gender are important factors that shape interpersonal communication, why would an effective leader *not* want to identify the race or the gender of a group member when discussing her/his ideas or position? How can an effective leader encourage members to acknowledge the importance of race and gender without lapsing into **exceptionalism** or **tokenism**?

NOTES

1. Silverstein, R., Bass, L. B., Tuttle, A., Knudson-Martin, C., & Huenergardt, D. (2006). What does it mean to be relational? A framework for assessment and practice. *Family Process,* 45, 391–405.

2. Gonzalez, R., & Griffin, D. (2002). Modeling the personality of dyads and groups. *Journal of Personality,* 70, 901–924.

3. Galanes, G. J. (2009). Dialectical tension of small group leadership. *Communication Studies,* 60, 409–425.

4. Barge, J.K. (1996). Leadership skills and the dialectics of leadership in group decision making. In R. Y. Hirokawa & M. S. Poole (Eds.), *Communication and group decision making* (pp. 301–342). Thousand Oaks: SAGE.

5. Collinson, D. L. (2005). Dialectics of leadership. *Human Relations,* 58, 1419–1442.

6. Stamp, G. H. (1999). A qualitatively constructed interpersonal communication model. *Human Communication Research,* 25, 531–547.

7. Wang, X. (2007). A model of the relationship of sex-role orientation to social problem solving. *Sex Roles,* 57, 397–408.

8. Johnson, A.J., Becker, J. A. H., Wigley, S., Haigh, M. M., & Craig, E. A. (2007). Reported argumentativeness and verbal aggressiveness levels: The influence of type of argument. *Communication Studies,* 58, 189–205.

9. Altman, I., & Taylor, D. A. (1973) *Social penetration: The development of interpersonal relationships.* New York: Holt, Rinehart & Winston.

10. Petronio, S. (2002). *Boundaries of privacy: Dialectics of disclosure.* Albany: SUNY Press.

11. Luft, J. (1969). *Of human interaction.* Palo Alto: National Press Books.

12. Kelly, A. E., & McKillop, K. J. (1996). *Psychological Bulletin,* 120, 450–465.

13. Berger, C.R., & Bradac, J. J. (1982). *Language and social knowledge: Uncertainty in interpersonal relations.* London: Arnold.

14. Ibid.

15. Berger, C. R. (1995). Inscrutable goals, uncertain plans, and the production of communicative action. In C. R. Berger & M. Burgoon (Eds.), *Communication and social processes* (pp. 1–28). East Lansing: Michigan State University Press.

16. Berger, C. R. (1979). Beyond initial interaction: Uncertainty, understanding, and the development of interpersonal relationships. In H. Giles & R. St. Clair (Eds.), *Language and social psychology* (pp. 122–144). Oxford: Blackwell.

17. Stewart, J. (1995). *Language as articulate contact: Toward a post-semiotic philosophy of communication.* Albany: SUNY Press.

18. Pacanowsky, M. E., & O' Donnell-Trujillo, N. (1990). *Communication and organizational cultures.* In S. R. Corman, S. P. Banks, C. R. Bantz, & M. E. Mayer (Eds.), *Foundations of organizational communication: A reader* (pp. 142–153). New York: Longman.

19. Giddens, A. (1984). *The constitution of society: Outline of the theory of structuration.* Berkeley: University of California Press.

20. Ting-Toomey, S. (1994). *The challenge of facework.* Albany: SUNY Press.

21. Ibid.

22. Ting-Toomey, S. Intercultural conflict training: Theory-practice approaches and research challenges. *Journal of Intercultural Communication Research,* 36, 255–271.

23. Cooper, P.J., & Symonds, C. J. (2003). *Communication for the classroom teacher.* Boston: Allyn & Bacon.

24. Gastil, J., Black, L., & Moscovitz, K. (2008). Ideology, attitude change and deliberation in face-to-face groups. *Political Communication,* 25(1), 23–46.

25. Wood, J. T. (2010). *Interpersonal communication: Everyday encounters.* Boston: Wadsworth.

26. McCroskey, J.C., & Richmond, V. C. (1991). *Quiet children and the classroom teacher.* Urbana: ERIC Clearinghouse on Reading and Communication Skills.

27. Ibid.

28. Allen, B. J. (1995). "Diversity" and organizational communication. *Journal of Applied Communication Research,* 23(2), 143–155.

29. Wang, X., Silverstein, R., Bass, L. B., Tuttle, A., Knudson-Martin, C., & Huenergardt. D.

30. Collins, P. H. (1990). *Black feminist thought: Knowledge, consciousness, and the politics of social empowerment.* Boston: Unwin Hyman.

31. Delpit, L. (1995). *Other people's children: Cultural conflict in the classroom.* New York: New Press.

32. Avolio, B. J., & Bass, B. M. (1999). Re-examining the components of transformational and transactional leadership using the Multifactor Leadership Questionnaire. *Journal of Occupational and Organizational Psychology,* 72, 441–462.

Goal Setting

GOAL SETTING

There is an old Chinese proverb, "If you don't know where you are going, any road will take you there." In group discussion, it helps to know where you are going, and setting goals and objectives gives the group the specific direction it needs to get to wherever it is the group should go. In an effective group or team setting, work is always planned out in advance. Planning is a way to establish performance expectations and goals for both the group and each member to direct their efforts toward achieving the group's charge. A good leader will include all members in the planning process. When members participate in this process, they come to understand their goals, what needs to be done, why it needs to be done, and how well it should be done. The process of planning tends to help a group reach consensus about who they are.

Understanding the Group Charge

Charge
The assignment given to a subordinate group by a higher authority.

As we've noted earlier, groups form for specific purposes. The ones that we are concerned with are problem-solving and decision-making. Your group is going to either solve a specific problem or recommend some sort of decision. Where is your group going? It is imperative that each and every member understand precisely why they are there and what they are expected to achieve. This is known as **understanding the charge**. A charge is the assignment given to a subordinate group by a higher authority. One major component of the charge is the group's area of freedom. The charge specifies what the group will accomplish, whereas the area of freedom defines both the authority the group has and limits on what the group may do to complete its charge.[1] Sometimes, though, such as in classroom group work, you may have to define your own problem or develop your own issue for which to decide a course of action. Either way, you will need to establish a set of goals and objectives. The following are examples of a group charge:

A university academic senate charge may read, "The Academic Senate of this university is constituted to formulate and evaluate policy and procedures on academic, personnel, and fiscal matters and make recommendations to the President."

The U.S. Food and Drug Administration is a subgroup of the U.S. Department of Health and Human Services. Its charge states, "The FDA is responsible for protecting the public health by assuring the safety, efficacy, and security of human and veterinary drugs, biological products, medical devices, our nation's food supply, cosmetics, and products that emit radiation."

The FDA is also "responsible for advancing the public health by helping to speed innovations that make medicines and foods more effective, safer, and more affordable; and helping the public get the accurate, science-based information they need to use medicines and food to improve their health."[2]

Nutrition Facts
Serving Size 1/6 package (60g)
Servings Per Container 6

Amount Per Serving	Mix	Prepared
Calories	260	360
Calories from Fat	80	150
	% Daily Value*	
Total Fat 9g*	14%	26%
Saturated Fat 3.5g	18%	30%
Cholesterol 0mg	0%	1%
Sodium 360mg	15%	20%
Total Carbohydrate 46g	15%	16%
Dietary Fiber 1g	4%	4%
Sugars 28g		
Protein 2g		
Vitamin A	0%	10%
Vitamin C	0%	0%
Calcium	15%	25%
Iron	6%	6%

*Amount in mix   based on a 2,000

© Anthony Berenyi, 2011. Under license from Shutterstock, Inc.

In each of these charges, you can see that there is a higher authority each entity reports to: the academic senate reports to the president of the university, and the FDA reports to Health and Human Services. You will notice that their charges are written as clearly defined statements.

Before we continue discussion regarding goals and objectives, you should be aware of a continuing controversy as to their definitions. Depending upon which discipline you study, or which business you work for, you may be given differing definitions of what a goal is. For some, a goal is unattainable because it is considered to be a direction you strive for. An example of a goal would be to travel east without a specified destination. However, if you say that you want to travel east, say from San Francisco to New York City, you have now set an objective, which is New York City. You travel east until you arrive at New York City. Objectives are measurable and achievable; goals are not. You cannot measure a goal, only objectives. So here's the dichotomy. Some people will refer to goals as being measurable and achievable, depending on who they are and where they work. I teach my public relations students that only objectives are achievable and goals are a direction to strive for. However, for our purpose, goals *are* achievable. Most, if not all, performance management literature refers to goals as being achievable, so we will remain constant with that notion.

Generally, any group that problem-solves or recommends a decision reports to some higher authority. A group should know what authority has empowered them and what output is required of them. All too often, groups lose sight of where they are going and have to be reminded about their charge. As leader, determine if there are any checkpoints you can use to make sure that the group stays on track. Either you can develop those, or they may be prescribed to the group.

Checkpoints are predetermined places the group should be at certain times. For example, the goal direction of going from San Francisco to New York City—before you leave on your trip, you estimate how many miles a day you want to travel. You then check on a map for a city or town within that range, and locate possible lodging for the night. You want to have an idea of how long the trip will take and where you may stop each night. You can change your travel plans along the way as long as you still arrive at your original destination. These are checkpoints. Group work has similar checkpoints. Each member should be at particular points by an approximate time. Since our culture is very linear in direction, we need to get from A to B by a certain time and should have a given amount of work done along some type of continuum, then from B to C, then C to D, and so forth.

Checkpoints
Predetermined places the group should be at certain times.

If, as leader, you have been given particular instructions, have you shared them with the group? If so, does everyone understand them? How many times have you explained a set of instructions to someone, and he or she acknowledged that he or she understood but really didn't? It's very frustrating. Take the time to explain to the group the instructions given to you, and make sure each and every member fully understands them.

Goal-Setting Theory

Dr. Edwin Locke pioneered research on goal setting and motivation in the late 1960s to understand how goals can influence an individual's performance. He believed that employees are motivated by clear goals and appropriate feedback, and that working toward a goal provides a major source of motivation for employees to actually reach the goal, which in turn, improves performance. Basically, the theory holds that human behavior is stimulated to act and is governed by goals and ambition. Much of goal-setting theory developments and goal-setting research has been done in connection to motivation in sports and business to help coaches get better results out of the players and managers to increase motivation and productivity of their employees.[3] However, even though goal-setting theory isn't a communication theory, much of the research findings have implications for communication. A summary of some of the most important findings of this research concludes that groups should:[4]

1. **Set clear and specific goals.** Clear goals have a greater positive influence on performance than do general goals.
2. **Set goals that are difficult but attainable.** They will lead to higher performance than will easy goals.
3. **Focus on participative rather than assigned goals.** When members volunteer for specific goals, they feel empowered and tend to perform better than if the goal was assigned to them.
4. **Give frequent feedback about the goal setting and work processes.** Frequent feedback is a performance reinforcer.

In order for goals to be effective, they must be clear and specific, group members must participate in their formulation, and the goals must be the subject of performance feedback. Feedback is essential to motivation because members have an opportunity to know how they're doing and how their efforts contribute to the success or failure of the group. Members who are given such feedback from group leaders tend to be more satisfied and perform better than those who don't get such feedback.[5]

SETTING AND ATTAINING GOALS

One common mistake groups make is to set goals and objectives that are not practical or achievable. In other words, they set the bar too high, making it impossible to achieve the goal. As we'll see later in this chapter, goal setting is all about human behavior. When you set the bar too high, you're asking the group to achieve the unachievable. A **goal** is a conceptual statement of what you plan to achieve—a clear, positive statement of intent to solve a significant problem or achieve a significant result within a specific time frame.[6] A goal is a desired outcome. Outside of the classroom, a goal is a statement rooted in the organization's mission or vision. It acknowledges the problem or issue and sketches out how the organization hopes to see it settled, and it is stated in general terms.

Goals are also subject to interpretation.[7] For example, a national food chain may be experiencing minority discrimination law suits or may have a negative public image for not hiring minorities. The company sends out directives to all of its outlets to hire more minorities. However, the local outlets may believe that this is merely a public relations ploy to gain favorable public image, and they don't take the goal seriously.

© my-summit, 2011. Under license from Shutterstock, Inc.

When you define a specified, or preset, level of performance that you expect the group to perform, we call that **goal setting**.[8] At its basic level, it allows the group to determine how it will accomplish its charge. When a group knows precisely what it wants to achieve, members know what they have to focus on and improve upon when necessary. Goal setting gives the group long-term vision and short-term motivation, and allows for the group to identify and organize its resources, and to acquire additional knowledge. By setting goals, the individual or group can:

1. Achieve more than they would if no goals were set;
2. Improve self-confidence;
3. Increase members' pride and satisfaction in their achievements;
4. Increase self-motivation to succeed;
5. Measure their success as they work toward fulfilling their charge.

Goal setting really is a desired outcome of performance. Depending on the length of time the group will be working on their charge, you may want to establish a set of subgoals. **Subgoals** are goals that you set along the way that lead ultimately to the overall goal, or charge. Once you have stated your goals, they should be evaluated by asking: (1) Do they really address the problem or decision to be made? (2) Are they realistic and achievable? (3) Can the success of achieving your goals be measured in meaningful terms? Your goal is stated in terms of group outcomes instead of group inputs. It is not a question of how much each member contributes or participates; these are known as **inputs**. The group inputs time, energy, reports, research, etc. Inputs are the means, but a goal is the end.[9]

Objectives are the single most important element in the goal-setting process. An objective is a statement originating from the group's goals and usually addresses a specific aspect of the problem with each of several objectives

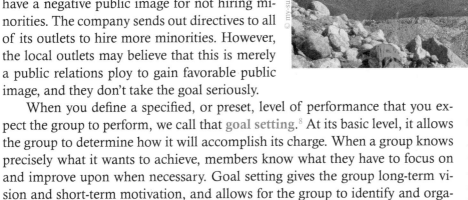

Goal
A conceptual statement of what you plan to achieve; a clear, positive statement of intent to solve a significant problem or achieve a significant result within a specific timeframe.

Goal setting
A specified, or preset, level of performance that you expect the group to perform.

Subgoals
Goals that you set along the way that lead ultimately to the overall goal, or charge.

Objectives
A statement originating from the group's goals, which usually addresses a specific aspect of the problem with each of several objectives contributing toward achieving the goal.

contributing toward achieving the goal.[10] The term objectives is often used as a substitution for subgoals. An objective is a specific and measurable destination that represents the achievement of a goal.[11] It is written to point the way toward particular levels of awareness, acceptance or action.[12] It states not what the group will do, but what the group will accomplish. Objectives must be stated in **clear language** so that each member knows precisely what he or she and the group are to accomplish. Objectives must be **measurable**. Measurement means that you can determine the progress as it occurs, that it can be measured along a predetermined continuum. How much data has been researched? How many pages of the proposal have been written? How many times has the group met to discuss its progress? How many sources were collected? Objectives should be obtainable given current resources. You should not have to purchase the data, equipment, etc., in order to achieve your stated objectives. And finally, objectives must be given a **timeline** for completion. Your group has a certain amount of time to accomplish their charge, which means each objective has to be met by its assigned time; otherwise, the group will never be able to move forward.

The following is a list of suggested standards for evaluating effective and practical objectives:[13]

1. **Goal-rooted.** Objectives are rooted in goals. They are based on the organization's goal statements, which themselves grow out of the mission or vision that the organization has defined for itself. Objectives are responsive to a particular issue that the organization has recognized as important to its effectiveness.
2. **Linked to research.** Good objectives are tied to research. Research provides the data with which the group will make its recommendations.
3. **Explicit.** Objectives are explicit and clearly defined. All members of the group must share a common understanding of where the objective is leading.
4. **Measurable.** Objectives are precise and quantifiable, with clear measures that state the degree of change being sought.
5. **Time-definite.** Objectives are time-definite. They include a clear indication of a specific time frame to be accomplished.
6. **Singular.** Objectives are singular, focusing on one desired response from the group.
7. **Challenging.** Objectives should challenge members a bit and inspire members to action.
8. **Attainable.** Objectives should be understood and supported by the entire group. The value of objectives is not that they are written, but rather that they are used.

Once the objectives or responsibilities are identified and understood, the leader must clearly specify what constitutes good performance in each area, so that the leader and each member know when performance is approaching the desired level. The leader must specify what good performance looks like.

Accomplishment is another term for performance, which necessitates some form of evaluation. Throughout this entire process, you should know how each member and the group as a whole are doing because along the way you will be evaluating their progress. To achieve the goals and objectives, a leader will assist the group in developing **action steps**. Action steps detail the necessary procedures and operations that each member takes in order to achieve the goals.

Karl Weick (1969) offers a novel approach to understanding goal setting. He says that planning (goal setting) can best be understood by thinking in the future perfect tense. It isn't the plan that gives reason or rationality to people's actions. It is the fact that those actions are to be accomplished in the future,

Goal Setting: Sample Goals and Objectives	**TABLE 10.1**
Goal: A broad statement of group hopes will be accomplished	**Goal 1:** Company X employees will continue to what the be trained in cost-saving seminars.
Objective: States how that goal will be accomplished	**Objective A:** Each employee of company X will be required to attend three complete seminars per year to remain employed at company X. **Objective B:** Each seminar will focus on cost-saving techniques. **Objective C:** Each employee will complete a satisfaction survey after each seminar.
Action step: The final step is the assignment of responsibility for carrying out the objectives and a time frame for its completion.	**Action Step 1:** The director, in consultation with continuing education directors at University Y, will develop a list of continuing cost-saving seminars available to employees. This will be distributed to management on January 1, 2010. The executive committee will review employees' participation quarterly. **Action Step 2:** Upon completion of the quarterly review, the executive committee will make its recommendations to the director regarding each employee's participation. **Action Step 3:** Within 30 days of the executive committee's recommendations, the director will terminate any employee not in compliance with objectives A and/ or C.

and therefore the means for accomplishing them are made explicit. It is not the stated goal per se that allows groups to perform in an orderly fashion, but rather the thoughtful and insightful way that the group meets its goal. Goal setting works because we can look back to member performance and evaluate it, not because goal setting accurately anticipates future performance.[14]

Before we move to the next section, let's do a quick review of what you've just read regarding critical points in the goal-writing process. You may discover that writing each objective and action step will take far more time than you anticipated. You may even stare at a blank screen for hours before writing something. If I didn't mention this in an earlier chapter, let me do so now because you probably will spend an inordinate amount of time trying to write the perfect objectives and action steps. There is no such thing as a perfectly written objective or action step. Art Buchwald, a syndicated journalist, once wrote about the "Art of Writing." He said that the "art of writing is applying the seat of the pants to the seat of the chair." In part, he was correct. What he forgot to mention was that you need to put a word on the computer screen—any word—just something to get you going. From my experience, writing not only includes applying the seat of the pants to the seat of the chair, it also includes writing something, anything, to get you started, and then rewrite, and rewrite, and rewrite again. Then you give what you've written to your colleagues and ask them to review and edit.

Review of Critical Points in the Goal-Writing Process

1. Goals are broad statements of problem-solving or decision-making issues for the group.
2. Objectives must be measurable on a quantifiable scale.
3. Action steps must assign responsibility and timeliness.
4. Goals are not realized without specific objectives and action steps.
5. The group must attempt to reach consensus on all goals and objectives. This suggests that each member can live with those goals or objectives, not necessarily that each would be most important to every member.
6. The goal-writing process takes time and a lot of discussion; don't rush it. This will probably be the first test of the group's ability to disagree and still come together to agree. Take your time! This is your road map, so do it right the first time.

As a leader, have you made sure that all members know specifically what their responsibilities are, their goals and objectives? Have you clearly defined and explained the objectives or member responsibilities? Once the objectives or responsibilities are identified and understood, it is your responsibility to clearly specify what constitutes good performance in each area so that both you and the members know when performance is approaching the desired level. And most importantly, you must specify what good performance looks like. For you and the group members to know how well someone is doing, good performance has to be clearly specified. In general terms, it is goal-directed.

Helping Members Choose a Realistic Group Goal

One important consideration when setting goals is the degree to which the goal is both challenging and attainable. Both of these elements are critical in the ultimate success of goal setting. The criterion of challenging refers to how high a goal is set, and attainable refers to how low a goal should be. The best goals meet both criteria.[15] The last thing a group wants to achieve is failure. Failure is a product of a number of things, but one of the primary considerations is setting unrealistic goals, especially if the group is a student group. It is the leader's responsibility to guide the group toward more rational and realistic choices. Ideally, the group should consider a goal that is moderately challenging, one that is neither too hard nor too easy. Student groups have a tendency to set difficult goals rather than easy ones. These actions usually cause the group to fail to achieve its goal, and the failures in turn generate ill feelings for individual members and group disharmony.[16] As a result, individuals tend to shy away from future group work.

Goals may be set unrealistically high for a number of reasons. Sometimes, the group lacks the authority to set its own goals. When this happens, some other body unfamiliar with the group and its members will set unrealistic goals based on what they want. Often, this is done because they don't know or understand the depth of the problem. The group may set unrealistic goals because of insufficient information. One way to avoid this is for each member to have a clear and realistic understanding of what it the group charge is. And sometimes people just believe that they will perform their best all of the time, not just some of the time. Many times, the group will base their goals on their best performance. They fail to take into account bad days, such as: not feeling well, too much homework that week, studying for exams, working overtime, partied too hardy the night before, roommate kept them up all night—the list is endless.

The opposite of setting goals unrealistically high is setting them unrealistically low. Why bother to be in a group at all? If goals are too low, then how do you

really solve the problem; that is, how are you really going to learn? Learning is thinking critically. In group work, we learn, in part, by using an evaluation process that consists of description, interpretation, recall and recognition, and comprehension and understanding.[17]

Descriptive Phase

A. Learners use content-specific methods to acquire specific facts that have meaning and value of themselves.
B. Learners must answer the questions:

1. What is it?
2. What is it related to? (What other concepts are connected?)

C. Learners describe by:

1. Defining the term
2. Classification (a kind of conflict behavior/kind of reasoning)
3. Identification of patterns (a complimentary relationship, chronological order)
4. Recognition of processes (relational deterioration/reasoning)
5. Generating criteria (elements of a human system/of an introduction)
6. Locating techniques (research techniques appropriate to the content)
7. Observing and listening

Interpretation Phase

A. The explanation or summarization of a set of facts derives from description.
B. The organizing and structuring of information, emphasizing interrelationships and patterns
C. The use of concepts and generalizations as organizing ideas
D. The learner must answer the following questions:

1. What behaviors are perceived?
2. What meanings may they have?

E. Learners interpret by:

1. Analysis: The breakdown of a body of information into constituent parts. The discovery of relationships.
2. Synthesis: Putting together the constituent parts so as to form a whole. The formulation of hypotheses based upon the analysis of factors. The formulation of generalizations. The process of extrapolation and prediction.

What do we mean by **recall** and **recognition**? Recall is the cognitive process of remembering what something is, and recognition is the ability to identify it.

What do we mean by **comprehension** and **understanding**? Comprehension is the ability to explain what something is—to understand its meaning; and to express it—to demonstrate how it works; and to interpret its functions.

Encouraging Realistic Group Goals

Alvin Zander, a psychologist at the University of Michigan and pioneer in the research of the individual and group dynamics, wrote extensively (1968, 1971, 1977, 1982) about group goals. He said that a moderately challenging goal is more beneficial than a very difficult or very easy one. Because of this, the group leader and its members should ensure that a group chooses and supports a goal that is moderately challenging. He cited six practices that foster the selection of such an objective:[18]

1. **Report to members how well their group is doing over time.** The leader should report to the group how well it is performing as it finishes each major phase toward completion of its task. Such feedback of a group's accomplishment is necessary if members are to have rational expectations about its chances of future success. Without reliable evidence about the group's progress, members have a tendency to believe that their group is highly productive, even when it isn't, and they tend to prefer goals typically chosen by successful groups.

2. **There should be a clear definition of the group's purpose.** State the group's purposes, the reason for its existence, as clearly and precisely as possible. Activities in the group should fulfill the group's charge, or purpose. Each group activity should therefore have a goal that describes how much the group is expected to accomplish in that work. Such a goal is also a criterion for evaluating the group's performance. The group's goal cannot be clearly stated unless the group's purpose and the activities undertaken toward those ends are clearly given.

3. **Members should understand the values of a group goal.** Demonstrate to members that a goal is useful because it stimulates the development of the skills, knowledge, and abilities necessary for group success. Members perform better if they have a specific target to achieve than if they try to reach an ambiguous end. A goal is a source of stimulation for either encouraging an individual's energy on tasks or reducing efforts when the objective is achieved. It is a beacon that guides the direction of members' efforts, and it justifies collaboration among members. A goal determines the distribution or rewards among members, whether they all share alike in that reward or whether some members gain more than others. It is clear that a realistic group goal ensures that benefits from its attainment will be achieved; an unrealistic goal does not.

4. **Encourage a desire for group success among members.** The leader should encourage a willingness among members to value the consequence of group success. A willingness can be stimulated by pointing out the attractiveness of conditions that accompany a good performance and by emphasizing their importance. Consequences may vary from group to group, but generally they promote members' pride in their group and the approval a group obtains after a success.

5. **The fear of failure should be played down among members.** Whether it's peer-to-peer or from the leader, goals should increase the strength of

members' desires for group success because members who have more desire develop a stronger preference for moderately challenging goals. The desire is stronger among persons who have a strong interest in attaining the satisfaction that follows a group success and who believe the chances are good that their group will succeed in its task. As a result, members need a goal they want to reach and think they can attain.

6. **The group should continually strive to improve the group's procedures so they are as efficient as possible and work to keep them that way.** The leader should encourage members to introduce changes within the group that enable colleagues to work more effectively. These changes improve members' skills, and the equipment available to them, their group, or the group's leadership.

Survey for Measuring Member Desire for Group Achievement

One way for determining each member's desire for group success is to take an unscientific survey of their attitudes. This doesn't have to be leadership driven; rather, any member may want to measure how strongly colleagues desire group success. You can create your own survey or look for one used previously by other groups or recommended by your instructor, or you may adapt any of the following useful questions.[19]

1. In your opinion, what are the chances that your group's output will give you a feeling of pride in the group this semester?

   a. never happen
   b. unlikely it will happen
   c. 50–50 chance it will happen
   d. likely chance it will happen
   e. will definitely happen

2. Among the various sources in the group, how important is it that you have pride in your group's output?

   a. not important
   b. somewhat important
   c. moderately important
   d. very important
   e. most important

3. From what you've experienced so far, what are the chances your group's output during this semester will give you a feeling of shame in your group?

   a. will definitely happen
   b. good chance it will happen
   c. 50–50 chance it will happen
   d. probably won't happen
   e. cannot possibly happen

4. Among the sources of dissatisfaction with your group, how important is it that you avoid a sense of failure or shame in the output of your group.

   a. not at all important
   b. not very important
   c. moderately important
   d. very important
   e. most important

5. Are you more interested in the quality of your own work or more interested in the quality of your group's work?

   a. my work
   b. group's work

6. When the group does well, do you have more pride in the group's performance or more pride in your own performance?

   a. group's performance
   b. my performance

7. When the group does poorly, are you more embarrassed by the team's performance or your own performance?

   a. group performance
   b. my performance

8. Are you usually more concerned about the accomplishments of your group as a whole or more concerned about your own accomplishments within the group?

   a. group performance (accomplishments)
   b. my performance (accomplishments)

The questions are premised on the assumption that the strength of the desire that a member has for group success is greater when a person is more confident the group will be successful and when the member places more value on the consequences of such success. Question 1 is a measure of confidence; Question 2 measures value and satisfaction; Questions 3 and 4 measure the desire to avoid group failure; and Questions 5 through 8 attempt to identify preference for output of the group or personal output.

As we have repeatedly stated, goals are all about performance. We have a tendency to want to perform our best. Our minds want us to make contracts that we subconsciously, or consciously, know we cannot fulfill; a little bit of egoism. As a result, we make goals that are unrealistic, one way or the other. When your group discusses goals and goal setting, compare your goals to the suggested practices and criteria in this chapter; you will never go wrong.

Let's assume that all members are highly motivated to perform their tasks. We can generally classify activities that are a result of high motivation as goal-directed activity and goal activity. When a person is motivated to reach a particular goal, we call that a **goal-directed activity**. For example, if a person's strongest need at a given moment is to eat, various activities such as looking for

Goal-directed activity

When a person is motivated to reach a particular goal.

a fast-food restaurant, café, hot dog stand, or taco truck would be considered goal-directed activities. A **goal activity** is the process of achieving the goal itself. With regard to eating, consuming food is the goal, and looking for food is the goal activity. Paul Hersey, et al (2001) aptly summarizes the differences between the two;[20] they state that an important distinction between these two classes of activities is their effect on the strength of the need. In goal-directed activity, the strength of the need tends to increase as one engages in the activity until the goal is reached or frustration sets in. Remember, frustration develops when one is continually blocked from reaching a goal. If the frustration becomes intense enough, the strength of the need may decrease until it is no longer potent enough to affect behavior—a person gives up. The strength of the need tends to increase as one engages in goal-directed activity; however, once goal activity begins, the strength of the need tends to decrease as one engages in it. In group work, goal-directed activity should be more intensified than the actual achievement of the goal. This is when tasks are performed; when members exert the most effort. Remember, good goal setting requires that goals be challenging and attainable.

Creating Goal Criteria

As we noted earlier, effective group and team work is all about performance management, getting people to improve their behavior to maximize performance and ultimately produce a superior proposal or product. From a PM perspective, the most important reason for setting goals is not only to meet group expectations for member performance, but also to create additional opportunities for reinforcement. Improved performance is the primary benefit of effective goal setting for groups, and increased reinforcement is the primary benefit of goal setting for individual members.[21] Remember, goals are antecedents for performance. We establish goals and then strive to achieve them. Goal setting occurs before we perform our tasks. Since reinforcement increases performance, goals are naturally a valuable performance improvement tool. Goals alone, as antecedents to performance, do not consistently produce improvement unless they are paired with reinforcement. Goals provide the opportunity for reinforcement. As leader, when you establish your goals and objectives, you should always include measures for reinforcement.

How to Set Good Goals

Before the group determines what they are going to set as good goals, members should consider three basic criteria to compare the suggested goals to in order to help them decide if those goals are actually good and attainable. There should be quite a bit of discussion about these criteria because it does more than merely help the group choose the best goals, but the ensuing dialogue also affords members the opportunity to learn more about the charge, process, tasks, etc. You hold this discussion prior to group consensus regarding the choice of those goals and commitment to achieving them. Those criteria are: keep it simple, keep goals action-oriented, and keep goals task-important.[22]

1. **Keep goals simple.** Make sure that the goals are simple enough to be understood by every member and can be reasonably implemented. Tasks should be divided into achievable components, and the leader should encourage group efforts to simplify procedures, especially if they appear to be complex and confusing. Keeping goals simple helps to avoid any unnecessary complications.

2. **Keep goals action-oriented.** Keeping goals action oriented communicates a positive sense of urgency about getting the job done. Keeping task performance moving in the right direction emphasizes the importance of day-to-day progress. It is a reinforcer that acts as an encourager for members to get things done and helps members concentrate on meeting deadlines.

3. **Keep goals task-important.** Build on task importance. This helps promote individual and group commitment to excellence in achieving task achievement. Instead of just something that has to get done, focusing on task importance makes the task meaningful and relevant. Once this happens, it has a tendency to encourage members to suggest innovative and creative suggestions for improving productivity. This helps prevent or reverse any impressions that the importance of what the group is doing is somehow downplayed or diminished.

The Value of an Agenda

Group discussion is more than just people getting together and talking about issues. People with different ideas and perspectives come together and work as a group to solve a problem. In order to resolve the different ideas and behaviors of group members, it is important to have some type of method or procedure that all members can follow. The group needs rules of order to prevent conflict or to resolve if it arises. In group work, members commit themselves to a common goal. It would be very difficult to get anything accomplished if people presented their ideas anytime they wanted, interrupted a presentation at anytime, or blurted out questions. This is why group work follows some type of agenda that allows a leader to facilitate members from individual commitment to group solution. When members follow an agenda, they can process their ideas intelligently, which increases their chances of achieving their charge.[23]

Hidden Agenda or Hidden Agenda Item

There may be times when confusion occurs within the group because of conflict or competition between the stated group purpose and hidden agendas of individual members or the group itself. The term hidden agenda refers to any objectives of individual members, subgroup of members, or even the entire group that are unannounced, covert, and different from the stated group purpose.[24] Hidden agendas can be harmful because they have the potential to prevent the group from achieving its charge. If members are dissatisfied with their roles, the purpose of the group, other members, or the group itself, these dissatisfied members need to be changed. Sometimes, a hidden agenda is apparent because one or more members will not seem to be working toward the same goal or discussing the same topics as the rest of the group. As leader or even as an

Hidden agenda
Any objectives of individual members, subgroup of members, or even the entire group that are unannounced, covert, and different from the stated group purpose.

individual member, if you suspect a hidden agenda, you need to get it out into the open. One way of doing that is to ask probing questions such as:

"Could you please tell me what the group's charge is, specifically?"
"Is there a purpose for calling today's meeting?"
"Can you tell me what we are trying to accomplish as a group?"
"How does this information directly relate to our objectives?"
"How does this research fit into our goals?"

You should get clear and concise answers to these questions. Let's state it another way: you should insist on getting clear and concise answers. Remember, this is all about performance. If a member feels that working toward the group goal is meaningless or insignificant, then that person's performance will be weak, at best.

GOAL-SETTING PLANNING MODEL

"To be successful, strategic planning process should provide the criteria for making day-to-day organizational decisions and should provide a template against which all such decisions can be evaluated."[25]

Pfeiffer, Goodstein, Nolan, 1986

It is a fact that planning is one of the most critical management functions a group or team leader has. Planning isn't just people jotting down things they may want to do at a given time. Planning is strategic; it leads to organization and the development of effective work plans, and it is a prerequisite to the achievement of goals and group accountability. Strategic planning is also an important part of effective time management.[26]

What Is Strategic Planning, Really?

Strategic planning came about from business in the 1970s as a way for helping managers make decisions that made the most out of organizational objectives. Similar to the thoughts of Karl Weick (1969), Pfeifer, et al. (1986) defined strategic planning as the process by which an organization provides both the direction in which the organization should move and the energy to begin that move. When an organization has envisioned its future, it has begun the process of strategic planning. Strategic plans are about seeing the future and finding a vision of what an organization might become in the future.[27]

Why Do We Construct a Strategic Plan?

A strategic plan is not only a blueprint for how we achieve our goals and objectives on a daily basis; it also guides or modifies member performance toward achieving those goals. A strategic plan is future oriented; it directs members' behaviors as to what they should do, not to what they did. It increases the likelihood that the group will achieve its charge on time. It is a performance management tool. There are a number of good planning models that work well; the following is a recommended Five Basic Step Model:[28]

Step 1: Ask the question, "How much commitment to the planning process is present?" All too often, groups have labored intensely and spent numerous hours developing plans, only to have them placed in a file or on some shelf where they collect dust and forgotten about. So the first question a leader asks is, "How much commitment to the planning process is present?" If the answer is little or none, stop; do not pass GO; do not collect your $200.00; and cancel any plans to move ahead into strategic planning steps. You will need to figure out how you and the group will get more commitment for the idea first. Commitment must be somewhat assured that your group's recommendations, or final proposal, may be acted upon, or at least reviewed by the appropriate body. Otherwise, you're doing a lot of busy work for nothing.

Step 2: Perform a values audit. A **values audit** identifies the significant group or organizational values that cannot be tampered with. This includes an assessment of the group or organizational culture and what type of change can be supported by that culture.

Step 3: Construct a **mission formulation**. There are three questions that need to be asked prior to constructing the plan.

1. What function does the group or organization serve? Any strategic plan must conform to the group or organization's function, or what it does, its reason for existence. It doesn't make any sense for the group to develop a plan that the organization may not be able to implement or one that does not complement its functions.

2. For whom does the organization serve this function? Is it the private or public sector that the organization serves, or both? This is where knowing who the targeted audience(s) is helps to better understand why and how the organization functions. Any proposal your group presents will not only have an impact on the organization that gave you your charge, but also on those whom the organization interacts with.

3. How does the organization go about filling this function? What type of valued product or service does the organization provide? What does it do? How does it make money or perform its function?

Step 4: **Strategic modeling** is the process by which the group or organization defines success. First, the group identifies one or more quantified objectives, for example, ensuring that the group's next agenda is distributed to all members by a certain time. Then it lists statements of how the quantified objectives will be achieved. For example, (1) the leader will have the next agenda written one week prior to the next scheduled group meeting; (2) the agenda will be distributed by email one week prior to the meeting to all members; and (3) the group note-taker will verify that all members received their email by contacting them directly. This type of planning is employed for every objective that the group endeavors. And for every objective, there should be two questions asked: "How do we accomplish this?" and "Why are we doing this?" If no one can satisfactorily answer these basic questions, then you shouldn't be pursuing the objectives. A strategic planning model should be specific enough for you to understand how the group or organization's mission; problem; or decision-making statements, goals, objectives, and tasks relate to one another. In public relations, we call it a strategic planning ladder.[29]

Step 5: The **performance audit** is something that the leader should perform on a regular basis. It examines the ongoing performance of each group member and the group as a whole regarding their tasks and task achievements. There exists a gap between where the group currently is and where it ultimately should be, as indicated by the strategic model. A performance audit provides the data that identify the gap between the current where and the ultimate where. This is the determination of the degree to which the strategic model is realistic and workable and can be conducted. If the gap is too wide, then the group may have set the bar too high on its goals and objectives, or there aren't enough resources or members to achieve the goals, or a host of reasons why the gap is too great. The point is, this should be done very early in the group's formation; otherwise, the group may spend a lot of time, energy, and resources trying to accomplish the unaccomplishable. The key question the audit must answer is whether the group or organization has the capability to successfully implement its strategic plan and to achieve its stated goals and objectives.

FIGURE 10.1
Applied Strategic
Planning Model

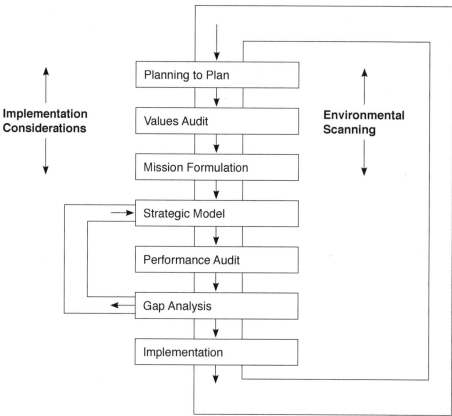

Adapted from Goodstein, Nolan, and Pfeiffer (1993). [30]

GOAL IMPLEMENTATION

Once the strategic plan—the means with which to achieve the group's stated goals and objectives—has been written, it needs to be implemented. How do you do that? By creating action steps. Action steps are specific task assignments that members must achieve by a certain time and date. This is when time lines are assigned on a daily, weekly, or monthly basis, whatever the planning model specifies. This is the final test of implementing the plan. It is the degree to which group leaders and members use the strategic plan in their daily decision-making. There are some common pitfalls to using this that are associated with these types of techniques. It is recommended that members not get assigned the same task repeatedly; rotate tasks so all members have an opportunity to complete each one, including that of leadership. People lose interest once a task becomes rote. Let everyone have an opportunity to experience all roles. Another pitfall is underestimating or overestimating the time, resources, energy, etc. that may be necessary to complete each task in the action plan. It is difficult to factor in unknown contingencies or unintended consequences. An action plan is a rational tool, which means it can create an illusion that the plan will be implemented exactly as it appears on the chart that members have created.[31] For example, the group may decide that it would take only a few days to compile a data sheet from extensive research, only to discover that the file has been corrupted or saved in an unknown format. This sets back any task contingent on that data sheet. Or just the opposite: too much time was allotted for compiling the data

Action steps
Specific task assignments that members must achieve by a certain time and date.

Weekly Strategic Plan — TABLE 10.2

Name	Task	Date Assigned	Start Date	Completion Date	Resources	Status
Tamara	research health stats	9/10/10	9/12/10	9/19/10	county health agencies	Presented report to group
Thomas	take meeting notes	9/10/10	9/21/10	9/21/10	laptop	Emailed proceedings to members
Yecenia	group observer	9/10/10	9/21/10	9/21/10	notepad laptop	Sent report to group leader
Kyla	research grassroots org.'s	9/10/10	9/12/10	9/19/10	web	Presented report to group
Jesse	research local media	9/10/10	9/12/10	9/19/10	web phone book	Presented report to group

sheet, and the group lost valuable work time waiting for it. Group time clocks rarely run smoothly.

How to Determine When Goals Have Been Achieved

When will the group know that they are successful? Having an established set of standards answers this question. We rely on standards and feedback to determine when goals have been achieved. Standards are important because they let the group know when the goal has been accomplished and they eliminate the guessing as to when the group has completed a goal. Without standards, it is anyone's opinion whether the goal was reached.[32] What is a standard? A standard can be defined as a degree or level of requirement, excellence, quality, or attainment. The standard of a group or team is an established measure or criterion (or set of criteria) against which the group is to be judged. It is the performance of the group in comparison to that standard that determines whether the group's work is of high quality or not. The distinction between standard and quality can be explained as outcomes and processes. The outcomes, what the group eventually produces, may not come up to the expected standard, or it may just comply with an acceptable standard, but the processes, how the group should go about its business, should remain at the higher quality.[33] Karl Weick (1969) stated that a leader should coordinate processes rather than groups because the way in which a group functions depends on the relationships that exist among processes rather than among groups. In order for the leader to coordinate the group, the leader needs to know the dynamics that govern the group, especially the direction of the causal ties between those dynamics and the flow of information. For Weick, the actions performed by the group are less important than are the processes they are related to, and the direction of those relationships.

Before adopting any set of standards, consider these three criteria:

"Are there clear and measurable performance standards?"
"Are those standards communicated so that members know how well they are supposed to perform?"
"Is work-related feedback provided?"

Standard
A degree or level of requirement, excellence, quality, or attainment.

Feedback
Indicates the quality and quantity of progress toward reaching a goal that is defined by standards.

Feedback indicates the quality and quantity of progress toward reaching a goal that is defined by standards. It is the process by which the group compares its performance to a predetermined standard and uses this comparison to control its output.[34] Feedback is essential when the group is considering its intended goals, that is, goals that the group has accepted as meaningful and worthwhile.[35] Feedback is a way for the group to regulate itself in order to adapt to its environment. Goals, standard, and feedback are all related. When it comes to feedback, consider the following questions:

"Does that feedback describe results consistent with the standards and not just behavior?"
"Is feedback provided soon enough to help members remember what they did?"

"Is feedback provided on a frequent basis?"
"Is feedback selective and specific?"
"Is feedback limited to a few matters of importance?"
"Is feedback vague and too general?"
"Is feedback positive and constructive?"
"Is feedback educational so that members learn from it?"

Leadership Tips

Every member will not pursue each and every task with equal enthusiasm and energy. There will be times when you will need to motivate member performance. As leader, you need to identify areas that you believe need motivating. Does each member know specifically what his or her responsibilities are, or the goals and objectives?

> "What area of my group's work or individual members' work do I need to influence?"

For you to know how well someone is doing, good performance has to be clearly specified. You cannot change and develop behavior in areas that are unclear. Please remember that no one (including you) learns how to do anything all at once. We learn a little bit at a time. We learn with each task completed. If you want someone to do something completely new, you should reward or reinforce the slightest progress the person makes in the desired direction. It is important to remember that motivational needs, such as Positive Reinforcement, must have value to the performer.[36] This cannot be stressed enough. The value of the reinforcer lies with the performer. Each individual member requires different rewards/motivation, but the *goals* always remain the same. What do they want from their roles/tasks? What do they need? We reintroduce terms from Chapter 8—Leadership and Team Building—here because they are relevant to goal setting and achieving goals.

Incentives

The term incentive refers to the member's task-relevant incentive—the motivation to complete the specific task successfully. We've discussed intrinsic and extrinsic rewards. Remember, members tend to be more motivated to successfully complete tasks that bring them either intrinsic or extrinsic rewards than to complete tasks that do not reward them personally.

If a member has an incentive problem, the first step is to check the use of rewards and punishments. People have a natural tendency to pursue tasks that are rewarded and to avoid tasks that are not.

Individualizing Reinforcement

Reinforcement depends on the individual. What is reinforcing to one person may not be reinforcing to another.

Dangers of Overgeneralizing

Just as "What is reinforcing to one person may not be reinforcing to another," don't assume that the same reinforcer will work for each situation. An individual may respond positively to one reinforcer in a particular instance, but may not in another. This is overgeneralizing.

Use Immediate Reinforcement

The more immediate the reinforcer is tied to the behavior, the more effective it will be. In order to do this, you must be aware of any progress so as to be in a position to reinforce this change appropriately.

Set Short-term Goals

Set short-term goals rather than final performance criteria, and then reinforce appropriate progress toward the final goals as they are met. In setting goals, it is important that they be obtainable so that the individual proceeds along a path of gradual and systematic development. Avoid making goals too easy to reach or too difficult.

Consequences

The type of consequence individuals experience as a result of their behavior will determine the speed with which they approach their optimum performance, or desired goals.

SUMMARY

In this chapter, we learned that the group charge is the assignment given to a subordinate group by a higher authority. It is the performance expected of the group. We explored how we set goals and objectives, and for what purpose. We learned about goal criteria and how to set good goals, and how to create and implement a strategic plan. And finally, we determined when the group would know that they are successful. Good goal setting is one of the first things a group does, before it starts satisfying its charge. Good goal setting is the group's roadmap for success.

DISCUSSION

1. Why is the setting of measurable goals so important in planning group work? When a group is in its initial stages and is setting participative goals that come from the group itself, why is there sometimes a strong tendency for the group to set goals that *cannot* be easily measured?

2. Identify a specific situation in which work may be organized around unrealistically high goals that cannot be achieved. Why is this *not* merely a good motivating tactic to "raise expectations?" In what ways do people respond when they cannot possibly achieve their goals? What contexts in our society sometimes create/reinforce this climate of goals set too high?

3. Identify a specific situation in which work may be organized around very low goals that are simple for anyone to achieve. Why is this *not* merely a good motivating tactic to "establish confidence?" In what ways do people respond when they have no trouble at all achieving their goals? What contexts in our society sometimes create/reinforce this climate of goals set too low?

4. Why is the second step of the Strategic Planning model in Figure 10.1, the Values Audit, so important for performance? What potential resources that can enhance group work are identified in a Values Audit? What potential constraints that can alter or reshape group work are identified in a Values Audit?

5. In what ways might it be possible to have too much feedback, or to have unhelpful feedback, as your group moves toward its goals? What negative consequences can arise if feedback loops are too tight, i.e. very little time elapses within feedback cycles? What are the hallmark characteristics of unhelpful, or even destructive, performance feedback?

NOTES

1. Brilhart, J.K. (1986). *Effective group discussion* (5th ed.). Dubuque, IA: Wm. C. Brown.

2. http://www.fda.gov/AboutFDA/CentersOffices/default.htm. Retrieved November 24, 2009.

3. http://www.time-management-guide.com/goal-setting-theory.html. Retrieved November 24, 2009.

4. Locke, E., & Latham, G. (1984). *Goal setting: A motivational technique that really works.!* Englewood Cliffs, NJ: Prentice Hall. See also Eisenberg, E.M., Goodall, Jr., H.L., & Trethewey, A. (2007). *Organizational communication: Balancing creativity and constraint* (5th ed.). New York: Bedford/St. Martin's.

5. Eisenberg, E.M., Goodall, H.L., Jr., & Trethewey, A. (2007). *Organizational communication: Balancing creativity and constraint,* (5th ed.). New York: Bedford/St. Martin's.

6. Austin, E.W., & Pinkleton, B.E. (2006). *Strategic public relations management* (2nd ed.). Mahwah, NJ: Lawrence Erlbaum.

7. Wheelan, S.A. (1994). *Group processes: A developmental perspective.* Boston: Allyn and Bacon.

8. Daniels, A.C. (1989). *Performance management: Improving quality productivity through positive reinforcement* (3rd ed.). Tucker, GA: Performance Management.

9. Wilcox, D.L., Cameron, G.T., Ault, P., & Agee, W.K. (2007). *Public relations strategies and tactics* (8th ed.). New York: Pearson.

10. Kendall, R. (1996). *Public relations campaign strategies: Planning for implementation* (2nd ed.). New York: Harper Collins College.

11. Austin, E.W., & Pinkleton, B.E. (2006). *Strategic public relations management* (2nd ed.). Mahwah, NJ: Lawrence Erlbaum.

12. Smith., R.D. (2005). *Strategic planning for public relations.* Mahwah, NJ: Lawrence Erlbaum.

13. Adapted from Hendrix, J.A. (2004). *Public relations cases* (6th ed.). New York: Wadsworth Thomson.

14. Weick, K. E. (1969). *The social psychology of organizing.* Menlo Park, CA: Addison-Wesley.

15. Daniels, A.C. (1989). *Performance management: Improving quality productivity through positive reinforcement* (3rd ed.). Tucker, GA: Performance Management.

16. Zander, A. (1982). *Making groups effective.* San Francisco: Jossey-Bass.

17. The definition of terms used in the evaluation process are notes from an undergraduate class I attended at California State University, Hayward, Ca. Source unknown.

18. Adapted from Zander, A. (1982). *Making groups effective.* San Francisco: Jossey-Bass.

19. Adapted from Zander, A. (1982). *Making groups effective.* San Francisco: Jossey-Bass.

20. Hersey, P., Blanchard, K. H., & Johnson, D.E. (2001). *Management of organizational behavior.* Upper Saddle River, N.J.: Prentice Hall.

21. Daniels, A.C. (1989). *Performance management: Improving quality productivity through positive reinforcement* (3rd ed.). Tucker, GA: Performance Management.

22. Hersey, P., Blanchard, K.H., & Johnson, D.E. (2001). *Management of organizational behavior.* Upper Saddle River, N.J.: Prentice Hall.

23. Wood, J.T., Phillips, G.M., & Pedersen, D.J. (1986). *Group discussion: A practical guide to participation and leadership.* New York: Harper & Row.

24. Brilhart, J.K. (1986). *Effective group discussion* (5th ed.). Dubuque, IA: Wm. C. Brown.

25. Pfeiffer, J. W., Goodstein, L. D., & Nolan, T. M. (1986). *Applied strategic planning: A how to do it guide.* San Diego: University Associates.

26. Smith, R.E. (2009). *Human resources administration: A school-based perspective.* Larchmont, NY: Eye On Education.

27. www.eyeoneducation.com. Retrieved November 13, 2009.

28. Adapted from the model presented by Pheiffer, J. W., Goodstein, L. D., & Nolan, T. M. (1986). *Applied strategic planning: A how to do it guide.* San Diego: University Associates.

29. Austin, E.W. & Pinkleton, B.E. (2006). *Strategic public relations management* (2nd ed.). Mahwah, NJ: Lawrence Erlbaum.

30. Goodstein, L.D., Nolan, T.M., & Pfeiffer, J.W. (1993). *Applied strategic planning: How to develop a plan that really works.* New York: McGraw-Hill.

31. Schwarz, R.M. (1994). *The skilled facilitator.* San Francisco: Jossey-Bass.

32. Hersey, P., Blanchard, K. H., & Johnson, D.E. (2001). *Management of organizational behavior.* Upper Saddle River, N.J.: Prentice Hall.

33. http://www.springerlink.com/content/vu159511hw42145j/. Retrieved November 20, 2009.

34. Trenholm, S., & Jensen, A. (1992). *Interpersonal communication.* Belmont, CA: Wadsworth.

35. Hersey, P., Blanchard, K. H., & Johnson, D.E. (2001). *Management of organizational behavior.* Upper Saddle River, N.J.: Prentice Hall.

36. Daniels, A.C. (1989). *Performance management: Improving quality productivity through positive reinforcement* (3rd ed.). Tucker, GA: Performance Management.

11

Critical Thinking, Problem Solving, and Decision Making

CHAPTER OBJECTIVES

- Describe the critical-thinking process
- Explain the role of critical thinking in group decision making
- Identify the symptoms of groupthink as barriers to decision making
- Identify structural barriers to decision making
- Explain how group processes can prevent barriers to decision making
- Describe and implement the five-step problem-solving process

KEY TERMS

Deliberation

Democratic participation

Groupthink

Brainstorming

CHAPTER OUTLINE

© Ilike, 2011. Under license from Shutterstock, Inc.

Nearly all small groups exist because they include people collaborating to make decisions. This is true not only of professional small groups charged with accomplishing new work-related tasks, but also, for example, of families that make decisions about how to share scarce resources like space or technology, friendship groups that make decisions about how to share time together with limited schedules, student groups that make decisions about new questions or assignments posed by teachers, and so on.

What links these examples of groups dealing with change is that each of them requires more from each group member than a mere individual **response** (see Chapter 9) to new information or different environments. Instead, making such decisions effectively requires **critical thinking** by individual group members. When the critical thinking process is applied collaboratively on the group level, it involves responding to perceived changes by conducting an organized examination of what the group already knows, what resources are available, what the group still needs, and how the group can evaluate its choices. This approach to making decisions on the group level is called **problem solving**. This chapter describes critical thinking and problem-solving processes and their relationship to group decision making.

CRITICAL THINKING

Critical Thinking and Effective Small Groups

Academic attention in Western cultures to the role of thinking in effective decision making dates back at least to the time of Socrates. Many researchers who currently work with the concept of critical thinking are interested in teaching, learning, and the ways that people can develop better critical thinking skills over time. A cogent, workable definition of critical thinking comes from just such an initiative: Paul, Elder, and Bartell, teacher education scholars, mark seven dimensions of critical thinking, explaining that when we think critically, we recognize that:

- All reasoning occurs within points of view and frames of reference.
- All reasoning proceeds from some goals and objectives.
- All reasoning has an informational base.
- All data when used in reasoning must be interpreted.
- Interpretation involves concepts.
- Concepts entail assumptions.
- All basic inferences in thought have implications.[1]

Learning how to think critically may seem challenging, given these seven dimensions and what they mean: we cannot take anything we hear, see, or even believe or know for granted. But critical thinking is consistently demanded, and increasingly highlighted, in business, management, and professional contexts as well as the educational programs that support them.[2]

One way we can explore the concept of critical thinking and its connection to group problem solving is to consider the ideas of John Dewey, a scholar who devoted much of his attention to mental activity and its relationship to human development. Dewey used the phrase *reflective thinking* in a similar sense to the definition of critical thinking above, characterizing this kind of thinking as something we must do carefully and consistently whenever we are confronted with any belief or supposed fact.[3] What should we be considering when we think reflectively about a specific thing we believe or know? According to Dewey, we should consider both how we came to know or believe this thing, and also what consequences follow from knowing/believing it.[4] He used the phrase reflective thinking to describe the process we now associate with critical thinking, because he emphasized reflection as the key part of this ongoing cycle of human development through thought and action:

- We reflect based on experience.
- We form goals based on these reflections.
- We act purposefully based on these goals.
- We reflect again based on the new experiences resulting from our actions.

Look at again Dewey's definition, above, of how we think reflectively. Notice that it includes both reflection on the past and reflection on the future. We reflect on the past when we think critically about how we came to know or believe what we do. We reflect on the future when we think critically about how we expect this knowledge or belief to affect the world. In short, critical thinking means considering the present in light of the past and in light of the future. Critical thinking is always poised between the past and the future. As in the seven dimensions of critical thinking above, when a person thinks critically, that person is acknowledging that all knowledge is **contingent** on our particular history (where we've been) and our particular goals (where we're going). A central skill that you should develop, as a small group member, is to acknowledge, consider, and encourage your group to consider the contingency of goals, plans, protocols, and even facts and values. Doing this will make your group communication more successful because the group will place its decisions in context. A small group makes effective decisions when it fully understands the past and when it fully considers the future.

This is a helpful way to understand the relevance of critical thinking to group communication, because all groups are also contingent. They have a particular group history, with memberships, practices, and accumulated knowledge that depend on group history and that vary from group to group. They also have a particular goal orientation, with new tasks, new challenges, and new procedures for evaluating outcomes that depend on group goals and that vary from group to group.

Dewey's model of thinking indicates that there is a constant loop, always cycling—what we do shapes what we think, and what we think shapes what we do. But this does not mean that we have to carry out a detailed test, through taking some action, every time we want to make a decision. When we think critically, we often make decisions among competing choices just by carefully and systematically reflecting and talking. Here, our work as group members becomes vital—small groups are extremely effective, more effective than individuals or larger organizations, at using communication to critically test choices and to make high quality decisions among those choices.[5] Small groups are so effective at this task because of the unique way they are poised between past and future. They are large enough to include multiple experiences among members, and therefore multiple ways of evaluating knowledge or belief; but they are small enough to include focused, collective goals, and therefore a common system for evaluating plans of action.

How Critical Thinking by Members Can Support a Small Group

However, small groups cannot simply achieve high-quality decisions automatically. The above definitions of critical thinking remind us that it is both **active** and **self-conscious**, like the dimensions of effective listening (see Chapter 9). This means that, like listening skills, critical thinking skills will develop only with dedicated practice. A small group's ability to make quality decisions depends on its individual members' abilities to listen and think critically, and those members' commitments to developing those skills in the group setting. Interestingly, though critical thinking is usually conceptualized as an individual process, small groups can foster critical thinking among their members, while members' development of critical thinking can foster the development of a high quality group; like the thought process described by Dewey, the relationship between individual critical thinking and group decision making is reciprocal, and individuals and groups reinforce one another in these ways.[6] This section focuses on individuals' use of critical thinking to support the group, while the following two sections focus on small group processes and structures that support individual critical thinking.

Individuals can practice critical thinking and support their group's ability to make quality decisions by making each of these choices as much as possible, both when in small group discussion and also when working independently:

(C1) Acknowledge your values, beliefs, prejudices, and biases.

(C2) Identify the assumptions, underlying statements and arguments, and the implications about the future that they entail.

(C3) Identify and evaluate supporting evidence for statements and arguments, and the context that produces this evidence.

(C4) Use effective listening skills (see Chapter 9).

(C5) Take time to reflect on what you have heard and what you have learned before advocating a single decision.

How Small Groups Can Support Critical Thinking

Norms: Three D's

Just as important, though, is that small groups themselves can also enhance their members' critical thinking abilities. The small group communication process includes three unique elements that can encourage critical thinking among members if they become **norms** for the group (see Chapter 2); we can remember these as the Three D's of small groups that encourage critical thinking by individuals: **divergent ideals, deliberation, and democratic participation**.

We can link these three D's to explore how their elements can foster individual critical thinking, and how all three D's are interrelated and must be present for the group to function most effectively.

1. A group that norms **divergent ideas** put forward by members in the initial stages of its problem-solving process (see the following **Problem-Solving Process** section) will have a broader range of options to consider as it evaluates potential solutions. Divergent potential solutions lead to higher quality choices compared with convergent potential solutions—not only because a wider range of possibilities is considered, but also because reflecting on divergent solutions actually deepens members' thinking about the problem itself.[7] This means that the group will have a much better chance to make a quality decision. When a group has a range of divergent alternatives to consider, it encourages additional deliberation and thereby encourages the reflective component of critical

Rina Piccolo

"Mom! My dollhouse melted!"

thinking among members. When a group seeks a range of divergent ideas, it encourages democratic participation among group members and thereby encourages the active, self-conscious component of critical thinking among members (C5).

Deliberation

A process that ensures that ideas are carefully considered over a meaningful period of time from multiple perspectives through extended group discussion.

2. A group that norms **deliberation** ensures that ideas are carefully considered over a meaningful period of time (depending on the task at hand) from multiple perspectives through extended group discussion (C5). According to Hirokawa, group deliberation also enables seven group functions, advocacy, discovery, clarification, unification, relationship management, norming, and impression management.[8] Four of these seven group functions are related to social elements of the group (see Chapter 2), and thus are indirectly related to individual critical thinking because they affect the communication climate (see Chapter 9) and democratic participation described as follows. But the first three functions identified by Hirokawa directly support critical thinking by individual group members in these ways:

- **Advocacy.** Deliberation that functions to change opinion or belief on an issue can lead individual members to attend to the contingency of their prior opinions or beliefs (C1).
- **Discovery.** Deliberation that functions to reveal shared meanings, such as a problem or a solution, can lead individual members to recognize the goals and objectives that are directing their thought (C2).
- **Clarification.** Deliberation that functions to clarify key points of potential conceptual fuzziness or dispute can lead individual members to attend to supporting evidence and the situated nature of knowledge (C3).

Democratic participation

A process that enables each individual group member to develop and maintain a unique voice within the group.

3. A group that norms **democratic participation** enables each individual group member to develop and maintain a unique voice within the group, and ensures that each member's voice has an opportunity not only to be heard but to have a meaningful role in the exchange of ideas.[9] Democratic participation increases the range of ideas exchanged, thereby promoting divergent ideas, and also makes the exchange of ideas itself more robust throughout the entire group, thereby promoting deliberation.

Small Group Structures

In addition to communication norms within the group, there are structural factors associated with each small group that influence critical thinking among members. These include:

1. External feedback and access to resources
2. Group roles
3. Communication environment
4. Systematic questioning

The first three of these structural factors are central subjects in earlier chapters:

1. Each group, as it functions as an interdependent system within a larger institutional, organizational, or social context, will differ in terms of these elements (see Chapter 2):

- Permeability of boundaries
- Access to external feedback
- Access to human resources
- Access to information

These factors influence critical thinking because they influence the ability of each member to evaluate information, form goals, and evaluate actions taken toward those goals.

2. Each group will differ in the roles members play within group discussion. Such roles include, for example, Devil's Advocate, Information Seeker, and Mediator (see Chapter 4). These three roles can support critical thinking among group members in these ways:

- **Devil's advocate.** A member who plays this role calls into question assumptions, beliefs, or values held widely within the group, and poses challenge or alternatives to new ideas offered within the group. This fosters critical thinking by sustaining reflection and deliberation as well as by providing divergent ideas.
- **Information seeker.** A member who plays this role requests additional evidence and support for proposed solutions. This fosters critical thinking by giving the group more chances to evaluate evidence and to put it in context.
- **Mediator.** A member who plays this role helps other members who may be communicating defensively to feel that their voices are valued. This fosters critical thinking by promoting critical listening, deliberation, and democratic participation.

3. Each group will differ in terms of the communication environment within the group (see Chapter 9). A supportive climate can be maintained by:

- Establishing and maintaining consistent group procedures
- Maintaining a provisional perspective rather than promoting one idea
- Providing concrete and explicit messages about goals and constraints
- Engaging in critical listening
- Listening with empathy

Supportive climates foster critical thinking by promoting critical listening, deliberation, and democratic participation.

4. Finally, when a coherent system for questioning information and decisions is the norm within a small group, the group has the opportunity to recognize and define **problems**, and to devise and implement solutions to these problems. Effective problem solving processes strongly parallel Dewey's description of the reflective thinking cycle, and so groups that engage members in problem solving foster individual critical thinking and establish a positive cycle of reciprocity for the group. Questioning, and its role in

problem solving, are the subject of the final section of this chapter; to show how problem-solving processes are meaningful, potential **barriers** to effective group decision making are discussed first.

BARRIERS TO EFFECTIVE DECISION MAKING

An Example of a Small Group Decision

Consider this small group's need to make a decision: Abbie, Rebecca, and Samantha are members of a group of seven program leaders in an afterschool program for first through third grade students. Afterschool program leaders change every few months; typically only one or two members change at a time while the rest remain. They only come together if there is a problem to be solved relating to the children; they do not meet regularly. One Friday afternoon was unexpectedly rainy, making the program's planned outdoor activities impossible. The afterschool leaders met to discuss how to plan alternatives; they had just 15 minutes to decide what to do with the children before the school day would come to an end and the children would arrive.

Rebecca, the most experienced program leader, offered the idea that each leader take twenty students and play games with them in separate classrooms. The newest program leader, Samantha, suggested doing something that would be fun and different for the kids, such as bringing all the students into the cafeteria to watch a movie and eat popcorn. Another leader excitedly noted that it would be easy to bring a television into the cafeteria, that the kids would enjoy eating popcorn, and that she knew where there was a selection of movies that would be perfect for Samantha's idea. Three other leaders then quickly agreed with Samantha as well, showing enthusiasm not only for the idea but for the chance to begin working on it. All the leaders looked at Rebecca, and Rebecca hesitantly said that Samantha's idea sounded good.

Abbie, reflecting to herself at this point, was a little concerned about the excitement of the rain and the fact that the students had been inside all day; though she tried to imagine about 150 young students all in the same room, she kept quiet. Samantha turned to Abbie and asked, "So you have any ideas of what we should watch?" Abbie decided it would be too much effort to argue that Rebecca had a better idea, because she did not want to ruin their fun, and because the group only had minutes to make a decision.

As the leaders gathered the students into the cafeteria, they experienced more than one obstacle. The television was too small to fit all the students around it; the leaders did not have enough popcorn prepared; and students were

© Diego Cervo, 2011. Under license from Shutterstock, Inc.

excited about the rain and hyper from being inside classrooms all day. The entire ordeal ended with wild students throughout the cafeteria yelling, not watching the movie, complaining and angry because they could not go outside.

This example provides a concrete foundation for exploring both group process and group structure, and for considering how group process and group structure can include barriers that thwart effective decision making.

Groupthink: A Process Barrier

In 1971, Irving Janis published an important study of decisions made by government leaders. He investigated the ways that a process called groupthink is brought on in group decision making, chiefly through feelings of personal commitment to the group. Janis describes groupthink as "a mode of thinking that people engage in when they are deeply involved in a cohesive in-group, when concurrence-seeking becomes so dominant that it tends to override critical thinking."[10] Groupthink can be recognized as a group's tendency to rush toward consensus for the sake of consensus, which impedes careful, conscious deliberation among alternatives—often leading to a poor final decision. Groupthink is a mode of thinking that people can begin to practice when they become part of a cohesive group and identify strongly with that group.

Groupthink
A mode of thinking that people engage in when they are deeply involved in a cohesive in-group; when concurrence-seeking becomes so dominant that it tends to override critical thinking.

Causes

The central initial cause of groupthink is unusually strong commitment to the group on the part of members, which results in members overemphasizing agreement and underemphasizing effective decision-making procedures. One reason is **homogeneity** among group's members—beliefs, attitudes, values, expertise, and communication styles that are widely shared among group members. This can also lead to closed-mindedness as well as an illusion of unanimity, or the false sense that members agree at each stage of the decision-making process.[11] A second reason such commitment develops is a long **group history** of members working together on a similar set of tasks within an organization; this can lead to overestimation of the group and closed-mindedness among members with respect to alternatives.[12] Also, a very short group history can lead to members rushing decisions in order to validate the existence of the group.[13] Finally, **group procedures** themselves may be faulty; this can lead to an inability on the part of the group to effectively frame problems, gather information, develop solution criteria, and evaluate choices.[14] As the prevention section below demonstrates, understanding these three causes is essential if a group hopes to avoid groupthink.

Symptoms

One of the most important practices that an effective group can attend to regularly is to identify symptoms of groupthink as they begin to develop. The afterschool leaders in the above example demonstrate these symptoms, and so reconsidering the example will give you the chance to practice recognizing these symptoms. Primary symptoms of groupthink include:

- **Concurrence seeking.** Similar ideas or opinions become prominently noted in the group and emphasized in discussion. This can give a false sheen of quality to the similar ideas while at the same time discouraging discussion of contrasting ideas.[15]

In the example, Samantha's idea for a movie and popcorn was followed rapidly by similar ideas and even supporting information such as the availability of a television and a good movie. This created within the group a false sense that the idea must be a good one, because supporting material was introduced before criteria for evaluating that material had even been decided. Several program leaders' rapid show of enthusiasm for Samantha's idea implies that this group values decisions simply because they have been made, rather than because they are of high quality—this is the hallmark of concurrence seeking.

- **Unusual cohesiveness.** Members' commitment to the group as an enduring unit is more important to them than their commitment to the function of the group in making decisions. Our human need to find acceptance among others can result in **affiliative constraints** on extended, meaningful group deliberation.

It is important for groups to have positive regard for one another to facilitate democratic participation, and to have a unique group identity, or cohesiveness, to facilitate collaborative goal setting and ensure collective responsibility for tasks. However, excessive cohesiveness can also impede a group's willingness to evaluate alternative if group members identify strongly with the group—especially in task-oriented professional groups, if that group identification derives from a mutual attraction among peer members as competent professionals rather than as close friends or superiors/subordinates.[16]

In the example, this group of afterschool leaders are not friends outside of this role; their only connection to one another is their work as afterschool leaders. They share power in the group, and the response to Samantha's idea, given that she is the newest member, suggests that the group wants her to feel accepted as an intelligent contributor and a competent afterschool leader. Notice that cohesiveness depends on the unique nature of the role the group plays in the social lives of members; groups that engage in groupthink because they are too cohesive are not necessarily just close friends or people who can broadly be said to get along well.

© Andrejs Pidjass, 2011. Under license from Shutterstock, Inc.

- **Illusion of unanimity.** Silence, or the absence of contradictory discussion, is treated as agreement by the group. This has both a structure and a process component: Some groups require consensus, such as juries, while other groups have developed a group history over time of treating silence as consent.[17]

In the example, Abbie's silence was taken by Samantha as agreement; rather than asking for Abbie's perspective, which Abbie was in the midst of formulating, Samantha asked for Abbie's help in developing Samantha's own idea. At the individual level, this choice short-circuited Abbie's effort to think critically, which appears to have had the chance to help the group establish decision criteria and better evaluate decisions. At the group level, this choice combined with Abbie's silence and Rebecca's subsequent assent to create the illusion of unanimity.

- **Pressuring dissenters.** Those who offer dissenting ideas or opinions are pressured to change. This can happen in cases where a majority rule is normed or when consensus is expected; in either case, explicit dissent is met, not with requests for clarification or elaboration, but with requests for the dissenter to change his or her mind and agree instead.[18]

In the example, Rebecca's initial games idea was never clarified; the next time Rebecca was invited to participate occurred when the group members looked to her to signal her agreement with the movie idea. Notice that pressure on dissenting members can be subtle in just this way; it is not always in the form of aggressive verbal or nonverbal communication.

- **Self-censorship.** Individual members choose not to ask questions or share ideas or opinions. This can take the form of silencing one's own participation in group discussion or rationalizing one's own agreement with the group, even when that agreement feels wrong. In other words, self-censorship can happen at the group level by abdicating one's responsibility to challenge ideas, or at the individual level by short-circuiting one's own critical thinking.[19]

In the example, Abbie chooses not to voice her concerns about the unique needs of young children who have been inside all day and are experiencing a sudden rainstorm. This not only weakens the group discussion, it also turns Abbie's own attention away from these issues until she is confronted with them later when the group implements their poor decision.

Prevention

Once your group has begun to identify emerging symptoms of groupthink using the concepts above, group members can use four different strategies to prevent groupthink from damaging its decision making. Two of these strategies involve the composition of the group, while the other two involve how the group uses the discussion process.

1. Composition of the group:

   a. **A diverse group.** When a group is composed of members who bring a variety of beliefs, values, and knowledge to the group, members will be less likely to signal premature agreement and will be more likely to pursue alternatives.[20]

In the example, we do not know for certain about the range of beliefs, values, and knowledge among the group. But the way the group makes its decisions, including Samantha's advocacy of fun and Abbie's reflection that she did not want to spoil [group members'] fun, suggests that many members of this group have a strong orientation to fun in their work with young people. The effort to foreground the fun aspects of working with young people seems to conflict here with more rigorous requirements of shaping the young people's behavior, sending consistent messages to them, responding to their unique needs at the end of a long school day, and so on. The group does not show any diversity, with the possible exception of Rebecca, in terms of this orientation to fun as a primary decision criterion.

    b. **Independent group members and an independent group.** When a group has a history of success, which is obviously a good thing, members can overestimate the group compared with their own role in it, leading to groupthink. Interestingly, when a group has little history as a group, group members can also overestimate the group because they have not yet established their own roles within it.[21]

Ideally, groups should be composed of members who have some independent success within the organization or institution, because each member then has a better chance to balance the importance of the group with his or her own importance as a member. A group's role should also be independently established in order to facilitate effective decision making.

In the example, the afterschool program leaders were part of a new group and charged with caring for 150 young students, a significant responsibility. Yet their only reason for meeting, in this situation, is due to the unforeseen outside pressure of a rainy day. The group has no meaningful history, yet groupthink develops anyway, perhaps because of self-consciousness connected to their sudden role as decision makers. Also, Samantha's excitement in offering a solution may result from her own personal self-consciousness as a young program leader, and the quick support for her idea may result from group members' efforts to affirm her in that role.

  2. Group process

    a. **Goal-setting** is one of the most important group processes in terms of preventing groupthink. Goal-setting is related to establishing decision criteria, discussed below, but goal-setting is important for a separate reason as well: Groups tends to set less rigorous goals for the group as a whole than individual members will set for themselves.[22] A group that sets clear goals early in the discussion process, or that has goals established for it by leadership prior to its taking up of a task, will be less likely to fall into the trap of setting goals that are simply easy to reach.

In the example, the afterschool program leaders approach their discussion with the apparent goal of finding an alternative to planned outdoor activities. They did not explore, even briefly, what the planned outdoor activities were originally designed to accomplish and how they could meet that burden; their goal was the much simpler one of finding anything that counted as an alternative to the outdoors. This overly simple level of goal-setting should be avoided in order to prevent groupthink.

b. **Problem-solving procedures** should be established and practiced on a systematic basis in order to prevent groupthink. The problem-solving process is the subject of the final major section of the chapter, and it will be treated comprehensively there; first, structural barriers to effective decision making are described.

Structural Barriers

As we have seen, groupthink and its prevention involve attention to group discussion processes and to how the composition of the group affects those processes. There are also barriers to effective decision making that are related to structural elements of the group—in other words, how the group stands in relation to the larger organization or institution that creates it and that depends on its decisions.

1. **Lack of information.** A group cannot make effective decisions when it does not have access to information from outside the group.[23] Successful groups must establish and maintain meaningful feedback loops (see Chapter 2).

In the example, the afterschool leaders group did not have access to plans for inclement weather, or consistent knowledge across all group members about the size of the television and the availability of popcorn quantities. These factors directly compromised its decision.

2. **Lack of institutional support.** A group cannot make effective decisions if it experiences adversity within the organization or institution, or threats from outside forces that damage the viability of the group.[24] Organizations and institutions must protect the group through such practices as providing a workspace, preventing interruptions of group work, and preventing unnecessary surveillance of the group by outsiders.

In the example, the group responds to an unforeseen event, the rain, by striving to find an alternative to outdoor activities very quickly. Are they the only authority figures in the school who have noticed it is raining? Given that 150 students are part of this afterschool program, should the school itself have alternative procedures (holding students after the bell, providing temporary space in a place like the cafeteria) to keep the children safe and dry while the leaders are given more than 15 minutes to plan new activities?

3. **Lack of effective leadership.** A group cannot make effective decisions if it lacks effective leadership. Ineffective leadership can take many forms, but two that commonly result in ineffective decision making are leaders who promote their own ideas and leaders who do not ensure that ideas are fully considered.[25] See Chapter 5 for more information about effective leadership.

In the example, group members seem to view Rebecca's as the most important voice in the group because they look to her for confirmation. Yet she does not take time to clarify the merits of her own idea or encourage meaningful deliberation on criteria for making the decision. Instead, she quickly assents to the alternative offered by other group members.

PROBLEM SOLVING

Problems and Their Role in Decision Making

As discussed in the introduction to this chapter, nearly all small groups make decisions. What it means to make decisions is to select among two or more competing alternative goals or objectives. Groups are impelled to make decisions for two primary reasons:

1. **Externally directed.** They are directed to do so by organizational or institutional leadership, such as when a creative team designs a new product for a company or when a special task force creates a plan for assessing learning outcomes in a school.
2. **Internally directed.** They direct themselves to do so, such as when a church committee plans a holiday event or when a family creates a budget to survive tough economic times.

Notice that whether a group makes decisions based on external or internal direction, the group must, in both cases, consider the future in light of present circumstances that have changed and therefore contrast with the past. Dewey argued that because change is unavoidable in human life, our decision-making systems must respond flexibly to changing circumstances. Interestingly, he characterized systems that make decisions flexibly, and that respect the needs of their members and stakeholders while doing so, as democratic.[26] This is why critical thinking is such an important part of the small group decision-making process. Critical thinking, as discussed in the previous section, always involves considering the present in light of the future and in light of the past.

So how does a group begin—whether given a task or given a changing environment? The most important way for a group to begin its decision-making process is to evaluate the fit between current resources and the changing situation. If your group is charged with designing a product, what resource would the product provide, and how has the need for this resource changed over time? If your family is working together on a budget, what have your primary expenses been in the past, and

THINKING INSIDE THE BOX

2008. Joe Martin.Dist. by Neatly Chiseled Features

Comic Videos www.MrBoffo.com

JOE MARTIN
7-12-08

how has your income changed? The first step in making a decision, then, is identifying a gap between existing resources and what is currently needed; this gap is the **problem** the group must initially solve, and it will form the basis for generating potential solutions and evaluating those solutions—in other words, it will form the basis for making decisions.

Problems are sometimes caused by the creation of simple gaps, over time, between existing resources and changing needs. But other times, problems can arise from the interaction of more complex forces, such as inequitable power relationships within a community or urgent material needs that require organized effort to meet them.[27] Also, identifying one problem frequently leads to the identification of secondary problems, and so solutions to the problems must be nested inside one another, like this:

The Problem-Solving Process

In addition to recognizing the nested nature of some problem-solution systems, small groups must also consider the **solution space** available: some problems have only a small number of possible solutions because of the nature of the problem itself, such as in the family budget example above, while other problems may have an almost infinite number of possible solutions, as in the new product example above.[28] The complex, sometimes interconnected, nature of the problems identified by small groups means that it is helpful to have a workable system for approaching problems. A commonly used system involves five steps[29]:

Five-Step Problem-Solving Process

1. Define the problem.
2. Analyze the problem.
3. Generate potential solutions.
4. Evaluate potential solutions.
5. Choose and implement the optimal solutions.

It is important to keep in mind that this five-step process is not equivalent to decision making—partly because decision making usually involves a loop in which groups are involved (alone or with wider communities) in testing and re-evaluating the solution produced by the five-step process. The five-step process is best understood as one central component of group decision making, with other components including group structure, group process, and the testing and reevaluation loop.

Defining the Problem

The most effective first step in this process is the same for both narrow and broad solution spaces: defining the problem.[30] Remember that recognizing a problem means recognizing a gap between existing resources and changing circumstances. Sometimes, this means that a group must develop and implement a new policy to marshal institutional resources that are used to confront

a problem, as in the example above when a school develops a plan for assessing learning outcomes. However, it is vital that groups consider other dimensions of a problem besides merely its ability to be solved with new policy—some problems are not problems of policy, even within large organizations.

Gouran identified four types of problems facing groups, arguing that each type requires a different frame for group problem solving[31]:

1. Policy. What can we do?

With these frames, groups confront a problem by identifying a range of actions that are within the scope of the group's control (see constraints below). The impact of possible actions on the problem is evaluated in terms of efficacy—asking, "Will the problem go away?"

2. Fact. What is true?

With these frames, groups confront a problem by identifying what is known about the supposedly changing circumstances and what is known about existing resources for dealing with those changes. The impact of these facts on the problem is evaluated in terms of validity—asking, "Is the problem what we first thought it was?"

3. Conjecture. What might happen?

With these frames, groups confront a problem by identifying a range of possible outcomes based on changing circumstances. The impact of these possible outcomes on the problem is evaluated in terms of predictability—asking, "How will this problem change the world?"

4. Value. What is right?

With these frames, groups confront a problem by identifying the values that are relevant to the situation created by changing circumstances. The impact of values on the problem is evaluated in terms of ethics—asking, "How will this problem affect people's lives?"

Though small groups are often characterized as policy makers, all four of these frames can become a part of a group's problem-solving process. A successful group will strive to frame the problem first, before moving forward with analysis or solutions.

Constraints must also be considered in this first step, because groups do not have complete freedom to solve problems in any way they wish. Three forms of constraints are:

1. **External constraints.** What institutional resources does the group have, in terms of money, time, access to information, and commitment from external networks?
2. **Internal constraints.** What expertise exists within the group? How committed are members to the problem-solving process? What group procedures are in place to foster problem solving? What is the tradition of leadership within the group?
3. **Solution space.** As described above, this is a mental concept, but it applies to group problem solving as well as individual thought: What range of possibilities exists in terms of possible solutions to this problem? For instance, an algebra problem has a limited solution space in traditional mathematics, whereas the creation of a poem has a much broader solution space—though not an infinite one, because language itself is limited.

Analyzing the Problem

The best way for a group to analyze a problem effectively, once a gap between resources and needs is initially identified, is to ask the right series of questions. Remember that to enable critical thinking, these questions must provide an understanding of the past, of how things came to be as they are, and of the future, of how things might change. For the past, this requires asking questions about existing **knowledge** associated with the problem as well as the evolving **process** that has shaped the problem itself over time. For the future, this requires asking questions about beliefs, attitudes, and **values**, as well as questions about **constraints** on possible solutions. One additional way to help organize these questions is to notice that they begin with the common question words:

Knowledge questions:

- What is [what counts as] [what do people think of] X?
- What do we now know about X?
- How do we know what we know about X?
- Who knows [in our group] [outside our group] about X?

Process questions:

- When did X become a problem?
- Why did X become a problem?
- How did people come to identify X as a problem?

Value questions:

- Why do we believe what we believe about X and our solutions to X?
- How do we feel about X and our solutions to X?

© SeDmi, 2011. Under license from Shutterstock, Inc.

- Who is affected by X and/or our solutions to X?
- Who benefits from X and/or our solutions to X?

Constraint questions:

- Who will evaluate our solutions to X?
- What internal resources do we have to implement our solutions to X?
- What external resources do we have to implement our solutions to X?
- How free are we to implement our solutions to X?
- How will we implement our solutions to X?
- Where will we need to implement our solutions to X?
- When will we need to implement our solutions to X?

Generating Solutions

The next step in the problem-solving process is group members generating solutions. As discussed above, the importance of this step is twofold: First, generating as wide a range of solutions as possible means that the group will have more options to consider, in terms of raw numbers. Second, the mere act of considering options has a positive effect on group members' depth of thinking about the problem.[32] So the key to this step is allowing ideas to come to the surface without any further limits than the ones already imposed in steps I and II; this process is often call brainstorming. **Brainstorming** is an open-ended process of generating as many ideas as possible

Four rules for brainstorming, modeled by Osborn[33], that can be adapted to the group setting include:

Brainstorming

An open-ended process of generating as many ideas as possible.

1. Express any and all ideas that come to any person's mind.
2. Do not criticize any ideas.
3. Generate as many ideas as the group can.
4. Combine ideas and parts of ideas into new ideas as the discussion continues.

It may seem strange to go through this *anything goes* process, but remember that this third step in the problem-solving process is embedded within two others. The previous step was an analysis step that will have already shaped ideas among members, and the next step is an evaluation step that can give the group the chance to modify or discard unwanted ideas or parts of ideas. Success in this step means a genuine trust in the process, believing that no idea should be overlooked.

Leaders play an important role in this process because most group members will need encouragement to allow ideas to flow freely; the group brainstorming process does not automatically lead to better idea generation, but it requires experienced facilitation.[34]

This is also a step in which democratic participation is essential; sometimes, this means more than simply effective facilitation during the discussion—good participation can also require opportunities for talk outside the group itself as well as time to build group commitment.[35] So it is important, for these reasons, to allow sufficient time for this step and not hurry past it in an effort to test solutions.

Evaluating Solutions

In this step, the group has the opportunity to examine the possible solutions proposed in the third step. The evaluation step, like all steps in the five-step process, depends on the successful completion of earlier steps—in this case, earlier steps provide the foundation for **evaluation criteria**. Groups must take the time to carefully develop evaluation criteria that are uniquely suited to the problem; otherwise, potential flaws in solutions may be overlooked, while some useful parts of other, unworkable solutions may be ignored. Below are four questions to consider when developing evaluation criteria, along with the earlier step when the group likely began to answer these questions.[36]

Evaluation criteria:

- What are the group's **goals** in solving this problem? [Step 1]
- What are the **standards** by which the solution will be judged? [Steps 1 and 2]
- What are the expected **positive consequences** of the solution? [Step 2]
- What are the expected **negative consequences** of the solution? [Step 2]

Once your group has developed criteria that are uniquely suited to evaluate the alternative solutions generated in Step 3, you can move forward to evaluating the solutions themselves. Common ways to do so include:

- A T-chart comparing benefits and drawbacks (pros and cons) for each alternative
- A grading system that the group uses to rank order alternatives
- An advocacy system that requires individuals or pairs to defend alternatives

Choosing and Implementing a Solution

Finally, the group must build on its evaluation step by making a decision—choosing among alternative solutions to the problem. This can take several different forms, depending on the needs, history, and leadership resources of the group. Groups may make decisions highly autocratically, based on the summative efforts of a single leader; they may strive to reach consensus, in which deliberation continues until all members agree on a solution; they may utilize voting procedures that identify the perspective of a majority; and they may combine these decision-making procedures in various ways as well, combining autocratic and democratic methods to solve various components of a problem (for instance, a plan for treating the substance of the problem may differ from a plan for implementing solutions).[37]

Again, the decision-making process does not come to an end when the steps of the problem-solving process have each been undertaken. Most groups will also take part in implementing and reevaluating their solutions, at least on some level within the organization. This ongoing feedback loop has dramatic effects on the cohesiveness of the group, and it can have positive effects on the task-oriented procedures of the group when it returns to the decision-making process.[38] This is why the ongoing decision making—which sustains and is sustained by individual critical thinking—plays such a key role in group success.

SUMMARY

Critical thinking, which is an individual activity, is nevertheless an important part of effective small group decision making, because each group member, through cultivating his or her own critical thinking, can support the group through identifying assumptions, examining the foundations for claims, and critically listening to others' perspectives.

Small groups, for this reason, should foster critical thinking among their members. Groups can do this by supporting members who share divergent ideas, by having establishing procedures to ensure careful deliberation, and by making democratic participation the norm in group discussion.

There are several barriers to effective decision making; chief among these is groupthink, the tendency of small groups to rush to consensus without examining alternatives carefully. Structural factors, such as how the group is connected to outside environments and how leadership works within the group, also influence decision making.

The most reliable way for a small group to foster high-quality decision making is to make a problem-solving process a consistent part of the group's efforts. One such process involves the five steps of defining and analyzing a problem, generating and evaluating solutions to the problem, and choosing the best solution through conscious deliberation among alternatives.

DISCUSSION

1. You learned in this chapter that divergent ideas are useful in problem solving; however, why might a group's boundaries be *too* permeable to allow for effective problem solving? In terms of the problem solving process outlined in this chapter, what are the drawbacks to a group that has constant, rapid flow of information and feedback in and out of the group?

2. Why is **concurrence seeking** such a common impulse in our work with task–oriented small groups, even when we are not coming together for social reasons and we know our job is to make a quality decision? What factors in society lead us to expect, and to try to achieve, agreement with others as quickly as possible?

3. Why do we often tend to equate silence with **unanimity**? What aspects of the democratic process, whether within groups or in larger society, encourage us to equate silence with consent, or silence with agreement? What can an effective group leader do to discourage this tendency?

4. What special risks are there to effective group deliberation when the choice to solve a problem is **externally directed**? How might the group's lack of choice in deciding to take up a problem negatively affect its problem solving process? Conversely, what special risks are there when the choice to solve a problem is **internally directed**? How might the group's interest in taking up a problem negatively affect its problem solving process?

5. Why would it be important to avoid criticizing another person's idea during a brainstorming session, even if that idea were obviously unmanageable in terms of the group's existing resources? What benefits can the group derive from leaving an obviously unmanageable idea "on the table" for later consideration?

NOTES

1. Paul, R., Elder, L., & Bartell, T. (2009). A brief history of the idea of critical thinking. In *The critical thinking community.* Foundation for Critical Thinking. Retrieved from http://www.criticalthinking.org/aboutCT/briefHistoryCT.cfm. Paragraph 22.

2. Page, D., & Mukherjee, A. (2007). Promoting critical thinking skills by using negotiation exercises. *Journal of Education for Business,* 82, 251–257.

3. Dewey, J. (1910). *How we think.* Lexington, MA: D. C. Heath.

4. Ibid.

5. Poole, M.S., & Hollingshead, A. B. (Eds.) (2005). *Theories of small groups: Interdisciplinary perspectives.* Thousand Oaks: Sage.

6. Kayes, D. C. (2006). From climbing stairs to riding waves. *Small Group Research,* 37, 612–630.

7. Harlan, J.N., & Kwan, J. L. (2006). Minority influence, divergent thinking and detection of correct solutions. *Journal of Applied Social Psychology,* 17, 788–799.

8. Hirokawa, R. Y., & Scheerhorn, D. R. (1985). The functions of argumentation in group deliberation. *Conference proceedings—National Communication Association/American Forensic Association (Alta conference on argumentation)*

9. Gastil, J. (1992). A definition of small group democracy. 1971 *Small Group Research,* 23, 278–301.

10. Janis, I. (1971).Groupthink among policy makers. In N. Sanford & C. Comstock (Eds.), *Sanctions for Evil* (p. 73). San Francisco: Jossey-Bass.

11. Moorhead, G., Ference, R., & Neck, C. (1991). Group decision fiascoes continue: Space shuttle Challenger and a revised groupthink framework. *Travistock Institute of Human Relations,* 44 (6) Retrieved from http://ils.unc.edu/~bwilder/inls500/challengerarticle.pdf

12. Ibid.

13. Schafer, M., & Crichlow, S. (1996). Antecedents of groupthink. *Journal of Conflict Resolution,* 40, 415–435.

14. Ibid.

15. Janis.

16. Hogg, M., & Hains, S. (1998). Friendship and group identification: A new look at the role of cohesiveness in groupthink. *European Journal of Social Psychology,* 28, 323–341. Retrieved from Academic Search Elite database.

17. Kameda, T., & Sugimori, S. (1993). Psychological entrapment in group decision making: An assigned decision rule and a groupthink phenomenon. *Journal of Personality & Social Psychology,* 65(2), 282–292. Retrieved from Academic Search Elite database.

18. Ibid.

19. Johnson, S., & Weaver, II, R. (1992). Groupthink and the classroom: Changing familiar patterns to encourage critical thought. *Journal of Instructional Psychology,* 19(2), 99. Retrieved from Academic Search Elite database.

20. Pi-Yueh, C., & Wen-Bin, C. (2008). Framing effects in group investment decision making: Role of group polarization. *Psychological Reports,* 102(1), 283–292. doi:10.2466/PRO.102.1.283-292; Von Hippel, C. (2003). Individual differences in inhibitions and its influence on group decision making. *Australian Journal of Psychology,* 55147-148. Retrieved from Academic Search Elite database.

21. McFarland, K. (2007, April 18). Where Group-Think Is Good. *BusinessWeek Online.* Retrieved from EBSCO Host database.

22. Hinsz, V. (1995). Group and individual decision making for task performance goals: Processes in the establishment of goals in groups. *Journal of Applied Social Psychology,* 25(4), 353–370. Retrieved from Academic Search Elite database.

23. Moorhead, G., Ference, R., & Neck, C.

24. Turner, M. E. (2001). The dilemma of threat: Group effectiveness and ineffectiveness under adversity. In *Groups at Work: Theory and Research* (pp. 445–470). New Jersey: Lawrence Erlbaum Associates.

25. Ahlfinger, N., & Esser, J. (2001). Testing the groupthink model: Effects of promotional leadership and conformity predisposition. *Social Behavior & Personality: An International Journal,* 29(1), 31.

26. Dewey, J. (1921). *Democracy and education: An introduction to the philosophy of education.* New York: MacMillan.

27. Freire, P. (200) *Pedagogy of the oppressed.* Trans. M.B. Ramos. New York: Continuum.

28. Xun, G.E., & Land., S. M. (2004). A conceptual framework for scaffolding ill-structured problem-solving processes using question prompts and peer interactions. *Educational Technology Research & Development,* 52(2), 6–7.

29. There is no single academically agreed upon method for an ideal problem-solving process; the one described here, like many other similar models, is adapted from G. Polya (1957). *How to solve It* (2nd Ed.). Princeton: Princeton University Press.

30. Xun & Land, pp. 6-7.

31. Gouran, J. (2003).Reflections on the type of question as a determinant of the form of interactions in decision-making and problem-solving discussions. *Communication Quarterly,* 51(2), 115–125.

32. Charlan, J.N. & Kwan, J. L.

33. Osborn, A. F. (1957). *Applied imagination.* New York: Scribner.

34. Oxley, N., Dzindolet, M. T., & Paulus, P. B. (1996). The effects of facilitators on the performance of brainstorming groups. *Journal of Social Behavior and Personality,* 11. 6336–46.

35. Gastil, J. (1993). Identifying obstacles to small group democracy. *Small Group Research,* 24, 5–27.

36. Orlitzky, M., & Hirokawa, R. Y. (2001). To err is human, to correct for it divine: A meta-analysis of research testing the functional theory of group decision-making effectives. *Small Group Research,* 32, 313–341.

37. Sager, K. L., & Gastil, J. (2006). The origins and consequences of consensus decision making: A test of the social consensus model. *Southern Communication Journal,* 71(1), 1–24.

38. Klein, C., Diaz-Granados, D., Salas, E., Huy, L., Burke, C. S., Lyons, R., & Goodwin, G. F. (2009). Does team building work? *Small Group Research,* 40, 181–222.

12

Conflict Management

CHAPTER OBJECTIVES

- Understand how conflict arises in groups
- Be familiar with the conflict continuum
- Comprehend the diversity of viewpoints and experiences
- Know the patterns of conflict
- Distinguish between the various coping styles
- Know how to identify the signs and stages of conflict
- Understand power in groups
- Be able to explain constructive conflict management
- Explain how the leader can assume the role of mediator

KEY TERMS

Conflict management

Tangibles

Mediation

Move

Contingent moves

Caucus

CHAPTER OUTLINE

We live in a world where disagreements happen every day. We disagree with others on a regular basis. A **disagreement** is a form or phase of conflict. We feel the effects of conflict often. It is ubiquitous. Just look around you'll notice at any given time a number of people involved in what are called fights, disagreements, spats, conflicts, arguments, heated discussions, or disputes. These occur whether a person is at home or at work. Conflict is natural and unavoidable. All of us are engaged in various forms or phases of conflict much of the time. Our conflict ranges from the intrapersonal or internal conflict, such as cognitive dissonance; to interpersonal conflict with others; to group conflict; and to intersocietal, cultural, and national conflict. When we talk about conflict, we mean rhetorical conflict and not forms of coercive or physically violent conflict. We do not show aggressive behavior, lack of respect toward members, or a competitive orientation. The conflict that groups encounter requires discourse, dialogue, or discussion. We emphasize mutual respect and collaboration in order to manage individual and group conflict.

What creates conflict? Conflict occurs when people have separate but competing or conflicting interests in attaining their goals. Interests are an

© bikeriderlondon, 2011. Under license from Shutterstock, Inc.

individual person's needs, wants, desires, concerns, and fear.[1] Interests motivate people to do things. They are the silent movers behind a person's actions. Conflicts of interest can cause anything from a mild disagreement of opinion, to a dispute, or to all-out war.

Disagreements and **disputes** usually occur when we have to make decisions and we find ourselves at odds with others over the nature of a decision. A disagreement becomes a dispute only when the two parties (disputants) are unable and/or unwilling to resolve their disagreement; that is, when either one or both of the parties are not prepared to accept the way things currently are or willing to accede to the demand or denial of demand by the other party. A dispute is usually precipitated by a crisis in the relationship.[2] The most common forms of conflict in group work are disagreements and disputes.

Conflicts of interest may arise from everyday things such as differing needs, wants, and opinions, to the more complex such as the distribution of scarce resources (money, water, food, and employment), different world views, competing value systems, cultural contradictions, failures in communication, and so on.[3] In a two-person dispute, one person can break off contact and eliminate conflict, but that means that person would have to give up whatever it was he or she wanted that caused the conflict to begin with. Usually, a disagreement is not resolved until the people involved in the conflict take charge and deal with it.

It must be noted that two or more parties do not have to be interdependent, as in group work, to be in a state of conflict. For example, the United States and Iran have been in conflict over Iran's ambitions to build nuclear facilities. The United States does not want a nuclear Iran. These two countries are not interdependent, yet there exists a conflict of interests. The interests of the United States and those of Iran were stated in the form of positions (intent of behaviors). The United States has said that it would not allow Iran to become a nuclear power, and Iran has said that it has the right to be a nuclear power. At some point in time, their interests will have to be satisfied. The question is, "How will both their interests be satisfied?"

When we talk about conflict resolution, you will discover that there are differing perspectives as to whether conflict is resolved or managed. This author teaches alternative dispute resolution (ADR). I have found over the years that group conflict really isn't resolved; rather, it is managed. As long as two or more people work together, there will always be some form of conflict. Ongoing relationships produce ongoing conflict. All conflict isn't bad or harmful. A lot of conflict in group work is constructive and helpful. You will always have different opinions in group work; otherwise, you would have groupthink. Conflict produced by differing opinions is managed by the parties; they discuss their differences, work them out, and

© Alexander Raths, 2011. Under license from Shutterstock, Inc.

Conflict management

The process of group planning to avoid conflict where possible and organizing to manage conflict where and when it does happen, as quickly and smoothly as possible.

move on. This is a never-ending process in group work; therefore, conflict is managed and not resolved. We can define conflict management as the process of group planning to avoid conflict where possible and organizing to manage conflict where and when it does happen, as quickly and smoothly as possible.[4]

Members can effectively manage conflict situations if they consciously choose appropriate behavior rather than reacting according to their normative habits. Many people learn how to deal with conflict at an early age by watching their parents. This is a form of social learning; we incorporate it as part of who we are, and we take it with us as when we become adults. When we do engage in conflict situations, especially when they become emotional, we fall back on the conflict management behavior we learned when we were young. This is our comfort zone, for better or for worse. If you have learned to **self-monitor**, that is, recognize how you react in a conflict situation as it occurs, ask yourself, "Is this the way I should be responding to the other person?" Knowing a better alternative to managing conflict, you may want to change that old behavior. Only you can change your behavior. By changing the way you act, you may affect the way others react to you.

As you read this chapter, think of conflict is terms of behavior and management, especially if you are the group leader. Will you try to resolve conflict between two or more members, or try to manage it? My bet is that by the end of this chapter you will adopt the perspective that group conflict is something to be managed.

CONFLICT WITHIN SYSTEMS

Conflict within a system consists of two basic elements: (1) substance of issue around which the disagreement takes place; and (2) pattern of interactive communication. The substance and pattern of the conflict are interrelated through the process. Harris and Sherblom (2005) state that it is:

> The pattern that gives meaning to the substance and the substance that manifests the pattern. In small group conflict, however, it is the pattern of the conflict that determines the quality of the outcome for the group, rather than the substance of the matter over which the conflict is engaged. Regardless of the issue under dispute, if the participants are open to new perspectives and are committed to maintaining their relationships and to resolving their disputes, they are likely to find a satisfactory solution. On the other hand, if they feel little or no relational concern and are afraid of giving up any of their position for fear that, if they don't win, they lose, they are less likely to achieve a satisfactory outcome. To the extent that the pattern itself becomes an issue, however, it can be addressed and resolved when all parties commit to working on it.[5]

Tangibles

Those things which are on the group's formal agenda, such as: scheduling of meetings, order of reports, task assignments, new business, old business, and so forth.

Substance of the issue refers to the substantive elements or tangible aspects of an issue. Tangibles are those things that are on the group's formal agenda, such as: scheduling of meetings, order of reports, task assignments, new business, old business, and so forth.[6] When members disagree with the leadership about their task or role assignments, disagree about the date or time for a future meeting, or about who delivers their report first, we call this a substance of issue conflict. **Patterns of interactive communication** are the relational issues between the participants engaged in the dispute. Relational issues within a system are usually produced by an authority to subordinate relationship. What style of communication does the organization use; is it top–down, bottom–up, or lateral? Does interactive communication exist, or is it strictly a top–down form of communication? That is, can the participants in the dispute, regardless of position in the organization, disagree openly and honestly without fear of reprisal, or does the subordinate remain silent? What are the relationships between the disputants? Does the boss dislike the subordinate; is it a strained relationship at best? Or does the boss condone and encourage dissent? On a larger organizational scale, take a corporation that has many vice presidents. What are their relationships to one another? Relational issues determine, in part, the type and degree of conflict that occurs.

CONFLICT WITHIN GROUPS

Conflict is an inevitable and a necessary part of group work. Contrary to popular belief, group conflict is a good thing, a positive thing, and not a bad thing, if it is managed appropriately. It lets the group know that there is something wrong. We may want to avoid a disagreement, but that doesn't make it go away. There are two types of group conflict: **constructive** and **destructive**. And there are two factors for constructive or destructive conflict[7]:

1. Flashpoint. This is the origin of the conflict.
2. Orientation of group members toward patterns of conflict resolution. This concerns the relational aspects of group members to one another.

If conflict (flashpoint) resides in substance of issues, then it has the potential for constructive management.[8] This is constructive conflict because substantive issues are reasoned through discourse. Members talk through the issues and may engage in dialogue or dialectics. This process has a tendency to separate emotions from substance because members must focus on facts, data, reports, opinion, and other materials. It is constructive because of the nature of discussion, which would center on problem-solving or decision-making. Members are asking other members to listen to and understand their reasoning or conclusions.

If conflict (flashpoint) resides in the interactive patterns of the group members, then it has potential for destructive conflict. Interactive patterns refers to the relationships members have with one another, how they feel about each other, their emotions, whether they like or dislike each other, and so forth.

By permission of Leigh Rubin and Creators Syndicate, Inc.

Whether or not Oscar actually possessed the gift of telepathy was beside the point. He was usually right.

Relational conflict can be very destructive because the focus of the conflict is about attitudes, feelings, egos, etc. People tend to see other people as the problem instead of focusing on the substantive aspects of the problem. This is all about personalities and perception—the relationship becomes the problem. That makes it destructive.

Every member needs to be aware of conflict and as a group make decisions about what they are going to do about it. Conflict becomes negative only when it is not addressed and properly managed. Group leaders and members need to be able to manage conflict successfully. As in any skill, conflict management can be learned. The group will need to develop ways of recognizing and managing conflict so that it does not become so serious that cooperation is impossible. A group needs to have ways of keeping conflict to a minimum and ways of solving problems caused by conflict before conflict becomes a major obstacle to its work. This could and does happen to many groups.

At times, conflict can get very emotional, and a leader often needs to overcome the emotions involved in a conflict. Any individual in the group can provide that leadership. The role is not designated solely to the group leader, and often there is a member who is skilled at mediating conflict between other people. Group leaders know that issues affecting one member usually have an impact on other members as well. Learning to manage conflict will always lead to a more productive team and more satisfied group members, who feel that they can openly communicate, take risks, and exchange ideas in a safe environment.[9] Telling someone that you disagree with him or her in group work is expected; however, lack of communication among members can lead to conflict avoidance. When that happens, the group can lose its effectiveness.

One of the first agenda items a newly formed group should have is a process for managing conflict. This process should be efficient, is governed by rules of conduct, is mediated, allows for open discussion, and promotes a neutral environment. An efficient process means that there is order to managing conflict that minimizes group time, energy, emotions, and resources. We don't want the conflict to consume the group or its work; it will negatively impact the group. Rules of conduct limit the interactions of the disputants. These usually include such things as: no name calling, no yelling, maintain respect for the other person, speak calmly, no personal attacks, and so forth. We want open discussion because members should feel free to express themselves—their feelings, thoughts, wants, needs, and fears. This includes the substantive issues as well as the relational aspects. They have a tendency to become entwined, and open discussion is a way to separate them. A neutral environment provides a safe atmosphere for discussion. The goal is to establish a positive tone of trust, cooperation, and common concern between the disputants. A safe environment allows members to express their emotions and at the same time prevent any destructive expression of emotions.

CONFLICT BETWEEN INDIVIDUALS

The Conflict Continuum

Conflict rarely begins at an extreme level; it has a tendency to grow over time if unaddressed. What starts as mild differences, irritations, or disagreements can grow to obvious tension with observable arguing or under-the-surface struggles. Communication in these situations may range from open and friendly and open but strained, to limited and tense. The relationship between members may be perceived as being that of partners, friends, and acquaintances, to rivals and eventually as opponents.

Toward the other end of the continuum are aggression, antagonism, explosiveness, undermining, and open hostility. Communication in these phases can range from tense, restricted and planned, to potential episodes of mild acts of violence. The relationship between members ranges from opponents and competitors, to antagonists and enemies. It is critical for the group to deal with conflict at the lowest possible level to prevent a mild disagreement or irritation from worsening.

Relationship Issues

Thompson (2001) argues that there are two basic types of conflict that occur in relationships. **A-type conflict**, which is also known as **emotional conflict**, is personal, defensive, and resentful. A-type conflict is said to be rooted in anger, personality clashes, ego, and tension. **C-type conflict**, also referred to as **cognitive conflict**, is mainly depersonalized. It centers on the process of argumentation regarding the merits of ideas, plans, and projects, and is independent of the identity of the people involved. C-type conflict can be effective for integrative agreement because it forces people to rethink problems and arrive at outcomes that the group can live with. Conversely, A-type conflict has a tendency to threaten relationships, whereas C-type conflict enhances relationships.[10]

There are times that relationships in group work deteriorate. This is a natural by-product of unmanaged conflict. The problem is that, left unaddressed, whatever anger and hostility that manifest themselves can spread throughout the group. Members become scapegoats or are bullied; polarization between members becomes a common occurrence, and conflict increases over time. Relationships often show signs of deterioration. Some of those signs include but are not limited to: (1) One member will go out of his or her way and attempt to be nice and accommodating in order to solve the problem. The person who tries to be nice will make substantive concessions in order to avoid or reduce the chances for conflict. The conflict will continue to exist, but the process of problem-solving will be diminished. (2) Frustration will build between the members in conflict, which may lead to finger pointing and blaming, followed by threats and defensive reactions. Communication becomes limited and tense, and the orientation between them becomes a win–lose hostile battle. (3) One issue suddenly becomes many issues with unrelated attacks from one person to another or behind his or her back. Communication becomes extremely restricted.

© Roi Brooks, 2011. Under license from Shutterstock, Inc.

Meetings have now become forums for attacking one another, and the group now suffers serious damage to its synergy and ability to be cohesive and viable. (4) If unchecked, labels related to personality characteristics can occur. Conflict management becomes difficult at this point. Pejorative name-calling becomes the norm. People say things about others they would never consider if conflict didn't exist. 5) The disputing parties begin to retaliate. Other members are drawn into the conflict and take sides. The disputing members begin to stretch the truth, tells lies about each other, look for any type of mistake or short-coming that they can point out, even tattle to superiors. It is now an all-out war. Disputing members see each other as enemies. The conflict has the propensity to become violent if left unchecked. These are all things that could happen, but don't necessarily have to happen. Identifying and dealing with relational conflict early can prevent escalation and preserve group integrity.

Cultural Differences

Contextual factors that contribute to group conflict are cultural and co-cultural differences. Differences in the way people dress, the languages they speak, world views, rituals, religions, and goals within close proximity to each other seem to trigger disagreements, disputes, or more. These differences occur in interpersonal relations and intergroup relations. When the group leader fails to provide for adequate communication in between cultures, this creates a framework for conflict.[11]

Identifying Conflict

You can't manage conflict if you don't know what it looks like. The first step in managing conflict is to identify it.

1. Do the group members know that a conflict exists?
2. Are the group members arguing over competing goals and/or objectives?
3. Are the members arguing over resources?
4. Are the arguments substantive in nature or relational?
5. Are the arguments clashes of personality or ego-driven?
6. Are members calling each other names and refusing to work with one another?
7. Are members talking behind each other's backs?
8. Are members lobbying other members against a particular member?

Common Causes of Conflict

There are a multitude of causes or sources for group conflict. The most common are:

1. Poor communication
2. Lack of teamwork
3. Lack of clarity in roles, tasks, and responsibilities
4. Different attitudes, values, and perceptions
5. Disagreements about interests, needs, priorities, goals, and objectives
6. Scarcity of resources (time, money, equipment, facilities, etc.)

THE SUBSTANCE OF CONFLICT

In group work, members feel empowered to speak their minds. Since no two individuals are the same, there is a diversity of viewpoints and experiences. These provide the grounds for constructive, issues-based conflict. When this occurs, we need to isolate and focus on the present issues that have given rise to the conflict and avoid dispelling that conflict as merely a personality clash or a continuation of some previous conflict that was not issue-based. There are at least three substantive causes that can lead to constructive conflict:[12]

1. **Scarce resources.** This includes a perceived lack of reliable, efficient, and safe instruments; lack of time; insufficient information; inadequate space or place; insufficient skills or training; limited rewards; inadequate materials, supplies, and assistance; limited access to financial, informational, or other resources; competition for leadership positions, etc.
2. **Diverse backgrounds or orientation of group members.** This includes conflict of values (such as religious, political, or socioeconomic); cultural orientations; value systems (which are the basis for behavior);[13] differing interests or abilities; varying knowledge or experience related to the subject matter; different information or opinions on the subject matter; sources of anxiety reduction (how we handle stress).
3. **Varying orientations to task accomplishment.** This includes cognitive styles (how we organize and process information); divergent definitions or understandings of the breadth or depth of the subject matter or of the group process to be used; locus of decision-making (by the leader or consensus as a group); and what each individual accepts as evidence.

Generally, these substantive causes are not separate influences; rather, they are interdependent and may appear as clusters. For example, the general population in the United States is extremely diverse. It is not uncommon to see in the workplace, in public, or in school, people from many cultures. Some are easy to differentiate because they may wear ethnic clothes, and some may have distinguishing physical attributes, while many are not so obvious. You may be in a group that has a member from India, one from Japan, one from Saudi Arabia, one from Mexico, and you, from a traditional U.S. background. When discussing which evidence or data the group will adopt, the person from India will rely

on personal feelings to form the basis for the truth or what data he or she will or will not accept. The member from Japan tends to be more subjective than objective when making a decision on evidence. Whereas, generally, the Saudi member's faith in Islamic ideologies shapes the truth; objective facts seldom overrule one's thinking. The member from Mexico relies on subjective feelings to form the basis for truth, and this leads to the truth changing depending on what one is perceived to want. And then there is you. For you, evidence is made through the accumulation of objective facts. These are sometimes biased by faith in the ideologies of democracy, capitalism, and consumerism, but seldom by your subjective feelings.[14]

When there is a confluence of substantive differences, it doesn't take much for this type of conflict to occur. The combination of diverse backgrounds and varying orientations to task accomplishment merge together with the potential to create substances for conflict.

FIGURE 12.1

FIVE STYLES AND TACTICS OF CONFLICT MANAGEMENT

Competition
Tough adversary
Aggressive
Personal criticism
Ask hostile questions
Power orientation–we/they
Win-lose

Collaboration
Problem-solver
Makes analytical remarks
Assertive
Integrator–us rather than you
Acceptance of responsibility
Win-win

Compromise
Conciliator
Appeals to fairness
Willing to cede interests
Suggests a trade-off
Offers a quick, short-term solution
Lose-lose

Avoidance
Interpersonal complier
Passive by nature
Denies conflict exists
Noncommittal behavior
Lose-win

Accommodation
Friendly helper
Giving up/giving in
Disengagement
Denial of needs
Need for harmony
Lose-win

PATTERNS OF CONFLICT MANAGEMENT

People approach conflict in a number of ways. When we see those people consistently use the same method for dealing with conflict, we call it a conflict style. Conflict styles reflect the way people use the same or similar conflict tactics in different contexts or with different people. Our conflict styles represent our routine ways for handling disagreements or disputes. They become first nature, and we use them without much thought.[15] The conflict management style you choose depends in part on how assertive and cooperative you are.

COPING WITH CONFLICT STYLES

Whether we like it or not, we must cope with conflict; it is inevitable, especially in group work. Conflict, when not dealt with appropriately, will become a destructive force. There are a variety of strategies available for dealing with conflict. We can develop skills to help implement these strategies. Conflict can be dealt with in several basic ways. They are: avoidance, accommodation, compromise, competition, and collaboration.

Avoidance

Some people attempt to avoid conflict by postponing it, hiding their feelings, changing the subject, leaving the room or quitting the project. They are unwilling or unable to deal with the conflict and they vacate themselves physically, verbally, or nonverbally.[16] They are low in assertiveness and low in cooperativeness. There can be a multitude of drawbacks to avoiding conflict: the conflict can escalate, the relationship may not improve, the person avoiding the conflict will internalize any ill feelings toward the other person and stew. This can lead to gunnysacking, which is a failure to confront conflict as it occurs, eventually building up and bursting; creating a greater conflict than if previous situations had been addressed.[17] Avoidance may be appropriate when: the conflict is small and not worth the group's time to respond, members need time to calm down because relationships are at stake, or time is needed to gather more information.[18] Avoidance may not be appropriate when the issue is very important, a decision is needed quickly, no decision has a major impact on the situation, or postponing the issue will only make matters worse. Avoiding the conflict is usually not satisfying to the individual nor does it help the group resolve a problem.

Accommodation

This is a conflict management style which is high in cooperativeness and low in assertiveness, where one person appeases or gives in to others.[19] These group members are easy going and willing to follow the group. Accommodation is a convenient strategy to satisfy an immediate need for individuals or the group. It emphasizes the things conflicting parties have in common and de-emphasizes the differences. A member who puts other members' needs or desires ahead of his or her own is accommodating that member. Accommodation is helpful for

© wavebreakmedia ltd, 2011. Under license from Shutterstock, Inc.

a group to review their common purpose in the midst of conflict. Accommodation should not be used if an important issue is at stake, one which needs to be addressed immediately. Accommodation can be detrimental if one or more members do not value the worth or importance of his or her own needs.[20]

Compromise

Compromise can be used as a conflict management strategy; it is a shared solution to a conflict situation. These group members are moderate in assertiveness and moderate in cooperativeness. Compromisers are willing to give and take to resolve conflict. Someone using this style demonstrates a high concern for group social relationships but low concern for task accomplishments.[21] When two members meet half way in negotiating the conflict, both give up something they want or need and meet somewhere in the middle.[22] Compromise is appropriate when all members are satisfied with a part of their requests and are willing to be flexible. Compromise is mutual for all parties. All members should receive something, and all members will need to give up something. Compromise works when both members are willing to reduce some demands or an intermediate solution saves time and effort for both sides. Compromise doesn't work when initial demands are too great from the beginning or there is no commitment to honor the compromise.[23] The disadvantage to this strategy is that members seldom get their interests satisfied; they leave feeling short-changed.

Competition

Unlike avoidance, accommodation, and compromise, competitive approaches to conflict often involve highly assertive and even aggressive individuals who see conflict as a win–lose situation.[24] They are high in assertiveness and low in cooperativeness. Competitive people want to win the conflict. It is driven by self-interest rather than the group's mutual interest, and by an assumption of a limited resource and limited possibilities for gain.[25] This particular conflict management style suggests that a member might be uncooperative and aggressive, and may attempt to dominate or force the outcome to his or her advantage.[26] During a conflict, competition is a strategy used to exercise power. It is a way to approach conflict, knowing that eventually someone wins and someone loses. Competition will enable one party to win. Before using competition as a conflict management strategy, one must decide whether or not winning the conflict is beneficial to the individual or the group. Competition will not enhance a group's ability to work together. It reduces cooperation.

Collaboration

The goal of a collaborative style of conflict management is to produce a win–win outcome. This is the ideal conflict management style for any group. This strategy encourages teamwork, cooperation, and consensus within a group. Collaborators are high in assertiveness and high in cooperativeness. These group members are active and productive problem-solvers. Collaborative communication requires the participation of all members, with each stating points of view as clearly and concisely as possible, and it requires active listening on the part of all members. Collaboration does not establish winners and losers. It does not gain power over others. Collaboration works best when members trust and respect one another, when there is time for all members to share their views and feelings, when members want the best solution for the group as a whole, and members are willing to change their positions on issues when more information is found and new options are suggested. Collaboration may not be best when time is limited and people must act before they can work through their conflict or there is not enough trust, respect, or communication among the group for collaboration to occur.[27]

HOW TO IDENTIFY SIGNS AND STAGES OF CONFLICT

Stages of Conflict

There are a number of stages of conflict. Sam Keltner (1992) identified six basic stages. They are: Stage 1: Mild Difference; Stage 2: Disagreement; Stage 3: Argument/Bargaining; Stage 4: Campaign; Stage 5: Litigation; and Stage 6: Fight or War.[28] As you can see, the handling of conflict requires awareness of its various developmental stages. If a group leader can identify the conflict issue and how far it has developed, he or she can manage it before it becomes much more serious. Typical stages in group conflict include:[29]

1. The most basic stage of group conflict—members recognize that a lack of resources, gender differences, diversity of thought, opposing values or cultural orientation may be cause for conflict if members do not recognize them as such or are not sensitive to these differences.

2. Latent conflict between two or more members occurs when a competitive situation may easily give into conflict. Unmanaged or unresolved conflict is carried over from previous situations and acts as tinder for future conflict. In this scenario, it wouldn't take much for two or more members to engage in conflict.

3. The most obvious stage is open conflict, which can be triggered by an incident and suddenly mushroom into full-blown conflict. At this point, it wouldn't take much for the disputing members to engage in open verbal hostility.

4. The aftermath conflict is a situation where a specific problem may have been successfully managed or resolved, at least on the surface, but the potential for conflict still exists. At times, the potential for future conflict may be even greater than previous conflict situations if one member or the group perceives itself as engaged in a win–lose situation.

Signs of Conflict Between Members

The group leader and members should always be alert to the signs of conflict between colleagues so they can be proactive in managing that conflict. Some of the more obvious signs are:

1. Colleagues stop or refuse to speak with one another or ignore one another during group meetings.
2. One of the disputing members will avoid coming to meetings, making excuses that other situations have priority over the group.
3. Members in conflict contradict one another and display poor behavior by bad-mouthing each other.
4. Personal interests overcome the group's interests when members deliberately undermine or refuse to cooperate with each other. This leads to the deterioration and possible disbanding of the group.

Signs of Conflict Between Groups of People

As with signs of conflict between members, the group leader and members can identify latent conflict between cliques or groups of members within the group and plan to address it before the conflict becomes open and destructive.

1. A clique or faction of members meets separately from the group itself to discuss issues. This may signal that the clique has a hidden agenda and may attempt to exert its will on the rest of the group.
2. One subgroup may be intentionally left out of the group process or event when all members should be included.
3. One subgroup may resort to threatening slogans or symbols to demonstrate that they are right and the other subgroups are wrong.

POWER IN GROUP CONFLICT

All groups have a continuing flow and exchange of influence among their members. Power is an intentional communicative influence process between two or more people in a group. It is not owned by the group. In group work, it is natural for individuals to assert some type of power over other members. Defining power is as elusive as power itself; however, there are certain basics that appear to define power: Power is a potential and actual process of intentionally influencing events, beliefs, emotions, values, and behaviors of others in order to satisfy self and/or others' needs and desires by performing some actions which are basically communicative in nature.[30] The source of power resides in relationships, not individuals, and within the contexts in which members operate. Effective leadership ensures empowerment of all members.

Power is a neutral term. What really defines power is how it is used. A group member can exercise power for the benefit of group by facilitating members of the group in reaching their goals or helping the group achieve its goals. We say that people who can do these things have the power to integrate. The opposite end of the spectrum is based on the perception of life in which people function from fear, positions of dominance, and control of submissive others for their own welfare and satisfactions. People who view power from this perception usually feel threatened and are generally more aggressive toward others.[31]

POWER IN CONTEXT

Individual Power in Groups

The ability of one member to influence the behavior of another member has several bases. French and Raven (see Chapter 3) distinguished five types of power: **expert power, reward** or **punishment power**, **positional** or **legitimate power, referent power,** and **charismatic power**. We've added two more to this list: **interpersonal linkage power and avoidance power**. We will explore other types of power not mentioned in Chapter 3 that are germane to group work.

1. Expert power is a result of special knowledge, skill, talent, and/or experience that a member brings to the group. The strength of the expert power that is given to someone varies with the knowledge or perception that others attribute to him or her.
2. Reward or punishment (coercion) power is defined as power whose basis is the ability to reward. If your manager gives you a raise because he or she says that you've worked hard, then that is a reward—that person has reward power. The degree to which your group leader has reward power is determined by his or her ability to provide that reward. Punishment or coercion power is the ability of the leader to gain compliance or influence others by threatening members with forms of punishment. The threat of punishment is a form of coercion; it is a negative consequence.
3. Positional or legitimate power is defined as that power that is inherent in an individual's position or office in which others have an obligation to accept his or her influence. In all forms of legitimate power, the notion of legitimacy involves some sort of established code or standard.
4. Referent power has its basis in the identification of one person with another. By identification, I mean the feeling of oneness that one person has for another or a desire for such an identity. It is the influence inherent in the respect and admiration others have for an individual. Individuals with referent power are perceived as credible, wise, and as role models.
5. Charismatic (or personal) power is as elusive to define as defining beauty; no two people hold the same perspective. We may agree that a particular person has charisma, but we may disagree as to what personal qualities

constitute that charisma. Attributes that contribute to the perception of charisma include physical attractiveness, expertise and mastery of certain persuasive and communication skills, dynamism, reliability, trustworthiness, similar values, and the charismatic individual's ability to create identification with the group. All contribute to a person's ability to influence or have power over others.[33]

6. **Interpersonal linkage power** is a set of currencies that depend on a member's interpersonal contacts. A member of one group also holds a position in a larger group. If that member is a liaison person between these two groups, then he or she serves as a communication bridge between these two groups that have information about each other. That member now serves as a linkage currency between the groups. He or she gains power through coalition formation.[32]

7. **Avoidance power** is characterized by a person's denial of the conflict, equivocation, changing and avoiding topics, being noncommittal, and making jokes rather than dealing with the conflict situation. Unfortunately, avoiding conflict does not prevent it from happening.[34] Although this is one way to deal with conflict, as noted earlier, it is also used as a power.

Rollo May (1972) and G. Ray Funkhouser (1986) continued researching power where French and Raven left off. Note the similarities and differences between their work and French and Raven's work. May argues that all of us have five different kinds of individual power, which we use at different times, while Funkhouser divides power into a spectrum comprising of four parts.[35]

May's Individual Power [36]

1. **Exploitive power** is the simplest and most destructive type of power, especially in group work. It is used to dominate and control others. A leader or member with a strong personality will use it to get others to submit to his or her will. Violence or the threat of violence is used for compliance gaining; other group members will feel that they do not have a choice, and they will comply.

2. **Competitive power** is the basis for the win–lose attitude. We see this type of power throughout society, and we see it in group work. At least one member must outdo or best someone else. Some people have a stronger desire to win than others; and, regardless of the context, they seek to be winners. This has both a positive advantage and a negative outcome. On the positive side, a competitive person can invigorate or energize the group, making it more productive. The negative outcome is that a member who is too competitive can be destructive to the group. Other members will feel alienated and will shy away from open participation.

3. **Manipulative power** is a way of changing or modifying member behavior by crafty and unfair means in order to control members and get them to behave the way the manipulator wants them to. People who use this form of power are deceitful but generally will not use threats of violence for compliance.

4. Nutrient power occurs when an individual shows caring for other group members. A member may provide various forms of support, resources, or information for the benefit of another member.

5. Integrative power recognizes that individuals who seek similar needs, wants, desires, and mutual goals will cooperate with each other in order to achieve them. Instead of being adversarial or competitive, these individuals join together, providing growth and advancement for them and the group.

Funkhouser's Spectrum [37]

1. Structural power is similar to legitimate power in that power originates from the structure or organization and the social roles that are associated with that organization. Every structure has a hierarchy of power, whether that be formal (such as a business, government, or even a family) or informal. Each structure has positions of power, some ascribed by title, such as father or mother, and others by formal authority, such as president and vice president.

2. Agreement power is the product of two or more parties coming to a mutual decision. During the negotiation process, each party agrees to stipulations or options of what each party can or cannot do. They agree to particular terms that govern their behavior or performance.

3. Persuasive power is influencing group members' attitudes and behaviors so that they perform the way the persuader wants them to. The persuader will generally use appeals to the various needs, wants, fears, and desires of members.

4. Performance power lies within each of us. It is our ability to make decisions to take action. Another term for it is taking the initiative, doing the right thing at the right time in order to accomplish goals and objectives.

The Leader's Role and Resources in Conflict Management

© Dean Mitchell, 2011. Under license from Shutterstock, Inc.

Just because the group or team leader has the role of leadership, it doesn't mean that he or she knows how to manage conflict. A leader should be skilled in identifying conflict early; he or she should be able to create an environment in which differences are accepted and addressed rather than avoided, be able to respond proactively to conflict, and be ready to act as a mediator in the event of conflict between group members.

When a leader acts as mediator, there are certain issues that can be discussed or negotiated, and issues that should not be. A leader should separate any substantive issues in conflict from the relational issues between the disputing members.[38] Often, negotiating is more about who's right and who's wrong. However, during any mediation process, there are some issues that should be discussed but not be negotiated; they include but, are not limited to, members' issues concerning: beliefs, values or principles, perceptions, feelings, trust, anger, blame or fault, and interpretation of events. There are certain behavioral guidelines that should be considered, and issues that should be negotiated include: the communication process regarding mediation, issue substance, group norms (how people treat each other), the speaking order, rules on how disagreements over data should be managed, task responsibilities, the various ways tasks are performed, and communicating about problems.

CONSTRUCTIVE CONFLICT MANAGEMENT

Group conflict cannot be managed properly if the environment does not provide a supportive climate. Members should accept the fact that conflict is going to happen; it's a normal part of group work. However, when conflict beyond mere disagreement does arise, there are some basic golden rules for constructive conflict management that the group, as a whole, can engage in:

1. **Positive group relations.** First and foremost, maintain a commitment to the importance of positive group relations. Group synergy works best when the group, even in times of conflict, stays committed to good relations and positive relationships.
2. **Communicate openly and willingly.** Individual members should not be afraid to state their positions directly and honestly. They should be able to state their ideas and opinions as to what they believe the conflict to be and how it came about.
3. **Respect and courtesy.** Members should respect the rights of others and be courteous to others, even when they disagree with them. Every member should be given the courtesy and respect to be heard.
4. **Act with civility.** A supportive climate demands that members speak to and behave toward each other with civility. Avoid name calling. Members do not use abrasive or foul language toward one another, nor do they threaten another member. Each individual is treated equally and fairly.
5. **A willingness to listen.** As each member wants to be heard, each, in turn, must be willing to listen attentively to the diverse opinions of others.
6. **Accept responsibility for one's own thoughts and feelings.** Don't put the blame on someone else for the way you feel or what you think. For example, instead of saying, "You made me feel angry," say, "I feel angry about..." or "I feel this way because..." No one makes you feel the way you do; only you make yourself feel that way or think the thoughts you have.
7. **Substantive versus relational or personality issues.** Separate the substantive issues from the relational (personality) issues. As we said earlier, we have a tendency to blend relationships with substance. Separate these two issues. At times, the relational aspects may need to be addressed before any

substantive issues can be, at least to the point where people can speak civilly with one another.[39] It is impossible to rationally discuss issues of substance when emotions are running wild, and that generally occurs when personalities clash.

8. **Look for areas of agreement that underlie the disagreement.** Begin with the easiest issues that members can agree to. The more "yeses" they get, the more cooperation to conflict management will occur.

9. **Don't blame one another for their problems.** Avoid holding the other side responsible for the problem.

10. **Generate alternatives.** Members should generate as many alternatives (options) as possible before coming to a resolution. A rule of thumb: don't reject alternatives as they are offered: wait until all viable options have been placed on the table, then discuss each one based on their merits.

11. **Address one issue at a time.** Each issue must be dealt with separately. Avoid blending issues since each one is distinct unto itself; otherwise, you'll never be able to manage the conflict.

12. **Deal with any past issues first.** These may be blocking current communication. A past issue should be listed as a current issue that needs resolution.

13. **Avoid reacting to unintentional remarks.** Words such as always and never are usually said when emotions run high. A member will take offense to those remarks and become defensive. Anger will increase the conflict rather than making it manageable.

14. **Agree to disagree.** Disagreement is what probably created the conflict to begin with. There will never be 100 percent consensus in group work, but members can respect one another even when disagreeing.

15. **Don't insist on being right.** There are always several options to every problem. Be open to alternative views.

16. **Put yourself in their shoes.** Members tend to see issues according to their perceptions and disregard or misinterpret those that call their perceptions into question. Put yourself in their shoes; mentally switch roles; and try to understand the problem from their side. Understanding their point of view is not the same as agreeing with them.

LEADER AS MEDIATOR

There are many types of mediators; however, in group work the preferred mediator role is called the **benevolent mediator**. This type of mediator is not neutral or impartial toward the disputants because the mediator has existing relationships with the parties, nor does the mediator serve at the pleasure of the parties. The leader as mediator has an ongoing relationship with the parties and seeks the best solution for all involved, including the group as a whole. However, the leader is generally impartial regarding the specific substantive outcome of the conflict and has the authority to advise, suggest, or make a decision.[40] For our purpose, we can define mediation as the intervention of a third party who is not directly involved in the dispute or the substantive issues in question, and who has limited authoritative decision-making power. The parties are encouraged to see and make clear, deliberate choices, while acknowledging the perspective

Mediation
The intervention of a third party who is not directly involved in the dispute or the substantive issues in question, and who has limited authoritative decision-making power.

of the other. The leader or the member acting as mediator helps the disputants discuss their differences, identify areas of agreement, and test options with a possible outcome that is mutually acceptable to the disputants. The mediator looks at specific content issues and encourages the parties to create their own solutions to the problem areas. The parties in this process are in control of the information and issues discussed while the mediator maintains control of the process. Mediators are often called process facilitators or process managers.[41] The parties in dispute voluntarily reach a mutually acceptable settlement of the issues that have caused the conflict. Unless the parties agree to have the mediator make a decision, the decision-making power lies primarily in the hands of the disputants, or, if there is a stalemate between the disputants, the mediator makes the decision in order to balance out the needs of the group versus the interests of the individuals.

The mediator provides a safe environment and a safe process for the disputants to manage their conflict. The goal of the process is to support the negotiation between the disputants as they move toward resolution. The goal of the mediator is to set guidelines that provide safety and balance for the parties involved and to assist each party in understanding himself or herself and the other party. One of the most important jobs of the mediator is to identify the differing goals that must flow together before a solution can be reached.[42] An effective mediator is tactful and diplomatic, and has the necessary powers of persuasion and strong character to nudge the disputants progressively towards an agreement.

How to Be an Effective Mediator

Many leaders lack mediation experience or knowledge. A leader can cause more damage than good if he or she attempts to mediate a conflict without having some of the basic skills necessary to do so. It takes quite a bit of time and experience to become a skilled mediator; however, that shouldn't prevent the leader, or any member of the group, from practicing the following basic skills necessary for competent performance as a mediator:[43]

1. **Create a safe environment.** The first thing a mediator must do is create a safe environment for the disputing parties. They must feel as though they can openly discuss their feelings, positions, and so forth.
2. **Listen actively.** It is important to use active listening skills. Not only does this entail what you hear from each party, but also how it is said.
3. **Analyze problems, identify and separate the issues involved, and frame these issues for resolution or decision-making.** This is where critical thinking skills become necessary. The mediator employs clear thinking in identifying the real problems and offers practical solutions.
4. **Use clear, concise, and neutral language in speaking with the disputing parties.** There should not be any ambiguity in what the leader says; words should be explicit and clear, and presented in such a way as to denote the mediator's neutrality between the parties.

5. **Be sensitive to strongly felt values of the disputants, including gender, ethnic, and cultural differences.** The mediator must suppress any biases, if any, that he or she may hold regarding these values. Values are motivators; they compel people to behave the way they do, and they must be respected during the mediation process.

6. **Understand power imbalances.** Seldom do disputants in group work have equality in power. Over time, power imbalances occur between members, whether that is a result of relational interactions, resources, information, and so forth. A good mediator can identify these imbalances and neutralize them.

7. **Earn trust, acceptance, and cooperation.** One of the qualities a mediator must have from the parties is their trust. Without trust, the parties will not feel safe and will reluctantly discuss their feelings and interests, which makes acceptance and cooperation by the parties problematic.

8. **Convert the parties' positions into needs and interests.** Positions are the stated things the parties want. Interests and needs are the underlying motivators that give rise to positions.

9. **Screen out nonmediable issues.** Not all issues can be mediated, nor should they. The mediator should be able to discern the difference between mediable and nonmediable issues. We discussed the differences earlier in this chapter.

10. **Help parties invent creative options.** When the parties seem fixated on an either–or, black or white, or fixed-pie mentality, that is, when there is only so much that each side can gain, the mediator helps the parties explore more alternatives.

11. **Help parties make their own informed choices.** There will be times when the parties are hesitant about making a choice as to which solutions are best for them. In times such as this, the mediator will want to ask probing questions, such as, "Does this option satisfy your interests? If it does, then why do you think so?" "Does this solution seem reasonable and rational to you? If so, why does it? If not, why not?" "Do you see any problems that this solution may cause you?"

Mediation Activities: Moves and Interventions

Move

A specific act of intervention or influence technique focused on the individuals in the dispute.

Contingent moves

Responses to problems specific to the parties that occur during the mediation process.

Throughout the process, the mediator may initiate moves that keep the process flowing. Keltner (1994) identifies a move for a mediator as a specific act of intervention or influence technique focused on the individuals in the dispute. These are meant to encourage the parties to select positive actions and to inhibit selection of negative actions relative to the issues in conflict. Mediators make two types of interventions in response to critical situations: general or **noncontingent moves** or activities, and contingent moves or activities. Noncontingent moves are general interventions that a mediator uses in virtually all disputes. They are linked to the overall pattern of conflict development and resolution. Noncontingent moves enable the mediator to:[44]

1. Gain entry into the dispute
2. Assist the parties in selecting the appropriate conflict resolution approach and arena
3. Collect data and analyze the conflict
4. Design a mediation plan
5. Assist the parties in beginning productive negotiations
6. Identify important issues and build an agenda
7. Identify parties' underlying interests
8. Aid the parties in developing resolution options
9. Assist in assessing options
10. Promote final bargaining, agreement-making, and closure

Contingent moves are responses to problems specific to the parties that occur during the mediation process. Contingent moves are interventions that manage intense anger, bluffing, bargaining in bad faith, mistrust, or miscommunication. Generally, the mediator will outline codes of conduct and discuss them with the parties at the very beginning of the process. Any code of conduct will detail behaviors that are acceptable and unacceptable. When a party displays unacceptable behavior, the mediator will use a contingent move to stop it.

Each mediator modifies his or her moves and interventions.

Code of Conduct for Participants

Caucus

The mediator speaks separately with each party outside of the presence of the other party.

The mediator should establish a code of conduct that the participants need to adhere to and he or she should discuss it with them prior to the parties engaging in the mediation process. The mediator can do this in two ways: first, the mediator can have both parties present when discussing the guidelines, and have them acknowledge that they understand and will comply with them; or second, the mediator can caucus each party separately to discuss the guidelines. A caucus occurs when the mediator speaks separately with each party outside of the presence of the other party. The mediator will speak with one party at a time in a separate room. The following is a list of rules and procedures which the mediator gets each side to agree to prior to starting the mediation session.

1. The parties will trust and respect the mediator and the role of mediator.
2. The parties agree to behave in a polite and disciplined manner.

3. The parties will speak only to the mediator and not to each other.
4. The parties will not be verbally abusive, shout at one another, or blame one another.
5. The parties will not use physical intimidation (e.g., pointing fingers) or threats of violence.
6. The parties agree to keep whatever is said during mediation confidential.

Conducting a Mediation Session

The mediation session consists of several stages, depending on the complexity of the problem(s), the number of disputants, and the constraint of time and resources. For our purpose, we will use a simple mediation process that can be easily implemented. We assume that the mediator and disputants know each other because they have been working together in the context of the group.[45]

Stage 1: Introduction to the process. During the first stage the mediator:

1. Establishes an open and positive tone.
2. Educates the disputants to the process of mediation; this includes a description of the process, the role of the mediator, and the different stages of mediation.
3. Establishes ground rules and behavioral guidelines, and has the parties agree to the rules and procedures. The mediator will also direct the parties not to talk directly to each other, but to the mediator, and he or she will then rephrase what was said to the other party. This eliminates direct confrontation between parties.
4. Assists the parties in venting emotions, also known as catharsis.

Stage 2: Collecting and analyzing background information. During the second stage, the mediator:

1. Creates common ground. It is important that the mediator have the parties begin by creating common ground with each other. Common ground is the basis for mutuality, and a starting point by focusing on the goals and values they can share and agree on. This acts as a way to ease tension and helps to create a safe atmosphere.
2. Identifies broad topic areas of concern to the parties. The mediator discovers the source(s) of conflict. The mediator will leave most of the talking to the disputing parties, but will actively listen and ask probing questions to pinpoint the causes of the conflict and obstacles to a possible settlement. Usually, in this stage, the mediator will ask the parties to describe how the conflict came about and to present their points of view. Each one will take his or her turn describing the conflict from his or her perspective and explain his or her position. The mediator will summarize their statements, allow for clarifying questions, and allow for responses from each party.
3. Obtains agreement on the issues to be discussed. The parties need to agree as to which issues will be openly discussed and which ones will not.
4. Determine the sequence for addressing the issues. The parties will identify and prioritize the issues according to their importance.

Stage 3: Uncovering hidden interests of the disputing parties. During the third stage, the mediator:

1. Identifies the substantive and psychological interests of the parties. It is here that the mediator asks probing questions to uncover the hidden or underlying interests of the parties.
2. Educates the parties about each other's interests. The mediator will restate the interests to the other party and ask if he or she understood them.
3. Intervenes more actively in guiding the process. The mediator becomes more vocal in his or her probing of underlying interests and guides the parties more actively through the process.

Stage 4: Generating options for settlement. During the fourth stage, the mediator:

1. Develops awareness among the parties of the need for multiple options. The mediator explains that the parties must look beyond the either–or solution or a one-size-fits-all solution, that they must be creative and generate multiple options.
2. Lowers commitment to positions or sole alternatives. By uncovering interests, the mediator shifts the parties from positional bargaining to principled bargaining, that is, to satisfying their interests instead of a firm position or alternative.
3. Generates options using interest-based bargaining. The parties invent options that will satisfy their interests instead of their positions, allowing them to be more creative and expansive.
4. Offers advice to the parties in order to discover areas in which compromise can be reached.

Stage 5: Assessing options for settlement. During the fifth stage, the mediator:

1. Reviews the interests of the parties. This allows each party to affirm or clarify his or her interests.
2. Assesses how interests can be met by available options. This is a diagnostic process in which the mediator gets each party to assess how the options each generated satisfy their interests.
3. Assesses the costs and benefits of selecting options. This is a diagnostic process in which the mediator gets each party to assess the cost/benefit ratio for each option. They weigh the benefits of each option to their costs to determine whether those options satisfactorily meet their interests.
4. The mediator will encourage parties to put forward proposals and counterproposals and (when a solution appears possible) will begin to urge or even pressure the participants toward acceptance of a settlement.

Stage 6: Final Bargaining. During this stage:

1. The parties reach an agreement. This is done in a number of ways, either through incremental convergence of positions, satisfaction of interests, development of a consensual formula, or establishment of procedural means to reach a substantive agreement.

2. Each party restates his or her options to the agreement and states why he or she thinks those options are viable solutions to the conflict.

3. The mediator has to be flexible and inventive, must ensure that his or her personal values are not imposed on the parties. At best, a mediator can advise, persuade, or cajole the parties toward agreement.

Stage 7: Achieving Formal Settlement. During this stage, the mediator:

1. Will use diplomacy or exert pressure toward final settlement of the dispute. Timing and sensitivity to personalities and strategic positions are important for the mediator to maintain credibility and avoid rejection by one or more parties in the process.

2. Identifies procedural steps to operationalize the agreement. The mediator details how the parties can commit to and enact the agreement. In the event of a final settlement being reached, the mediator usually assists the parties in the drafting of their agreement, ensuring that both sides are satisfied with the wording, terms, and conditions of the agreement.

3. Establishes an evaluation procedure. The mediator creates a procedure that will evaluate the extent to which the parties are complying with the agreement.

4. Closes mediation. The mediator thanks the parties for their participation and cooperation, and reminds them of the evaluation procedures which the mediator will monitor to ensure that the parties are adhering to their commitments.

With any kind of luck, the mediator will be successful. As we said earlier in this chapter, there are a number of mediation processes. This is one method and, we believe, a very effective way, for mediating group conflict.

SUMMARY

In this chapter, we learned about the many aspects of conflict management, from disagreements to disputes. We compared the differences and similarities between conflict within systems and conflict within groups, to conflict between individuals. We learned how to identify conflict and understand some of the common causes of conflict. We came to understand the substance of conflict, patterns of conflict management, and methods of coping with conflict styles. We also learned how to identify the signs and stages of conflict, and how individual power in groups is contextualized. We focused on the leader's role and resources in conflict management, and what constructive conflict management means. We looked at the leader as mediator, from how to be an effective mediator, mediation activities (moves and interventions), to a code of conduct for participants, and conducting a mediation session.

DISCUSSION

1. In this chapter you learned that conflict with a **substantive flashpoint** has the potential to be **constructive** for group work, while conflicts with flashpoints based in **interactive patterns** among group members has the potential to be **destructive**. Consider exceptions to these claims: What circumstances can you describe in which substantive conflict might be destructive to group work? What circumstances can you describe in which interaction–based conflict might be constructive for group work?

2. Imagine that your organization has assigned to your group a new member who has been publically, and vocally, critical about the work ethic of several members of your group in the past. What are some specific choices an effective group leader might make at the next group meeting, the new member's first group meeting, to help discourage **emotional conflict** within the group?

3. Recall that in Chapter 1 you learned about how cultural differences can result in some members orienting to messages seeking **agreement** during brewing conflicts and other members orienting to messages maintaining **autonomy**. Now consider the questions designed to help you identify conflict on page 8: How might these questions be complicated, or made more difficult for leaders to answer, depending on members' possible differing orientations to agreement and autonomy in the early stages of conflict? How might an effective leader take such cultural differences into account when attempting to trace the sources of an emerging conflict?

4. Why is **collaboration** not necessarily always the most productive approach to conflict in group work, given that successful collaboration typically fosters positive cohesiveness and a strong sense of group accomplishment? If a leader recognizes circumstances in which collaboration might not be the most valuable approach to resolving a conflict, how might s/he help the group choose other resolution strategies without, at the same time, damaging group cohesiveness?

5. Why would an effective leader not simply use **manipulative power** to resolve conflicts if s/he could gain agreement quickly by doing so? What are the drawbacks of a leader relying on manipulation to resolve conflicts among members?

NOTES

1. Fisher, R., & Ury, W. (1981). *Getting to yes* (2nd ed.). New York: Penguin.

2. Gulliver, P.H. (1979). *Disputes and negotiations.* San Diego, CA: Academic Press.

3. Keltner, J.W. (1997). The management of struggle (2nd ed.). Cresskill, NJ: Hampton.

4. Moore, C.W. (1986). *The mediation process: Practical strategies for resolving conflict.* San Francisco: Jossey-Bass.

5. Harris, T.E., & Sherblom, J.C. (2005). *Small group and team communication* (3rd ed.). New York: Pearson. P. 245–46.

6. Lewicki, R.J., & Litterer, J.A. (1985). *Negotiation.* Homewood, IL: The Irwin Series in Management and The Behavioral Sciences.

7. Moore, C.W. (2003). *The mediation process: Practical strategies for resolving conflict* (3rd ed.). San Francisco: Jossey-Bass.

8. Harris, T.E., & Sherblom, J.C. (2005). *Small group and team communication* (3rd ed.). New York: Pearson.

9. Cupach, W.R., & Canary, D.J. (1997). *Competence in interpersonal conflict.* New York: McGraw-Hill.

10. Thompson, L. (2001). *The mind and heart of the negotiator* (2nd ed.). Upper Saddle River, NJ: Prentice-Hall.

11. Keltner, J.W. (1997). *The management of struggle* (2nd ed.). Cresskill, NJ: Hampton.

12. Adapted from Harris, T.E., & Sherblom, J.C. (2005). *Small group and team communication* (3rd ed.). New York: Pearson.

13. Morrison, T., Conaway, W.A., & Borden, G.A. (1994). *Kiss, bow, or shake hands: How to do business in sixty countries.* Avon, MA: Adams Media.

14. Ibid.

15. Cupach, W.R., & Canary, D.J. (1997). *Competence in interpersonal conflict.* New York: McGraw-Hill.

16. Domenici, K. (1996). *Mediation: Empowerment in conflict management.* Prospect Heights, IL: Waveland.

17. Trenholm, S., & Jensen, A. (1992). *Interpersonal communication.* Belmont, CA: Wadsworth.

18. Borisoff, D., & Victor, D.A. (1989). *Conflict management: A communication skills approach.* Englewood Cliffs, NJ: Prentice-Hall.

19. Galanes, G.J., Adams, K., & Brilhart, J.K. (2004). *Effective group discussion: Theory and practice.* New York: McGraw-Hill.

20. Domenici, K. (1996). *Mediation: Empowerment in conflict management.* Prospect Heights, IL: Waveland.

21. Rothwell, J.D. (2007). *In mixed company: Communicating in small groups and teams* (7th ed.). Boston, MA: Wadsworth.

22. Ibid.

23. Wilmot, W.W., & Hocker, J.L. (2001). *Interpersonal conflict* (6th ed.). New York: McGraw-Hill.

24. Domenici, K. (1996). *Mediation: Empowerment in conflict management.* Prospect Heights, IL: Waveland.

25. Harris, T.E., & Sherblom, J.C. (2005). *Small group and team communication* (3rd ed.). New York: Pearson.

26. Galanes, G.J., Adams, K., & Brilhart, J.K. (2004). *Effective group discussion: Theory and practice.* New York: McGraw-Hill.

27. Forsyth, D.R. (2006). *Group dynamics* (4th ed.). Belmont, CA: Thomson-Wadsworth.

28. See Keltner, J.W. (1997). *The management of struggle* (2nd ed.). Cresskill, NJ: Hampton Press.

29. Tubbs, S.L. (1995). *A systems approach to small group interaction* (5th ed.). New York: McGraw-Hill.

30. Keltner, J.W. (1997). *The management of struggle* (2nd ed.). Cresskill, NJ: Hampton Press.

31. Ibid.

32. Wilmot, W.W., & Hocker, J.L (2001). *Interpersonal conflict* (6th ed.). New York: McGraw-Hill.

33. Keltner, J.W. (1997). *The management of struggle* (2nd ed.). Cresskill, NJ: Hampton.

34. Wilmot, W.W., & Hocker, J.L. (2001). *Interpersonal conflict* (6th ed.). New York: McGraw-Hill.

35. Keltner, J.W. (1997). *The management of struggle* (2nd ed.). Cresskill, NJ: Hampton.

36. May, R. (1972). *Power and innocence: A search for the sources of violence.* New York: W.W. Norton. See also Keltner, J.W. (1997). *The management of struggle* (2nd ed.). Cresskill, NJ: Hampton Press.

37. Funkhouser, G.R. (1986). *The power of persuasion: A guide to moving ahead in business and life.* New York: Random House. See also Keltner, J.W. (1997). *The management of struggle* (2nd ed.). Cresskill, NJ: Hampton.

38. Fisher, R., & Ury, W. (1981). *Getting to yes* (2nd ed.). New York: Penguin.

39. Ury, W. (1993). *Getting past no: Negotiating your way from confrontation to cooperation.* New York: Bantam.

40. Moore, C.W. (2003). *The mediation process: Practical strategies for resolving conflict* (3rd ed.). San Francisco: Jossey-Bass.

41. Domenici, K. (1996). *Mediation: Empowerment in conflict management.* Prospect Heights, IL: Waveland.

42. Ibid.

43. Adapted from Keltner, J.W. (1997). *The management of struggle* (2nd ed.). Cresskill, NJ: Hampton.

44. Adapted from Keltner, J.W. (1997). *The management of struggle* (2nd ed.). Cresskill, NJ: Hampton.

45. Adapted from Moore, C.W. (2003). *The mediation process: Practical strategies for resolving conflict* (3rd ed.). San Francisco: Jossey-Bass, and from Keltner, J.W. (1997). *The management of struggle* (2nd ed.). Cresskill, NJ: Hampton.

13

Virtual Groups

CHAPTER OBJECTIVES

- Understand how mediated groups function in an electronic age
- Be familiar with information literacy
- Understand what constitutes virtual dimensions
- Explain how to build a virtual group
- Know how to conduct a virtual meeting
- Be familiar with virtual rules

CHAPTER OUTLINE

KEY TERMS

Synchronous
  communication

Asynchronous
  communication

Information literacy
  (IL)

Information literacy
  gap

Place

Time setting

Space

Distance

Sequence of
  communication

VIRTUAL GROUPS

Mediated Groups in an Electronic Age

There is no question about it: we live in an ever-expanding world of technology that has brought us within seconds to the farthest reaches of the planet without leaving our homes. This technology has become ubiquitous, and we are just in its infantile stage. At some time in the immediate future, nanotechnology will make today's technology obsolete. The next generation, those who will use nanotechnology, will view us as Neanderthals and wonder how we were able to do the things we now do with such crude tools, just as we view those before the advent of the computer. But for now, ever-evolving technology has brought communication to new heights through not only the use of the computer, but through satellites and the World Wide Web. No longer do we need to mail letters and wait days, sometimes even weeks, for a response. Nor do we need to write so many checks to pay our bills and hope that the post office delivers them on time. The personal telephone landline will soon disappear like the dinosaur. Our cell phones will be all-encompassing, and the need for separate electronic devices, such as credit cards, proof of identification, driver's license, and so forth, will be obsolete. I am of the opinion that all of this will be electronically performed through our personal cell phones.

Technology not only affects our communication, but also our relationships with others, and our lives in general, both public and private. For example, Google Earth has the ability to track people and objects in real time through satellites, just as governments do with their satellites. Many workplaces monitor employee email. We use YouTube to post videos, and Twitter and Facebook to develop and maintain relationships. We purchase goods online, such as books from Amazon.com, clothing, equipment, movies, and so forth. We even play virtual computer games globally. We use instant messaging (IM) instead of the telephone and email in place of snail mail. And we can get our college degrees online through platforms such as eCollege and Blackboard. Communications as we now know it will dramatically change, one hopes for the better, for technology, in and of itself, is neutral. What determines if it is good or bad is the user, how it is applied. It would be naïve for us to think that we can avoid the changes that are coming our way.

This chapter is about virtual group communication. **Virtual groups**, or V-groups, depend on technology to communicate across geographical boundaries, time boundaries, and organizational boundaries. Members of virtual groups can be

separated merely by a wall or by thousands of miles. They can share the same time, be hours apart, or even a day apart (international time zone), and they don't have to be a part of the same organization. Virtual groups are flexible and responsive, and they have a diversity of perspectives that may be quite different from traditional groups. Members may be more diverse because of cultural backgrounds, ability to speak multiple languages, and membership in various organizations. For example, I have been a member of the American Communication Association almost since its incorporation in 1993; I am a past president, and a former executive director, and a board member. What began as a virtual group that was primarily asynchronous, meeting annually, has morphed into one that is completely asynchronous. Membership includes scholars and practitioners from Israel, Portugal, China (PRC), Taiwan (ROC), England, Peru, Mexico, Argentina, Iran, Canada, and the U.S., just to name a few countries. In addition, ACA has created a virtual public speaking text that is free for students and faculty alike, accessible on the Web.

Members of virtual groups generally use computer-mediated communication (CMC), but they are not limited to just the computer as a means to communicate. They may use, for example, audio, video, or teleconferencing. The use of CMC as a means to communicate transcends physical space and time. Members can literally be next to each other, sitting side-by-side, or they can be separated geographically or geographically mixed.[1] As V-groups become more popular in organizations, at this time they cannot replace traditional face-to-face group work because they lack the synergy and interpersonal bonds that are created when people physically get together to work as a group. V-groups, for now, sacrifice these bonds.[2] Face-to-face communication occurs when members are physically together in a room. They can see and touch one another; they share a physical proximity; they work face-to-face. When members of a group communicate at a distance, whether that is by email, telephone, FAX, or video conferencing, for example, they are working virtually. Perhaps when nanotechnology becomes pervasive, the issues that surround bonding may no longer be issues.

In V-group work we have two types of communication: synchronous and asynchronous communication. Teleconferencing (conference calls), video conferencing, and Internet chat rooms are examples of synchronous communication because group members interact simultaneously in real time. This type of communication does have its advantages. Because of its virtuality, group members may be able to brainstorm more quickly, analyze a problem more effectively, or propose a broader array of options more efficiently than traditional groups. However, for every benefit V-groups may have, they also have their costs. When I attempt to rapidly respond to an IM, I become all thumbs, and my message is distorted. "I know it's what I said, but that's not what I meant," takes on a whole new meaning. My typing skills become problematic when I attempt to type too quickly. How about you? And if it is a group IM or chat room, then you have responses that generally are out of sequence. Unlike face-to-face communication, group IM makes it difficult to know when topics have been changed; some members may be discussing topic B while others are still on topic A. This can make group discussion quite confusing.

 Synchronous communication

Interaction that takes place in same time settings; asynchronous communications refers to different time settings.

 **Asynchronous communication**

Sends data in one direction; it is linear (one character at a time) and is not interactive.

Asynchronous communication sends data in one direction. It is linear, one character at a time, and it is not interactive. This is the opposite of synchronous communication. Traditional patterns of communication no longer apply, making CMC a social and psychological phenomenon besides a technological one.[3] When someone sends a message asynchronously, he or she posts it for the group to look at. Members will view it and post a response, often at their convenience, and usually within 24 hours. Email, bulletin, and white boards are examples of asynchronous communication. These forms of CMC have their advantages. Members have the opportunity to think about how they might respond to a question or provide solutions to a problem. It gives members time to research and/ or collaborate in order to provide carefully thought-out responses. It is especially useful when members must edit and rewrite proposals or reports. Copies are simultaneously emailed to each member; they work on it, sending it back and forth until a final copy is produced. This is more efficient than the traditional method for handling a proposal or paper. One of the courses I regularly teach is Public Relations Campaigns. This course is taught asynchronously. The class is divided into groups of four or five students, and they conduct their research and create their campaigns outside of the classroom and between themselves. We meet periodically (synchronous communication) throughout the semester to observe student progress. During these meetings, each group presents their work for critique and direction. All group members work together to edit proposals, brochures, and contact letters. Combining these two forms of communication has proved to be very effective and efficient for the type of group work it serves. Students learn new ways to interact to solve problems and be creative.

INFORMATION LITERACY

With the advent of the Internet, we have discovered that there is no lack of information in the world. Some of that information is reliable, but most of it probably is questionable, at best. How do you determine what information is reliable and what is not? Do you know where to retrieve that information? Individual skills needed to search, select, evaluate, and use information can vary from a complete lack of information skills to some level of literacy. The term information literacy, sometimes referred to as information competency, is generally defined as the ability to access, evaluate, organize, and use information from a variety of sources. Being information-literate requires knowing how to clearly define a subject or area of investigation, select the appropriate terminology that expresses the concept or subject under investigation, formulate a search strategy that takes into consideration different sources of information and the variable ways that information is organized, analyze the data collected for value, relevancy, quality, and suitability; and subsequently turn information into knowledge.[4] This involves a deeper understanding of how and where to find information, the ability to judge whether that information is meaningful, and ultimately, how best that information can be incorporated to address the problem or issue at hand.[5] Information literacy requires an awareness of the way in which information systems work, of the dynamic link between a particular information need and the sources and channels required to satisfy that need.[6]

Information Literacy (IL) refers to a set of information and knowledge age skills that enable individuals to recognize when information is and is not needed and how to locate, evaluate, integrate, use, and effectively communicate that information. These skills are critical for members of virtual groups in order to assist them with the broad selection of tools to search, organize, and analyze results, and to communicate and integrate them for problem-solving or decision-making.[7]

Information literacy skills help an individual to:

1. Determine the nature and extent of the information needed.
2. Access needed information effectively and efficiently.
3. Evaluate information and its sources critically.
4. Use information effectively to accomplish a specific purpose.
5. Understand the economic, legal, social, and ethical issues surrounding the use of information in a virtual world.

There is a gap between an individual's understanding and his or her ability to access what he or she needs from the external environment. The information literacy gap is the space between availability of information and an individual's ability to access it, understand it, and apply it. Information Literacy, at times referred to as meta-information (or information about information), helps close that gap and provides ways of increasing a member's ability to access what he or she needs from the external information environment. To determine your IL gap, the first thing to do is to self-assess and learn what areas you need to target for improvement. Anyone can assess his or her strengths and weaknesses in IL, build on existing strengths, and turn weaknesses into strengths in order to become information literate. For example, assess your knowledge by answering the following questions:[8]

1. Do you recognize when you need information? All of the time?
2. Can you name at least two search engines?
3. Can you find basic facts on the Internet?
4. Can you analyze the data you get on the Internet for validity and reliability? Are you always sure where your information comes from?
5. Do you know how to identify a computer hoax or urban legend?
6. Do you know how to request permission to use information under copyright?
7. Do you know basic steps to ensure your online privacy?
8. Do you know what browser you are using?
9. Do you know what the deep Web is and that it has 500 times more information than the surface Web we usually surf?

Improving Information Literacy

There are things you can do to improve your information literacy. These apply not only to V-group work, but to learning overall. When you are working on a project, paper, problem, or task, ask yourself the following questions from these six categories:[9]

Information literacy (IL)

Refers to a set of information and knowledge-age skills that enable individuals to recognize when information is and is not needed and how to locate, evaluate, integrate, use, and effectively communicate that information.

Information literacy gap

The space between availability of information and an individual's ability to access it, understand it, and apply it.

Defining Your Problem and Asking Meaningful Questions

1. What is my task, project, paper, or problem?
2. What information do I need?
3. What do I already know?
4. What more do I need to find out?

Remember: Try to make the most out of any research project, paper, problem, or task. The more focused your question is, the more specific your information will be and the more you will learn.

Information-Seeking Strategies

1. Where can I find the information I need? Which are the best possible sources? Which databases are the best choices?
2. Which types of sources will best help me solve my information problem? Which sources do I already have?
3. Do I need help to find the resources or to make sure I haven't overlooked any critical sources?

Selecting and Evaluating Your Resources

1. How can I search these sources effectively?
2. After reading, can I identify better keywords or subject headings to refine my electronic search?
3. Do the resources I found really answer my questions or offer evidence to support my project, paper, problem, or task?
4. Have I carefully examined my selected sources for significant details and concepts?
5. Have I examined my sources for currency, relevance, accuracy, credibility, appropriateness, and bias?
6. Can I defend all of the resources I am considering for inclusion in my Works Consulted page?
7. Do the scope, depth, and quality of my research meet my group's and my own expectations?
8. How will I credit my sources?

Organizing and Restructuring Information

1. How much of the information I collected is truly relevant?
2. Do I see any patterns emerging in the information I collected?
3. How can I organize this information so that it makes sense to me and to others? Do I have a strategy for note-taking?
4. Can I construct a visual tool or written outline to help me structure my work?
5. Have I solved my information problem and answered the related questions?
6. Do I have enough information?

Communicating the Results of Your Research

1. Who receives my work product?
2. How can I most effectively share this information with this audience?
3. Which would be the best format for communicating the results of my information, by PowerPoint, video-conference, email document, tele-conference, or some other form of transmission?
4. What do I need to do this presentation? Hardware? Software?
5. Have I included everything I want to share?
6. Have I proofread, edited, and truly finished my project, paper, problem, or task?

© Arcady, 2011. Under license from Shutterstock, Inc.

Evaluating Your Work

The product:

1. Am I proud of the product? Was it effective?
2. Did I meet the guidelines or follow the rubric for the project, paper, problem, or task?
3. Am I sure I did not plagiarize from any of my sources?
4. Is this the best work I could have done?

The process:

1. Did I explore the full scope of available resources and select the best?
2. Did I approach the research process energetically?
3. Did I search electronic resources (the Web and licensed databases) using effective, efficient, strategic, search strategies?

Working in a virtual group requires skills beyond using email or surfing the Web. For V-groups, technology provides tools that will allow members to potentially perform faster and more effectively, whereby increasing productivity. Remember, group work is all about performance, and, in the working environment, the cost–benefit ratio. At this time, V-groups will not replace face-to-face groups; however, they both have their functions.

VIRTUAL DIMENSIONS

New communications technologies have enabled virtual group work to be conducted across many dimensions, including place, time, space, and through distance. These communication dimensions are important because information

must be transferred through time, space, and distance to enable virtual communications. This information is transferred through one of several technologies, which include telephone lines, cable lines, local and wide area networks, satellites, or wireless signals. Each of these forms of transmissions has strengths and weaknesses that influence the quality of information being transferred across different dimensions.[10]

Place

Place refers to the organizations, especially multinational organizations, that operate in many countries around the world, and the location of people who work for those organizations. In virtual communications, group members are considered to be either co-located (same place) or remote (different places). The dimension of place, where people and organizations are located, has a number of important implications for virtual communications. Before the Internet, groups relied on the telephone, fax machines, and the mail services to send and gather information from people in other places. However, new information technologies have allowed groups to share, gain access to, exchange, and view information irrespective of their group's location.

There are a number of technological tools that help members in virtual groups; however, before any are chosen, the group must take into consideration the locations of all the participants. Some virtual tools enable only same place interaction. Some examples of this include technologies that require all participants to have access to a network, some messaging tools, and electronic white boards. Any-place technologies include the Internet, intranets, discussion boards, listervs, newsgroups, chat, telephones, video teleconferencing (VTC), cable, and wireless.

Place

The organizations, especially multinational organizations that operate in many countries around the world, and the location of people who work for those organizations.

FIGURE 13.1
Electronic meeting systems to support group work.

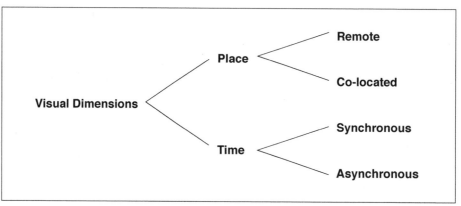

Adapted from Nunamaker, J. F., Dennis, A. R., Valacich, J. S., Vogel, D. R., & George, J. F. (1993).

Time

Virtual communications take place either in same time or different **time settings**. Synchronous communications, as noted earlier, are interactions that take place in same-time settings, and asynchronous communications refers to different time settings. Virtual groups frequently work across many time zones. V-group members have to take into consideration the time factors that influence group communication because this is an integral part of information literacy.

Communication technologies have enabled groups to work around the challenges of time through the ability to store information in databases on Internet portals, intranets, LANs, and so forth. To communicate virtually at different times, the technology must enable any-time access to information. This will allow one member to send a message at one time and have another member receive information at a different time. Same-time-only technologies include video teleconferencing, telephone communication, chat, and instant messaging, for example. Any-time technologies include Internet-based collaboration and team-ware products, decision support technologies, discussion boards, listservs, news groups, and calendars, and project management tools.

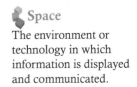

Time settings
The time zones or other time factors that need to be taken into consideration when working in a group.

Space

The dimension of **space** in virtual communications refers to the environment or technology in which information is displayed and communicated. A simple example of this is the electronic white board, which allows members to view and communicate information. Other examples of shared space are Internet pages and applications where communities meet to share information. The practice of shared display or shared space has been studied by experts in the field of group dynamics, and it indicates that when information is shared so that people can view it and alter it, group dynamics improve.[11] In addition, when members can visually interact with information, they begin to feel empowered and take ownership of their ideas and contributions. Teleconferencing does not encourage this dynamic, because the group can only hear but can't see the information being communicated.

Space
The environment or technology in which information is displayed and communicated.

Shared space also refers to a physical environment where members interact, such as a conference or meeting room. Group work in same-time, same-place meetings is best conducted in an environment that allows members to sit facing each other in a circular formation and with colorful visual displays on the walls. The same principle is true in virtual communications. In video teleconferencing, if a room is poorly lighted and some members can't see other members, it will negatively impact the experience for all members. To optimize an effective virtual communication session, it is important to consider how well the technology and/or the environment adequately displays information.

Distance

Distance
How far group members are away from each other, such as telephone and wireless communication versus physical proximity.

Distance, or how far group members are away from each other, can affect the quality of information transmission. This is especially true for some forms of communications such as telephone and wireless communications, where communication can be interrupted. How many times have you been talking on your cell phone and suddenly you read on your display "call lost." Distance doesn't affect all technologies used in V-groups, but it can be frustrating when it does happen.

SEQUENCE OF COMMUNICATION

 **Sequence of communication**

The ordering of communication acts in group processes.

Sequence of communication refers to the ordering of communication acts in group processes. For example, when V-group members communicate, there is a sequence of interaction between them that may begin with making introductions, reviewing an agenda, setting the context, and so forth. Next, the group might move to brainstorming activities, such as generating ideas, options, or solutions, followed by their prioritization, and then decision-making. By understanding and planning the sequence of group communication acts, members can improve the flow, quality, and productivity of virtual communications, thus improving V-group performance. Depending on the size of the group, each phase of the communication process should be mapped and assessed, then sent to all members in advance of the virtual meeting so that enough time can be allotted for each phase. This will allow all participants to be included in the process.

Preparing for a Virtual Group Meeting

One of the cardinal sins that a member can commit is to come to a meeting unprepared or ill-prepared. Shame on the person who forgets to create an agenda or does not follow the agenda to achieve his or her desired outcomes. Not only is it embarrassing, it wastes the group's time, members become irritated, and little gets accomplished. And if the group is in synchronous time and its members are in different time zones, a lack of preparation can damage the group's vitality. Members will be reluctant to set aside time that may be inconvenient for them. Always prepare for each V-group meeting. It is better to be over prepared than under prepared. The following guidelines may be useful when preparing for a V-group meeting:[12]

1. Have someone review your content prior to sending out a message. We tend to overlook our mistakes. Take a few moments ahead of time to have a second opinion when it comes to sending out a group communication; otherwise, you may learn the hard way that you offended someone or broke cultural norms, after the fact.

2. As group leader, create and send a clear and detailed agenda of what you plan to accomplish before your V-group meeting. This gives every member an opportunity to be prepared.

3. Create and send a clear statement of the time and date of the virtual session, and indicate who will be participating.

4. Notify members in advance, either by email, phone, or other means, of the virtual session. Sometimes, it is best to send several invitations as reminders. Meetings are usually calendared at least three months ahead of time.

The leader should send a reminder one week prior to the meeting, and then follow up with another reminder two days prior. If the agenda is modified prior to the meeting, then the leader should send those modifications soon after they are made.

5. Consider the chain of command when creating a virtual message. Some V-group meetings are moderated; that is, all messages are sent to a designated leader, who then forwards them to all members. There may also be unwritten protocols about who will receive or act upon a message in an organization. Rules governing communication processes are generally established very early in group formation.

6. Establish clear ground rules for participation in the virtual session. Many organizations have defined the rules and protocols for using messaging systems, such as to restrict sending organization-wide messages unless they meet certain criteria (for instance, not sending out jokes or personal news via email). In other virtual sessions, such as conferencing, Webcasts, chat, and discussion boards, it is critical to post rules about the use of profanity or the criticism of group members. Ground rules should also include a code of ethics—guidelines for appropriate behavior. What may be funny to one person may be insulting to another.

7. The leader should enforce a timeline for participation. Virtual collaboration has a short lifespan, especially if it is synchronous. It is important to advise a group members involved in problem-solving, decision-making, or brain-storming, that their contributions must be made quickly because of time constraints. When you do this, members are more likely to stay engaged because they have an opportunity to contribute.

8. It is imperative that all members understand how to use the technology and make technical support available for those who may not have the appropriate skills or experience to use the tools. Make sure instructions for participation are included in the advance messages about the virtual communication and again immediately prior to the session. This will help participants feel more confident that they will receive adequate support for their efforts.

9. For online group meetings, prepopulate the communication tool with engaging and interesting content. Think of the virtual space as if it were a newspaper or movie trailer; it should capture people's interest by drawing attention to matters that they care about. Where possible, use graphics supported by small amounts of text.

10. If the group is collaborating on a sensitive matter and is able to use an anonymous collaboration or discussion tool, make sure participants know this in advance. And, if some comments will be designed to be anonymous and some attributed, be sure to make those distinctions apparent within the tool.

11. Design the content using open-ended questions, and avoid short-answer or yes and no questions, especially if the group is engaged in fact-finding. Members will want to discern as much information as possible. Designing engaging content for virtual communication is an art, but it can be achieved with practice and thought.

Virtual Communication Ethics

There are some special rules that apply to communicating virtually. The most important is to remember that you are communicating with real people, not a computer. Dr. Raymon C. Barquin (1991) argued for the need for a set of standards to guide and instruct people in the ethical use of computers. He offered the following ten commandments of computer ethics:[13]

The Ten Commandments of Computer Ethics

1. Thou shalt not use a computer to harm other people.
2. Thou shalt not interfere with other people's computer work.
3. Thou shalt not snoop around in other people's computer files.
4. Thou shalt not use a computer to steal.
5. Thou shalt not use a computer to bear false witness.
6. Thou shalt not copy or use proprietary software for which you have not paid.
7. Thou shalt not use other people's computer resources without authorization or proper compensation.
8. Thou shalt not appropriate other people's intellectual output.
9. Thou shalt think about the social consequences of the program you are writing or the system you are designing.
10. Thou shalt always use a computer in ways that ensure consideration and respect for your fellow humans.

Virtual Communication Tasks

Similar to face-to-face group work, V-groups share many of the same tasks. Because of the nature of V-groups, some of those tasks may have greater priority, and some of those tasks may have no importance at all. For example, V-groups may not have a need for an observer, but the need for information-sharing is critical. Some of the tasks that V-groups should consider are:

1. **Information sharing and knowledge exchange.** Some groups may be thousands of miles apart and separated by a number of time zones. It is essential that all information deemed relevant and pertinent to the group be shared with all members on a timely basis. The lack of timely sharing or the lack of sharing of information and knowledge exchange prevents the group from achieving its goal. Therefore, it is incumbent upon each and every member to fully participate in the sharing of information and knowledge.
2. **Collaborating and team work.** V-groups cannot exist without members collaborating and working as a team 100 percent of the time. This is a task imperative.
3. **Decision making/voting.** All members must participate in the decision-making process, and all members must vote. Members cannot defer to other members to make decisions for them; their voice must be heard. The same applies for voting. There should never be an abstain vote in V-group work.

4. **Document sharing.** As with collaborating and teamwork, members must share all documents that are relevant to the group. The more informed the group is, the better the decision-making process and the better the decision.

5. **Project management.** Every group charge has to have a group leader to facilitate group performance and the group process. The project manager does not have to be the group leader, but it should be someone who has been authorized by the leader to oversee a project. A project can be a task performed by a few members. For the project manager, frequent communication is essential. Failure to communicate effectively and frequently with the group's project team is a recipe for disaster. The project manager who does not take proactive steps to keep the lines of communication fluid will not be protected from surprises, nor will he or she have the opportunity to intercede before little problems become big ones.[14]

6. **Scheduling.** Meetings have to be scheduled; tasks have a beginning and an end; documents have to be completed by certain dates; decisions have to be made; and votes have to be cast. Scheduling is as integral to V-group tasks as collaboration.

When to Use a Virtual Group

How do you know when a V-group should be used? A V-group, in a sense, is a tool to accomplish something, just as a face-to-face group is. Each tool has its own uniqueness and its own purpose. You wouldn't want to use a hammer to secure a bolt; you would use a wrench. Groups are the same. You wouldn't use a V-group if a face-to-face group does the job just as well and more quickly. Answer the following questions to determine if a V-group is appropriate to use:

1. Why should we use virtual communications? What is the purpose or charge that must be accomplished? What are the desired outcomes?

2. Who are the group members? Where are they located? What are their needs? What are the group dynamics that will influence communications? What is the level of their technological experience?

3. What technological tools are available? What tools will best facilitate group communication? Is there any usability issues related to the tools? What technologies are available, and which are best for facilitating the group process?

4. Which technology best facilitates communication? What standards regulate the best practices and principles for virtual communications? What does a communications plan include?

Virtual Group Tools

When we refer to virtual tools, we mean communication technologies as tools. There are many technological tools available to V-groups, with new ones emerging almost on a regular basis. When you think you've seen the last of a technological innovation, along comes another one, appearing to be more amazing than its predecessor. I would assume by the time this book goes to print, new communication technologies will be unveiled. For now, the following are available for V-group use:

- **Email** has become the communication technology of choice. It is easier, cheaper, and quicker than writing and mailing a memo. Unlike memos, which must be sent to each individual separately, emails can be distributed in mass. Emails have their advantages and disadvantages. Their advantages: emails travel at the speed of an electrical impulse. Person A in New York City can communicate in synchronous real-time with Person B in Beijing, China, at the fraction of the cost of a postal stamp. In addition, Person A can attach documents, digital photographs, stream video, and so forth, whereas memos cannot. Plus Person A can fax Person B through emails. Disadvantages: emails are not private. Organizations may monitor employee emails.[15] Once they are in cyberspace, they no longer belong to the sender; anyone who knows how to access them can read them. Confidentiality between sender and receiver is based on the honor system. The receiver has no obligation not to make them public. Emails are never guaranteed to reach their intended targets. A full mailbox will bounce new emails back to the sender; a server could be down; a wrong address entered to recipient would cause a bounce-back; or the recipient doesn't bother to open his or her inbox for weeks at a time.[16]
- **Text-messaging** is an alternative to email. Text-only messaging application includes cell phones besides the computer. Texting has become globally ubiquitous, but it does not facilitate good V-group communication.
- **Teleconferences** (combination with computer display) are electronically mediated meetings that let group members meet regardless of geographic location. Teleconferencing includes: **audioconferences**, commonly known as the conference call, which lets members hear each other but not see each other; **videoconferences**, which are more technologically sophisticated than teleconferences[17] (they let members see and hear each other); and **computer conferences**, which allow members to send messages to each other that are displayed on the computer screen.[18]
- **Voice mail** is an asynchronous form of communication. It is a good way to leave a message for someone when you cannot have an interactive conversation. For the receiver, it may be a good way to avoid answering the telephone or cell phone, or speaking with someone you don't want to speak with.[19]
- **Web pages** are what make up the World Wide Web. These documents are written in HTML (hypertext markup language) and are translated by your Web browser. Web pages can either be static or dynamic. Static pages show the same content each time they are viewed. Dynamic pages have content that can change each time they are accessed. These pages are typically written in scripting languages such as PHP, Perl, ASP, or JSP. The scripts in the pages run functions on the server that return things like the date and time, and database information. All the information is returned as HTML code, so when the page gets to your browser, all the browser has to do is translate the HTML. Please note that a Web page is not the same thing as a Web site. A Web site is a collection of pages. A Web page is an individual HTML document.[20]

- **Web site** is a set of interconnected Web pages, usually including a homepage, generally located on the same server, and prepared and maintained as a collection of information by a person, group, or organization.[21]
- **Bulletin board** is an electronic communication system that allows users to send or read electronic messages, files, and other data, and to download software and information to the user's own computer.[22]
- **Electronic chat**, or chat rooms, are also known as desktop conferencing, real-time conferencing, and Internet relay chat (IRC), just to name a few. Chat rooms are places where participants can discuss all kinds of topics and issues.
- **PDF** (portable document format) is a file format that has captured all the elements of a printed document as an electronic image that you can view, navigate, print, or forward to someone else. PDF files are especially useful for documents such as magazine articles, product brochures, or flyers that you want to preserve in the original graphic appearance online. A PDF file contains one or more page images, each of which you can zoom in on or out from. You can page forward and backward. Some situations in which PDF files are desirable include graphic design development in which group members are working at a distance and need to explore design ideas online, and the online distribution of any printed document in which you want to preserve its printed appearance. Acrobat's PDF files are more than images of documents. Files can embed type fonts so that they're available at any viewing location. They can also include interactive elements such as buttons for forms entry and for triggering sound and QuickTime or AVI movies. PDF files are optimized for the Web by rendering text before graphic images and hypertext links.[23]

© Africa Studio, 2011. Under license from Shutterstock, Inc.

Impact of Virtual Groups

Many V-groups are made up of members from different geographic areas, as we noted earlier. There are a number of implications that need to be considered when we speak about geographic areas, such as different work environments, different social structures, different cultures, different organizational cultures, different conflict management protocols, and the limitations of CMC. These differences are affected by the types of communication tools V-groups use. Unlike face-to-face group work where members interact interpersonally in the physical context, V-group interaction is mediated, making interaction challenging. In traditional group work, members can observe both verbal and nonverbal behaviors of other members. Relationships are developed over time, and members learn to read behavioral cues and know how other members respond to comments and suggestions. However, V-group work makes these observations problematic. Careful consideration must be given to the words members choose, the way they are delivered, and the contextual meaning that they are couched in. You may be comfortable in your group using colloquialisms or jargon, but they can have a debilitating affect in V-groups because members from other cultures or geographic areas may not understand their meanings. Members must be sensitive to cultural differences, especially language. There are many cultural norms (which are addressed in Chapter 1) that members need to be aware of. In addition to cultural differences, members need to be aware of various organizational cultures, especially power and political structures, and communication structures. Power and political structures refer to the power hierarchy (who has the authority to make decisions and provide resources), and political structures tie in with power (who has the ability to influence whom). Communication structures refers to the protocols that a culture has developed for individuals to communicate with one another. Communication structures complement power structures, in that a hierarchical society will generally have a hierarchical communication structure, and an individualistic culture will possess an egalitarian communication structure. A culture's social structure tells us many things about that culture, such as power differences between people—individualism versus collectivism, male-dominated versus egalitarian, communication behaviors between the sexes, and so forth. Ignorance of these differences can cause irreparable damage to the group. Conflict management is both idiosyncratic and culturally defined. Idiosyncratic refers to how individual people manage conflict—it is their personal conflict styles. Culturally defined conflict management refers to the formal and informal structures that a culture has established for addressing conflict.

Building and Adapting to the Virtual Group

- **Basics of group work.** V-groups are extremely interdependent. Members wholly rely on other members to complete their tasks and share all information, documents, and so forth, and to do this on time. It may take more time to accomplish tasks because of the nature of V-groups, but it doesn't impede interdependence. This is one reason why scheduling is so important. Windows of opportunity for meetings may be limited by time, making be prepared more than just a slogan. It would be very difficult for other members to take up the work of a member who is a slacker. The group works as one.
- **Performance and productivity.** Members must do what they are supposed to do when they are supposed to do it. This means that they are self-motivated. Performance and productivity rely on the individual. Members must perform optimally and contribute their share of the work on time if the group is to be successful. It is difficult for a leader in one geographic area to use traditional consequences effectively on a member who is in another geographic area.
- **Tasks and skills.** Each member brings certain skills to the group that other members may not have. Similar to face-to-face groups, however, one skill that is generally universal is computer literacy. Tasks may be assigned by

capability instead of being assigned by the group leader. A survey of member skills may be appropriate prior to task assignment.

- **Cohesion and trust.** These are much more difficult to cultivate in V-groups simply because of the nature of the group. In traditional groups, cohesion and trust are developed over time through continuous member interaction and performance. Members develop interpersonal relationships, becoming interdependent and forming a cohesive bond. Trust is developed through performance—doing what you're supposed to do. Over time, members *trust* that other members will perform accordingly.

- **Communication.** V-group communication challenges traditional group communication in several ways: (1) **Relational communication** is quite different in V-groups. Unless you know the individual, have a working relationship with that person, it is difficult to form relational bonds in the traditional sense. The depth of relational communication is based on levels of self-disclosure—things about you that only you know and are willing to share with someone else. The more you disclose to that member, and the member reciprocates in kind, the deeper the relationship becomes. (2) **Lack of nonverbal communication** presents quite a communication problem for V-groups. We observe the nonverbal cues that people give when communicating; it's a part of the transactional communication process, and we react and adjust our messages to those cues. We know when people are sad by their frowns, when they are happy by their smiles, and their states of confusion by their wrinkled foreheads. Unless V-group meetings are televised in some manner, we will not be able to see these nonverbal cues. A new language has been developed to replace the nonverbal cues—smiley faces, exclamation points, and so forth. However, they may be substitutes for nonverbal cues, but they don't replace the actual meanings of nonverbal cues. Members need to be careful when they use these symbols because, like nonverbal cues, they can be culturally dependent. (3) **Social orientation** refers to one's place in society. As mentioned in Chapter 1 and in this chapter, each culture determines a person's position in that society. In a collectivist society, the individual is one of many and generally has a hierarchy of status, a pecking order so to speak, which affects communication patterns and protocols. This also has implications for the organizational culture and communication processes. In an individualistic society, the individual is egalitarian, and communication is generally one across; there are no hierarchy protocols as in the collectivist culture. (4) **Text messaging** is language-dependent. This includes not only the symbols used, but the level of language competency. For members who speak English as a second language, care must be given to the types of words used and their context. It is always safe to use concrete, neutral language to reduce the chances of misunderstanding. (5) **Computer video imaging** is a great tool to have, but it has its limitations. Some view the camera like public speaking—they fear it, are

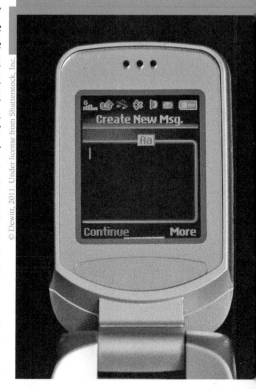

intimidated by it, and feel discouraged to participate, and this increases the overall sense of anxiety. The mere presence of a camera makes people change their rate of speaking, tone of voice, and physical composure. Usually, practice, practice, practice helps reduce these fears.

CREATING SUCCESSFUL VIRTUAL GROUPS

In many ways, the world of V- group work is far different from face-to-face group work. V-groups comprise of people you may never see and may have never met except in the virtual sense. Moreover, people come and go from employment in companies with astonishing rapidity. One or more members of a V-group with one company may disappear by the next meeting, only to be replaced by someone who doesn't know the group's history. All of this complexity adds up to one certain issue: good communication has become more difficult than ever. How do you ensure that it happens successfully, and often enough to get the job done? What are the new ground rules of communication in the virtual age?

At its heart, virtual communication puts stress on three competencies that have always been important: accountability, trust, and adaptability. The following is an excerpt from Psychologist Tom McDonald, who stresses the need for accountability, in an article in *Successful Meetings,* the *Harvard Management Communication Letter* (December 2000). He offers expert insight into the new communications rules for V-groups in these three essential areas.[24]

Ensure Accountability

Psychologist Tom McDonald stresses the need for accountability in an article in *Successful Meetings.* "Ironic as it may seem, virtual teamwork starts with a high emphasis on individual responsibility, rather than on group thinking," McDonald argues. "Team members are very clear about what their individual jobs are, and, frankly, want to be left alone to do them. Achievement is uppermost in their minds. They take their jobs seriously and expect each team member to do the same."

McDonald cautions, however, that "at times this individualism can be overdone. When you have a group of these powerful individuals hell-bent on doing their own thing, you've got a real coordination challenge on your hands. The best way to approach it is to give team members a lot of room, and rest secure that they'll do the job well, even if it's done in their own way."

There are pitfalls to the focused approach of the virtual team, McDonald admits. "Being so task-focused," McDonald notes, "team members can easily miss the subtleties of tricky interpersonal dynamics." To counteract this potential problem, give your teams practical training in how to listen and other communication skills. But keep it practical—these virtual workhorses don't want their time wasted.

Build Trust

For Dennis S. Reina and Michelle L. Reina, principals in an organizational development research and consulting firm and authors of *Trust and Betrayal in the Workplace: Building Effective Relationships in Your Organization,* the basic issue is the establishment of a solid trusting relationship. Without that, virtual work is impossible. They identify three kinds of trust that employers must address to be successful: contractual, communication, and competence trust.

Contractual trust is, fundamentally, doing what you say you will do. You need to manage expectations, establish clear boundaries, delegate appropriately, honor your agreements, and, above all, be consistent in your words and actions. This kind of trust is especially frail in today's workplaces because of the legacy of layoffs, downsizing, and reorganization that reengineering and economic problems have brought to the modern corporation.

You simply cannot keep the trust of your workers if you exhort them to work hard on behalf of the corporation, on the one hand, and lay hundreds or thousands of them off on the other. No matter how sincere your intentions, your employees will see inconsistency and indeed hypocrisy in those two sets of behaviors—and judge you accordingly. The result will be a workplace that focuses more on internal politics than on getting the job done.

Communication trust is, at its heart, a question of honesty and disclosure. You have to be willing to share difficult truths with your employees, admit your mistakes, give honest feedback, and at the same time maintain confidentiality. That's a tricky path to negotiate, and one on which many an executive has stumbled while trying to find the right balance between openness and company confidentiality.

The third kind is competence trust—respecting your teammates' abilities and skills, as well as your own, and helping others learn new skills. It means involving others rather than trying to do it all yourself.

Learn to Adapt

Finally, William E. Fulmer, author of *Shaping the Adaptive Organization,* finds adaptability to be at the core of the new communication style needed in today's workplace. At the heart of Fulmer's argument is the idea that corporations today will succeed or fail depending on how well they can constantly take in data about their changing business landscape and then communicate that understanding throughout their organizations.

Business leaders must scan the terrain with attention and insight as never before, because the terrain is changing so fast, and because it is so important to business success in a consumer-driven marketplace. But that's only half the story. Companies then must build their organizational communications—indeed their very organizations—around this understanding of the terrain. Once the terrain is understood, the business leader must articulate a clear sense of direction forward, without becoming locked into one path and one way of doing things. Every employee needs to know precisely what the company's business is every day in order to be empowered to realize opportunities and correct mistakes at ground level.

Fulmer writes, "The leaders at several large organizations I have examined have been especially successful at articulating a clear direction for their employees." The secret to making things clear? Keep it simple, communicate your goals to everyone, and incorporate your values in everything that you do. Further, Fulmer offers strategies for bringing this clarity to your everyday practice: encourage individual learning and then share it, promote responsible risk-taking, create an atmosphere of openness, treat employees as owners—and continually "listen" to what's going on out there in the business terrain you inhabit, committing yourself to the painful job of being willing to change direction precisely when things seem to be going well, and there is every reason to take success for granted.

As Andy Grove, the famously paranoid chairman of Intel Corporation says, "You have no choice but to operate in a world shaped by globalization and the information revolution. There are two options: Adapt or die. You need to plan the way a fire department plans. It cannot anticipate fires, so it has to shape a flexible organization that is capable of responding to unpredictable events."

Virtual Group Rules

The following are some basic rules to live by when working in a V-group:

Rule 1: Don't procrastinate—get started right away. Avoid putting off your task until the last moment.

Rule 2: Communicate frequently—keep the flow of communication going. This keeps members well informed and helps build cohesiveness, trust, synergy, and so forth, and it reduces uncertainty.

Rule 3: Multitask getting organized and doing substantive work simultaneously—although this challenges your skills, you'll avoid the linear mentality of performing one job at a time, and you'll improve your performance and productivity.

Rule 4: Overtly acknowledge that you have read one another's messages—the second worst thing you can do is to not read the messages; the worst thing you can do is tell a member that you've read the messages only to have him or her find out in dialogue that you haven't. Not only is this embarrassing for you

© Feng Yu, 2011. Under license from Shutterstock, Inc.

and the group, but you lose all credibility and trust. Messages are sent out so members can act upon them before discussion.

Rule 5: Be explicit about what you are thinking and doing—avoid using generalities. Members need specificity from you. They need to know explicitly what you are thinking and your current progress.

Rule 6: Set deadlines, and stick to them—this falls under scheduling. Remember the chapter on Performance Management (do what you say you are going to do); this establishes the antecedent. When you set a deadline, stick to it, don't change it. Members will quickly learn that they can't put things off and will have their tasks performed on time.

THE FUTURE

What we currently consider to be virtual communications tools—email, networks, and telephones and cell phones—will undoubtedly evolve technologically. The costs of these new technologies will decrease sufficiently to allow geographic areas that have not been able to afford today's technology to be a part of a new network. There is no doubt that the new tools on the horizon will make existing virtual communication pale in comparison. Reliable wireless communications seem to be the future. This author believes that the future of communications is in nanotechnology. This will have the ability to move large volumes of data with the near speed of light, and hand-held devices, similar to the Blackberry, will replace our laptops, desktops, landlines, and so forth. Wireless companies will probably continue to invest billions of dollars to build infrastructures that services run on. In the future, wireless will become the mode of communication for a number of devices. Wireless will become a standard option for PDAs, MP3 players, and digital cameras. Author Robert W. Brodersen believes that we are now on a threshold of wireless connectivity, which will become the dominant method of interconnecting countless future devices that will consume and produce data. These communications will range from the high end involving computers, high-quality video, cameras and displays, to simple internet access devices and appliances for reading and listening; for communications between people and the control of utilities to the lowest end in which very low bandwidth communications will be used to extract information from large numbers of distributed sensors. A fundamental belief that Brodersen has is that many new applications will evolve when inexpensive wireless communications become available, and it is in these new areas that the most important new developments will occur. The future of virtual communication will depend heavily upon the wide-spread implementation of wireless technology.[25]

SUMMARY

This chapter has given us insight into virtual groups and the two types of communication that it uses, **synchronous** and **asynchronous communication**. We learned about information literacy and the things we can do to improve this literacy. We now know that new communications technologies have enabled virtual group work to be conducted across many dimensions, including place, time, space, and through distance, and that these communication dimensions are important because information must be transferred through time, space, and distance to enable virtual communications. We discovered the need for a set of standards to guide and instruct people in the ethical use of computers, labeled the Ten Commandments of Computer Ethics. We see that similar to face-to-face group work, V-groups share many of the same tasks, but unlike face-to-face group work, V-groups use more technological tools. And we have the sufficient knowledge to create successful virtual groups, including group rules.

DISCUSSION

1. What distinct advantages to productive group work would a V–group have when using **synchronous** communication tools? What distinct advantages to productive group work would a V–group have when using **asynchronous** communication tools?

2. Why is a clear agenda, prepared and distributed in advance, more significant in a virtual group meeting than in a face-to-face group meeting? What aspects of our experience in virtual environments make agenda clarity and task ordering distinctively important in these environments?

3. Consider the "10 Commandments of Computer Ethics" list on page 314: Given that most, if not all, of these are ethical claims that apply to non–computer contexts as well, why would there be a need for such a specifically computer–focused list? What unique aspects of the experience of using computer–based technologies make unethical behavior riskier or more likely? Why should an effective group leader take the special risks of unethical use of computers into account?

4. Imagine that your local group, here in your home city, needs to communicate an important assignment to a group supervisor overseas: that group supervisor must fire, immediately (this same work day) because of a financial deadline, three members of the group she supervises. Discuss the advantages and disadvantages of each of the following communication choices when giving this overseas supervisor the assignment to fire three members today: Email; text message; phone call; videoconference.

5. Why is it so important to overtly acknowledge that you have received other group members' messages in a virtual context, according to Rule 4 on page 322? What experiences have you had in which friends, family, or co–workers have not overtly acknowledged receipt of your virtual messages, and how has it affected communication?

NOTES

1. Jarvenpaa, S.L., & Leidner, D.E. (1999). Communication and trust in global virtual teams. *Organizational Science* 10(6), 791–815.

2. Rees, F. (2001). *How to lead work teams.* San Francisco: Jossey-Bass/Pfeiffer.

3. Shedletsky, L., & Aitken, J.E. (2004). *Human communication on the internet.* Boston: Allyn & Bacon.

4. American Library Association Presidential Committee on Information Literacy. 1989. Final Report. Washington, DC.

5. http://www.libraryinstruction.com/infolit.html. Retrieved December 27, 2009.

6. Gilton, D. L. (1994). A world of difference: Preparing for information literacy instruction for diverse groups. *Multicultural Review*, 3(3).

7. Bennet, A. (2001). http://www.chips.navy.mil/archives/01_fall/information_literacy.htm. Retrieved December 27, 2009.

8. Ibid.

9. Adapted from http://www.joycevalenza.com/questions.html. Retrieved December 30, 2009.

10. Adapted from http://www.doncio.navy.mil/iltoolkit/default.htm. Retrieved December 26, 2009. Adapted from Nunamaker, J. F., Dennis, A. R., Valacich, J. S., Vogel, D. R., & George, J. F. (1993). *Electronic meeting systems to support group work.* Morgan Kaufmann,

11. Engleberg, I.N., & Wynn, D.R. (2007). *Working in groups: Communication principles and strategies* (4th ed.). Boston: Houghton Mifflin.

12. Adapted from http://www.doncio.navy.mil/iltoolkit/default.htm. Retrieved December 28, 2009.

13. Engleberg, I.N., & Wynn, D.R. (2007). *Working in groups: Communication principles and strategies* (4th ed.). Boston: Houghton Mifflin.

14. http://business-project-management.suite101.com/article.cfm/project_management_communication_tools. Retrieved December 28, 2009.

15. Hacker, K.L., Goss, B., Townley, C., & Horton, V. (1998). Employee attitudes regarding electronic mail policies: A case study. *Management Communication Quarterly,* 5 (4), 379–402.

16. Engleberg, I.N., & Wynn, D.R. (2007). *Working in groups: Communication principles and strategies* (4th ed.). Boston: Houghton Mifflin.

17. Rothwell, J.D. (2010). *In mixed company: Communicating in small groups* (7th ed.). Boston, MA: Wadsworth.

18. Galanes, G.J., Adams, K., & Brilhart, J.K. (2004). *Effective group discussion: Theory and practice* (11th ed.). New York: McGraw-Hill.

19. Modaff, D.P., & DeWine, S. (2002). *Organizational communication: Foundations, challenges, misunderstandings.* Los Angeles, CA: Roxbury.

20. http://www.techterms.com/definition/webpage. Retrieved December 29, 2009.

21. http://www.thefreedictionary.com/website. Retrieved December 29, 2009.

22. http://www.thefreedictionary.com/Bulletin+Boards. Retrieved December 29, 2009.

23. http://whatis.techtarget.com/definition/0,,sid9_gci214288,00.html#. Retrieved December 29, 2009.

24. Adapted from *Harvard Management Communication Letter,* December 2000. http://hbswk.hbs.edu/archive/2122.html. Retrieved on December 28, 2009.

25. Adapted from http://www.doncio.navy.mil/iltoolkit/default.htm. Retrieved December 30, 2009.

Glossary

A

Abstract words Those that refer to general ideas, attributes or qualities.

ACORN test An acronym for five qualifications of every good description of the mission or charge of the group (at the policy level).

Action steps Specific task assignments that members must achieve by a certain time and date.

Active listening Choosing to focus attention in a conscious way.

Agentic state When a group member or members exhibit undesirable, destructive, or evil behavior.

Anchors Reference points, are the beliefs, attitudes, and biases of the individual; they are key elements in deciding what type of message will be most effective.

Antecedent A condition that precedes and is associated with a specific outcome—but does not necessarily cause the outcome.

Appropriate language Language that is deemed suitable for a given situation that others will be able to comprehend.

Asynchronous communication Sends data in one direction; it is linear (one character at a time) and is not interactive.

Attitude Considered to be an accumulation of information about an object, person, situation, or experience, often shaped very early in life.

Attribution theory Attempts to explain how people account for the actions of others.

Authoritarian leader Controls the direction and outcome of discussion, gives orders, and expects group members to follow those orders.

B

Behavior Any observable and measurable act—or simply, anything you can see a person do.

Behavioral consequences Can be explained as events that follow behaviors and change the probability that those behaviors will recur in the future.

Behavioral interdependence Each member influences and is influenced by other members as they work together to achieve that common goal.

Beliefs The hundreds of thousands of statements that we make about self and the world.

Brainstorming An open-ended process of generating as many ideas as possible.

Bullying A dysfunctional behavior which ignores the rights of others.

C

Caucus The mediator speaks separately with each party outside of the presence of the other party.

Charge The assignment given to a subordinate group by a higher authority.

Charisma A trait called "charm, personality, appeal, or personal magnetism."

Checkpoints Predetermined places the group should be at certain times.

Closed system A system that has fixed and impervious boundaries that does not allow for much interaction between itself and its environment.

Cognitions The beliefs a person might have.

Cohesiveness Individual members bonding to one another.

Communication apprehension A feeling of discomfort that some people have when asked to participate in communication settings.

Communication competence The extent to which a leader communicates in a personally effective and socially appropriate manner with group members and others outside of the group who are relevant to achieving the group's goals.

Communication The process by which people create and transmit messages that are received, interpreted, and responded to by other people.

Competence The leader's ability to get a job done effectively and efficiently.

Compliance gaining Trying to get people to do what you want them to do, or to stop doing something you don't like.

Conception The private or personal understanding of a symbol.

Concepts Shared meanings among communicators.

Concrete language Words that best describe or are most specific to tangible objects (people, places, and things.)

Conflict management The process of group planning to avoid conflict where possible and organizing to manage conflict where and when it does happen, as quickly and smoothly as possible.

Connotative meaning In contrast to denotative, is a word's figurative or associated meaning.

Consequence The effect, result, or outcome of something that occurred earlier.

Context interdependence Members work within a particular environment which they influence, and which also has an influence on them.

Contingent moves Responses to problems specific to the parties that occur during the mediation process.

Credibility The degree to which a leader is believable.

Critical listening Using the listening process to contextualize and evaluate messages within the decision-making process.

Cultural assumptions A cluster of beliefs that govern behavior and are viewed as fundamental by those who hold them.

Cultural norms The collective expectations of what constitutes proper or improper behavior in a given interaction situation.

Culture The dominant set of learned behaviors, values, beliefs, and thinking patterns we learn as we grow and develop in our social groups.

D

Data-oriented Means that we use data to evaluate the effectiveness of motivational strategies.

Deliberation A process that ensures that ideas are carefully considered over a meaningful period of time from multiple perspectives through extended group discussion.

Democratic leader Promotes the interests of group members and practices social equity.

Democratic participation A process that enables each individual group member to develop and maintain a unique voice within the group.

Denotative meaning The literal meaning of a word.

Dependability The reliance people have in the leader's word.

Descriptive belief Describe to us the world around us.

Desired outcomes A plan of action designed to solve a specific problem or policy that is the group's charge.

Dissonance theory Predicts that when two things do not follow from each other, we will experience psychological tension, which we will try to reduce in some way.

Distance How far group members are away from each other, such as telephone and wireless communication versus physical proximity.

Dynamic system A system constantly changes the environment and is changed by the environment.

E

Empathy Voluntarily adopting the perspective of the other person within an interaction.

Equilibrium A system monitors itself to ensure that it is always in balance.

Ethics A code of conduct based on moral philosophy.

Evaluative belief Belief that focuses on our judgments of what is good and bad.

Expectancy theory The specific outcomes, or rewards, achieved by a person are dependent not only on the choices that he or she makes but also on the events which are beyond his or her control.

F

Face The public image we have for and with others.

Facework Actions that we take to negotiate the public image we want or that another person wants.

Feedback Indicates the quality and quantity of progress toward reaching a goal that is defined by standards.

Field theory Also known as force field analysis, this theory comes from the idea that in order to explain behavior one must look at all dynamic interactions (behavior) between individuals and their environment; that all interactions influence outcomes.

Formal role A position either assigned by an organization or specifically designated by the group itself.

Fundamental attribution error The tendency to underestimate the importance of external group pressures and to overestimate the importance of the individual's internal motives and personality when we interpret his or her behavior.

G

Goal A conceptual statement of what you plan to achieve; a clear, positive statement of intent to solve a significant problem or achieve a significant result within a specific timeframe.

Goal activity The process of achieving the goal itself.

Goal interdependence Groups share accomplishing a common goal.

Goal setting A specified, or preset, level of performance that you expect the group to perform.

Goal-directed activity When a person is motivated to reach a particular goal.

Goals What the group plans on accomplishing.

Group charge The purpose or final outcome for group work.

Groupthink A mode of thinking that people engage in when they are deeply involved in a cohesive in-group; when concurrence-seeking becomes so dominant that it tends to override critical thinking.

H

Hidden agenda Any objectives of individual members, subgroup of members, or even the entire group that are unannounced, covert, and different from the stated group purpose.

I

Identification When group members identify with the power holder. They begin to act like him or her; they create a nexus with that person.

Individual role Refers to the idiosyncratic behavior of each individual member.

Informal role A role that emerges from interactions between group members and is not appointed.

Information literacy (IL) Refers to a set of information and knowledge-age skills that enable individuals to recognize when information is and is not needed and how to locate, evaluate, integrate, use, and effectively communicate that information.

Information literacy gap The space between availability of information and an individual's ability to access it, understand it, and apply it.

Instrumental values Values we try to live life by on a daily basis.

Interaction process analysis Aims to explain the pattern of responses in which groups work toward a goal of a group decision-making problem.

Internalization Group members are no longer carrying out the power holder's orders; rather, their behaviors reflect their own personal beliefs, opinions, and goals as conscious or subconscious guiding principles.

K

Kinesics The study of body movements.

L

Laissez-faire leader Empowers the group to take control of all decisions and actions.

Leadership Defines what the future should look like, aligns people with that vision, and inspires them to make it happen despite obstacles.

M

Maintenance role The relationships which the activity of one member of the group has to that of another; they are the communication behaviors that occur between people in performing those tasks.

Measurement Refers to the assessment of performance and results achieved by both the group as a whole and individual members.

Mediation The intervention of a third party who is not directly involved in the dispute or the substantive issues in question, and who has limited authoritative decision-making power.

Motives Needs, wants, desires, drives, or impulses within the individual; they are directed toward goals, which may be conscious or subconscious.

Move A specific act of intervention or influence technique focused on the individuals in the dispute.

N

Needs Appeals to human motivations and values.

Nonsummativity When a system is greater than the sum of its parts.

O

Objectives A statement originating from the group's goals, which usually addresses a specific aspect of the problem with each of several objectives contributing toward achieving the goal.

Open system A system that does not have fixed and impervious boundaries that allows for much interaction between itself and its environment.

P

Particular other A person who influences our communication because we expect to, or choose to, continue and deepen our relationship with this person over time.

Personal power Those who get their influence from their personality and behavior.

Pinpointing Accurately identifying the problem.

Place The organizations, especially multinational organizations that operate in many countries around the world, and the location of people who work for those organizations.

Position power Those who can get others to comply because of their positions.

Power A resource that enables a person to bring about compliance from others or to influence them.

Premack Principle States that high-probability behaviors (those performed frequently under conditions of free choice) can be used to reinforce low-probability behaviors.

Prescriptive belief Belief concerning how people should behave.

Proactive behavior Can be a combination of behaviors designed to facilitate and enhance group synergy.

Process Generally a prescriptive set of guidelines on how to conduct or manage group behavior toward achieving objectives and goals.

Promotive interaction When members of productive groups promote each other's success and well-being.

Pseudolistening When a member merely pretends to listen but is not actually listening.

Psychographics The internal state of an individual.

Punishment Weakens a behavior because a negative condition is introduced or experienced as a consequence of the behavior.

R

Reinforcement The process in which a person receives a reinforcer.

Relationship role or social emotional role Relates to the group climate and working relationships among members.

Response styles Cognitive-behavioral responses to cope with stressful events; divided into two types: ruminative and distractive.

Risk-averse People who refuse to take risk.

Risk-taker People who aren't afraid of risk.

Role A name we give to a complex of many different kinds of behavioral observations.

Role May be defined as a set of expectations, or a pattern of appropriate behavior, of a person in a position toward other related positions.

Role conflict A state of tension caused when an individual's behavioral expectations of that role conflict with the group's expectations associated with that role or is contradictory to his or her role performances in other groups.

Role performance The actual conduct of someone within a particular role.

Roles The general behaviors expected of people who occupy different status positions within the group.

S

Sanctions Motivate individuals through the use of punishments and rewards.

Self-centered role Serves individual needs or goals while, at the same time, disrupting or impeding group goal achievement.

Self–disclosure Voluntarily sharing information about oneself that is not otherwise available to others.

Self-monitoring Thinking about what we will say and how we will say it, and considering how our behavior will be perceived.

Sequence of communication The ordering of communication acts in group processes.

Situational leadership Leaders must adapt to the particular environmental and individual needs of the moment.

Social loafing The tendency of individual group members to reduce their work effort as groups increase in size.

Space The environment or technology in which information is displayed and communicated.

Standard A degree or level of requirement, excellence, quality, or attainment.

Static system Neither system elements nor the system itself changes much over time in relation to the environment.

Status The prominence or position someone has within the group.

Structure Determines how the group will function.

Subgoals Goals that you set along the way that lead ultimately to the overall goal, or charge.

Subsystem A self-contained unit; that is, a part of a wider and higher order, and one which can be understood only within the context of the entire system.

Symbolic interaction Creating the meanings, through interacting with others and reflecting on ourselves, that motivate all of our actions.

Synchronous communication Interaction that takes place in same time settings; asynchronous communications refers to different time settings.

Systematic Means that in order to determine if any particular management procedure is effective, you must specify the behaviors and results to be affected.

T

Tangibles Those things which are on the group's formal agenda, such as: scheduling of meetings, order of reports, task assignments, new business, old business, and so forth.

Task leader Coordinates and facilitates the task-related discussions and directs energy toward achieving the task.

Task role The tasks that people perform; the elements of social behavior.

Teamwork Cooperative behavior between group discussion members.

Terminal values Values that we try to live life by and the ones we pass on from generation to generation.

Theory of reasoned action Helps explain how attitudes guide behavior.

Time setting The time zones or other time factors that need to be taken into consideration when working in a group.

Transactional process The process by which individuals create and transmit messages that are simultaneously received and interpreted by group members, who then create and transmit messages in response to the sender.

U

Uncertainty An inability to predict and/or explain others' behavioral choices; divided into two types: cognitive and behavioral.

V

Value-added work The activities that team members engage in that further the goal of the team by generating and delivering the appropriate solution or fulfilling the group's charge.

Values Our central, core ideals about how to live or conduct our lives.